European Private Law after the Common Frame of Reference

European Private Law after the Common Frame of Reference

Edited by

Hans-W. Micklitz

European University Institute, Italy

Fabrizio Cafaggi

European University Institute, Italy

Edward Elgar
Cheltenham, UK • Northampton, MA, USA

Published by
Edward Elgar Publishing Limited
The Lypiatts
15 Lansdown Road
Cheltenham
Glos GL50 2JA
UK

Edward Elgar Publishing, Inc.
William Pratt House
9 Dewey Court
Northampton
Massachusetts 01060
USA

KJA 700.E8

A catalogue record for this book is available from the British Library

Library of Congress Control Number: 2009937921

Mixed Sources
Product group from well-managed
forests and other controlled sources
www.fsc.org Cert no. SA-COC-1565
© 1996 Forest Stewardship Council
FSC

ISBN 978 1 84844 407 2

Typeset by Cambrian Typesetters, Camberley, Surrey
Printed and bound by MPG Books Group, UK

Contents

Contributors

Fabrizio Cafaggi, European University Institute, Italy.

Fernando Gomez, Professor of Law and Economics, Universitat Pompeu Fabra, Spain.

Stefan Grundmann, Professor for Private Law, European and International Private and Business Law, Humboldt University, Germany.

Martijn W. Hesselink, Professor of European Private Law and Director of the Centre for the Study of European Contract Law, Universiteit van Amsterdam, the Netherlands.

Nils Jansen, Professor of Roman Law, Legal History and European Private Law and Director at the Institut für Rechtsgeschichte, Westfälische Wilhelms-University, Münster, Germany.

Hans-W. Micklitz, European University Institute, Italy.

Florian Möslein, Senior Research Fellow, Faculty of Law, Humboldt University.

Horatia Muir Watt, Professor, Global and Comparative Legal Studies, Law School, Sciences-Po, Paris, France.

Norbert Reich, Professor Emeritus, University of Bremen, Germany; Dr. h.c., University of Helsinki, Finland; and Braudel Senior Fellow at the European University Institute, Florence, Italy (January–May 2009).

Ruth Sefton-Green, Maître de conférences, Université Paris 1 (Panthéon-Sorbonne), UMR de droit comparé de Paris, France.

Jan M. Smits, Professor of European Private Law and Comparative Law, Tilburg University, the Netherlands and Visiting Professor of Comparative Legal Studies, University of Helsinki, Finland.

Alessandro Somma, Professor, University of Ferrara, Italy.

Giuseppe Vettori, Professor in Civil Law, Florence University, Italy.

Introduction

Hans-W. Micklitz and Fabrizio Cafaggi

I. AFTER THE CFR – A PLEA FOR A SECOND GENERATION OF RESEARCH

The heading of the book reflects the future programme of research in European private law. The draft version of the so-called 'Academic' Draft Common Frame of Reference[1] is not even two years old and it seems as if at least the 'Political' Draft Common Frame of Reference is dead. The mandate of the European Parliament and the European Commission has expired in 2009 and no one knows to what extent the then elected new European Parliament is again willing to push the European Commission to transform the Academic DCFR into a political tool. What remains, however, is the academic input from the study group and the *acquis* group, merged in the DCFR.

The DCFR and the authors deserve respect and praise for having accomplished such a huge task in such a short time. The DCFR contributed to change the legal landscape in European private law. One might even go as far as arguing that there is a particular European legal field.[2] The most far-reaching importance of the DCFR is only about to become clear. The DCFR has established a network of more than 200 researchers who will continue to enrich academic exchange far beyond the mandate given by the European Commission, in particular in Eastern Europe.[3] The set of rules laid down in the DCFR are a most valuable tool for interesting solutions. Each and every researcher working in that field will have to take them into account when discussing his or her opinion.[4]

---

[1] See R. Schulze, 'The Academic Draft of the CFR and the EC Contract Law', in R. Schulze (ed.), *Common Frame of Reference and Existing EC Contract Law* (2008), p. 3.

[2] See for a first attempt to structure the European legal field in private law matters, H.-W. Micklitz, 'The European Legal Field in Private Law Matters', in B. de Witte and Antoine Vauchez (eds.), *The European Legal Field* (forthcoming, 2009).

[3] See the diverse contributions of the Tartu conference held in November 2007. The results are published in *Juridica International, Law Review University of Tartu* (2008).

[4] Such as in the field of consumer contract law or anti-discrimination, see

This book should be understood as an attempt to pave the way for and to initiate *second generation research* in European private law subsequent to the DCFR. It is, however, not discussing the dogmatics of the various proposed solution – its pros and cons and compatibilities or incompatibilities with particular national concepts,[5] nor the most far-reaching question of whether a European Civil Code in any form is needed in a global political and economic environment where private law is getting ever more extra-territorialised.[6] This book takes a middle range theoretical perspective. It aims at giving a voice to the growing dissatisfaction[7] in academic discourse that the DCFR as it stands in 2009 does not represent available knowledge as to the possible future of European private law. The theoretical level is therefore middle range, focusing on the legitimacy of law-making through academics now and in the future and on possible conceptual choices in the future European private law.

In the light of the experience gained through the DCFR the authors advocate the competition of ideas and concepts. In less than six months the DCFR has turned from a political academic draft into a true academic project which has to withstand academic discourse. The DCFR stands side by side with the Principles of European Contract Law,[8] the Gandolfi-Project, the work of the Trento Group,[9] the Principles of European Tort Law (PETL)[10] and the European Insurance Group.[11] This reduction in status, if it is one – or is it an upgrade? – will facilitate academic debate over the future European private

---

H.-W. Micklitz and N. Reich, 'Crónica de una muerte anunciada: The Commission Proposal for a "Directive on Consumer Rights"', 47 *Common Market Law Review*, (2009), 471.

[5] This discussion will take place and it already takes place at various levels.

[6] R. Michaels and N. Jansen, 'Private Law Beyond the State? Europeanization, Globalization, Privatization', 54 *American Journal of Comparative Law* (2006), 843.

[7] See M. Hesselink who is a member of the study group, but formulated a strong plea for a true democratic debate of the 'academic' rules.

[8] Ole Lando and Hugh Beale (eds.), *Principles of European Contract Law, Parts I and II* (2000).

[9] M. Reimann, 'Of Products and Process – The First Six Trento Volumes and Their Making', in M. Bussani and H. Mattei (eds.), *Opening Up European Law, The Common Core Project towards Eastern and South Eastern Europe* (2007), p. 83.

[10] European Group of Tort Law (eds.), *Principles of European Tort Law, Text and Commentary* (2005), see Alpa, *EBLR* 2005, 957; Wagner, (2005) 42 *CMLR*, 1269; van den Bergh and Visscher, *ERPL* 2006, 511; Jansen, *ZEuP* 2007, 398; Schulz, *EBLR* 2007, 1305.

[11] Helmut Heiss, 'The Common Frame of Reference (CFR) of European Insurance Contract Law', in: Schulze (ed.), *Common Frame of Reference and Existing EC Contract Law* (2008), p. 229. See now the set of contributions on 'European Insurance Contract Law and DCFR' in *ERA Forum* (2008), *Scripta iuris europaei, European Contract Law*, Special Issue, 'Towards a Common Frame of Reference (CFR) European Insurance Contract Law and the CFR', 595 ff.

law. Therefore a second round of research does not and cannot mean merely to develop another set of rules which would have to compete with those already existing, but to use the existing research which has already been realised as a starting point in further research on the possible outlook of the European private legal order.

There is one common element of conceptual critique which will trigger the second generation research: this is the backwards-looking character of the DCFR.[12] First and foremost, it does not take the European legal integration process fully into account which affects the concept of private law. The DCFR stands side by side with national private legal orders. The understanding of the EU as a multi-level governance structure is today commonplace. One might therefore have expected that the DCFR would deal with the multi-level structure and the interrelationship between the DCFR and the national private legal orders. The opposite is true. The DCFR does not incorporate tools designed to foster legal integration in a constitutional framework of legal pluralism. It sets aside the multi-level dimension of private law which should be reflected in the structure of the DCFR with rules concerning neither the impact of the DCFR on national legal systems and the governance of spill-over effects nor the impact of national systems on the DCFR and the potential effect of their legal disintegration.

This does not mean that the DCFR does not contain substantial innovative elements. Already the *acquis* group had put much emphasis on anti-discrimination rules and had developed a set of articles meant to give shape to anti-discrimination as a legal principle in private law matters.[13] To that extent, the *acquis* group paved the way for the infiltration of the anti-discrimination principle into the DCFR. Here the DCFR is overtly modern and openly addresses one of the most delicate issues in private law. Unsurprisingly the EC-induced integration of the anti-discrimination principle has raised strong objection in parts of private law academia,[14] but also gained cautious support.[15] So far the debate is very much concentrated on whether and to what extent a principle evolved in labour law can and should become a general principle of private law. The growing number of references in EC sector-related

---

[12]   See R. Schulze, 'The Academic Draft of the CFR and the EC Contract Law', in R. Schulze (ed.), *Common Frame of Reference and Existing EC Contract Law* (2008), p. 3.

[13]   See S. Leible, 'Non-discrimination' in R. Schulze (ed.), *Common Frame of Reference and Existing EC Contract Law* (2008), 127.

[14]   See F.J. Säcker, 'Vertragsfreiheit und Schutz vor Diskriminierung', *ZEuP* (2006), 1 and J. Basedow, 'Grundsatz der Nichtdiskriminierung', *ZEuP* (2008), 230.

[15]   See D. Schiek, *Differenzierte Gerechtigkeit, Diskriminierungsschutz und Vertragsrecht* (2000).

rules are thereby more or less neglected.[16] The resulting more ambitious question with regard to the relationship between (social) justice and anti-discrimination remains largely unanswered.[17]

The integration of anti-discrimination rules in the DCFR cannot, however, overcome the second major deficiency which so overtly documents its backward-looking conceptual outlook: its deep grounding in the dominating conceptual ideas of 19th century codifications: free will in contract law[18] and personal liability in torts.[19] We do not want to be misunderstood. There is no reason to argue that free will and personal liability have no role to play in a 'codification' which is meant to set the standards for the 21st century. However, what is missing in the DCFR is a deeper reflection of the changes which occurred in the 20th century and which affected both the concept of free will and that of personal liability. In the light of its backward-looking character, the emerging debate on the future of European private law after the DCFR could be structured around the following issues: a modern concept of contract and tort, the EC initiated paradigm shift from codification to regulation and competition, the changing patterns of methods and discourse in European private law, the new forms of private law-making in a multi-level EU and the missing dimension of collective redress in the DCFR, respectively in European private law.[20]

---

[16]   See the different sets of directives on regulated markets, F. Cafaggi, 'Una governance per il diritto dei contratti', in F. Cafaggi (ed.), *Quale Armonizzazione per il Diritto Europea dei Contratti* (2003), p. 183; ibid. 'Il diritto dei contratti nei mercati regolati', *RTDPC* (2008); and with regard to anti-discrimination in the field of universal services, P. Rott, 'A New Social Contract Law for Public Services? – Consequences from Regulation of Services of General Economic Interest in the EC', 3 *European Review of Contract Law* (2005), 323; ibid. 'Consumers and Services of General Interest? Is EC Consumer Law the Future?', *JCP* (2007), 8; C. Willett, 'General Clauses on Fairness and the Promotion of Values Important in Services of General Interests', in C. Twigg-Flesner, D. Parry, G. Howells and A. Nordhausen (eds.), *Yearbook of Consumer Law 2008* (2008), 67; N. Reich, 'Crisis or Future of European Consumer Law', in D. Parry, A. Nordhausen, G. Howells and C. Twigg-Flesner (eds.), *The Yearbook of Consumer Law 2009* (2009), 1.

[17]   See my attempt to develop an understanding of the genuine European concept of social justice, 'Social Justice in European Private Law', *Yearbook of European Law 1999/2000*, 167 and in this volume with regard to the anti-discrimination principle, N. Reich.

[18]   See on the role of free will in the 19th century, D. Kennedy, 'Two Globalisations of Law and Legal Thoughts: 1850–1968', 36 *Suffolk University Law Review* (2003), 632.

[19]   G. Brüggemeier, *Haftungsrecht, Struktur, Prinzipien, Schutzbereich, Ein Beitrag zur Europäisierung des Haftungsrechts* (2006).

[20]   See F. Cafaggi and H. Muir Watt, *Making European Private Law: Governance Design* (2008).

II.   QUESTIONS ON THE CONCEPTS OF 'CONTRACT' AND 'TORT'

As is generally known, the DCFR is based on two pillars, on the comparative research of the study group and on the analysis of what is being understood as *acquis communautaire* in European private law. The final version of the DCFR published in Spring 2009 looks like a fully fledged European Civil Code, quite different from the mandate given to the groups to develop 'a common frame of reference' on contract law, but property, family and wills are still missing. The DCFR must be understood as a law of obligations, covering contract and tort. The drafters concede that the DCFR can quite easily be reduced from a law of obligations into contract law alone.[21]

Be that as it may, the question then is what exactly has been the basis of research on which the proposed rules are grounded. The rather backwards-looking concept of the DCFR may be demonstrated with regard to the understanding which underpins the notion of contract in the work of the study group and the way in which it is conceived. For a couple of decades contract lawyers all over Europe have discussed new forms of contracts and new modes of contracts which are not regulated in the old codifications, but which determine economic transactions. As far as we can see, the Study Group did not take these new forms and modes of contract into consideration when drafting the DCFR, although the question was raised relatively early in the debate over European law-making of what concept of contract should be laid down in the DCFR.[22] This may be due to the fact that they have not pursued a bottom-up approach.[23]

A first category concerns the so-called relational contracts[24] where the parties engage in long term commitments contrary to on the spot transactions. Relational contracts deserve a different contractual design which takes into

---

[21]   H. Schulte-Nölke, 'Contract Law or Law of Obligations? – The Draft Common Frame of Reference ("DCFR") as a Multifunctional Tool', in R. Schulze (ed.), *Common Frame of Reference and Existing EC Contract Law* (2008), p. 47.

[22]   S. Grundmann, 'European Contract Law(s) of What Colour', *European Review of Contract Law* (2005), 187; F. Cafaggi (ed.), *The Institutional Framework of European Private Law* (2006).

[23]   W. van Gerven, 'Codifying European Private Law: Top Down *and* Bottom Up', in S. Grundmann and J. Stuyck (ed.), *An Academic Green Paper on European Contract Law* (2002), p. 403.

[24]   S. Macaulay, 'Non-Contractual Relations in Business: A Preliminary Study', 28 *American Sociological Review* (1963), 55; for a German view see C. Joerges, 'Vertragsgerechtigkeit und Wettbewerbsschutz in den Beziehungen zwischen Automobilherstellern und – händlern: Über die Aufgaben richterlicher Rechtspolitik in Relationierungsverträgen', *Festschrift R. Wassermann* (1985), p. 697.

account the fact that parties are willing or have to continue to cooperate even in times of conflicts.[25] The academic debate in Europe focused very much on distribution agreements.[26] A second category constitutes network contracts, where more than two parties are involved. Network contracts appear in various sectors of the industry. They play a dominant rule in the energy, telecommunications, transport and financial services sectors.[27] Whilst network contracts have gained academic attention, the legal category is not yet really specified. However, one of the key issues in network contracts is how to shape rights and duties, and in particular how to assign responsibilities between contract parties. One striking example is the credit-financed transaction, where at least three parties are involved: the supplier, the lender and the buyer/debtor. By way of the *Heiniger*-saga, this issue reached EC level.[28] Four ECJ judgments within a couple of years bore witness to the helplessness of judges to decide over conflicts where the codified law provides insufficient guidance. A third but certainly not the last category is contract governance, which should not be confused with corporate governance. Contract governance transfers the governance debate which arose in the area of public law to the private law forum. It cuts across relational and network contracts: it even affects traditional bilateral contracts and seeks new modes of contractual management which meet the standards of accountability, transparency and legitimacy.[29] We will come back to this issue in more detail later.

Whilst this lack is obvious, there are more questions to be raised on the concept of contract as it stands and as it has been used in the DCFR. One

---

[25] See C. Goetz and R. Scott, *Principles of Relational Contracts*.

[26] C. Joerges (ed.) 'Franchising and the Law: Theoretical and Comparative Approaches in Europe and the United States' [Das Recht des Franchising: Konzeptionelle, rechtsvergleichende und europarechtliche Analysen] (Schriftenreihe der Gesellschaft für Rechtsvergleichung Bd. 153) (1991).

[27] See G. Teubner, 'Networks as Connected Contracts', *Theoretical Inquiries* (2007); F. Cafaggi, 'Contractual Networks and the Small Business Act', *ERCL* (2008), 493. With regard to the triangular relationship between credit card issuers (banks), companies and customers see D. Voigt, *Die Rückabwicklung von Kartenzahlungen* (2007); with regard to the triangular relationships with regard to bank transfers. The 2009 conference of SECOLA, held in June 2009 in Florence, was devoted to network contracts.

[28] See for a reconstruction in the English language, H.-W. Micklitz, 'The Relationship between National and European Consumer Policy – Challenges and Perspectives', in C. Twigg-Flesner, D. Parry, G. Howells and A. Nordhausen (eds.), *Yearbook of Consumer Law 2008* (2007), 35.

[29] F. Cafaggi and H. Muir Watt (eds.), *Making European Private Law: Governance Design* (2008); F. Möslein and K. Riesenhuber, 'Contract Governance – A Draft Research Agenda', *European Review of Contract Law* 5 (2009), 248–289.

important issue is the relationship between the general part and specific contracts. The general part seems to be drafted having sales in mind while many important specific contracts regulated in Book IV have different features not captured in the general part. As is well known, the DCFR is based on extensive comparative research, in particular with regard to specific contracts. Book IV integrates this research, initiated and elaborated by different working groups. Part C on Services may serve as an example.[30] The concept of the contract for services is based on mutual cooperation between the parties, as documented in the pre-contractual duties to inform and to warn as well as in the obligation to cooperate. This concept of contract does not fit to the under-standing of the general part, where duties of mutual information and coopera-tion are not explicitly foreseen. If any they can be deduced from the principle of good faith.[31]

A related question concerns the ambiguous position on the distinction between btob and btoc contracts. The DCFR partly integrates the mandatory consumer law into the body of the rules. This seems to be very much in line with the German approach, where the legislator decided in the Law on the Modernisation of the Civil Code to insert consumer law into the German Civil Code,[32] contrary to the French and Italian approach, where consumer law rules are codified in a separate piece of legislation, standing side-by-side with the 'codice civile'.[33] However, just as in German law, it remains to be examined whether and to what extent there are different concepts of contract behind, which do not fit together. The German experience suggests that the DCFR might accommodate two different concepts of contract without there being a conceptual link.

Similar trends in conceptual deficits can be identified with regard to tort law. Book VI of the DCFR competes with the Principles of European Tort Law (PETL), published in 2005 and elaborated by a group of tort lawyers, joined together in ECTIL. The conceptual question is whether liability in tort should be based on personal responsibility alone or whether outside and beyond personal responsibility a new category is needed which pays tribute to modern forms of organisations in economy and society – organisational liability or

---

[30]   M. Barendrecht, C. Jansen, M. Loos, A. Pinna, R. Cascao and S. van Gulijk, *Principles of European Law, Study Group on a European Civil Code, Service Contracts (PEL SC)* (2007).

[31]   See from the literature before the adoption of the CFR, B. Lurger, *Vertragliche Solidariät* (1998); B. Heiderhoff, *Grundstrukturen des nationalen und europäischen Verbrauchervertragsrechts* (2004); C. Meller-Hannich, *Verbraucher-schutz im Schuldvertragsrecht* (2005).

[32]   H.-W. Micklitz, T. Pfeiffer, K. Tonner and A. Willingmann (eds.), 'Schuldrechtsreform und Verbraucherschutz', *Band 9 der VIEW Schriftenreihe* (2001).

[33]   See F. Cafaggi, 'Il diritto dei contratti nei mercati regolati', *RTDPC* (2008).

enterprise liability. Whilst the PETL deal with these new forms of liability, at least in a rudimentary form, Book VI of the DCFR fully relies on personal liability as the starting point for assigning responsibilities. This does not make Book VI immune to critique from opening up the floodgates of court litigation intending to make the wrongdoer liable beyond all boundaries.[34] At least two further deficiencies can be identified which deserve to be analysed with scrutiny: the role and place of product liability rules and the interplay between liability and insurance systems.

The famous EC Directive 85/374/EC on product liability has set a common standard not just for Europe; it has also influenced product liability laws in the world. However, it is a success on paper alone, as the rules are largely not applied by the courts.[35] This would be reason enough to investigate the relationship between product liability rules and tort law as well as to pay tribute to a globalised business world where dealers, wholesalers, large retailers and importers have often become the key players. The producers establish businesses in countries where the product liability rules are not applicable or where transborder law enforcement is still hard to imagine. Whilst the EU is taking steps in re-organising the market surveillance system, paying due regard to the cooperation of market surveillance authorities and custom authorities,[36] the liability regime under the Directive 85/374/EEC remains the same. The European Commission[37] did not recognise any need to reform the law on the liability of the dealer, and that seems to be the position of the drafters of the DCFR. Similarly disappointing is the examination of the role and function of insurance systems in liability claims. Those seeking answers on these two issues must go to China, where a reform of the Civil Code concerning tort law has just been approved. Here a draft has been presented which claims to provide a liability regime which is fit for the 21st century.[38]

---

[34] H. Eidenmüller, Florian Faust, Hans Christoph Grigoleit, Nils Jansen, Gerhard Wagner and Reinhard Zimmermann, 'Der Gemeinsame Referenzrahmen für das Europäische Privatrecht – Wertungsfragen und Kodifikationsprobleme', *JZ* (2008), 529, 539.

[35] M. Reimann, 'Product Liability in a Global Context: the Hollow Victory of the European Model', 11 *European Review of Private Law* (2003), 128.

[36] See Regulation 768/2008 OJ L 218, 13.8.2008, 30, thereto F. Cafaggi and H.-W. Micklitz, 'Introduction' in F. Cafaggi and H.-W. Micklitz (eds.), *New Frontiers of Consumer Protection – the Interplay between Private and Public Enforcement* (2009) and F. Cafaggi, 'Coordinating civil liability', in *The Institutional Framework of European Private Law* (2006), p. 191.

[37] COM(2003)718 final.

[38] G. Brüggemeier and Zhu Yan, *Entwurf für ein Chinesisches Haftungsrecht, Text und Begründung, Ein Beitrag zur internationalen Diskussion um die Reform des Haftungsrechts* (2009).

III.   FROM CODIFICATION TO REGULATION AND COMPETITION

The critique mainly against the DCFR and to a lesser extent against the *acquis* group can be broken down into two aspects: first the inadequate analysis of the impact of primary Community law on private law matters, and secondly the setting aside of those areas outside consumer and anti-discrimination law where the 'Transformation of European Private Law from Autonomy to Functionalism in Competition and Regulation'[39] is most obvious.

With regard to the first it must be clearly said that the drafters remain behind the findings of E. Steindorff,[40] published in 1996, where he analyses the case law of the ECJ with regard to market freedoms, competition and property rights in its implications on private law. We may concede that time pressure and the huge amount of case law posed a huge challenge. However, private lawyers all over Europe must accept, whether they like it or not, that European private law as it stands today, the famous *acquis communautaire*, is much broader than the few contract and private law related Directives and Regulations designed to constitute this by the European Commission in its 2001 Communication 'Contract Law'.[41] If we follow the ECJ in its understanding that the EC Treaty is more than a European legal order, it is a 'Constitution',[42] then European private law, more precisely the *acquis communautaire*, is paradigmatic for a process of constitutionalisation of private law which has been taking place for decades. European private law is a strange mixture of remote secondary Community law and ECJ case law on the four freedoms: competition, state aids, property rights and, last but not least, rights, remedies and procedures.[43]

In 1971 L. Raiser published a little book, *Die Zukunft des Privatrechts* (the future of private law). Here he developed the idea of the 'Funktionswandel des Privatrechts', from private law to economic law. The development started more than 50 years ago, but gained pace through the European integration process. It is perhaps one of the most obvious deficiencies of the DCFR that it

---

[39]   See for a deeper account of what might be understood as the 'Visible Hand of European Regulatory Private Law', H.-W. Micklitz in *Yearbook of European Law* (2009).

[40]   *Gemeinschaftsrecht und Privatrecht* (1996).

[41]   See the website of DG Sanco where the history is well documented, http://ec.europa.eu/consumers/rights/contract_law_en.htm.

[42]   ECJ, 25.2.1988, Case C-249/83 *Les Verts* [1988] ECR 1017.

[43]   The heading of W. van Gerven's seminal article, 'Of Rights, Remedies on Procedure', 37 *Common Market Law Review* (2000), 501. A dimension again excluded from the DCFR. See F. Cafaggi and H. Muir Watt (eds.), *The Regulatory Functions of European Private Law* (2009).

does not link the European codification project to 50 years of European legal integration, via primary and secondary Community law. The paradigm change is most overtly documented in the set of secondary law dealing directly or indirectly with private law matters. Most of secondary EC law is private regulatory law, meeting various purposes, but nearly all ruled do no longer reflect the economic image of the free market, or alternatives to the market, but 'the pragmatically regulated markets'.[44]

The following list of subjects to be taken into account in a complete analysis of the *acquis communautaire* is no more than a first stock-taking. Each of the four areas touches upon different areas of European private law, new principles, new modes of contract conclusion, new remedies, contractual standard setting and liability standards.[45] Whether and to what extent possible new legal categories may be generalised or not must be subject to research which the *acquis* group escaped by concentrating its activities entirely on consumer and anti-discrimination law.

(1) Regulated Markets

Network law: the privatisation (liberalisation) of former state monopolies in the sector of telecommunication, energy and transport has raised the importance of contract law.[46] The overwhelming majority of the literature dealing with network law sets aside the contractual dimension be it b2b or b2c.[47] It focuses on the public law side, i.e., on the concept, the regulatory devices meant to open up markets and to establish a competitive structure, as well as on the availability of an appropriate decentralised enforcement structure. The regulatory role of contract law as a device between the regulated markets to serve the overall purpose of liberalisation and privatisation belongs to the core

---

[44] D. Kennedy, 'Two Globalisations of Law & Legal Thought', 36 *Suffolk University Law Review* (2003) 630 at 633. See F. Cafaggi and H. Muir Watt (eds.), *The Regulatory Functions of European Private Law* (2009) and F. Cafaggi (ed.), *The Institutional Framework of European Private Law* (2006).

[45] See for a more developed analysis of the possible effects of the different areas of regulatory private law on the private law, H.-W. Micklitz, 'The Visible Hand', *Yearbook of European Law* (2009) and F. Cafaggi, 'Private Regulation in European Private Law', *RSCAS* w.p. 2009/31.

[46] Keßler and Micklitz, Kundenschutz auf den liberalisierten Märkten für Telekommunikation, Energie, Verkehr, VIEW Schriftenreihe, Vol. 23, 24, 25, 2008. See F. Cafaggi and H. Muir Watt (eds.), *The Regulatory Functions of European Private Law* (2009).

[47] Paradigmatic, Cameron (ed.), *Legal Aspects of EU Energy Regulation* (2nd edition 2007).

of the project.[48] This may be explained by the fact that the different set of EC directives deal only to a very limited extent with private law relations. The concept of universal services implants new principles and new legal concepts into private law relations.[49]

Insurance law (which is usually regarded as a subject of its own)[50] and capital market law (investor protection law):[51] the policy behind and the regulatory technique – with an emphasis on establishing the market via publiclaw regulations – resembles the approach chosen in the field of telecommunications, energy and transport. However, the regulatory approach is different. The EC Directive 2004/39/EC[52] on Markets in Financial Instruments – the so-called MIFID – lays down a broad framework which serves to establish a coherent European capital market within level 1 ofthe Lamfalussy approach. In line with the Lamfalussy procedure two level 2 pieces of law have been adopted; Directive 2006/73/EC[53] on organisational requirements and operating conditions for investment firms and the implementing Regulation 2006/1287/EC.[54] These Directives and Regulations already establish a dense network of rules which contain strong links to the contractual relations, where a professional or a private investor engages with his or her investment firm. The third level rules to be developed by the national regulatory agencies are of primary interest for the

---

[48]   A first attempt has been made by Gijrath and Smits, 'European Contract Law in View of Technical and Economic Regulation', in Boele-Woelki and Grosheide (eds.), *The Future of European Contract Law* (2007), p. 53; Bellantuono and Boffa, *Energy Regulation and Consumers' Interests* (2007); Cafaggi, 'Il diritto dei contratti nei mercati regolati', *RTDPC* (2008); Bellantuono, *Contratti e regolazione nei mercati dell'energia* (2009).

[49]   See W. Sauter, 'Services of General Economic Interests and Universal Service in EU Law', *European Law Review* (2008), 167; P. Rott, 'A New Social Contract Law for Public Services? – Consequences from Regulation of Services of General Economic Interests in the EC', *ERCL* (2005), 323; T. Wilhelmsson, 'Services of General Interest and European Private Law', in C.E.F. Rickett and T.G. Telfer (eds.), *International Perspectives on Consumers' Access to Justice* (2003), 149; see H.-W. Micklitz, 'Universal Services: Nucleus for a Social European Private Law?' in M. Cremona (ed.), *Collected Courses of the European Academy of Law* (forthcoming, 2009).

[50]   See Basedow and Fock (eds.), *Europäisches Versicherungsrecht* (2002), vols 1 and 2 (show the particularities of EC insurance law).

[51]   Hopt and Voigt (eds.), *Prospekt- und Kapitalmarktinformationshaftung* (2005); Keßler and Micklitz, 'Anlegerschutz in Deutschland, Schweiz, Großbritannien, USA und der EG', 15V *IEW Schriftenreihe* (2004).

[52]   OJ L145, 30.4.2004, 1.

[53]   OJ L241, 2.9.2006, 26.

[54]   OJ L241, 2.9.2006, 1.

research.[55] In the aftermath of the financial crisis, however, the Member States agreed on a reform of the institutional architecture.[56]

Company law: there are two dominating perspectives at the Member States level which clash in the harmonisation efforts of the European Community. There are those Member States where company law is in essence regarded as dealing with the inner organisation and the correct shaping and sharing of responsibilities; there are others where company law is seen as forming an essential market of the capital market law. Last but not least, due to the failure of the European Commission to merge the two conflicting perspectives, the ECJ has become the key actor in de-regulating national company law.[57] The possible impact of the ECJ's case law, as well as the few Directives and Regulations which have been adopted to give shape to European company law, in particular Directives 77/91/EEC,[58] 78/855/EEC,[59] 82/891/EEC,[60] 89/666/EEC,[61] 89/667/EEC,[62] 2001/86/EC,[63] 2005/56/EC[64] and Regulations 2137/85/EC[65] and 2157/2001,[66] has not yet been analysed with regard to its possible effects on private law, e.g., on the concept of natural persons and legal persons.[67]

(2) Commercial Practices and Contract Law

Commercial practices law: this is a field where the ECJ sets the tone in numerous judgments in which it tested the compatibility of national commercial practices (trading rules or marketing practices rules) with market freedoms, in

---

[55] Ferrarini, *Contract Standards and the Markets in the Financial Instruments Directive (MIFID)* (2005), p. 19; Ferrarini and Wymeersch, 'Investor Protection in Europe, Corporate Law Making, the MIFID and Beyond', *EBLR* (2006), 235.
[56] See COM(2009)204 and COM(2009)252.
[57] ECJ, 9.3.1999; Case C-317/99 *Centros* 1999 ECR I-1459, ECJ, 5.11.2002; Case 208/00 *Überseering* 2002 ECR I-9919; ECJ 30.9.2003; Case C-167/01 *Inspire Art* 2003 ECR I-10155; ECJ 16.12.2008 Case C- 210/06 *Cartesio*, not yet reported.
[58] OJ L26, 31.1.1977, 1.
[59] OJ L295, 20.10.1978, 36.
[60] OJ L378, 31.12.1982, 47.
[61] OJ L395, 21.12.1989, 36.
[62] OJ L395, 30.12.1989, 40.
[63] OJ L294, 10.11.2001, 22.
[64] OJ L310, 25.11.2005, 1.
[65] OJ L199, 25.7.1985, 1.
[66] OJ L294, 10.11.2001, 1.
[67] In that sense see Schulze, 'The Academic Draft on the CFR and the European Contract Law', in R. Schulze (ed.), *Common Frame of Reference and Existing EC Contract Law* (2008), p. 20.

particular the concept of misleading advertising.[68] It is here where the ECJ developed the notion of the average consumer.[69] Commercial practices law is heavily regulated by secondary law.[70] The most important rules are Directive 2005/29/EC[71] on unfair commercial practices dealing with b2c relations, and the Directive 2006/114/EC[72] on misleading and comparative advertising in b2b relations. Again the ECJ seems ready to set the benchmarks.[73] The e-commerce Directive 2000/31/EC[74] and the Directive 99/44/EC[75] on consumer sales affect the modalities under which the contract is concluded, the pre- and post-contractual stage (disclosure of information, role of third parties) and oversteps boundaries between commercial practices and private law. Some of these effects have already been taken into account by the *acquis* group and have been integrated into the DCFR.[76] However, a more coordinated system between European contract law and European unfair practices law is missing.

Intellectual property rights: intellectual property rights law is subject to control under the competition rules of the Treaty, in particular Article 82.[77] More important in our context is the EC policy to extend the existing intellectual property rights law and give it a European outlook coupled with appropriate legal redress mechanisms to sanction violations of property rights (Directive 2004/48/EC[78]). The considerable expansion[79] of intellectual prop-

---

[68]   See for an analysis of the ECJ case law, Münchener Kommentar/UWG-Heermann, EG B (2006).
[69]   The literature is no longer to overlook, see in particular the writings of S. Weatherill, 'Who is the Average Consumer?', in S. Weatherill and O. Bernitz (eds.), *The Regulation of Unfair Commercial Practices Under EC Directive 2005/29* (2007), p. 115.
[70]   See for a full account of the different Directives and Regulations, Münchener Kommentar/UWG-Micklitz, EG E-Q (2006).
[71]   OJ L149, 11.6.2005, 22.
[72]   OJ L376, 27.12.2006, 21.
[73]   ECJ 23.4.2009, C-261/07 and C-299/07 *VTB-VAB NV v. Sanoma*, not yet reported, thereto H.-W. Micklitz, 'VTB v. Sanamo – Vollharmonisierung im Lauterkeitsrecht', *VuR* (2009), 110.
[74]   OJ L178, 17.7.2000, 1; in particular Grundmann, 'European Contract Law(s) of What Colour', *European Review of Contract Law* (2005), 187 emphasises the key role of that directive for European contract law, because it contains default rules as well.
[75]   OJ L171, 7.7.1999, 12.
[76]   See for example DCFR II.-9:102.
[77]   See ECJ, 29.4.2004, Case C-418/01, *IMS Health* ECR 2004, I-5039.
[78]   OJ L195, 2.6.2004, 16.
[79]   See for a critical analysis R. Hilty, 'Entwicklungsperspektiven des Schutzes geistigen Eigentums', in Behrens (ed.), *Stand und Perspektiven des Schutzes geistigen Eigentums* (2004), p. 139.

erty rights at the same time restricts the users' rights.[80] These exclusive rights are enforced via contract law, often via standard terms which form part of the licence contract, which the consumer concludes, for example, via the internet.[81]

(3) Competition Law, State Aids and Public Procurement

Private competition law (*Kartellprivatrecht*)[82] is another neglected domain, although the *acquis* group decided to integrate the subject matter in its forthcoming work programme. Block exemptions are a well established means used by the European Commission to shape the admissibility of vertical agreements by means of competition law. The diverse regulations on exclusive and selective distribution, the umbrella Regulation 2790/1999,[83] Regulation 1400/2002[84] on the car sector, and Regulation 772/2004[85] on technology transfer, however, intervene indirectly in contract-making: indirectly, because the parties to the vertical agreement are free to define their contractual relations. In practice, however, the content of the rights and duties in vertical agreements is determined to a large extent by block exemptions. The parties will often literally copy the Articles in the block exemptions into their contracts to avoid discrepancies between the EC rules and the contractual rights. This is particularly true with regard to 'hard core restrictions'.

State aid law: state aids are submitted to a control under Arts. 87 *et seq.* of the European Treaty. The huge bulk of case law constitutes a prominent field of research in order to investigate the indirect effects of primary EC law on contractual relations.[86] The new economic approach has led to the adoption of

---

[80] See from the consumer/user perspective Guibault and Helberger, 'Copy Rights and EC Consumer Protection Law ECLG', 035/05, available at http://212.3.246.142/docs/1/BNGJCMJAHCODHMBAJGKMFMFNPDB19DBYCY9DW3571KM/BEUC/docs/DLS/2005-00181-01-E.pdf; in the same context see Rott, 'Die Privatkopie aus der Perspektive des Verbraucherrechts', in Hilty and Peukert (eds.), *Interessenausgleich im Urheberrecht* (2004), p. 267.

[81] Kreutzer, *Verbraucherschutz bei digitalen Medien, Studie im Auftrag des vzbv* (2006).

[82] S. Grundmann, *Europäisches Schuldvertragsrecht* (1999); Schumacher, *Recht des KfZ-Vertriebs in Europa* (2005).

[83] OJ L336, 29.12.1999, 21.

[84] Commission Regulation (EC) No 1400/2002 of 31 on the Application of Article 81(3) of the Treaty to Categories of Vertical Agreements and Concerned Practices in the Motor Vehicle Sector, 2002 OJ L203, 1.8.2002, 30.

[85] OJ L123, 27.4.2004, 11.

[86] See the list of case law in Mestmäcker and Schweitzer, *Europäisches Wettbewerbsrecht* (2nd edn, 2004), p. 1177 and Beljin, '§ 28 B. Rechtsprechung ("leading cases")', in Schulze and Zuleeg (eds.), *Europarecht, Handbuch für die deutsche Rechtspraxis* (2006).

the *de minimis* Regulation 1998/2006.[87] European state aid law may be divided into a substantive and a procedural part. The terminology differs: sometimes the procedural law is dealt with under the heading of 'remedies',[88] though it is sometimes simply termed procedural rules on state aids.[89] What really matters are the possible effects of illegal state aids, that is to say the question of repayment of unlawful state aids[90] and the possible remedies of third parties.[91]

Public procurement law: public procurement affects market freedoms. It is heavily regulated by secondary law. As early as 1971 the EC adopted Regulation 1182/71.[92] The two major pieces of EC law which have determined public procurement law since its entering into force on 31 January 2006 are Directive 2004/17/EC[93] dealing with procurement procedures of entities operating in the water, energy, transport and postal services and Directive 2004/18/EC[94] on the coordination of the procurement procedure on public works contracts, public supply contracts and public services contracts. Both are currently under revision.[95] The emphasis in academic research is put on competition and market freedoms.[96] Whilst the purpose of these directives is clearly to enhance competition and strengthen market freedoms, at the same time, they shape contractual relations.[97] This is particularly true with regard to appropriate remedies.[98] Most recently the ECJ held in a landmark decision that a Member State is obliged to cancel contracts which have been concluded

---

[87]   OJ L379, 28.12.2006, 5, thereto Nordmann, 'Die neue de minimis Verordnung im EG-Beihilferecht', *EuZW* (2007), 752.

[88]   Beljin, '§ 28 B. Rechtsprechung' ("leading cases"), in Schulze and Zuleeg (eds.), *Europarecht, Handbuch für die deutsche Rechtspraxis* (2006).

[89]   Mestmäcker and Schweitzer, *Europäisches Wettbewerbsrecht* (2nd edn, 2004), paras 42–47.

[90]   Already Micklitz and Weatherill, *European Economic Law* (1997), pp. 226 ff.

[91]   For an early account of the issue see L. Gormley, 'Public Interest Litigation and State Subsidies', in Micklitz and Reich, *Public Interest Litigation before European Courts* (1996), p. 159.

[92]   OJ 1971 L124, 3.6.71, 1.

[93]   OJ 2004 L134, 30.4.2004, 1.

[94]   OJ L134, 30.4.2004, 114.

[95]   COM(2007)23 final, 24.1.2007.

[96]   See Mestmäcker and Schweitzer, *Europäisches Wettbewerbsrecht* (2nd edn, 2004), para 36; Noch, '§ 29', in Schulze and Zuleeg (eds.), *Europarecht, Handbuch für die Rechtspraxis* (2006).

[97]   Some references may be found in Noch, '§ 29 Rn. 172 et seq.', in ibid.

[98]   See already Arrowsmith, 'Public Procurement: Example of a Developed Field of National Remedies', in Micklitz and Reich (eds.), *Public Interest Litigation Before European Courts* (1996), p. 125.

in violation of EC procurement obligations.[99] This judgment challenges *pacta sunt servanda* and the protection of confidence (*Vertrauensschutz*). Again, the ECJ is using private parties to strengthen the European Economic Constitution.

(4) Health, Food Safety and the Regulation of Services

Product safety and food safety law. Directive 2001/95/EC[100] on product safety enhances the role of contract law as a means to shape contractual relations.[101] Even more interesting are liability rules hidden in various fields of food law.[102] This is particularly true with regard to liability rules, which may be found in the Feed Hygiene Regulation 183/2005,[103] the Food Hygiene Regulation 852/2004;[104] the Regulation on Official Feed and Food Controls 882/2004[105] and Regulation 178/2002[106] on Food Law.[107]

Consumer law and services: the so-called Services Directive 2006/123/EC[108] enhances the elaboration of 'technical standards' by the European standard bodies CEN/CENELEC as well as by National Standards Bodies that come near to some sort of standard contract conditions with a rather unclear legal status.[109] These technical standards are developed within and under the Services Directive which defines a fully harmonised frame for the regulation of services. Technical standards, however, are generally not directly binding. What happens if these technical standards contradict national unfair contract

---

[99] ECJ, 18.7.2007, Case C-503/04 ECR 2007 I-6153; *Mitrenga/Rubach-Larsen*, available at http://www.bblaw.com/Broschueren.507.0.html?&L=1.

[100] OJ L11, 15.1.2002, 4.

[101] See F. Cafaggi, 'A Coordinated Approach to Regulation and Civil Liability in European Law. Rethinking Institutional Complementarities', in F. Cafaggi (ed.), *The Institutional Framework of European Private Law* (2006), 191; G. Spindler and F. Cafaggi in Cafaggi and Muir Watt (eds.), *The Regulatory Function of European Private Law* (2009).

[102] See for an overview Basedow, 'EC Regulation in European Private Law', in *Private Law in the International Arena, Liber Amicorum Siehr* (2000), p. 17.

[103] OJ L35, 8.2.2005, 1.

[104] OJ L139, 30.4.2004, 9, as amended.

[105] OJ L191, 30.4.2004.

[106] OJ L1.2.2002, 1.

[107] See Civic Consulting, Liability in the food and feed sector, p. 50; taken out of 'Financial Guarantees in the Feed Sector', SANCO/2004/D1/SI2.398887, Final Report, Berlin, 6.09.2005, European Commission, DG SANCO, unpublished.

[108] OJ L376, 27.12.2006, 36.

[109] See H.-W. Micklitz, 'Service Standards: Defining the Core Consumer Elements and their Minimum Requirements', Study commissioned by ANEC, the European Voice in Standardisation, 2007 available at http://www.anec.eu/attachments/ANEC-R&T-2006-SERV-004final.pdf.

Table 0.1   The changing functions of European regulatory private law

Anti-discrimination in private law	• New values • Fairness of market access • Freedom of contract and obligation to contract • Human rights dimension in private law • Enforceability of anti-discrimination rules
Regulated markets • Financial services • Energy • Transport • Telecommunication	• New principles • Competition • Accessibility and affordability (for financial services?) • Best practices • Proceduralisation of conflicts in relational contracts (disconnection and late payment)
• Commercial practices • Intellectual property rights	• Average consumer • Pre- and post-contractual duties (disclosure of information) • The decrease in the importance of when exactly the contract is concluded • Beyond privity in contractual relations
• Private competition law • State aids • Public procurement	• Contract shaping via competition and regulation • Competitive elements: right and obligation to cancel illegal contracts • Legal effects on trilateral contracts • *Pacta sunt servanda* and protection of confidence (*Vertrauensschutz*)
• Product safety • Food safety • Regulation of (other) services	• Contract law-making via technical standard setting • Lack of harmonised contract law • Compensatory function of tort law and product liability

terms legislation? So far it is even unclear whether the technical standards can be measured against the scope of application of Directive 93/13/EEC[110] on unfair contract terms.

The survey over the following 10 issues provides a first insight into those questions which have to be much more fully analysed before the *acquis communautaire* can be formulated. It shows that private law regulation is shifting the balance at various levels.[111] The proposed categorisation provides for a rough overview of the changing patterns. European private law regulation no longer hinges upon distributive justice. The key concept seems today to be anti-discrimination being understood as a horizontal value which cuts across all areas of private law. Regulated markets yield new legal principles. Commercial practices and intellectual property rights regulation overstep the boundaries to contract law. Regulation on selective distribution systems, state aids and public procurement enhances competition in private law relations. Health and safety regulation is closely interlinked with standardisation which is now expanding into matters of contract law.[112] This is not to say that the traditional private law concept as enshrined and largely condensed in the DCFR no longer has a role to play. However, the relationship between the regulatory private law and the traditional private law, even more so in a multi-level order, is still awaiting clarification.

IV. METHODS AND DISCOURSE

The elaboration of the DCFR was in the hands of 200 academics. At least the study group made an effort to make the elaboration, the shaping and the solution of possible conflicts transparent.[113] What matters in our context is the resemblance of the DCFR law-making process to the 19th century *Professorenmodell*. The question is whether legal academics at the turn of an era – the shift from the second to third globalisation of law and legal thought

[110] OJ L95, 21.4.1993, 29.
[111] The following tendencies are elaborated in more detail in H.-W. Micklitz, 'The Visible Hand of European Private Law', *Yearbook of European Law* (forthcoming 2009).
[112] H.-W. Micklitz, 'The Service Directive – The Making of Consumer Contract Law via Standardisation, the Example of the Service Directive', in *Liber Amicorum für G. Brüggemeier* (2009), 483.
[113] See M.-R. McGuire, 'Ziel und Methode der Study Group on a European Civil Code', in Ulrich Ernst (ed.), *Auf halbem Weg – Vertragsrecht und europäische Privatrechtsvereinheitlichung, Deutsch-Polnisch-Ukrainisches Seminar in Krakau* (2007), p. 225.

– can be and are still the appropriate legal agents to codify the law, and if not what their role could and should be in the early 21st century?

So far the debate has very much focused on the democratic legitimacy of a set of rules which have not been submitted to parliamentarian discussion. Such a perspective falls short of getting to grips with the problems behind law-making at the EU and reaches too far as it overstretches the boundaries of EU-like democracy. The focus overreaches because it indirectly equates law-making at the national level with law-making at the EU level. The institutional design of law-making, however is not comparable. At the same time the emphasis on democratic legitimacy misses the point in that the particularities of EC law-making are set aside. It has been suggested to understand the drafting process of the DCFR as initiated by the European Commission as just one variant of the new approach type form of law-making.[114] Such a parallel allows one better to understand the inner mechanism of how law-making in the EU works in practice and where it derives its legitimacy, if any, from.[115] This has not to be reiterated.

What is more important is the authority the *Professorenmodell* claims to have is rather questionable.[116] The answer to this question has even gained importance after the predictable political failure of the CFR. The inherent logic of the *Professorenmodell* is that legal academics claim to know much better than politicians what the rules for the 21st century look like. It is therefore the claim of supremacy of legal *academic* expertise over political involvement of the executive *and* the legislative. The rise of 'The Social' in the 20th century and the decline of the *Professorenmodell* went hand in hand. Law-making shifted away from legal academic expertise and ended up in the hands of legislators and more and more regulators. In today's legal landscape, regulators are the key figures. This is true with regard to the European Commission, where individual public officials benefit from a degree of power national administrators usually do not have. This is due to the monopoly the Commission has in initiating legislative activities. But it is equally true with regard to national administrations where no such monopoly exists. The German Law on Modernisation of the Civil Code (BGB) goes back to the initiative of a single administrator in the German Ministry of Justice, Dr. Schmidt-Rentsch, who was, however, backed up by the then Minister of Justice, Däubler-Gmelin. Academic expertise is still needed and even desired,

---

[114]   See H.-W. Micklitz, 'Review of Academic Approaches on the European Contract Law Codification Project', in Mads Andenas, Silvia Diaz Alabart, Sir Basil Markesinis, Hans Micklitz and Nello Pasquino (eds.), *Liber Amicorum Guido Alpa Private Law Beyond the National Systems* (2007), 699–728.

[115]   See F.W. Scharpf, *Governance in Europe, Effective and Democratic* (1999).

[116]   See N. Jansen in this volume.

but it fulfils a different role. Academic expertise provides a service mainly to the administrations and sometimes to parliaments which might be taken into consideration or which might *not* be taken into consideration. The recent Commission Proposal on Consumer Rights which largely neglects the DCFR as well as the *aquis* Principles may serve as an example of this trend.[117]

The EU's or, more precisely, DG SANCO's initiative in 2001 seemingly provided a chance for European academia to take the law-drafting power away from the administration and to restore it to academia. The short halcyon of European academia collapsed as early as 2006 when it became clear that there was not enough political support for a European codification and that the European Commission would limit its efforts to the revision of the consumer *acquis*.[118] The 2008 draft proposal on a directive on consumer rights does not even refer to the DCFR, let alone the *acquis* principles.[119] The DCFR represents an academic draft, but one without political teeth. It claims to be of European origin and to unite different legal traditions and cultures. This implies sensitive issues such as the correct balancing of nations and cultures in the drafting of solutions. But how common is the Draft Common Frame of Reference? The strong institutional German bias has already been highlighted.[120] But the question remains whether the elaboration of the DCFR is based on a particular German variant of the *Professorenmodell*. At the very least it would mean competition between legal orders in the proper sense. At one end of the spectrum, there would be the German law-based and German idea-shaped model of a coherent and consistent European Civil Code reaching beyond contract law and advocating a German law type of law of obligations. Such a model is indirectly claiming supremacy over other national codifications. It issues from the pre-eminent role of German civil law science in the 19th and early 20th century which might *inter alia* explain the strong reactions in France against the European codification project[121] and even personalised

---

[117] COM(2008)614 final, Micklitz and Reich, Cronica de una muerte annunciada, CMLR 2009, 471.

[118] COM(2006)744 final.

[119] See Micklitz and Reich, *CMLR* (2009), 471.

[120] H. Eidenmüller, Florian Faust, Hans Christoph Grigoleit, Nils Jansen, Gerhard Wagner and Reinhard Zimmermann, 'Der Gemeinsame Referenzrahmen für das Europäische Privatrecht – Wertungsfragen und Kodifikationsprobleme', *JZ* (2008), 529; 'The Common Frame of Reference for European Private Law – Policy Choices and Codification Problems', 28 *Oxford J Legal Studies* (2008), 659–708; see also S. Grundmann in this volume.

[121] Y. Lequette, 'Quelques remarques à propos du projet de code civil européen de Monsieur von Bar', *Recueil Le Dalloz* (2002), 2202. But see Fauvarque-Cosson and Mazeaud (eds.), *European Contract Law, Materials for a Common Frame of Reference: Terminology, Guiding Principles: Model Rules*, Sellier (2008).

criticism.[122] At the other end of the range of options would be the common law system which the World Bank claimed to be superior to the old continental codification models.[123]

The *Professorenmodell* of the DCFR at the same time yields far-reaching legal methodological consequences as it eliminates social sciences and economics from the law-finding process.[124] The dominating legal technique in CLT thought was deduction within a coherent and autonomous legal order. 'The Social' relied on rational development of law as a means to a social end. Law-making was triggered by empirical evidence. The law was instrumentalised to achieve particular politically designed purposes. The development started mainly in labour law before the Second World War and reached private law and economic law in the rising consumer society after the Second World War. A substantial number of these special pieces of legislation were designed to compensate for various deficiencies in the private law system.[125] Empirical research constituted the trigger point for the law makers.[126] The administration sought advice with social jurisprudence and then proposed legislation meant to solve particular social problems.[127] The drafters of the DCFR did not start from the premise that empirical evidence can be a useful piece of knowledge. The comments and notes are not available yet. But nowhere in the documents published so far by the study group and the *acquis* group did empirical evidence concerning the national courts and, more generally the European judiciary, play a role, be it as a reference point for particular solutions or be it as a claim to initiate empirical research. Empirical evidence proving how common the DCFR is and where the sources of commonality are to be found is still missing. The deficiencies and shortcomings of laws designed to particular political ends have been subject to extensive theoretical debate, condensed in all sorts of 'failures' theories.[128] Socio-legal research as a

---

[122]   P. Legrand, 'Antivonbar Code', 1 *Journal of Comparative Law* (2006), 13.

[123]   See http://www.henricapitant.org/rubrique.php3?id_rubrique=24 for further information.

[124]   V. Nourse and G. Shaffer, *Varieties of New Legal Realism: Can a New World Order Prompt a New Legal Theory?* (2009).

[125]   See D. Kennedy, 'Two Globalisations', loc. cit.

[126]   D. Trubek, 'Where the Action is, Critical Legal Studies and Empiricism', 36 *Standard Law Review* (1984), 575.

[127]   The German Ministry of Justice had a particular unit on 'Rechtstatsachenforschung' which was led by D. Strempel, who had considerable financial resources to initiate fact finding legal research.

[128]   Market failure, regulatory failure, see e.g. N. Reich, 'The Regulatory Crisis: Does it Exist and Can it be Solved? Some Comparative Remarks on the Situation in Social Regulation in the USA and in the EEC', *Environment and Planning, Government and Policy* (1984), 117.

trigger point for law-making is therefore on the decline at least in the Member States. However, the drafters overlook that law-making at the EC level has been and still is based ever more firmly on empirical research via so-called impact assessments which were first undertaken by political scientist and which are now taken over by economics.[129] What matters more, however, is that the drafters of the DCFR did not cope with the new developments in empirical research, in particular with regard to behavioural economics and information economics.[130] The legal agents in their methodological approach are the academics (*Professorenmodell*) and the judges (strategic litigants). The drafters jump from the 19th century into post-modernism, setting aside private regulators and administrators. This explains why the DCFR combines positivistic norms (designed by academics) with open textured general clauses (applied by judges). The power granted to judges in the DCFR has not always been well appreciated.[131] The drafting style implies the ability of national judiciaries to cope with different interpretations of open textured general clauses. But nowhere is the question of modes of judicial cooperation in civil matters addressed. The lack of any institutional framework suitable to administering the DCFR constitutes a serious drawback of the project.

Outside and beyond the methodological implications of the *Professorenmodell* there is a second line of criticism which turns round the particularities of a European private legal order which is not or no longer bound to a particular territorial national state. The European Community is at the very most a *quasi*-state,[132] a union of nation states which are tied together by a genuine European legal order, if not a European Constitution, which, however, is still incomplete. This would imply ideally that the DCFR deals with three different though interlinked issues: first, how the particular values enshrined in the DCFR may and should be made compatible with the underlying values of

---

[129]   As part of the 'better regulation' policy of the EU, see http://ec.europa.eu/governance/better_regulation/index_en.htm, S. Weatherill (eds.), *Better Regulation* (2007); more particularly with regard to the role and function of the Impact Assessment Procedure in the drafting of the Commission Proposal on consumer rights, see H.-W. Micklitz, 'The Targeted Full Harmonisation Approach: Looking behind The Curtain', in Howells and Schulze (eds.), *Modernising and Harmonising Consumer Contract Law* (2009), 47–86.

[130]   See not on the theory but on its importance in practice D. Kohlert, *Anlageberatung und Qualität – ein Widerspruch?* (2008); see now the project 'Behavioural Approaches to Contract and Tort: Relevance for Policy Making' by W. van Boom and M.G. Faure at the University of Rotterdam, http://www.frg.eur.nl/english/research/research_programmes/behavioural_approaches_to_contract_and_tort_relevance_for_policymaking/.

[131]   See Eidenmüller et al, 537.

[132]   See Micklitz and Weatherill, *European Economic Law* (1996).

national legal orders; secondly, how the DCFR manages the problem that the guiding sociological unit of today is no longer – alone – the nation state but the civil society; and, thirdly, how the DCFR intends to handle the multi-level – federal – character of the European Community.[133]

The underlying values of the DCFR – the balance between private autonomy and social justice – may compete with values enshrined in national legal orders, be it from the side of more social elements – more and even deeper social distributive justice towards a need orientated concept, as in the Scandinavian countries,[134] or less social elements – not social distributive but commutative justice[135] – as in the common law countries. The drafters of the DCFR have found a bewildering answer. As the DCFR is said to become the optional 28th legal order, it is for the parties to decide whether or not they are willing to substitute the respective national order or national legal orders in transboundary relationships by the DCFR. The so-called blue button[136] will solve all problems resulting from legal pluralism, from national private legal orders standing side by side with the DCFR. Choice is reduced to the rather technical question of how to find the 'appropriate legal order'. The blue button approach overlooks the fact that each national legal order is embedded in a particular historical and cultural environment which shapes the relationship of the citizen towards his or her state, be it to the good in the meaning of strong reliance on the fairness of the national legal order, be it to the bad in the meaning of distrust in the national legal order.[137] A proper European legal order as enshrined in the DCFR would have to gain a particular reputation as being a reliable order satisfying the particular expectations of the parties to a transborder or even national conflict. A European legal order representing the institutional framework of DCFR would need legitimacy and political support. Does European academia have the authority to guarantee legitimacy, accountability and transparency? It is hard to see how these difficulties can be overcome by pushing or not push-

---

[133]   The categorisation goes back to D. Kennedy, 'Two Globalisations'.

[134]   See T. Wilhelmsson, *Critical Studies in Private Law* (1992).

[135]   Of paradigmatic importance is the conflict over the question whether the concept of good faith provides for the substantive control of contract terms or whether it is limited to procedural control, see H.-W. Micklitz, 'Judgment of the House of Lords of 25 October 2001, The General of Fair Trading v First National Bank plc [2001] UKHL 52', *European Review of Contract Law* (2006), 471.

[136]   See H. Schulte-Nölke, 'EC Law on the Formation of Contract – from the Common Frame of Reference to the "Blue Button"', *European Review of Contract Law* (2007), 332.

[137]   See T. Wilhelmsson, 'The Abuse of the Confident Consumer as a Justification for EC Consumer Law', 27 *Journal of Consumer Policy* (2004), 317.

ing the blue button even if one concedes that such a European civil law culture is in the offing.[138]

The pluralism of values is linked to the multi-level structure of the European Community.[139] The DCFR does not deal with the multi-level structure at all. To put it bluntly, where is the 'state' at the EU level which could fulfil a function similar to that of the nation state? The answer to this question relates to the sources of law at the EU level. It is obvious that, in particular at the EU level, there is more than one source of law to be considered. Co-regulation and soft law mechanisms[140] are at the forefront of the development but have not been touched upon by the DCFR. Private law, which is more and more detached from national boundaries, from nation states, from national institutions, leaves more and more room for civil society and private law making. The de-nationalisation of private law enhances and enlarges the leeway for civil actors developing proper rules beyond nation state bound private laws. This is the deeper reason why it has been suggested to build a true European private legal order from the 'bottom up'.[141]

How are the different legal orders, the DCFR and the national private legal orders institutionally or even constitutionally interlinked? As is generally known, the United States has no federal private law, although the US Uniform Commercial Code sets out largely common though not identical standards throughout the 50 US states. International private law rules decide on the applicable law.[142] With regard to the EU it is still unclear whether and to what extent the DCFR could be regarded as a chosen legal order within the Rome I

---

[138] See O. Lando, 'The Structure and the Legal Values of the Common Frame of Reference (CFR)', 3 *European Review of Contract Law* (2007) 245 against P. Legrand, 'European Legal Systems are Not Coverging', 45 *International and Comparative Law Quarterly* (1996), 52

[139] See F. Cafaggi and H. Muir Watt, *The Making of European Private Law* (2008).

[140] F. Cafaggi (ed.) *Reframing Self-regulation in European Private Law* (2006); D. Schiek, 'Private Rule Making and European Governance: Issues of Legitimacy', *European Law Review* (2007), 443; P. Zumbansen, 'The Law of Society: Governance through Contract', CLPE Research Paper 2/2007 and in more detail under V.

[141] See J. Smits in this volume and H. Collins (2008).

[142] Forum shopping is subject to stricter rules, however, with regard to class actions: see R. Nagareda, 'Aggregation and its Discontents: Class Settlement Pressure, Class-Wide Arbitration, and CAFA', Vanderbilt Law and Economics Research Paper, No. 06-14, available at http://ssrn.com/abstract=920833; C. Sharkey, 'CAFA Settlement Notice Provision: Optimal Regulatory Policy?', 156 *University of Pennsylvania Law Review* (2008), available at http://ssrn.com/abstract=1133137; H. Erichson, 'CAFA's Impact on Class Action Lawyers', 156 *University of Pennsylvania Law Review* (2008), available at SSRN: http://ssrn.com/abstract=1083819.

Regulation.[143] The EC legislator was obviously not willing to treat the DCFR as a legal order which is comparable to that of the Member States.[144] If the DCFR cannot become a chosen legal order under the Rome I Regulation how else can it be treated? What is the legal nature of the DCFR in case the parties pushed the blue button? Can the DCFR be treated as standard terms?

The 'federal' dimension alludes predominantly to the preliminary reference procedure as the classical means by which the EU interlinks the national with the European legal order. It is by no means clear, however, whether the ECJ would have jurisdiction over the DCFR as a chosen order and/or whether the ECJ might apply Directive 93/13/EEC on Unfair Terms in Consumer Contracts or Directive 2005/29/EC on Unfair Commercial Practices to the DCFR. The DCFR remains silent. But there are more open issues which need to be solved in that vein. Quite contrary to the secondary EU law which is condensed in the *acquis* principles, the DCFR does not deal with enforcement, neither individually nor collectively. Again this is an issue which deserves more scrutiny.[145] Politically, enforcement ranks high on the agenda. The plea that Member States benefit from procedural autonomy[146] is not really helpful, as the EU legislator in tandem with the ECJ is narrowing down the procedural autonomy not only by imposing EU standards on litigation but also by introducing new remedies.[147] Whilst the DCFR does not deal with 'procedural rules' it lays down rights and remedies in contract and in tort law.[148] Do the procedural standards as developed by the ECJ apply to the enforcement of these DCFR remedies? Or is it possible to imagine different procedural standards for remedies under the DCFR and for those remedies under (not necessarily) harmonised EC private law? The question reaches beyond the more technical issue of whether Article 234 of the European Treaty applies or not. In the minds of the drafters the DCFR is the 28th legal order, but as a European legal device it does not stand side by side with the 27 others, it has to face the multi-level, i.e. federal, structure of the European Community.

---

[143]   Regulation 593/2008 OJ L177, 4.7.2008, 6. See F. Cafaggi and H. Muir Watt (eds.), *The Regulatory Functions of European Private Law* (2009).

[144]   See on the applicability of the Rome I Regulation to the DCFR, H. Muir Watt and R. Sefton-Green in this volume.

[145]   See below, section VI.

[146]   W. van Gerven, 'Of rights, remedies on procedure', 37 *Common Market Law Review* (2000), p. 501.

[147]   See F. Zoll, 'The Remedies for Non-Performance in the System of the Acquis Group', in R. Schulze (ed.), *Common Frame of Reference and Existing EC Contract Law* (2008), 189; F. Zoll, The Remedies for Non-Performance in the Proposed Consumer Rights Directive and the Europeanisation of Private Law', in G. Howells and R. Schule (eds.), *Modernising and Harmonising Consumer Contract Law* (2009), p. 279.

[148]   See below, section VI.

V.   PRIVATE LAW-MAKING AND EUROPEAN PRIVATE LAW[149]

The DCFR is designed to operate in a framework based on the conventional actors: private, individual, parties, judges and the legislator. Collective actors have been left out of the picture. Regulators, both public and private, are missing. Collective private organisations are not considered. And a theory of sources that would be able to incorporate them is absent. This approach fails to reflect the evolution of European private law as a multi-level system both descriptively and normatively.[150]

The role of public regulation in EPL is relevant at both the European and Member States level The interplay between competition, regulation and consumer protection has become an important source of new rules and principles shaping EU and domestic laws.[151] The two most common examples are provided by Directive 93/13 on unfair contract terms, which applies also to regulated markets and Directive 2005/29, which also has general application and the enforcement of which has been primarily attributed to regulators. Competition authorities and sector specific authorities have shaped many principles of European private law. New contract law rules concerning duty to deal and long-term contracts in both BtoB and BtoC frameworks have been devised while applying competition law principles. In the field of competition law the recent development of private enforcement has certainly contributed to the emergence of rules concerning remedies and damages in the area of consumer protection.[152] Regulated markets provide additional rules affecting private law: from the duty to deal until the right to terminate contracts, sectors specific regulators have designed new rules affecting not only consumer contract law but also BtoB contracts.[153] The DCFR does not explain why these principles developed in newly liberalised markets should not be integrated in European private law. Is there a strong theoretical reason why private law in regulated markets should be kept separate? To what extent does (or should) the concrete level of liberalisation and competition define the boundaries and the domains of EPL and thus of DCFR? The separation between unregulated or free market and regulated market is an artefact of XIX legal thinking and the role of

---

[149]   This section builds on F. Cafaggi, 'Private Regulation and European Private Law', in A. Hartkamp et al (eds.) *Towards a European Civil Code* (4th edn, 2010).

[150]   See F. Cafaggi, 'Private Regulation in European Private Law', *RSCAS* w.p. 2001/31; F. Cafaggi and H. Muir Watt (eds.), *The Regulatory Functions of European Private Law* (2009).

[151]   See *supra* section III.

[152]   See N. Reich, 'Rights without Duties', EUI Working Paper (forthcoming).

[153]   See F. Cafaggi, 'Diritto dei contratti nei mercati regolati', *RTDPC* (2008).

private law as an agent of European legal integration makes it necessary to reach a coordinated system of rules, including those of regulated markets.

Not only contract law in regulated markets but also property and civil liability rules constitute an important part of the European *acquis* affecting the identity and functions of EPL. Partially liberalised markets include rules that have been and could be reference points for other markets, when the assumption of full competition falls short.

The role of private law-making in EPL is rather relevant as well. It contributes to the creation of internal market and, in a complementary fashion with public regulation, to address market failures.[154] It influences contract, property, civil liability, unfair competition and many other areas. Examples ranging from the Euro payment system to the technical standardisation, from environmental to food law, from advertising to warranties. Private regulation consists of different forms. It encompasses pure self-regulation and different forms of co-regulation from delegation of regulatory tasks to private bodies to *ex post* approval.[155]

Private regulation constitutes a multi-level system articulated in different ways depending on whether it is promoted by associations or by market players.[156] Often when trade associations draft regulatory principles there is a coordination between the state and the European levels at which these associations operate. Some initiatives are promoted at EU level while implemented at national level, others start at the state level, to be subsequently endorsed at EU level.

Private regulators often compete while supplying rules and standards. Often there are many organisations which produce standards and rules competing over regulated enterprises. In other contexts, rules are generated by the dominant European market players outside and at times even against trade associations. In this case often the main driver is the exclusion of competitors. Private actors are often conflicting and multiple regimes are in place in forms that certainly reflect normative pluralism, but at times increase regulatory costs overburdening the enterprises without real benefits for the 'beneficiaries'. Whether private regulation operates as an agent of European legal inte-

---

154   See F. Cafaggi, 'Self-regulation in European Contract Law' (2007), available at www.eui.eu and H. Collins, *Standard Contract Terms* (2008), p. 93; see also H. Collins, *The Right to Circulate Document* (2004); F. Cafaggi, 'Private Regulation in European Private Law', *RSCAS* w.p. 2009/31.

155   For a definition of self- and co-regulation see the Interinstitutional Agreement 31.12.2003. On the role of self-regulation in EPL see F. Cafaggi, 'Rethinking Private Regulation in the European Regulatory Space', in F. Cafaggi (ed.), *Reframing Self-Regulation in European Private Law* (2006), p. 3.

156   See F. Cafaggi, 'Private Law Making and European Legal Integration', in D. Oliver, T. Prosser and R. Rawlings (eds.) (forthcoming 2010).

gration or as a multiplier of fragmentation depends on the market structure and on the anti-competitive goals promoted by the players. Clearly the higher the presence of different stakeholders in the law-making process the lower the probability that private regulation may produce fragmentation instead of integration.

These private regulatory regimes often reflect the need to integrate markets, but may also present anti-competitive features. Competition authorities, both at EU and national level, have contributed to define principles and boundaries of private regulatory activity, ensuring that private regulation does not translate into market fragmentation but rather into market integration.[157]

Self-regulation operates in the field of contract standardisation but also in that of unfair trade practices, for example in deceptive advertisement law and in civil liability both in the area of professional malpractice and in that of product liability. Co-regulation is emerging in many fields but has a long-standing tradition in professional services, sports and to some extent in product safety regulation. We may distinguish between legislative and judicial co-regulation. The former is a relatively recent phenomenon although forms of legislative co-regulation go back to the Middle Ages in Europe.[158] The latter is an older form and it is based on judicial recognition of standards defined by collective actors accessing the legal system by way of custom or trade usages.[159] It plays an important role in the law of negligence and strict liability where standards of care are defined by professional bodies or by industry associations where judges can refer to customs for evidentiary purposes. Compliance with these standards never excludes liability, while violations of them can constitute the basis for tort and breach of contract.[160] Many regimes of liability in European tort law are co-designed by private organisations and judges but no references to this source is made in the DCFR.

Co-regulation is eroding some of the spaces traditionally occupied by self-regulation thereby signalling an increasing degree of public legislation, especially at EU level, but it also covers fields earlier occupied by legislation and command and control regulation.

---

[157] See F. Cafaggi, 'Self-Regulation in European Contract Law', in H. Collins (ed.), *Standard Contract Terms* (2008), p. 93.

[158] See F. Van Waarden, 'Where to Find a Demos for Controlling Global Risk Regulators from Private to Public Regulation and Back', in J. C. Graz and A. Nolke (eds.), *Transnational Private Governance and its Limits* (2008), p. 84 ff.

[159] See J. Basedow, *American Journal of Comparative Law* (2008).

[160] See G. Spindler, 'Interaction Between Product Liability and Regulation at the European Level' and F. Cafaggi, 'Product Safety, Private Standard-setting and Information Networks', in F. Cafaggi and H. Muir Watt, *The Regulatory Functions of European Private Law* (2009).

What are the implications of the increasing role of private regulation for the design of European private law? There are at least three dimensions, namely:

a) on the theory of sources of law;
b) on substantive law, in particular on the relationship between rule-making and enforcement involving collective actors; and
c) on the importance of the governance dimension.

The multi-level structure of EPL, reinforced by the reference to private regulation suggests that the traditional institutional framework through which coordination among different layers occurs has to be revisited. EPL, in the DCFR approach, has mainly been conceived as legislated private rules. But many, if not the majority of, rules in the domain of private law are privately produced by both individual and collective actors. Failure to consider private law-making as a legal format of EPL poses several problems concerning institutional design and effectiveness of the regulatory functions. In particular the focus on legislative harmonisation and the shift towards full harmonisation does not address the real factors contributing to divergent implementation.[161] Full harmonising legislation deploying general clauses and principles is bound to bring about different outcomes in Member States with different legal traditions and judicial styles. A governance design is needed to address different interpretations of European legislation not amounting to infringements but also spillover effects on the domestic legislation of Member States. For this reason we have proposed the creation of a European Law Institute, with a section devoted to European private law, which will foster judicial cooperation in civil and commercial matters and contribute to the creation of a 'real' legal European community including judges, lawyers, notaries and other legal professionals.[162]

VI.   DCFR AND COLLECTIVE REDRESS

One of the most relevant omissions in the DCFR is related to collective

---

[161]   For further elaboration see F. Cafaggi, 'Making European Private Law. Governance Design', in F. Cafaggi and H. Muir-Watt, *Making European Private Law* (2008), p. 289 ff.

[162]   For references see F. Cafaggi, 'The Making of European Private Law: Governance Design', in F. Cafaggi and H. Muir-Watt, *Making European Private Law* (2008), p. 289; H. Collins, *The European Civil Code. The Way Forward* (2008), p. 210 ff.

redress.[163] Neither in relation to contract nor to extra-contractual liability is collective redress considered. The focus is exclusively on individual remedies. It is hard to explain the reasons for this choice. Collective redress is certainly part of the Consumer *acquis*.[164] In particular injunctive relief constitutes a pillar of the Unfair Contract Terms Directive 93/13, Unfair Commercial Practices UCPD 2005/29, and, more generally, Directive 98/27 which applies to the main directives in the consumer field.[165]

In the area of consumer protection public enforcement has gained momentum and, as the case of UCPD shows, Member States have chosen primarily administrative enforcement to ensure collective redress.[166] The interplay between administrative enforcement, concerning the collective dimension, and judicial enforcement relating to individual harm, implies the necessity to coordinate the rules of DCFR with different forms of collective enforcement including administrative enforcement.[167]

The omission of collective redress concerns not only injunctive relief but also pecuniary remedies. In the last decade, many Member States have introduced legislation concerning group actions mainly choosing opt-in systems.[168] The enactment of new legislation on enforcement has generated a multi-level system where injunctions are mainly regulated at EU level, displaying a relative degree of uniformity, while group actions are regulated at Member State level, with a greater level of divergence. Collective redress goes far beyond the procedural aspects. These group and representative actions are likely to promote the development of new rules in the area of tort and contract, and the DCFR should take these developments into account.

---

[163]   See Principles, Definitions and Model Rules of European Private Law, Draft Common Frame of Reference (DCFR) Outline edition, Sellier, 2009 B.I I.-I.101, Intended field of application. In particular the reference to procedure and enforcement.

[164]   See Green Paper COM(2008)794 final.

[165]   On the application of Directive 98/27 see H.-W. Micklitz, Peter Rott, Ulrike Docekal and Peter Kolba, 'Verbraucherschutz durch Unterlassungsklagen, Rechtliche und Praktische Umsetzung der Richtlinie Unterlassungsklagen 98/27/EG in den Mitgliedstaaten', *VIEW Schriftenreihe* (2007).

[166]   See F. Cafaggi and H. Micklitz, 'Collective Enforcement of Consumer Law: a Framework for Comparative Assessment', *European Review of Private Law* (2008), 391.

[167]   See F. Cafaggi and H. Micklitz, 'The Way Forward' in F. Cafaggi and H. Micklitz (eds.), *New Frontiers of Consumer Protection* (2009).

[168]   See the Green Paper. For a detailed analysis see F. Cafaggi and H. Micklitz, *New Frontiers of Consumer Protection* (2009); 'The Globalization of Class Action', in *The Annals of the American Academy of Political and Social Sciences* (2009); C. Hodges, *The Reform of Class and Representative Actions in European Legal Systems. A New Framework for Collective Redress in Europe* (2008).

Failure to consider collective redress has strong policy implications. It is now well recognised that European private law has an important regulatory function.[169] The regulatory dimension, earlier emphasised in relation to information and contract law, has in fact a broader spectrum.[170] Enforcement plays a very significant role in ensuring that this regulatory function is correctly implemented. In particular, collective enforcement and aggregate litigation contribute to respond to market failures: asymmetric information and externalities.[171] An injunction concerning deletion of an unfair contract term, recommended by a trade association, polices the market and ensures that btoc standard form contracts do not externalise costs on consumers. These externalities would produce inefficient results by reducing the level of trade, discouraging consumers to enter into the transaction in the first place. Affirmative injunctions concerning information about consumer rights or risks associated with products reduce asymmetric information, ensuring that consumers will make informed choices and thus achieve or at least approach market efficiency.[172] But other regulatory dimensions are also touched by collective redress. Deterrence can only be pursued through collective redress when the value of individual claims is low but the aggregate value is high.[173] Failure to consider collective redress can undermine the deterrence goal, leaving it only to administrative enforcement. The most recent developments in the field of private collective enforcement show that deterrence, more than compensation, is the main aim.[174]

In the field both of contract and extra-contractual liability the collective dimension of enforcement has become quantitatively and qualitatively the most important factor and certainly a key element in designing and regulating the internal market. This omission also partly reflects the structure of substantive law in relation both to contract and extra-contractual liability laid out by the authors of DCFR.

---

[169]   See F. Cafaggi and H. Muir Watt, *The Regulatory Functions of European Private Law* (2009); H. Collins, *The European Civil Code* (2008); F. Cafaggi (ed.), *The Institutional Framework of European Private Law* (2006).

[170]   See S. Grundman, W. Kerber and S. Weatherill, *Party Autonomy and the Role of Information in the Internal Market* (2001).

[171]   See G. Miller in F. Cafaggi and H. Micklitz, *New Frontiers of Consumer Protection: The Interplay Between Private and Public Enforcement.*

[172]   See F. Cafaggi, 'Duties to Inform and Collective Redress. The Role of Enforcement in the Regulatory Function of EPL', paper presented at Helsinki seminar on DCFR and collective redress, April 2009.

[173]   See ALI Principles on aggregate litigation (2009).

[174]   See the different essays in F. Cafaggi and H. Micklitz, *New Frontiers of Consumer Protection: The Interplay Between Private and Public Enforcement.*

In the contractual domain where the main structure of contract, including its definition, provided in Book II, 1:101 mainly refers to individual, i.e., bilateral, contracts. The core of DCFR contract law, reflecting an approach close to national codifications, is still centred around the classical bilateral contract, while mass transactions and multilateral contracts constitute the exception more than the rule. Unfortunately this omission follows a similar failure in the PECL where collective enforcement remedies in mass transactions both in btob and btoc have not been sufficiently considered. The omission of injunction in the field of contract law breaks the unitary approach undertaken by current European legislation where – as it is the case in the Unfair Contract Terms Directive – both individual and collective remedies have been included. Regrettably, a similar choice has been made in the proposal of the Directive concerning consumer rights where only individual remedies have been included.[175]

In the extra-contractual domain a similar deficiency emerges but its consequences are even more serious. Mass torts are a reality in the environmental field, in product liability, in service provisions, in the financial market; a legal framework of extra-contractual liability limited to individual remedies does not capture the central functions of the contemporary tort systems. Both deterrence and compensation are promoted, mainly in the context of mass torts, while the traditional bilateral unlawful interaction plays an ever more minor role. Mass torts often require some type of aggregate litigation even in the context of personal injuries.[176]

The omission of collective redress begs a question: are there good reasons to separate the body of European private law concerning individual remedies from that related to collective remedies? Two potential rationales can be provided to justify the omission. Neither seems to be persuasive.

The first rationale may be institutional. According to the conventional view, while substantive law is Europeanised, remedies should be left at the national level following the principle of procedural autonomy.[177] This potential justification is flawed because on the positive side there is already legislation at EU level concerning collective redress.[178] At least for the injunctive relief there should be no institutional obstacle to including it in the DCFR. However, more

---

[175] See Proposal on Consumer Rights, COM(2008)614 final, on which see Micklitz and Reich, *CMLR* (2009), 471.
[176] On the relationship between mass torts and aggregate litigation, see J. Stapleton and A. Bernstein.
[177] See on these questions T. Tridimas, *Principles of EU Law* (2nd edn, 2006); M. Dougan, *Remedies for EU Law Breach* (2004).
[178] See W. van Gerven, 'On Rights, Remedies and Procedure', *CMLR* (2000); N. Reich in Micklitz, Reich and Rott, *Understanding Consumer Law* (2009), p. 317.

generally the separation between substantive and remedial rules at different institutional levels should be limited, because it generates divergences in the application of European legislation at Member State level, undermining the regulatory objectives of consumer protection and promotion of competition.

The second rationale may be substantive. The collective dimension of contractual and extra-contractual violations concerning not only the remedial but also the substantive side, would require a separate body of rules. The US experience shows that the use of class action and aggregate litigation has generated, especially in the area of tort law, a specific body of rules concerning liability, causation, remedies, different from those related to individual harm. Collective enforcement could be integrated and certainly should be coordinated with the general body of principles in contract and extra-contractual liability.

Often collective and individual remedies have to be coordinated. The most frequent example is provided by an injunction followed by a claim to seek damages. The relationship between collective and individual enforcement varies. There may be simultaneous enforcement with claims sought before the same or different courts, or there may be sequential enforcement, when collective redress comes first and individual remedies follow.[179]

The regulatory function of European private law would be seriously undermined if the collective enforcement dimension were separated from that of individual remedies. The institutional design of future European legislation should thus consider different forms of coordination between collective redress and substantive rules in the area of contract and civil liability.

a) Full integration. This is the most radical form and implies that both individual and collective remedies are included, specifying, if necessary, which substantive rules should be applied in relation to collective redress. This is the current legislative solution for unfair contract terms, and there are no good reasons to change as proposed in the DCFR.
b) Strong coordination. Strong coordination should occur when the level of specificity of collective redress is such that a separate body of rules, including substantive and evidentiary, should be designed. This may be the case in the area of product liability where product recall and withdrawal are available, at EU level, as administrative remedies. The experience in other legal systems shows that collective redress in this area may call for specific rules concerning causation and damages for future and latent harms.[180] Thus coordination between the individual and collective

---

[179] See on the policy implications of sequential enforcement F. Cafaggi and H. Micklitz, *Way Forward*.
[180] See J. Stapleton.

dimensions, including substantive and remedial rules, may be preferable to full integration

c) Light coordination. This is desirable especially when collective enforcement operates through administrative entities. As it is the case in many areas of consumer protection, administrative enforcement, consisting of injunctions but also on undertakings by enterprises, is often deployed. This probably leads to forms of sequential enforcement where individual litigation seeking damages, restitution or contract invalidity, follows issuance of the administrative remedy. Coordination should be designed between administrative and judicial enforcement so as to minimise litigation costs and maximise consistency of outcomes. This coordination cannot be limited to the remedial aspects because often the definition of unfair terms or practices or of a defective or unsafe product may vary, therein, leading to divergent or conflicting results.

The next round of research should include collective redress in the design of European private law and address the different forms of integration and coordination between individual and collective remedies.

VII. EUROPEAN PRIVATE LAW LEGAL INTEGRATION AND A LEGAL EUROPEAN COMMUNITY

The DCFR clearly represents an important juncture of the development of European private law. However several questions concerning the domain, the institutional framework and the governance design have been left unanswered. The search for a common private law for Europe needs to be carried on. We believe that a second round of research is needed in order to provide clear directions at least on these five dimensions:

1. the domain: i.e., the definition of the *acquis communautaire* relevant for EPL and the role of the common core of national legal systems;
2. the constitutional dimension of EPL. In particular the role of fundamental rights and common constitutional principles;
3. the role of private law-making;
4. the relationship between general private law and private law in regulated markets;
5. the role of enforcement and the rules of civil procedure.

a) The Institutional Question

The formation of European private law which includes partly the regulated markets needs to define which role national regulators and their coordinating institutions will play. In national legal systems the sector-specific and competition regulators contribute to the implementation of European private law. Specific devices for coordination are needed both among regulators and between them and the national judiciaries. Perhaps the most urgent improvements concern judicial cooperation in civil and commercial matters. To operationalise the current judicial networks and make them coordinate the judicial applications of European law, but also address spillovers into areas which are not technically within the European competences is of utmost relevance.

b)   The Governance Dimension

The creation of European private law is part of a broader process of European legal integration which cannot proceed solely on legislative paths. Legal integration must be based on a European community made up of European and national institutions where judges and practising lawyers together with legal academics contribute to the process. The drafting process of the DCFR with the distinction between drafters and stakeholders needs to be reconceived in the light of processes where the judiciary will be directly involved, both in finding the common law and designing the new rules. For these reasons a European Law Institute (ELI) is needed. Within the ELI, European private law should play an important role. A general ELI not limited to private law will enable better coordination with related fields and promote the creation of a community of European lawyers. The next months should be devoted to design structure and tasks of such an independent institution which, in collaboration primarily with the European Commission, the European Parliament, the Council and the Court of Justice, will have to contribute to non-legislative harmonisation and to coordination among Member States' legal systems.

VIII.   SHORT SUMMARY OF THE VARIOUS CONTRIBUTIONS

Somma's analysis focuses on the tension between different economic and political models which underpin the development of the DCFR. EC law refers on the one hand to the 'principle of an open market economy with free competition' (Article 4 of the EC Treaty) and on the other to 'fundamental rights' as they result from 'the constitutional traditions common to the Member States' (Article 6 of the EC Treaty). One might associate these fundamental principles with different visions of the market economy and of the political system.

Somma draws a distinction between principles and rules discussed in the introduction to the Articles of the DCFR. He then coordinates the principles with some model rules, selected, as is explained, because of their mandatory nature and therefore their high degree of ability to restrict a party's autonomy. The DCFR claims, this is the argument, to combine two different sets of fundamental principles, ordo-liberal ones and alternatives of solidarity and social justice enshrined into the constitutionalisation process of European private law. The conflict between the two models, however, is not openly addressed. Somma defends the need to put the DCFR in a constitutional perspective which respects the constitutional traditions and in particular the role and importance of social rights.

Vettori in a sense takes up and continues the debate triggered by Somma. Vettori uses the principle of good faith in the DCFR and the Italian to demonstrate the tensions which result from the interpretation of such general concepts. The DCFR's reference to interpretative criteria in the event of diversity between parties' rights, and to the general role of good faith, he argues, is certainly important. Looking at the said reference and the legal criteria laid down by the Italian legislator, it can be inferred that the judge must (under Article 1366 of the Italian Civil Code and under DCFR, when the text has a binding value) construe the contract in line with the parties' common intention and ascertain the rights deriving from special laws. This must be done in accordance with fundamental freedoms which, through good faith, become exegetic criteria and conformity parameters for the legal meaning of the contract. This does not conflict with the foundation of the provision which protects a party's reliance on the reasonable meaning and content of the parties' statements and conducts, and thus their conformity to the parties' common intention, integrated by fundamental rights and freedoms.

Grundmann starts from the assumption that the (Academic) Common Frame of Reference is intended to serve – albeit among others – as a first model for a European Civil Code: however, that the process which led to the ACFR was such that competition of ideas and designs was largely excluded. He argues that, quite to the contrary, competition would be paramount in the development of a European Code and identifies three reasons which may be particularly important, namely: the method to be employed is not clear: should it rather be a traditional comparative law approach, a social sciences based approach, one where constitutional or EC Treaty values are meaningful or one of sound dogmatic thinking? The subject matter is not clear: should it rather be a grand old Civil Code, although family law, wills and estates, property law, and even torts and unjust enrichment can easily be dissociated from contract law and contract law has become so complex that finding a good structure for contract law is a question of just enough complexity anyhow. Finally, should a modern European Contract Code not be such that it reflects at least the modern problems and developments of the last three or four decades already? In his second core section, Grundmann, very tentatively, investigates some possible ways of how finally to introduce the competition needed.

Reich insists on the specific contribution of EU/EC law in distinguishing private and public law. Even though it was initially mostly concerned with 'vertical' relations governed by public law, with competition law as the only exception, the later case law of the ECJ and secondary law have extended its impact on 'horizontal relations' supposed as governed by private autonomy. The first section is meant to demonstrate both the extent and the limits of this development, consequent to which the author pleads for a reconsideration of the doctrine of 'horizontal direct effect'. A further section, devoted to substantive concepts, insists on the importance of the non-discrimination principle for private law relations which, in the interest of legal certainty must however find its concretisation in secondary law. As an overall conclusion, EC law is seen to be oriented towards 'communitative justice' in private law relations, supplemented by 'corrective justice', and less towards distributive justice. Under the impact of the internal market imperatives, the public/private divide, Reich argues, becomes more and more blurred. Private law thereby assumes a public function.

For *Smits* the DCFR suffers from so-called methodological nationalism: the DCFR adopts a view of law and law making developed for national jurisdictions and in doing so, it takes too little into account the fact that what is best at the national level may not be optimal at the European one. This contention is justified with reference to three different features of the DCFR: the idea of comprehensive codification, the choice of the relevant rules and the way in which law is represented. For Smits the DCFR should be presented in a differentiated way, dependent on whether its function is to create binding rules, offer a source of inspiration for legal scholarship and teaching or take the first step towards the creation of an optional contract code.

Gomez argues that the model rules in the DCFR, like other legal rules, have the intention of affecting the behaviour of relevant parties subject to them. Thus it seems *prima facie* wise to consider how the latter would likely respond to the rules. In recent years, social scientists in economics and psychology, primarily, have studied human interaction in contracting and similar environments. They have studied such types of behaviour both in laboratory settings and in real-world markets using rigorous empirical techniques. The main source of empirical information for the DCFR, however, seems to be comparative legal analyses of EU law and the laws of European countries. But if the impact of contract law on social welfare is taken seriously, empirical studies of contracting behaviour, both in consumer markets and in firm-to-firm interaction, should carry some weight in assessing legal solutions in contract law and in crafting them in an informed way.

Hesselink analyses the ideas of Friedrich von Hayek in shaping the future of European private law. In response to a manifesto on social justice in European contract law which was concerned about the CFR process as it had been announced by the European Commission, some legal scholars have defended by reference to Hayek that law making is a long process of *trial* and *error* through which a partly spontaneous order has come into being. Hayek wrote extensively, not only on economics, political science and psychology, but also on law. His style is crystal clear and cogent and his rhetoric superb. But Hesselink asks whether he is convincing. In particular, should his ideas play an important role in the current debate concerning the future of private law in Europe? Should European private law indeed become a spontaneous order? And what does Hayek's theory of law have to offer for the choices which are currently on the table concerning European contract law?

Jansen asks to what extent the academic draft of a Common Frame of Reference (DCFR) could and perhaps should become a text of legal authority for the present and future European private law. It is based on the observation that the authority of legal texts has never been determined by political authorities, outside the legal system, alone: the authority of a legal text – legislation, precedent and academic writing – is ultimately decided on from within, by the participants to legal discourse and by their attitude towards the text in question. On the basis of these observations, it is argued that the present proposal for a DCFR should not be furnished with the inner-legal authority of a European reference text. It is not a homogeneous text, but an – normatively and systematically – incoherent compilation of divergent 'text-masses'; it cannot be understood as a fair restatement of European private law; and it leaves the decisive question of the law to the judge instead of deciding it itself; at the same time, it unnecessarily and unconvincingly dogmatises private law.

The contribution of *Möslein* is primarily concerned with the process of legal innovation that the DCFR might trigger. The question is, will it provide a dynamic framework for legal innovation? Legal innovation implies more than the reaction of the legal system to changes in social values and economic conditions. Legal innovation, it is argued, requires some new, creative element which was not formerly part of the relevant legal framework. It requires some sort of intellectual advance relative to the current state of the law. As regards contract law, such intellectual advances can originate in the creativity of private parties, their lawyers, the business community at large, national or supranational legislators, the courts or legal academia. Legal innovation can literally occur at any level of the legal hierarchy. Yet both the process and likelihood of legal innovation depend on the institutional framework in which these actors operate.

Muir Watt and *Sefton-Green* test the consequences of the DCFR being seen as an optional instrument. They come to the conclusion that if too many areas of contract law rules are categorised as default, or rather, dispositive rules, then freedom of contract will prevail. If, however, default rules are restricted to real gap-filling rules, as suggested, the parties' choice and margin for manoeuvre are severely curtailed. Reducing party choice may sometimes be necessary and can often be justified on the grounds of social justice. If a more accurate analysis is carried out to identify which rules are really dispositive, then the whole idea of an optional instrument may fall apart. Offering the parties an additional choice of an optional instrument is said to run the risk of dressing up a wolfish market-functional liberal ideal of contract law in sheep's clothing.

1. Towards a European private law? The Common Frame of Reference in the conflict between EC law and national laws

Alessandro Somma

1. ACADEMICS AND STAKEHOLDERS IN THE MAKING OF EUROPEAN PRIVATE LAW

About three years ago, the European Commission appointed an international network of research groups (Joint Network on European Private Law) to develop 'a Common Frame of Reference for European Contract Law' (Cfr), expected to be presented in the form of a 'draft' (Dcfr). The aim is to provide 'principles, definitions and model rules', identified by 'taking into account national laws', including both case law and established practice, as well as 'the EC *acquis* and relevant international instruments' (FP 6 – Contract n. 513351).

The Cfr will assist in the improvement of 'the quality of legislation already in place' towards 'a modernisation of existing instruments' and may form the basis of an 'optional instrument not limited to particular sectors', which would provide parties to a contract with 'a modern body of rules particularly adapted to cross-border contracts in the internal market' (COM(2001)398 final and COM(2003)68 final). Its immediate purpose is to act as a 'guide or tool box' for the EC legislator in the revision of the *acquis* (Von Bar et al., 2008a, p. 37).

The Cfr will also contribute to the making of a European legal science, something which is considered by many an essential condition for the development of European private law.

The first results are now available in an interim edition (Draft Common Frame of Reference – Interim edition (Dcfr-Ie). Articles without further indication belong to this text) (Von Bar et al., 2008b) which allows academics and other interested parties to comment before the final version is published. In the final edition, which is expected by the end of 2008, this text will be completed with additional material and accompanied by 'comments and comparative notes'.

The draft proposal, apart from a brief introduction, contains only Articles.

The Dcfr-Ie is the result of work by two research teams co-operating in the Joint Network: the Study Group on a European Civil Code and the Research Group on the Existing EC Private Law (the so-called Acquis Group).

The Study Group continues and supplements the work of the Commission on European Contract Law, which presented the well-known Principles on European Contract Law (Pecl) (Lando and Beal, 2000). The Study group has the task of formulating the 'Principles of European Law' (Pel), derived from the existing private law rules in the various legal systems of the Member States, whereas the Acquis Group is required to 'present and structure the bulky and rather incoherent patchwork of EC private Law' (Von Bar et al., 2008a, p. 28).

The Dcfr-Ie is therefore a synthesis of two groups of rules: on one hand, rules which form part of the so-called new European *ius commune*, collected from identifying commonalities in national contract laws, and on the other hand, rules of EC law, the coordination of which is one of the main problems that its authors have to face. As I aim to demonstrate, in contrast to the position generally held in Italy, the two groups express policies that are difficult to reconcile (Somma, 2003, p. 7 ff.), or at least that can be considered a unity only through the creation of a 'façade' (Blanc, 2008, p. 566). This creates the risk of cancelling the cultural identity of national laws, threatened more by so-called top-down harmonisation than by the process of identifying what they have in common (Sefton-Green, 2007a, p. 207 ff. and 2007b, p. 37 ff.).

Another five groups which are part of the Joint Network and called upon to contribute to the work from specific points of view did not take part in compiling the Dcfr-Ie, for reasons we shall look at shortly. Each group has its own tasks. The Research Group on the Economic Assessment of Contract Law Rules is responsible for the evaluation of the economic impact of the Dcfr, 'taking into consideration the needs of the economic operators in the internal market'. The Common Core Group is responsible for the assessment regarding the applicability of the Dcfr, to be achieved through the method of factual approach. The *Association Henri Capitant* together with the *Société de Législation Comparée* and the *Conseil Supérieur du Notariat* focus on the philosophical underpinnings of the Dcfr as well on the different conceptions of law (FP 6 – Contract n. 513351).

It is noteworthy that not only scholars collaborate on the construction of the Dcfr-Ie: stakeholders also play a crucial role. This expression usually indicates any group or individual which is conditioned by or can condition the achievement of an organisation's aims, and therefore groups and individuals that tend to be represented in various social areas (Freeman, 1984, p. 5). However, the stakeholders that have been involved mainly represent the world of business and the legal profession, and no role has been allocated to social actors affected by contract law and its distributive effects (Somma, 2007, p. 17 ff.).

As the introduction to Dcfr-Ie shows, some changes in the Pecl Articles resulted from the input from stakeholders to workshops held by the European Commission on selected topics (Von Bar et al., 2008a, p. 25). These changes imply a reduction in the normative political matrix of the European *ius commune* in favour of a value system embodied by EC law.

In this light, the Dcfr can be considered, as its authors underline, an academic and not a political product (Schulze, 2008, p. 3). However, the label 'academic' simply attributes the draft to the profession of its authors, academics who joined together to form an international network, and does not mean that it is an independent creation of legal science, produced on the basis of considerations that aspire to be of merely technical value.

2. STRUCTURE AND FUNCTION OF THE COMMON FRAME OF REFERENCE

The Dcfr-Ie deals with areas of private law that do not coincide with all those classically considered by national codifications of the nineteenth century (Schulze, 2008, p. 11), but which are, however, broader than those – all regarding the subject of contracts – the European Commission referred to. The latter has sometimes considered the interaction between contract laws and property laws, however only to affirm that, in preparing the Dcfr, there is a need to evaluate the possible problems arising from the interaction between contract law and property law (COM(2004)651 final). Only the European Parliament seems to be closer to the formulation of the Joint Network (A5-0384/2001). Yet it has so far not been given a sufficiently large role to play in the making of the European private law (a complaint made in P6_TA/2007/0615).

In a certain way, the Pecl – a point of reference for the drafting of the Dcfr – also went beyond the area of contracts. They could be applied 'by analogy, also to other juridical acts' (Von Bar et al., 2008a, p. 19). Equally, the Dcfr-Ie, in addition to contract as a type of juridical act (Book II) and as a legal relationship (Book III), some specific contracts (Book IV), addressed sources of obligation other than the contract. The areas regulated include the benevolent intervention in another's affairs (Book V), non-contractual liability arising out of damage caused to another (Book VI) and unjustified enrichment (Book VII). The Dcfr will also deal with topics related to property law, such as acquisition and loss of ownership in movables (Book VIII), security rights in movables (Book IX) and trusts (Book X). There are no provisions, however, on immovable property, either concerning family relationships, including matrimonial relationships, or similar relationships and employment relationships (art. I.-1:101 (2)).

The distinction between act and legal relationship is also noteworthy. This is highlighted in the introduction to the Dcfr-Ie as characterising its approach to contract law (Von Bar et al., 2008a, p. 22 f. and 2007, p. 359). Yet, the distinction does not appear to imply any reference to the presuppositions from which it has taken its inspiration, i.e. the view of the contract as an act of social communication, to which one can attribute a meaning in the wake of further elements than the intention of the parties (Betti, 1950, p. 51 ff. and Scognamiglio, 1969, p. 83 ff.). The distinction, in fact, appears functional to the development of a general part of the law of obligations – a choice refused when the Pecl were drawn up (Lando, 2006, p. 475 ff.) – in harmony with what is a particularly German trait, according to which one must cultivate a taste for abstraction and favour the precision of the text over its comprehensibility (Lando, 2007, p. 249 f. and Shulze, 2008, p. 13).

Yet, these aspects, like the debate on the structure of the Dcfr, are destined to be of merely academic interest. The European Commission is not interested in rules concerning areas of private law in which it has not asked for intervention. On the contrary, it seems to be focussed on much more limited aspects than those to which it referred in its early documents: the mere regulation of consumer contracts and sectors of general contract law directly applicable to it (Kuneva, 2007, p. 955 ff. and Hesselink, 2007, pp. 325 and 345). The most recent efforts by the EC have indeed been concentrated on these regulations (COM(2006)744 final) and this was the basis for the invitation 'to ensure that materials related to the consumer *acquis* are treated as a priority' (COM(2007)447 final. See also P6_TA/2007/0615).

All this occurred while, within the debate on the law applicable to contractual obligations, the initial favour shown towards the free choice of a 'possible future optional Community instrument' seems to have waned (COM(2005)650 final. See also Fauvarque-Cosson, 2007, p. 100 f.); furthermore, the Council of the European Union has just recommended that the Commission consider the Cfr a text to which to attribute a function that would be, if possible, more limited than the original idea of a 'tool box'. It was rather to be a tool amongst others to improve the production of legislation at the EC level: a 'non-binding' instrument, to be considered merely as a 'source of inspiration' (8092/08 JUSTCIV 64 CONSOM 37).

3.   COMMON AND FUNDAMENTAL PRINCIPLES OF EUROPEAN PUBLIC LAW

The reference to 'principles' in the title of the Dcfr-Ie – evidently comparable with the 'general rules' mentioned during the descriptions of the tasks entrusted to the Joint Network – appears also in European Commission documents dedicated to European private law. These speak first of 'common principles' (and sometimes of 'common denominators') of national contract laws (COM(2001)398 final and COM(2003)68 final) without, however, clarifying what it is intended to refer to, or clarifying it only in an allusive manner. It limits itself, in fact, to speaking of principles of the same 'open texture' (Chamboredon, 2001, p. 5) of the US Restatements (COM(2001)398 final and COM(2003)68 final).

This seems to many to exhaust the field of possibilities for referring to the work of the American Law Institute; in other words, there can be no further analogies, given that national legal systems often do not correspond, and therefore that these principles necessarily come from a more creative process the aim of which is that of identifying 'a common core' (Lando and Beal, 2000, p. xxvi).

The same cannot be said about the work of the *Acquis* Group, the members of which are explicitly inspired by the 'classic Restatement of the American Law Institute' (Ajani-Schulte-Nölke, 2007, p. IX). It is well known that EC law is by tradition meant to be developed autonomously (art. I.-1:102 (1)).

Yet, EC law refers both to the 'principle of an open market economy with free competition' (Art. 4 EC Treaty) and to 'fundamental rights' as they result from 'the constitutional traditions common to the Member States' (Art. 6 EC Treaty). We are dealing with principles and rights (the latter are also referred to in the Dcfr-Ie when it identifies aims to be evaluated during its interpretation (art. I.-1:102 (2)) which may be in conflict. This means that the task of building the EC *acquis* is one which involves facing incompatibilities similar to those involved in selecting principles drawn from national legal systems.

The most recent Community documents do not speak of 'common principles of contract law' *tout court*, but of 'common fundamental principles of contract law' and likewise of their conceptual difference from 'key concepts' (COM(2004)651). It is thus not clear how to understand the notion of principles, which is in any case, at an EC level, a notion as much used as it is vague (Toriello, 2000, p. 99 ff.). Neither can indications be obtained on what EC documents dedicated to the construction of European private law intend by fundamental principles, even where they give examples: they allude only to the 'principle of contractual freedom' (COM(2001)398 final, COM(2003)68 final and COM(2005)456 final) and only in one case, for a 'mainly informative' purpose, to 'the principle of good faith and fair dealing' (COM(2006)744 final and COM(2007)447 final).

4.   THE LACK OF FUNDAMENTAL PRINCIPLES OF EUROPEAN CONTRACT LAW

The authors of the Dcfr-Ie state that the principles which converge in the Dcfr-Ie are such (and this was also highlighted when the Pecl were drafted) because they constitute 'general rules'. In this sense, they are different from 'fundamental principles', as EC documents seem to indicate: only the latter are 'underlying principles' which denote 'essentially abstract basic values' (Von Bar et al., 2008a, p. 9).

Fundamental principles do not, therefore, converge in the Dcfr-Ie, which rather contains 'model rules of more general nature' (Von Bar et al., 2008a, p. 32). Identifying them will be the final phase of the task of identifying existing law (Von Bar et al., 2008a, p. 37 f. and Ajani-Schulte-Nölke, 2007, p. XI). All this is despite the fact that the European Commission and the Joint Network had agreed that support groups should have provided, from the very beginning, interdisciplinary stimuli, and should above all analyse 'the results of the research' (FP 6 – Contract n. 513351) from their own points of view.

Yet, there is no doubt that work completed up to now was at least implicitly inspired by non-explicit fundamental principles. One could only realistically affirm the opposite if the activity of identifying existing law ended up being a mere reproduction of it. However, this was evidently not the case. Even establishing rules with a low level of abstraction compared to those the content of which was intended to be reproduced constitutes both a cognitive and creative activity, necessarily affected by policies: whether they are those to which scholars refer independently or those that can be obtained from EC documents on contract law.

In other words, the drafting of the Cfr can be thought of as a neutral activity, but only to the extent that it is aimed at evaluating solutions in line with a given normative political framework: the result that is referred to in stating that, given the diversity between national legal systems, there is a need to evaluate the 'best solutions found in Member States' legal orders' (COM(2004)651 final. See also Oderkerk, 2007, p. 321). Evidently, these are only those solutions in line with ordoliberal theory (see below, section 5).

This is the sense in which we should understand EC documents where they state that 'policy decisions should be clearly identified and explained'. Meanwhile, it appears that the only decisions regarded as 'political' are those not in line with the indication according to which 'the principle of freedom of contract needs to be emphasised as crucial' (COM(2005)456 final).

It is the lack of debate, if not the lack of questioning, of the given economic system which is to be criticised, i.e. the lack of discussion of the conception of contract law and, above all, of social justice, by which the construction of the Dcfr is necessarily inspired from the outset. This is what has been widely denounced not only by the European Parliament (P6_TA/2006/0109) and authoritative participants in the Joint Network (Schulze, 2007, p. 143 f.), but also numerous European scholars: in particular members of the Study Group on social justice in European private law (Somma, 2007, p. 1 ff.).

The truth is that the theme of fundamental principles in European private law is seen as central. It has inspired numerous formal and informal debates within the Joint Network (Ajani-Schulte-Nölke, 2007, p. XII) which have, however, been conducted with stealth and which have not resulted in sufficient consensus around possible solutions. These debates have, furthermore, inevitably provided an influential background with respect to numerous choices (for example, as to the manner of filling in gaps or resolving antinomies in the EC *acquis*, or when settling contrasts between EC law and national laws).

In this respect we can affirm, as the authors of the Dcfr-Ie do, that it has been inspired to 'identify best solutions' and take a 'balanced position' (Von Bar et al., 2008a, pp. 12 and 31). On the other hand we cannot affirm or let it be understood, as the authors of the Dcfr-Ie do, that this does not imply choices of substance.

The same can also be said of the intention to develop 'a coherent terminology' (Von Bar et al., 2008a, p. 31) which led to the definitions collected in an Appendix to the Dcfr-Ie, an integral part of the text (art. I.-1:103 (1)). That providing terminology and definition is an activity with notable political implications was well-known to supporters of extreme, technical approaches to the phenomenon of law, such as exponents of scientific positivism with pandectist beliefs. Indeed, they accepted the codification of German civil law, but not the inclusion of a definition of the central concepts in the BGB. It is moreover known, as Iavolenus reminds us, that *omnis definitio in iure civili periculosa est* (D. 50, 17, 202), principally because it removes the creative power of each hermeneutic action.

5. REGULATING THE MARKET BETWEEN EFFICIENCY AND DISTRIBUTIVE EFFECTS

All things considered, we are not dealing with a text that is completely without indications concerning its essential background. In fact, in the introduction to the Dcfr-Ie, there is a brief list of 'some possible fundamental principles', the normative importance of which in terms of policy I will address shortly. Yet, as the authors specify, these principles are so abstract that they 'tend to contradict one another' and 'have to be weighed up against one another more exactly' (Von Bar et al., 2008a, pp. 9 and 13). Furthermore, it should be pointed out that 'where there is a general rule and a special rule applying to a particular situation within the scope of the principle, the rule prevails in any case of conflict' (art. I.-1:102 (5)).

I shall thus illustrate the fundamental principles discussed in the introduction to the Articles. I shall then coordinate the principles with some model rules, selected, as will be explained, because of their mandatory nature and therefore their high degree of ability to restrict a party's autonomy.

The list of fundamental principles is preceded by an underlining of their vagueness, proved by the circumstance that they can be seen as tending towards correcting 'market failures', but also as 'forms of social engineering': they can respectively promote efficiency or 'social justice' and 're-distribution of wealth' (Von Bar et al., 2008a, p. 11).

Such an alternative typically characterises all the measures of market regulation, a reason for which it would be opportune to take an in-depth look at the theme of fundamental principles. The measures under discussion can in effect have the function of being a sort of compensatory mechanism, destined to absorb or annul the destructive effects that economic freedom could have on society. These measures of market regulation can nevertheless also constitute a condition of historical and social possibility for a market economy (Foucault, 2005, p. 133 f.), i.e. they can embody the forms of ordered capitalism – or of ordoliberalism – developed at the end of the nineteenth century to face the failure of the invisible hand, and studied from a theoretical point of view in the first half of the twentieth century (Gerber, 1998, p. 232).

It should be noted from the outset that the introduction to the Dcfr-Ie seems to regard interventions in contract law as being attributable to the ordoliberal model or, given that private law always performs distributive functions, as a tool of redistribution of wealth according the intention of preserving market stability, and only indirectly what is considered 'social engineering' (Mazeaud, 2006, p. 136).

It could not be otherwise, since EC law has built a system of functionalised freedoms: incentivised if they 'help competition', and restricted if they 'harm competition' (Eucken, 1949, p. 52 ff.). All of this is in line with the ordoliberal scheme of the society of private law (*Privatrechtsgesellschaft*) according to which the state is ensured powers only as long as they are necessary for defending the functioning of the private mechanisms: in particular the freedom of action and the freedom of contract (Mayer-Scheinpflug, 1996, p. 75).

This scheme implies a cooperative vision of contractual relations, for which the behaviour of parties has to be regulated for reasons of the stability of the given economic system but not in relation to their specific interests. In other words, consumers and professionals are seen, respectively, as efficient selectors and multipliers of the supply of goods and services: they are both market players who are attributed with functions that we could call 'economic policing'. In this sense, consumer law is aimed at promoting self-determination, on the supposition that consumers are able to choose freely only if they have an adequate level of information, and company law is called upon to defend the mechanism of competition (Somma, 2003, p. 66 ff. and 2008).

Thus the protection of the weak parties becomes a tool through which to strengthen the free market in a functionalist manner, as it is also synthesised in the ordoliberal EC formula of the 'social market economy' (Müller-Armack, 1946 [1990], p. 60 ff. and Somma, 2006, p. 181 ff.) A different scenario would be one where, in the wake of both conflictual and solidarity oriented models, contract law is seen as a means of balancing social weakness through legal strength, i.e. not as a means of transforming individuals into instruments for achieving ultra-individual aims nor of reproducing and defending the result of the free interaction of market forces (Monateri, 2005, p. 67 ff.). To this end, the abstraction by which private parties are capable of self-determination is abandoned in favour of a different abstraction: that for which they are inexorably imbued with typical, structural weaknesses which have to be balanced *vis-à-vis* those that are imbued with typical, structural strength (Wilhelmsson, 1995, p. 31 ff. and Fabre-Magnan, 2004, p. 88 ff.).

6.   COMMON FRAME OF REFERENCE AND SOCIAL JUSTICE

The option for one of the two models of contract law mentioned, or at least a preference for one of them, is an important element in evaluating the conception of social justice that has inspired the Dcfr-Ie. It can be maintained that private law should not take on its distributive effects, but evidently this cannot lead us to deny that it has these kinds of effects (Wagner, 2007, p. 180). At most, it can be seen as an invitation to consider contractual justice first and foremost (i.e. the economic or normative balance in the contract), and to neglect, or consider as merely secondary, the theme of social justice.

This was perhaps acceptable in the era in which, alongside the market, there were alternative tools of redistribution, such as those ensured by the welfare state. It cannot be so under today's circumstances, characterised by the privatisation of welfare and therefore by the expansion of the contract into sectors concerning the satisfaction of needs linked to social rights (Marella, 2006, p. 259).

However, let us proceed to consider principles discussed in the introduction to the Dcfr-Ie and, first of all, its statements on 'justice', mainly intended in the commutative sense, but sometimes (at least according to the authors of the Dcfr-Ie) also in the distributive sense, for instance where the principle of good faith and fair dealing is invoked (Von Bar et al., 2008a, p. 14).

If we think about what is stated as regards the principle of good faith and fair dealing, along with the considerations mentioned below, we must end up doubting its use as an instrument of social policies. It is said – in a 'moralistic' way (Alpa, 2007, p. 38 and Vettori, 2007, p. 249 ff.) – that good faith and fair dealing are linked to the 'promotion of honest market practice' (Von Bar et al., 2008a, p. 17). Accordingly, distributive effects are secondary, or in any case subordinate to preserving market stability through an invitation to cooperate.

The discussion of 'freedom of contract' is also unclear. This should be understood in a substantive sense: we must take into account the contractual power of the parties. Therefore interventions are only permitted provided they aim at re-establishing such power, in particular in the contractual relations between businesses and consumers and in those between businesses. It is stated, however, exemplifying situations for which such interventions could be envisaged, that a contract concluded as the result of inequality of information, or which involves unfair discrimination, can be set aside by the aggrieved party (Von Bar et al., 2008a, p. 14 f.).

The first hypothesis fits well with an ordoliberal approach, even if it could be a prelude to alternative views: at least with reference to the statement that, in some cases, the party to the contract 'will not be able to make effective use of the information' and therefore 'restrictions on the parties' freedom to fix the terms of their contract may be justified' (Von Bar et al., 2008a, p. 15). The second hypothesis should be evaluated in the light of the forms of discrimination considered: I will discuss them soon to document how, here too, while we can glimpse references to both approaches, it is the ordoliberal one that dominates (see below, section 11).

Of a clearly ordoliberal orientation is also the formulation through which 'general welfare' is promoted 'by strengthening market forces' and, at the same time, 'allowing individuals to increase their economic wealth'. This, it is specified, has inspired the statement of many non-mandatory model rules which in this sense indicate 'efficient' solutions (Von Bar et al., 2008a, p. 16). Thus it becomes clear that efficiency concerns optimisation of behaviour from the point of view of market stability, which is to be maintained through a sort of visible hand, called upon to fulfil the same tasks once fulfilled by the invisible hand, that is, guiding the individual to pursue an aim that was not part of his intentions, i.e. 'the public good' (Smith, 1776 [1993]).

Another idea that can be traced to ordoliberal thought is that the promotion of individual economic well-being can be imposed against the tenor of the agreement, as far as it is useful to prevent or remedy 'market failures' (Von Bar et al., 2008a, p. 16). This idea was illustrated by the US Supreme Court in the era of the New Deal, when it said that the exploitation of a class of workers 'is not only detrimental to their health and well being, but casts a direct burden for their support upon the community', and therefore 'the community may direct its law-making power to correct the abuse which springs from the . . . selfish disregard of the public interest' (*West Coast Hotel v. Parrish*, 300 US 379 (1937)). It was later further clarified in ordoliberalism, which gave rise to the notion of the redistribution of wealth through contract law as an indirect effect of measures actually aimed at protecting the mechanism of the market in a functionalist manner (Eucken, 1949, p. 52).

Finally, the principle according to which there is a need to promote 'the solidarity and social responsibility' with measures which 'allow for altruistic and social activities' seems simply innocuous. In fact, amongst examples of this purpose in private law, only 'benevolent intervention' and 'contracts of donation' are mentioned (Von Bar et al., 2008a, p. 17).

Finally worthy of note is the identification of some fundamental principles to which 'formal aims' are attributed, in particular 'rationality' and 'efficiency'. According to these principles, it seems that restrictions of individual freedom are allowed if inspired by the typical and structural condition of the parties to the contract. It should be pointed out, however, that these restrictions are seen as aimed at ensuring that the general purposes of European contract law are effectively achieved (Von Bar et al., 2008a, pp. 13 and 18). They therefore reinforce the idea that the Dcfr must be interpreted functionally, its objective being the prevention of market failures.

7. CONTRACT LAW AND CONSTITUTIONAL HERITAGE IN EUROPE

Let us return to reflecting on the conflict between EC law and new European *ius commune* and the tendency of the Dcfr-Ie authors to hide this conflict. All things considered, even amongst the most authoritative participants of the Joint Network, there are more or less explicit references to the possibility that the Articles can lead to a scenario that is much less obvious and reassuring. This applies to those who observe that the reconstruction of EC *acquis* eases the comparison of legal principles and institutions created by Community law to sets of rules based upon national laws (such as the Pecl). Of course, such comparison principally highlights a 'methodological leap' between the provisions of the Dcfr, constructed from the comparison of national legal systems, and those taken from EC law (Schulze, 2008, pp. 7 and 11).

In the introduction to the Dcfr-Ie there are also passages formulated by those who are evidently aware of the problem and, above all, of its relevance in terms of policy. It is said that there are, in fact, some differences between the Dcfr and the Pecl on important issues and that these differences are due to the influence of stakeholders (Von Bar et al., 2008a, p. 25). The impression is that, in any case, the aim is to hide conflicts between the two sets of rules, by stating that improvements only 'occasionally go to substance' (Von Bar et al., 2008a, p. 27).

As we know, concealment of the conflict between EC law and new European *ius commune* results from the provision of the Dcfr-Ie prescribing that rules are to be interpreted 'in the light of any applicable instruments guaranteeing human rights and fundamental freedoms and any applicable constitutional laws' (art. I.-1:102 (2)).

Nevertheless, European constitutionalism includes references to horizontal solidarity and therefore to the principle according to which market relations must be adapted to aims that at least cannot be directly linked to avoiding its failure (Somma, 2004a, p. 263). It is also well-known that continental new European *ius commune* has developed from national codifications that have been reinterpreted in the light of constitutional law, and that as a result it cannot but clash with an EC law developed on the basis of ordoliberal frameworks (Mak, 2008, p. 5 ff.); frameworks which, moreover, will sooner or later be able to influence the decisions of the courts of the Member States (Cherednychenko, 2006, p. 500) and therefore Europe's constitutional heritage.

8. SOFT LAW AND HARD LAW IN THE MAKING OF EUROPEAN PRIVATE LAW: THE ROLE OF PRIVATE INTERNATIONAL LAW

I now turn to evaluate the model rules of a mandatory nature and, with them, the restrictions on the party autonomy implemented by the Dcfr-Ie. Together with rules explicitly declared mandatory, I consider those to which the Articles refer when they affirm the nullity of the contract when it 'infringes a principle recognized as fundamental in the laws of the Member States of the European Union' (art. II.-7:301). This formula, inspired by the Pecl (Art. 15:102), includes the concept of morality, violation of mandatory rules, public interest, public policy and *boni mores* developed by national laws and also by EC law (Lando et al., 2003, p. 219).

As one can imagine, the set of provisions directly or indirectly declared mandatory by the Dcfr-Ie is hence characterised by the conflict between EC law and new European *ius commune*. To understand the significance of this, we must briefly recall the considerations that refer to EC mandatory rules.

These considerations are in line with the ordoliberal recipe applied to the international unification of law. On one hand, they are aimed at promoting the harmonisation of rules that, being mandatory, could lead, if differences were maintained, to distortions of competition in the internal market. On the other hand, these rules are intended to be limited to cases where there is a need to strengthen the conditions on which the free market is founded: cases of market failure, which should be faced by functionalising the system of economic freedoms (COM(2003)68 final). According to this view, all remaining cases shall be ruled by the principle of the free choice of legal systems, i.e. there should be no harmonisation of rules, but rather competition between them, as long as they do not harm the competition within the economic system (Somma, 2004b, p. 58 ff.).

All this is to be strengthened by promoting private international law reforms, in order to ensure that harmonised mandatory rules prevail over contrasting mandatory provisions of national law. This is the sense of the repeated attacks on the rules on conflict of laws applicable to contracts that forecast outcomes different from those envisaged by the country of origin principle and the mutual recognition clause (Albath-Giesler, 2006, p. 38 ff.).

If this is the situation, beyond the question of the necessity of building EC contract law, at stake is its pursuit of the delimitation of intervention necessary to avoid market failure and therefore also of the range of cases in which mandatory regulation of the market ought to be undertaken.

This is one of the reasons for which the EC legislator now prefers to concentrate on sectoral intervention. It has also expressed the intention of considering the Cfr as nothing more than a simple tool box, at the same time specifying that any future optional instrument will be midway between the strict alternative of private autonomy and mandatory rules (Bachmann, 2008, p. 11. Cfr. also COM(2004)651 final). It will therefore be a new, supranational law, through recourse to international private law mechanisms (Rutgers, 2006, p. 201 ff. and Brödermann, 2007, p. 322).

Consequently, even if the most European of the positions should prevail, the result will be in any case 'to lay the success' of the Cfr 'into the hands of the stronger parties on the market' (Lurger, 2007, p. 144). This would be in line with the growing preference for recourse to soft law – an ambiguous, but seductive, expression that alludes to the many forms of self-regulation within the market (Senden, 2004, p. 107) and therefore to neo-corporative mechanisms, now called on to shape areas formerly reserved for democratic give-and-take (Trubek-Trubek, 2005, p. 343 ff. and Di Robilant, 2006, p. 499 ff.)

9. MANDATORY RULES AND FUNCTIONALISATION OF THE EC FREEDOMS: THE GOOD FAITH PRINCIPLE

Let us now move on to analysing the mandatory rules explicitly considered as such by the Dcfr-Ie. This will lead to analysing further aspects of the system of functionalised freedoms on which European contract law is to be based.

We can start from the provision according to which 'parties are free to make a contract or other juridical act and to determine its contents, subject to the rules on good faith and fair dealing and any other applicable mandatory rules' (art. II.-1:102 (1)). This is completed by the specification that 'parties may exclude the application of any of the following rules relating to contracts or other juridical acts, or the rights and obligations arising from them, or derogate from or vary their effects, except as otherwise provided' (art. II.-1:102 (2)).

The main provisions explicitly considered mandatory by the Dcfr-Ie are therefore those concerning the duty of good faith and fair dealing.

References to good faith and fair dealing concern the negotiation (art. II.-3:301 (2)), the performance of the obligation (art. III.-1:103 (1) (2)) and the interpretation of the contract (art. II.-8:102 (1)). From the comments to the Pecl (the indications of which are supposed to be shared by the authors of the Dcfr-Ie) one infers that good faith and fair dealing refers to cooperation and 'reasonableness in commercial transactions', in particular, in the hypothesis in which 'strict adherence' to the Pecl 'would lead to a manifestly unjust result' evident from the point of view of market praxis (Lando and Beale, 2000, p. 113).

Certainly, references to the duty of good faith and fair dealing – exploited in the development of a notion of contract centred on the theme of reliance – can also be a prelude to the construction of a law which is both conflictual and solidarity-oriented. It is, however, reasonable to assume that this meaning would not be in line with the overall framework of the Dcfr-Ie and, in particular, with the sense of other provisions in which the duty under discussion is set.

We are led to this belief by the consideration that, according to the Dcfr-Ie, and also to the Pecl (Art. 4:103), 'a party may avoid a contract for mistake of fact or law' if the other party, acting contrary to good faith and fair dealing, 'knew or could reasonably be expected to have known of the mistake' (art. II.-7:201 (1) (b)). In this context it is affirmed that the principle of freedom of contract shall be understood in a substantive and, more precisely, ordoliberal sense. It is suggested that 'a party should not be bound to a contract unless its consent to it was informed', and therefore to protect reliance and the 'security of transactions' only in order to reinforce the myth of self-determination of individuals (Lando and Beale, 2000, p. 230).

Also in harmony with the Pecl (Art. 4:107), it is established that a party may avoid a contract when the other party has induced the conclusion of the contract by 'fraudulent non-disclosure of any information which good faith and fair dealing required' (art. II.-7:205 (1)). Worries concerning the efficiency of the market are even more explicit here, as shown by the emphasis on the informative mechanism. So much so, in determining whether good faith and fair dealing required a party to disclose particular information, regard should be had to all the circumstances including 'the cost to the party of acquiring the relevant information' and 'whether the other party could reasonably acquire the information by other means' (art. II.-7:205 (3)).

Good faith and fair dealing are the measures the courts must use to adapt a contract induced by unfair exploitation, upon the request of the party entitled to avoidance (art. II.-7:207 (2)). The motivation for this is found in the comment on the corresponding Pecl provisions (Art. 4:109) which specify that the court should adapt the contract only if this is an appropriate remedy in the circumstances, and this is not the case when the contract is 'unfair', but the price is 'reasonable' (Lando and Beale, 2000, p. 262).

We know that, in the Pecl, the provision under examination lends itself to becoming both conflictual and solidarity-oriented, based on the possibility of presuming the disadvantage of the weaker party. However, given the ordo-liberal approach of the Dcfr-Ie, the provision just mentioned is considered 'a reasonable price to be paid for extending the market mechanism to weaker participants', in the face of the 'much more serious limitation of freedom of contract, consisting of regulation of the contents of contracts, strict price control, etc.' (Storme, 2007, p. 242).

Good faith and fair dealing are finally mentioned with reference to the effects of unfair terms, considered as non-binding if, to the disfavour of the protected party, they cause a 'significant disadvantage' in a contract between a business and a consumer or non-business parties, and a 'gross deviation' in those between businesses (art. II.-9:404 ff.). Under the current hypothesis it is possible to interpret this provision also as an expression of visions of contracts which are both conflictual and solidarity-oriented only if one invokes the foundations of consumerism developed by national laws (Somma, 2003, p. 66 ff.). Considering the overall structure of the Dcfr, here too it is reasonable to believe that this is not the case.

10.   THE PROTECTION OF THE CONSUMER

It is obvious that model rules concerning the duty of good faith and fair dealing do not exhaust the set of mandatory rules contained in the Dcfr-Ie. There are others that are also in line with the overall structure of the text. Examples are found in the provisions dedicated to the consumer protection system.

The provisions on identifying the moment in which electronic communication is said to have reached its addressee are mandatory (art. II.-1:106 (7)), as are the remedies for breach of information duties in the phase preceding the formation of the contract (art. II.-3:107 (5)). The same is true for provisions regarding the right to withdrawal (art. II.-3:107 (5) and II.-5:101 (2)) which are specified with reference to contracts away from the business premises and to timeshare contracts (art. II.-5:201 s.).

The ordoliberal matrix of such provisions, all derived from EC *acquis* and not contained in the Pecl, result from their being conceived as instruments of protection aimed at promoting the substantive freedom of contract, that is, to reinstate the capacity for self-determination, needed to transform what is considered the weaker contracting party into an efficient selector of goods and services offered on the market. Certainly this is what the emphasis on the information mechanism is aimed at, together with valorisation of the right to withdrawal: a tool of 'competitive contract law' (Micklitz, 1998, p. 257) founded on the belief that a cooling off period is an effective form of protection against the supplying of goods and services while consumers cannot effectively discharge their system function.

Also relevant for consumers is the provision, derived from the Pecl (Art. 2:105), concerning the protection of reliance and, in particular, the manner of identifing the intention to establish a legally binding relationship or one that produces legal effects. Usually the intention is found in the 'party's statements or conduct as they were reasonably understood by the other party' (art. II.-4:102). This is not the case, however, where there is a merger clause, which must be 'individually negotiated'. Otherwise, and this is a specification of a mandatory nature, there is only 'a presumption that the parties intended that their prior statements, undertakings or agreements were not to form part of the contract' (art. II.-4:104 (2)).

Such provisions evidently restrict the scope of the protection of reliance on the contract, expressed through references to reasonableness in the context of interpretation of contracts (art. II.-8:101 (3)) or of the identification of precontractual statements regarded as contract terms (art. II.-9:102). These provisions contribute to defining the contractual model to which EC law refers, which aims at maintaining a balance between the contracting parties, but only emphasising the self-determination of the weaker contracting party. All this is made possible by a system of functionalised freedom, which in many aspects makes contract law designed by the Dcfr-Ie appear a product of Neo-Pandectism (Cappellini, 1986, p. 523 ff.).

11.   THE RIGHT TO FREEDOM FROM DISCRIMINATION

We now need to evaluate the mandatory nature of provisions regarding fundamental principles of national laws and of EC law, to which the Dcfr-Ie allude or refer (art. II.-7:301).

It is useful to highlight that the fundamental principles we are talking about here seem to be only those shared by all national legal systems, as well as at

EC level, and not those found only in some legal systems. The Dcfr-Ie does not in fact include the provision of the Pecl which, according to the Rome Convention on the law applicable to contractual obligations and the future Rome 1 regulation, guarantees the application of national mandatory rules 'which, according to the relevant rules of private international law, are applicable irrespective of the law governing the contract' (Art. 1:103): rules which are expressive of a 'fundamental public policy of the enacting country and to which effect should be given when the contract has a close connection to this country' (Lando, 2000, p. 101).

It should also be noted that the nullity that the Dcfr-Ie speaks of, unlike that stated in the Pecl (Art. 15:101), is set out only as far as it 'is required to give effect' to a 'principle recognised as fundamental in the laws of the Member States of the European Union' (art. II.-7:301). It is in this way that, as has been said with reference to the Italian Civil Code at the time it was drawn up, mandatory rules act so that the 'individual contract' is effectively 'organised through its link with the general economic system' (Putzolu, 1941, p. 343).

This involves the explicit conformation of economic freedoms in the ordoliberal sense and, in line with this, a preference for the legal reaction considered the most suitable for preserving the stability of the system. It does not involve, however, any favour for both conflictual and solidarity-oriented contract law models characterising national legal systems and the new European *ius commune*.

We can document all this in an exemplary manner focusing on the prohibition of discrimination, a prohibition of a mandatory nature as it can be traced back to a fundamental principle of national laws and EC law, and to its impact on contractual relations.

A prohibition of discrimination appears in the Charter of Fundamental Rights of the European Union below the affirmation of the principle of formal equality before the law (Art. 20): '[a]ny discrimination based on any ground such as sex, race, colour, ethnic or social origin, genetic features, language, religion or belief, political or any other opinion, membership of a national minority, property, birth, disability, age or sexual orientation shall be prohibited' (Art. 21).

As we can see, this provision takes a decisive step backwards compared to the principle of substantive equality combined with the public duty to remove any impediment to its realisation, and entails an incisive reduction of the constitutional heritage of Europe, which is both conflictual and solidarity-oriented (Barcellona, 1965, 1971, p. 285).

The EC prohibition of discrimination is based on considerations that are incompatible with this model. It concerns the circumstance that the ordered development of the market mechanism is prejudiced by the behaviour of the economic operator who selects his collaborators in the wake of criteria other than merit, or who precludes a category of consumers from carrying out their function as selectors of goods supplied on the market. This economic operator determines a hypothesis of market failure: the drawback the discrimination causes to the public interest is an obstacle to a meritocratic society and to the achievement of the aims of progress and well-being (Maffeis, 2007, p. 367 and Vandenberghe, 2007, p. 410 ff.).

In line with such an approach, the Dcfr-Ie establishes that 'a person has a right not to be discriminated against on the grounds of sex or ethnic or racial origin in relation to a contract or other juridical act the object of which is to provide access to, or supply, goods or services which are available to the public' (art. II.-2:101). The text takes up what has already been established in two EC directives (2000/43/EC and 2004/113/EC), which state that one shall consider 'available to the public' only goods and services 'which are offered outside the area of private and family life and the transactions carried out in this context' (Directive 2004/113/EC) – a limitation that is, strangely, not however contained in the *acquis* principles, which limit themselves to establishing the prohibition of discrimination, which is very different from the right not to be discriminated against. The *acquis* principles furthermore, do not consider it a 'hard' rule (Research Group on the Existing EC Private Law, 2007, p. 108).

From this we can obtain further confirmation of the conflict between EC law and new European *ius commune* and, likewise, signals of the probable outcome of that conflict. The protection from discrimination is, in fact, a recent worry, and for this reason it refers to frameworks that are strongly influenced by the political climate at Community level (Haberl, 2008). It is a consequence of that climate (Meli, 2008, p. 65) if only a few national legal systems understand the protection from discrimination as referring to aspects such as individuals' social and economic strength (Schiek, 2007, p. 69), and if they limit themselves to promoting only an equality of chances useful for the functioning of the market.

12. EUROPEAN PRIVATE LAW BETWEEN SUPPRESSION OF POLITICAL LIBERALISM AND REFORM OF ECONOMIC LIBERALISM

New European *ius commune*, together with the constitutional heritage of Europe, also takes into consideration the individual's chances within the market. However, this is because individuals are viewed as carriers of a typical structural weakness, which cannot be balanced through the reinstatement of some kind of mythical capacity for self-determination. Yet, the market is seen in essence as a tool of redistribution of wealth, which is to be regulated in order to give the possibility of accessing resources guaranteed by the system of social rights, and not in order to ensure the market's survival.

In other words, new European *ius commune* does not aim to render individual freedoms functional in terms of cooperation towards purposes directly related to the stability of the economic system. The issue that it first undertakes is an individual one, i.e. to redress imbalances among individuals taking part in the social conflict without attempting to compel them to achieve any predetermined economic goal. European *ius commune* promotes their '*capacitas*', intended as an 'institutional precondition of a Market Economy' (Deakin, 2006, p. 317 ff.). To use the terminology of the Italian constitution, all of this leads to a reinterpretation of private duty towards political, economic and social solidarity (Art. 2) in the light of the public duty to remove all economic and social obstacles that, by limiting the freedom and equality of citizens, prevent full individual development and the participation of all workers in the political, economic and social organisation of the country (Art. 3).

For this reason, new European *ius commune*, in contradistinction to EC law, aims to formulate norms of a mandatory nature, having in mind distributive justice rather than commutative justice, or social justice rather than contractual justice. In this sense it combines the 'necessary connection between risk and company initiative', with the consideration that the protection of weaker parties corresponds to a public interest, even if the interest is not directly referred to the State (Panza, 1974, p. 338 ff.). This stems from the fact that the conflictual and solidarity-oriented contract law model conceives of conformation of economic freedom in a social and not in a statist way (Azzariti, 1999, p. 11 ff.).

This also entails the groundlessness of accusations usually levelled against the constitutional heritage of Europe, for instance, which refer to a 'totalitarian' approach, on the basis that 'it entrusts to laws and therefore to the State the global plan of the economy' (Irti, 1998, p. 19 f.). On the contrary, if forms of totalitarianism are developing, they come from the reappearance of the frameworks that at the outset of the last century followed the so-called third way between traditional liberalism and socialism, a third way based on a change in liberal economic arrangements – to ordoliberalism – and on the suppression of political liberalism, and therefore on the re-socialising of the economy realised apart from the democratic mechanism (Polanyi, 1944 [1974], p. 297 ff.).

This is not surprising if we consider the forms and methods chosen to produce the Dcfr: i.e. entrusting it to a commission of stakeholders which, in line with past contempt for 'the disintegrated and amorphous mass domination', feed 'the action of organised groups'. These methods determine the shelving of suffragist representation and the development of representation of interests of a neo-corporative matrix that from 'the basis of our economic life', can begin to become 'the basis of our political life' (Rocco, 1919 [1938], p. 479 f.). With just one difference – the identification of consumers as a category called upon to interact with the world of production, together with the exclusion of the world of labour as its legitimate antagonist – symbolising an adaptation to the present age of that model, rather than the will to distance oneself from it.

This is certainly no coincidence. Without the contribution of the world of labour, the process of implementing social rights would not have led to the development of forms of solidarity that characterise the constitutional heritage of Europe, given the roots that historically link the welfare state and trade unions (Romagnoli, 2005, p. 524 and Sciarra, 2004, p. 283). And this is exactly what ordoliberalism is aiming to avoid when it hides the conflict between EC law and new European *ius commune* and strengthens the prevalence of the former over the latter.

REFERENCES

Ajani, Gianmaria and Schulte-Nölke, Hans (2007), 'The Principles of the Existing EC Contract Law: A Preliminary Output of the Aquis Group', in Research Group on the Existing EC Private Law, *Contract I – Pre-contractual Obligations, Conclusion of Contract, Unfair Terms*, Munich, Sellier, pp. IX–XIII.

Albath, Lars and Giesler, Martina (2006), 'Das Herkunftslandprinzip in der Dienstleistungsrichtlinie', *Europäische Zeitschrift für Wirtschaftsrecht*, 17, 38.

Alpa, Guido (2007), 'I Principi Unidroit 2004 e i Principi di diritto europeo dei contratti', in Alessandro Somma (ed.), *Giustizia sociale e mercato nel diritto europeo dei contratti*, Turin, Giappichelli, 38.

Azzariti, Gaetano (1999), in Natalino Irti et al., *Il dibattito sull'ordine giuridico del mercato*, Rome and Bari, Ed. Laterza.

Bachmann, Georg (2008), 'Optionsmodelle im Privatrecht', *Juristen Zeitung*, 63, 11.

Barcellona, Pietro (1965), 'I controlli della libertà contrattuale', in Stefano Rodotà (ed.), *Il diritto privato nella società moderna*, Bologna, Il Mulino, 285.

Betti, Emilio (1950), *Teoria generale del negozio giuridico*, Turin, Giappichelli.

Blanc, Dominique and Deroulez, Jérôme (2007), 'La longue marche vers un droit européen des contrats', *Recueil Dalloz*, 23, 1615.

Brödermann, Eckart (2007), 'Betrachtungen zur Arbeit am Common Frame of Reference aus der Sicht eines Stakeholders: Der weite Weg zu einem europäischen Vertragsrecht', *Zeitschrift für Europäisches Privatrecht*, 15, 304.

Cappellini, Paolo (1986), 'Scienza civilistica, rivoluzioni industriali, analisi economica del diritto: verso una neopandettistica involontaria?', *Quaderni Fiorentini per la storia del pensiero giuridico moderno*, 15, 523.

Chamboredon, Anthony (2001), 'La "texture ouverte" d'un code européen du droit des contrats', *Journal du droit international*, 128, 5.

Cherednychenko, Olha (2006), 'Fundamental Rights and Contract Law', *European Review of Contract Law*, 2, 489.

D'Angelo, Andrea (2005), 'La buona fede ausiliaria del programma contrattuale', in Andrea D'Angelo, Pier Giuseppe Monateri and Alessandro Somma, *Buona fede e giustizia contrattuale. Modelli cooperativi e modelli conflittuali a confronto*, Turin, Giappichelli.

Deakin, Simon (2006), 'Capacitas: Contract Law and Institutional Preconditions of a Market Economy', *European Review of Contract Law*, 2, 317.

Di Robilant, Anna (2006), 'Genealogies of Soft Law', *American Journal of Comparative Law*, 54, 499.

Eucken, Walter (1949), 'Die Wettbewerbsordnung und ihre Verwirklichung', *Ordo – Jahrbuch für die Ordnung von Wirtschaft und Gesellschaft*, 2, 1.

Fabre-Magnan, Muriel (2004), *Les obligations*, Paris, Thémis droit privé.

Fauvarque-Cosson, Bénédicte (2007), 'Droit européen et international des contrats: l'apport des codifications doctrinales', *Recueil Dalloz*, 14, Chronique, 96.

Foucault, Michel (2005), *Nascita della biopolitica. Corso al Collège de France (1978–1979)*, Milan, Feltrinelli.

Freeman, Edward R. (1984), *Strategic Management: A Stakeholder Approach*, Boston, Pitman.

Gerber, David J. (1998), *Law and Competition in Twentieth Century Europe*, Oxford, Oxford University Press.

Haberl, Sonja (2009), 'Antidiscriminazione e stato liberale di diritto', *Rivista trimestrale di diritto processuale civile*, 63, 233ff.

Hesselink, Martijn W. (2007), 'European Contract Law: A Matter of Consumer Protection, Citizenship, or Justice?', *European Review of Private Law*, 15, 323.

Irti, Natalino (1998), *L'ordine giuridico del mercato*, Rome-Bari, Ed. Laterza.

Kuneva, Meglena (2007), 'The European Contract Law and Review of the Consumer Aquis', *Zeitschrift für Europäisches Privatrecht*, 4, 955.

Lando, Ole (2006), 'On Legislative Style and Structure', *European Review of Contract Law*, 14, 475.

Lando, Ole (2007), 'The Structure and the Legal Values of the Common Frame of reference', *European Review of Contract Law*, 3, 245.

Lando, Ole and Beal, Hugh (2000), *Principles of European Contract Law*, The Hague, Kluwer Law International.

Lando, Ole, Clive, Eric, Prum, André and Zimmermann, Reinhard (eds) (2003), *Principles of European Contract Law – Part III*, Prepared by the Commission on European Contract Law, The Hague, Kluwer Law International.

Lipari, Nicolò (1974), *Diritto Privato, una ricerca per l'insegnamento*, Rome-Bari, Ed. Laterza.

Lurger, Brigitta (2007), 'Il futuro del diritto europeo dei contratti: tra libertà contrattuale, guistizia sociale e razionalità del mercato', in Alessandro Somma (ed.), *Giustizia sociale e mercato nel diritto europeo dei contratti*, Turin, Giappichelli, 141.

Maffeis, Daniele (2007), *Offerta al pubblico e divieto di discriminazione*, Milan, Giuffré.

Mak, Chantal (2008), *Fundamental Rights in European Contract Law: a Comparison of the Impact of Fundamental Rights on Contractual Relationships in Germany, the Netherlands, Italy and England*, Austin etc., Kluwer Law International.

Marella, Maria Rosaria (2006), 'The Old and New Limits to Freedom of Contract in Europe', *European Review of Contract Law*, 2, 257.

Mayer, Klaus and Scheinpflug, Jörg (1996), *Privatrechtsgesellschaft und die Europäische Union*, Tübingen, Mohr-Siebeck.

Mazeaud, Denis (2006), 'Le droit de la consommation est-il un droit social ou un droit économique?', *Revue Lamy de la concurrence*, 9, 136.

Meli, Marisa (2008), 'Armonizzazione del diritto contrattuale europeo e Quadro comune di riferimento', *Europa e diritto privato*, 2, 59.

Micklitz, Hans W. (1998), 'Perspektiven eines europäischen Privatrechts – Ius Commune Praeter Legem?', *Zeitschrift für Europäisches Privatrecht*, 1, 257.

Monateri, Pier Giuseppe (2005), 'Contratto rugiadoso e contratto rude nel diritto europeo e comunitario', in Andrea D'Angelo, Pier Giuseppe Monateri and Alessandro Somma, *Buona fede e giustizia contrattuale*, Turin, Giappichelli.

Müller-Armack, Alfred (1946 [1990]), *Wirtschaftslenkung und Marktwirtschaft*, Munich, Kastell.

Oderkerk, Marieke (2007), 'The Cfr and the Method(s) of Comparative Legal Research', *European Review of Contract Law*, 3, 315.

Panza, Giuseppe (1944), 'Impiego del contratto e disciplina degli affari', in Nicolò Lipari (ed.), *Diritto privato. Una ricerca per l'insegnamento*, Rome and Bari, Laterza.

Polanyi, Karl (1944 [1974]), *La grande trasformazione*, Turin, Einaudi.

Putzolu, Antonio (1941), 'Panorama del Codice civile fascista', *Rivista di diritto civile*, 393.

Research Group on the Existing EC Private Law, *Contract I – Pre-contractual Obligations, Conclusion of Contract, Unfair Terms*, Munich, Sellier.

Rocco, Alfredo (1919 [1938]), 'Il congresso nazionalista di Roma', in Alfredo Rocco, *Scritti e discorsi*, 2, Milan, 473; in Alessandro Somma (2005), *I giuristi e l'Asse culturale Roma-Berlino. Economia e politica nel diritto fascista e nazionalsocialista*, Frankfurt am Main.

Romagnoli, Umberto (2005), 'I diritti sociali nella Costituzione', *Diritti lavori mercati*, 3, 521.

Rutgers, Jacobien W. (2006), 'An Optional Instrument and Social Dumping', *European Review of Contract Law*, 2, 199.

Schiek, Dagmar (2007), *Allgemeines Gleichbehandlungsgesetz: ein Kommentar aus europäischer Perspektive*, Munich, Sellier.

Schulze, Reiner (2007), 'Gemeinsamer Referenzrahmen und acquis communautaire', *Zeitschrift für Europäisches Privatrecht*, 11, 130.

Schulze, Reiner (2008), 'The Academic Draft of the Cfr and the EC Contract Law', in Reiner Schulze (ed.), *The Common Frame of Reference and Existing EC Contract Law*, Munich, Sellier, 3.

Sciarra, Silvana (2004), 'La costituzionalizzazione dell'Europa sociale. Diritti fondamentali e procedure di "soft law"', *Quaderni costituzionali*, 2, 281.

Scognamiglio, Renato (1969), *Contributo alla teoria del negozio giuridico*, Naples, Jovene.

Sefton-Green, Ruth (2007a), 'Diversità culturale e codice civile europeo', in Alessandro Somma (ed.), *Giustizia sociale e mercato nel diritto europeo dei contratti*, Turin, Giappichelli, 207, 205.

Sefton-Green, Ruth (2007b), 'The European Union, Law and Society: Making the Societal-Cultural Difference', in Thomas Wilhemsson, Elina Paunio and Annika Pohjolainen (eds), *Private Law and the Many Cultures of Europe*, Alphen aan den Rijn, Kluwer Law International, 37.

Senden, Linda (2004), *Soft Law in European Community Law*, Oxford etc., Hart Publishing.

Smith, Adam (1776 [1993]), *An Inquiry into the Nature and Causes of the Wealth of Nations*, Oxford, Oxford University Press.

Somma, Alessandro (2003), *Diritto comunitario vs. diritto comune europeo*, Turin, Giappichelli.

Somma, Alessandro (2004a), 'Diritto comunitario e patrimonio costituzionale europeo', *Politica del diritto*, 2, 263.

Somma, Alessandro (2004b), 'Mercificare il diritto, in Andrea Zoppini (ed.), *La concorrenza tra ordinamenti giuridici*, Rome-Bari, Laterza, 58.

Somma, Alessandro (2006), 'Social Justice and the Market in European Contract Law', *European Review of Contract Law*, 2, 181.

Somma, Alessandro (2007), *Introduzione critica al diritto europeo dei contratti*, Milan, Giuffré.

Somma, A. (2008), 'La cittadinanza nella società del diritto privato', *Politica del diritto*, 29, 507ff.

Storme, Matthias E. (2007), 'Freedom of Contract: Mandatory and Non mandatory Rules in European Contract Law', *European Review of Private Law*, 15, 233.

Toriello, Fabio (2000), *I principi generali del diritto comunitario*, Milan, Giuffré.

Trubek, David M. and Trubek, Louise G. (2005), 'Hard and Soft Law in the Construction of Social Europe: the Role of the Open Method of Co-ordination', *European Law Journal*, 11, 343.

Vandenberghe, Ann-Sophie (2007), 'The Economics of the Non-Discrimination Principle in General Contract Law', *European Review of Contract Law*, 3, 410.

Vettori, Giuseppe (2007), 'Giustizia e rimedi nel diritto europeo dei contratti', in Alessandro Somma (ed.), *Giustizia sociale e mercato nel diritto europeo dei contratti,* Turin, Giappichelli, 249.

Von Bar, Christian (2007), 'Coverage and Structure of the Academic Common Frame of Reference', *European Review of Contract Law,* 3, 350.

Von Bar, Christian, Beale, Hugh, Clive, Eric and Schulte-Nölke, Hans (2008a), 'Introduction', in Christian von Bar, Eric Clive and Hans Schulte-Nölke (eds), *Principles, Definitions and Model Rules of European Private Law. Draft Common Frame of Reference*, Munich, Sellier, 1.

Von Bar, Christian, Clive, Eric and Schulte-Nölke, Hans (eds) (2008b), *Principles, Definitions and Model Rules of European Private Law. Draft Common Frame of Reference*, Munich, Sellier.

Wagner, Gerhard (2007), 'Die soziale Frage und der Gemeinsame Referenzrahmen', *Zeitschrift für Europäisches Privatrecht*, 11, 180.

Wilhelmsson, Thomas (1995), *Social Contract Law and European Integration*, Aldershot etc., Dartmouth.

Wilhelmsson, Thomas, Paunio, Elina and Pohjolainen, Annika (eds) (2007), *Private Law and the Many Cultures of Europe*, Alphen aan den Rijn, Kluwer Law International.

2. The interpretation according to human rights, fundamental freedoms and constitutional laws (art. 1:102 DCFR)

Giuseppe Vettori

1. INTERPRETATION AND RIGHTS

Whenever there is an artistic, literary or legal objective expression, our interpretation comes into play. This has led some authoritative authors to search for a common element therein[1] – to reproduce someone else's thought and thus discover the spectacular, orchestral, literary and philosophic key to the work that is the object of exegesis. Within such a hypothetical *genus*, legal interpretations play a specific role dictated by the peculiarity of each text. They must lay down a principle so as to decide on or to take stands over a conflict of interests, over a demand for protection or over a relevant ascertainment.

The DCFR confirms well-known rules and lays down some new provisions. Article 1:102 says that the rules are to be read in the light of any applicable instruments guaranteeing human rights and fundamental freedoms and any applicable constitutional laws. Chapter 8 on the *Interpretation of contract*[2] includes a number of ambiguous provisions, some compromises and some new provisions.

The fundamental principle is the need to reconstruct the common intention of the parties, even where this differs from the literal meaning of the words (8:101 I). Importance is attached (according to a common law rule, embodied in Article 8 1 CVIM) to awareness of the true intention of a party if, at the time of the conclusion of the contract, the other party was aware, or could reasonably be

---

[1]   E. Betti, *Interpretazione della legge e degli atti giuridici (teoria generale e dogmatica)*, Milan, 1949.
[2]   Section I contains seven provisions: *General rules* (8:101), *Relevant matters* (8:102), *Interpretation against party supplying term* (8:103), *Preference for negotiated terms* (8:104), *Reference to contract as a whole* (8:105), *Preference for interpretation which gives terms effect* (8:106), *Linguistic discrepancies* (8:107). Section 2 contains only one provision among *General rules* on the issue of interpretation of juridical acts and a provision on analogy.

expected to have been aware, of such intention (8:101 2). An objective criterion is thus once again applied (8:101 3) as to the meaning a reasonable person
would give to the contract, thus adding a further specification with respect to
the Lando Principles. Such an application is allowed if the intention cannot be
established under the previous criteria, and if the question arises with a person
who is not a party to the contract or who, by law, has no wider rights than such
a party, provided the former has relied on the contract's apparent meaning
(8:101 3 a and b). Regard may be had, in particular (8:102 I), to the circumstances in which the contract was concluded (including preliminary negotiations), to the conduct of the parties (even subsequent to contractual
conclusion), to similar terms and practices established between the parties, to
the meaning commonly given to such terms, to the nature and purpose of the
contract, to usages and good faith. We thus find another new provision with
respect to the Lando principles. It is specified (8:102 2) that where an issue
arises in relation to a person, first, who is not a party to the contract (or an
assignee) or, second, who, by law, has no better rights than such a party, but
who has relied on the contract's apparent meaning, regard may be had to external circumstances only to the extent that those circumstances were known to,
or could reasonably be expected to have been known to, that party, subject to
the general principle of good faith.

These criteria are followed by a provision on non-individually negotiated
contract terms (8:103–8:104), by a reference to the contract as a whole
(8:105), a principle on the preference for interpretation which gives terms
effect (8:106), and a provision on linguistic discrepancies (8:107).

I will deal with one issue only: the role of good faith and the importance of
such a criterion where one party, by law, has better rights than the other (8:101
3 lett. b; 8:102 DCFR).

2. INTERPRETATION IN ACCORDANCE WITH GOOD FAITH AND FAIR DEALING (8: 102 I LETT. G, DCFR AND ARTICLE 1366 ITALIAN CIVIL CODE)

The rule has always given rise to doubts and questions, especially when identifying which solutions are in line with good faith, and how such a criterion adds
a further meaning to what is already envisaged in subjective and objective interpretative criteria (8:101, 8:102; Articles 1362 and 1367 Italian Civil Code).[3]

---

[3]   See on this point and the following reasoning, R. Sacco and G. De Nova, *Il
contratto*, in *Tratt. dir. civ.*, UTET (ed.), Turin, 2004, p. 369 ff.; N. Irti, *Testo e contesto*,
Padua, 1966, p. 25; but also C. Grassetti, *L'interpretazione del negozio giuridico con*

According to Italian law, interpretation in accordance with good faith is that which is in line with 'the intentions of the parties and the purpose they pursue in their negotiations'. Yet, it has been observed that respect for the parties' common intention is already requested by Article 1362. Hence, if an intention exists and is well-known, 'there is no need for art. 1366 to give it further strength'.[4]

Having abandoned the equivalence between good faith and intention, a more objective meaning has been upheld, whereby good faith underlines the importance of 'mutual fair dealings between the parties'.[5] Yet, this definition adds nothing to the meaning of Article 1366.

The idea of a link between good faith and the principle of reliance is very widespread. According to Cesare Grassetti, 'if a party is entitled to interpret a given statement in a given way . . . , such a way shall be relevant for the law, and the person who has made the statement cannot claim a different meaning'.[6] According to this view, to interpret a statement in accordance with good faith means to put oneself in the position of the person who takes cognisance thereof. Yet, such an argument is not convincing, since 'the contract is not the isolated statement of one person to another, rather a set of mutual statements: a unitary text endorsed by both parties. There is not a declarant and an addressee; rather, the two contractors assume both roles.'[7] What is more, there is not only an intended and communicated plan, but rather a heteronomous content to be identified in practice.

The reliance theory has been enriched by two further ideas. On the one hand, priority is given to the meaning that both parties wanted the text to have – although this mirrors either 'a code that is common to the parties or an objective meaning' which Article 1362[8] already implies. Hence, once more, Article 1366 amounts to a repetition. On the other hand, relevance is given to the predisposition of the contract, though this is already governed by Articles 1341 and 1370 of the Italian Civil Code, and by special laws on consumers. This leads to the claim that Article 1366 has not been subject to interesting developments since 'the applications which it gave rise to before 1942 are now

---

particolare riguardo ai contratti, Padua, 1983, p. 108; M. Casella, *Il contratto e l'interpretazione. Contributo ad una ricerca di diritto positivo,* Milan, 1961, p. 143; V. Rizzo, *Interpretazione dei contratti e relatività delle sue regole*, Naples, 1985, p. 163 ff.; C. Scognamiglio, *Interpretazione dei contratti e interessi dei contraenti*, Padua, 1992, p. 273; see the essay by V. Calderai, 'La teoria classica dell'interpretazione dei contratti. Origini, fortuna e crisi di un paradigma dogmatico', *Diritto Privato*, 2003, p. 344.

4   R. Sacco, n. 3 above, p. 375 ff.
5   C. Grassetti, n. 3 above, p. 197.
6   *Ibid.*
7   R. Sacco, n. 3 above, p. 408.
8   *Ibid.*

converted into specific legal rules and have thus become autonomous with respect to the matrix that produced them'.[9]

It is not surprising, therefore, that deeper meanings have been ascribed to Article 1366, which are not commonly upheld, albeit they surely have a justifiable basis. Some argue that Article 1366 applies to the case of unforeseen (and thus unfair) damages, leading to contractual revision or repetition, without altering the risks and duties laid down by the parties. Article 1366 is used 'to rectify contractual details, cancelling what was included therein by claiming the abuse of the other party's weakness, ingenuousness or shyness, or the temporary lack of said party's reason'.[10] In legitimacy judgments, it has been held that the general clause enlarges the parties' rights and obligations, so that the interpretative criterion that refers to it requires the interpreter to pay attention to that integration, to identify the actual content of the parties' rights and obligations, and to seek the meaning that is most consistent with the contractors' fair dealing.[11] Interpretative good faith is thus given a complete and useful meaning.

This has been confirmed by a recent judgment of the Italian Court of Cassation,[12] which has held that, when a party claims bad faith dealing and this is ignored by the judge when dealing with the merits, the infringement of the interpretative rule must be claimed in the appeal, or such a right is lost. Hence, there is a strong connection between ascertaining the unfairness of one's conduct and the interpretative rule.

This may appear to be in conflict with the DCFR, Article III 1:103 of which is rather ambiguous and introduces a new provision with respect to the Lando Principles. After confirming the role of the general clause in the *General provisions* (I 1:102) and its impact on *Obligations and corresponding rights*, its application is narrowed. Article III 1:103 3 says that breach of the duty to act in accordance with good faith does not give rise directly to remedies for non-performance of an obligation, but may preclude the person in breach from exercising or relying on a right, remedy or defence which that person would otherwise have had.

---

[9]   *Ibid.*

[10]   *Ibid.*, p. 410.

[11]   The Court of Cassation has expressed doubts, in the ambit of contractual interpretation, as to the opportunity of using other criteria when the literal meaning of the words leads to a certain result. Yet, quite recently, reference has been made to the necessary hermeneutical criterion evoked by the many contractual clauses (Art. 1363 Italian Civil Code) (Cass., 11 June 1999, n. 5747, in *Giur. It*, 2000, p. 705) and grounded on a set of behavioural rules of loyalty and fairness (Art. 1366 Italian Civil Code) (Cass., 12 November 1992, n.12165, in *Giust. civ. Mass.* 1992, dossier 11) which can lead to identifying instrumental duties to the satisfaction of the contractors, even in the event of mere 'conscious and voluntary inertia' (Cass., 17 February 2004, n. 2992, in *Dir. e giust.*, 2004, 13, p. 34).

[12]   Cass., 11 August 2000, n. 10705, in *Giust. civ. Mass.*, 2000, 1778.

Such a specification is clearly meant to curb the idea that the clause is a general instrument for control,[13] so limiting scope for the judge to draw new rights and obligations for the contractors from it.[14] Yet the text, precisely because of its ambiguity, is open to different interpretations. In contrast to the principle upheld by Italian case law, it says that breach of good faith does not imply non-performance, though this does not mean that the duty of good faith cannot give rise to new obligations and rights. Indeed, the provision grants the person acting in good faith the right to prevent the other party in bad faith from exercising a right, remedy or defence. Such a broad formulation encompasses the integrating capacity of the clause, which concerns a procedural evaluation of the parties' conduct, enriching the contractors' rights and duties.

The wording of Article III 1:103 3 clearly epitomises the different approach of common law and civil law jurists.[15] The Anglo-Saxon culture is naturally led to argue in terms of remedies and limits to remedies, while it has always feared the proliferation of rights, especially of unspecified origin. Continental jurists, instead, are used to constructing reasoning based on the definition of subjective positions; according to this approach, the autonomous role of good faith cannot but determine the rise of new rights and duties.

By going beyond both approaches, we may reach agreement on a key point. Good faith is the procedural instrument for the control of the parties' conduct. It is given a general value by Article 8:102 1 lett. g and 2, even where one party has stronger rights than another, and this may be important in outlining the limits of the content of good faith which can emerge from the parties' common intention, but also from rights and duties to be reconstructed in the concrete regulation of the case, by applying special rules in the field and the principles of Article 1:102. Let us examine both cases.

---

[13]   H. Beale, 'General Clauses and Specific Rules in The Principles of European Contract Law: the Good Faith Clause', in S. Grundman and D. Mazeaud (eds.), *General Clauses and Standard in European Contract Law*, Kluwer Law International, 2006, p. 205, excludes the possibility that good faith may be an all-inclusive instrument of control and limits its content to a judgement of reasonableness. Conversely, see O. Lando, 'Is Good Faith an Over-Arching General Clause in the Principles of European Contract Law?', *European Review of Private Law*, 2007, p. 841.

[14]   See M. Hesselink, *Common Frame of Reference & Social Justice*, Centre for the Study of European Contract Law Working Paper Series No. 2008/04, at http://ssrn.com; and, by the same author, 'The Concept of Good Faith', in A.S. Hartkamp et al. (eds.), *Towards a European Civil Code*, Kluwer Law International, 2004; and S. Whittaker and R. Zimmerman, 'Good Faith in European Contract Law: Surveying the Legal Landscape', in R. Zimmerman and S. Whittaker (eds.) *Good Faith in European Contract Law*, Cambridge, 2000, p. 7, 32.

[15]   See F. Viglione, 'L'interpretazione del contratto nella common Law inglese. Problemi e prospettive', *Riv. dir. civ.*, 2008, p.134.

3. IF ONE PARTY HAS STRONGER RIGHTS THAN THE OTHER

3.1 Interpretation in Accordance with Good Faith in France

The French *code civile* does not expressly refer to *bonne foi* as a criterion for interpretation. Its provisions on execution (Article 1134)[16] and on contractual integration (Article 1135)[17] contain a reference to the general clause. However, quite gradually, the idea of a *procédé de forçage* of contract and of an intervention on its content have gained ground.[18]

Besides, the entire section of the *Code civil* dealing with interpretation (the current Article 1154[19]) is based on the idea of identifying the contractors' common intention ('*La règle des règles*' according to Demolombe) and the most recent doctrine specifies that, when construing such common intention, the interpreter must refer to other criteria, including good faith.[20] There follows the traditional separation between *interprétation subjective*, which is meant to 'reveal' the contractual content, and *interprétation objective (ou constitutive)*, which 'determines it'. It is precisely with respect to the last criterion that good faith acquires relevance, through Articles 1134(3), 1135, and 1160.

---

[16]   According to Art. 1134(3) 'Elles doivent être exécutées de bonne foi' where reference is made to 'conventions légalement formées'. These provisions remain unaltered in the Avant projet.

[17]   The provision states: '*les conventions obligent non seulement à ce qui y est exprimé, mais encore à toutes les suites que l'équité, l'usage ou la loi donnent à l'obligation d'après sa nature*', where the notion of 'equity' is interpreted more or less like that of good faith.

[18]   V. L. Mestre and A. Laude, 'L'interprétation "active" du contrat par le juge', in Michel Buy et al., *Le juge et l'exécution du contrat*, Aix–Marseille, 1993. A relevant scope of application concerns information obligations, especially of professional figures, which have been extended by case law through Art. 1135. The same reference represents the basis for new developments in the case law on surveillance obligations (e.g. of hoteliers for their clients' chattels, Civ. Cass., 13 October 1987, Bull. civ., I, n. 262, p. 190).

[19]   According to this provision '*[o]n doit dans les conventions rechercher quelle a été la commune intention des parties contractantes, plutôt que de s'arrêter au sens littéral des termes*'. The wording remains unaltered in the *Avant projet*, just like the 'position' of the Article at the beginning of the section on interpretation. The numbering of Articles changes, since the interpretation provisions are included immediately after the 'General Provisions' relating to 'Contractual Effects'.

[20]   J. Ghestin, C. Jamin and M. Billiau, *Traité de Droit Civil, Les effets du contrat*, 3rd edn, Paris, 2001, p. 18.

The *Avant-projet de réforme* contains some important new provisions. It suggests including the section '*De l'interprétation et de la qualification*', immediately after the '*Dispositions Générales*', in Chapter III (*De l'effet des obligations*), numbered from Article 1136 onwards. The wording of Article 1135 is unaltered, while an extremely important new point is included in the provisions on interpretation. A new provision (Article 1139) is formulated, whereby '[t]he contract shall be interpreted according to reasonableness and equity';[21] the comment in the notes specifies that such criterion is viewed as a useful instrument for the '*contrôle de l'équilibre contractuel*', according to objective criteria of interpretation: *raison* and *équité*. Thanks to the latter, one must 'first seek the grounds for the existence of the agreement, which are in themselves evidence of the parties' intention, their interests and will, which cannot however be *inéquitable*'.

In this respect, Article 1140-1 is emblematic: derogating from Article 1140 ('in case of doubt, the contract is to be interpreted against the creditor and in favour of the debtor'), it says that, 'when the contractual content results from the dominant influence of a party, the contract shall be interpreted in the other party's favour'. This is defined as *contrôle de l'unilatéralisme licite,* and is frequently applied to consumer contracts as well as 'business to business' relationships.[22]

3.2 The Relevance of the Text in Common Law

The essential criterion for the English judge's interpretation is his strict endorsement of the literal meaning of the contract (parol evidence rule). It is this principle that case law has always referred to, ignoring all criticisms of the idea of language univocality. Hence, the judge's interpretation follows merely technical criteria that are intended to reconstruct the parties' will, as evidenced in the contract. Such an idea is in line with the classic conceptualisation of the contract as the synthesis of two autonomous wills (individually identifiable), and an expression of the parties' natural contrast.

The goal which is thus pursued is that of guaranteeing the certainty of the contract's effects, since no judicial intervention can change them in a way

---

21   '*Le contrat s'interprète en raison et en équité*'.

22   Equally significant is the formulation of Art. 1141, which is not included in the current structure of the Code: '[t]he interpretation of the contract is grounded on the analysis of all its elements. Failure to consider its essential elements entails misinterpretations (*dénaturation*).' The provision expresses the division of powers between judges deciding on the merits and legitimacy judges, in line with the theory of *dénaturation*. The latter gives rise to an evaluation under law, which may be censured before the *Cour de Cassation*, unlike the interpretation which is left to judges deciding on the merits of the case.

which is not in line with the parties' express will. There follows the exclusive role of the contract, the irrelevance of the context and, in general, of any elements that are external to it. Hence, jurists are generally distrustful of flexible and apparently indefinite concepts such as good faith.[23] This clause, as has been said, implies 'a systematic analysis or a subjective approach', and thus 'unquestionable negative effects on the efficiency of decision-making processes',[24] as well as longer proceedings and a greater number of disputes between private individuals.

However, such basic considerations do not exhaust the issue of interpretation in the English legal system, since the common law tradition has been integrated with rules which in fact often overlap with those used in civil law systems,[25] even without expressly resorting to the idea of good faith. Casebooks are certainly lacking in precedents on the use of good faith for interpretation purposes,[26] in line with the general diffidence towards it as a criterion.[27] Still, since the late 1980s, this situation has changed as the result of some important judgments[28] and, most of all, due to the European Union's regulations expressed through Directives. A lively doctrinal debate has ensued.[29]

---

[23]   G. Teubner, 'Legal Irritants: Good Faith in British Law of How Unifying Law Ends up in New Divergences' (1988) 61 *Modern Law Review* 1, MLR11; R. Brownsword et al., 'Good Faith in Contract: Concept and Context', in R. Brownsword et al. (eds), *Good Faith in Contract: Concept and Context*, Dartmouth Ashgate, 1999.

[24]   F. Viglione, 'L'interpretazione del contratto nel Common Law inglese. Problemi e prospettive', *Riv. dir. civ.*, 2008, fasc. S1, p. 142.

[25]   F. Viglione, n. 24 above, p. 157 ff.

[26]   Recently, K. Lewison, *The Interpretation of Contracts*, 3rd edn, London, 2004.

[27]   The sole relevant exception is R. Powell, 'Good Faith in Contracts' (1956) 9 *Current Legal Problems*, 16.

[28]   *Banque Financière de la Cité SA v Estgate Insurance Co. Ltd* [1987] 2 All ER 923; *Interfoto Picture Library Ltd v Stiletto Visual Programmes Ltd* [1989] QB 433.

[29]   Compare with R. Brownsword, 'Positive, Negative, Neutral: the Reception of Good Faith in English Contract Law', in R. Brownsword, N.J. Hird and G. Howells (eds.), *Good Faith in Contract, Concept and Context,* Dartmouth, Ashgate, 1999; R. Brownsword, *Contract Law. Themes for the Twenty-First Century*, Oxford, 2006; R. Brownsword, 'Good Faith in Contracts. Revisited' (1996) 49 *Current Legal Problems* 111. The author reconstructs three doctrinal approaches to the idea of good faith as a general principle: a negative one, a neutral one and a positive one, and evidences the reasons underpinning them. We first need clearly to identify the idea of good faith. In this respect, the doctrine mentions three models: *good faith requirement*, which is applied to the idea of fair dealings, already recognised in given fields; *good faith regime*, which concerns the standards for fair dealings resulting from a cooperation principle; lastly, the so-called *visceral justice*, a model however to be excluded (see in this respect M. Bridge, 'Good Faith in Commercial Contracts', in *Good Faith in Contract, Concept and Context*, above, p. 140. See also J. F. O'Connor, *Good Faith in English Law*, Dartmouth, Ashgate, 1991.

The lack of a general principle of good faith does not prevent judges from intervening in the contract (*construction*) and integrating it, through hermeneutical experiments of an objective kind, and affecting the traditional role given to the will expressed in the contract. This is occurring together with the emergence, in recent case law, of a tendency to underline the contractors' duty of diligence even in the pre-contractual stage.[30]

3.3   Interpretation in Accordance with Good Faith and Sectoral Regulation in Italy

The reference in the DCFR to interpretative criteria in the event of a disparity of power reflects a problem felt in every national system, the general laws[31] of which must be re-assessed in light of special laws on consumer contracts and on business contracts.

Italian doctrine has delivered different interpretations on the matter. For some, a non-negotiated contract between a professional and a consumer should be interpreted by reconstruing the 'parties' common intention' (meant as 'the parties' intended result'[32]). Other authors believe that the criterion of subjective interpretation cannot be applied to non-negotiated contracts between professionals and consumers, giving various reasons for this.[33]

However, while the criterion of the parties' common intention is not very useful if the contract is not individually negotiated, the good faith criterion remains useful nonetheless. Indeed, as indicated above, the criterion has a key role in fixing the contract's content and in underlining the parties' rights and obligations arising from the contract and from law. Such a role is very useful in the interpretation of contracts between professionals and consumers.

As regards business to business contracts, the two conclusions outlined above apply. The notion needs to be subdivided into a different number of

---

[30]   On the point see R. Goode, *Il diritto commerciale del terzo millennio*, Milan, 2003, pp. 49, 52 ff.

[31]   The articles on contractual interpretation are affected, in each legal system, by these different positions. See, in particular, Arts 1362–1371 Italian Civil Code; Art. 1140-1 of the French *Avant projet* whereby '*[t]outefois, lorsque la loi contractuelle a été établie sous l'influence dominante d'une partie, on doit l'interpréter en faveur de l'autre*'; and the articles of the DCFR 8:103 on *Interpretation against party supplying term* and 8:104 *Preference for negotiated terms*.

[32]   For a useful reconstruction of the different positions see B. Sirgiovanni, 'Interpretazione del contratto non negoziato con il consumatore', in *Rass. dir. civ.*, 2006, p. 729 and note 28.

[33]   A. Genovese, *Contratti standard e interpretazione oggettiva*, Milan, 2004, p. 26 ff.; G. Stella Richter, 'L'interpretazione dei contratti dei consumatori', in *Riv. trim.*, 1997, p. 1027.

negotiations, depending on whether we are dealing with unilaterally negoti-ated contracts (between professionals and consumers), where the considera-tions just outlined apply, or bilateral contracts, which in turn need to be separated into contracts between businesses, free from significant asymme-tries (B to B) and contracts where the parties' positions differ substantially due to subjective or objective circumstances (B to b).[34] Indeed, it is now increas-ingly obvious that the interpretative criteria must be diversified according to the specific way in which private autonomy is expressed.[35]

The doctrine has supported different theories.[36] As already noted, we need to diversify the many contractual figures. In these contracts, we need to exam-ine the special laws that are meant to protect the entrepreneur-contractor (against abuse of economic dependence, franchising and payment terms) and the juridical regulation of the market which each single negotiation is part of.[37] The relevant provisions can help us integrate the rights and duties prescribed by law or by the contract, and this cannot but affect interpretative criteria. Once more, then, good faith has a positive role, since it requires the interpreter to consider the parties' different power, which is made relevant by special laws, and to interpret the contract in line with relevant special criteria.

4.   ARTICLE 1:102 AND INTERPRETATION ACCORDING TO HUMAN RIGHTS, FUNDAMENTAL FREEDOMS AND CONSTITUTIONAL LAWS

The interpretative rule on respect for fundamental rights and freedoms requires a premise. The Charter of Fundamental Rights confirms the distinc-tion between rights and principles. The explanation of Article 52, referred to by the new Article 6 of the Treaty of Lisbon, is extremely clear. According to Article 51, principles may be implemented through legislative or executive acts, so that they are relevant to judges only when the regulations concerned are construed or subject to control, without leading to direct claims against the

---

[34]   See C. Scognamiglio, 'I contratti di impresa e la volontà delle parti contraenti', in P. Sirena (ed.), *Il diritto europeo dei contratti d'impresa. Autonomia negoziale dei privati e regolazione del mercato*, Milan, 2006, p. 493; G. Vettori, 'I contratti di distribuzione', in *ibid.*, p. 482.

[35]   See A. Rizzi, *Interpretazione del contratto e dello statuto societario*, Milan, 2002.

[36]   A. Genovese, *Contratti standard e interpretazione oggettiva*, Milan, 2004, p. 70.

[37]   G. Vettori, 'Autonomia privata e contratto giusto', in *Riv. dir. priv.*, 2000, 5, p. 21.

European Union institutions or the authorities of Member States.[38] This is said to be in line with the European Court of Justice's case law,[39] and with the approach to 'principles' taken by the constitutional systems of Member States, especially in the field of social laws. By way of example, we may refer to the principles recognised in Articles 25, 26 and 37 of the Charter. Moreover, in some cases, an Article of the Charter may contain elements of both a right and a principle, such as Articles 23, 33 and 34.[40]

Certainly,[41] the distinction between rights and principles is an expedient way to limit creative interpretations. In truth, however, it only prompts a careful specification of the desirable relationship between the contract, the Charter and case law, which is now meaningfully dealt with by Article 1:102, whereby all provisions of the DCFR are to be read in the light of any applicable instruments guaranteeing human rights, fundamental freedoms and any applicable constitutional laws.

Such a provision gains importance if we specify how an interpretative criterion, grounded on a principle, should apply. In order for the criterion in question to apply, a rule must be laid down by the legislator or created by the judge through an act of interpretation, i.e. without creating a new right, since the case falls within his juridical scope if there exists a principle. Such a method uses a *canon for juridical construction* derived from the case through different kinds of interferences and deductions.[42] This creates the rule for the decision, though it may also be used as an exegetic canon of the contract, provided the points mentioned here are borne in mind.

---

[38]   G. Vettori, 'La lunga marcia della Carta dei diritti fondamentali dell'Unione europea', in *Riv. dir. priv.*, 2007, 4, p. 5; by the same author, 'Il diritto dei contratti fra Costituzione, Codice civile e Codici di settore', in *Riv. trim. dir. proc. civ.*, 2008, p. 784.

[39]   Cf., in particular, the case law about the 'precautionary principle' of Article 174, paragraph 2 of the EC Treaty (replaced by Article III-233 of the Constitution): judgment of the CFI of 11 September 2002, Case T-13/99 *Pfizer v Council*, with many references to earlier case law; and a series of judgments on Article 33 (formerly Article 39) on the principles of agricultural law, e.g., judgment of the Court of Justice, C-265/85 *Van den Berg* [1987], ECR 1155: scrutiny of the principle of market stabilisation and of reasonable expectations, C-310/458 EN Offical Journal of the European Union 16.12.2004.

[40]   See G. Vettori, *La lunga marcia della Carta dei diritti fondamentali, op. cit.*, n. 38, p. 5, from which I draw my remarks.

[41]   In the European Council conclusions (Brussels, 21–22 June 2007), it is said that the Charter of Fundamental Rights has a juridical value, by referring to Art. 6 of the Treaties, by recalling Chapter VII on interpretation and application (without prejudice to Poland's unilateral declaration and to the additional protocol requested by the United Kingdom).

[42]   G. Vettori, *Il diritto dei contratti fra Costituzione, Codice civile e codici di settore, op. cit.* n. 38, p. 787.

The judge is subject only to the law,[43] which also governs the relationship between citizens' equality and disparity of power (Article 3).[44] The Constitution guarantees the equality of subjective situations (rights, obligations, powers, duties) before the law and the judge, since each right and interest is equally recognised (Article 24) and is assessed by an independent and impartial judge (Article 111). This means that eventual disparities of power between contractors cannot be ascertained and decided on the level of subjective situations, which are equal for all. Equality needs to be guaranteed through the judicial ascertainment of disparity, which will be exclusively based on the implementation of a provision, on the proper use of general clauses, and on the juridical qualification of a fact which justifies a differential treatment.[45]

Hence, the DCFR's reference to interpretative criteria in the event of a diversity between parties' rights, and to the general role of good faith is important. From it, and the legal criteria laid down by the Italian legislator, it can be inferred that the judge must (under Article 1366 Italian Civil Code and under the DCFR, when the text has a binding value) construe the contract in line with the parties' common intention and ascertain the rights deriving from special laws. This must be done in accordance with fundamental freedoms which, through good faith, become exegetic criteria and conformity parameters for the legal meaning of the contract.

This does not conflict with the foundation of the provision that protects a party's reliance on the reasonable meaning and content of the parties' statements and conducts, and thus their conformity to the parties' common intention, integrated by fundamental rights and freedoms.

---

[43]   Jurisdictional value is thus connected to popular sovereignty, and the idea of being subject to the law specifies such a connection. The judge's activity does not take the shape of political participation; rather it is an intellectual activity and any other power or judge cannot interfere with it. The judge is not even subject to Parliament, since he can raise a question of constitutionality with respect to an ordinary law. Therefore, the judge participates in enforcing the general will, often treading a subtle line reserved to politics which, together with law, is a social science after all.

[44]   See A. Orsi Battaglini, *Alla ricerca dello Stato di diritto. Per una Giustizia 'non amministrativa'*, Milan, 2005, pp. 115, 116, 117–118, 121–122.

[45]   *Ibid.*, p. 117.

3. The role of competition in the European codification process

Stefan Grundmann

I. CODIFICATION? QUALITY?

Most notable contract lawyers in countries such as Germany and Italy (countries which are still rather positive about a European contract law, and even about its codification in an optional instrument) seem to be highly sceptical about the outcome of the (Academic) Common Frame of Reference ('ACFR').[1] They have different concerns, reflecting their differing approaches to contract law. Amongst the concerns they have identified are that there is little new in the ACFR; it contains an abundance of vague decisions or non-decisions on core questions; it lacks a convincingly coherent structure; and it contains virtually no input from other branches of the social sciences which engage substantially with contract; and, more generally, it inadequately reflects concerns for 'social justice'.[2] Furthermore, the ACFR has been seen as

---

[1]   C. v Bar, E. Clive, H. Schulte-Nölke et al. for the Study Group on a European Civil Code and Research Group on EC Private Law (Acquis Group) (eds.), *Principles, Definitions and Model Rules of European Private Law – Draft Common Frame of Reference (DCFR)* (Munich: Sellier, 2008). Irrespective of the impact of the ACFR on it, this chapter does not deal with the so-called 'horizontal directive' in the core area of consumer law, consolidating the four directives on Sales, Unfair Terms, Doorstep and Distance Selling, in one; see now Proposal for a Directive of the European Parliament and of the Council on Consumer Rights, COM(2008)614 final. This directive mainly concerns the restructuring of a well established part of the *acquis communautaire*.

[2]   See, for instance, special issue of the *European Review of Contract Law* 3/2008 (contributions by S. Grundmann at 225, M. Hesselink at 248, J. Smits at 270, R. Sefton-Green at 281, B. Fages at 304, H. Beale at 317, M. Mekki and M. Kloepfer-Pelèse at 338, K. Langenbucher at 375, A. Carrasco at 389, S. Whittaker at 411 and P. Sirena at 445, those from outsiders all highly critical); H. Eidenmüller, F. Faust, H. Grigoleit, N. Jansen, G. Wagner and R. Zimmermann, 'Der Gemeinsame Referenzrahmen für das Europäische Privatrecht – Wertungsfragen und Kodifikationsprobleme', *Juristenzeitung* 2008, 529; summary in *Franfurter Allgemeine Zeitung* of 5 June 2008, p. 8 (R. Müller, 'Ungesteuerte Richtermacht'): 'Für einen politisch legitimierten Text ist die Zeit noch lange nicht reif'. See as well H. Collins, *The European*

too large an endeavour, conducted in isolation from the rest of European legal academia. And these countries, Germany and Italy, are amongst the most positive about the ACFR process!

My contribution to the special issue on 'The Structure of the DCFR: Which Approach for Today's Contract Law?' addressed the fact that the draft includes many areas with little significant intersection with contract law, while conversely it omits to answer most modern contract law questions which the old Codes do not tackle. Though the authors of the ACFR (after ten years' work, in the case of the Study Group) deplore the lack of time available to the process, they approach a host of subjects which could have easily been dissociated from contract law – for which alone a draft was requested. The Study Group thus would appear to have had the 'grand' Code in mind rather than advancing 'merely' European contract law. As in many other commentaries, my conclusion was that simply repairing the (Academic) Common Frame of Reference is not appropriate, because the existing structure and material do not provide a good enough basis. So there must be a fresh foundation and a more open start. It is to this end that the current chapter is addressed.

The chapter starts from the assumption that there are good chances that the process currently under way is aimed at or will aim at a European Code in the area of private law. This perspective is legitimate because core authors of the ACFR do intend this work to serve as a draft for such a Code. However, it is in addition assumed that the ACFR will ultimately principally serve as a quarry of legal ideas to be regarded, in a comparative law perspective, as an interesting contribution which brings a certain drive into the European discussion, but no more than this. On the other hand, if the ACFR really remains the exclusive basis for further development of European contract law, that is, if the political organs want a quick conclusion of the procedure, this chapter is pointless. This outcome is one I would regret, because my view of the European Contract Code is that it could indeed provide a new model for contract law at the beginning of the 21st Century, and be received as such also internationally – which would be a major development, given that society has altered so radically in recent decades. Finally, this chapter assumes that as early as 2001–03, a better way forward would have been that of a competition of legal ideas about a new European contract law. It strongly advocates this path at least for five, perhaps even ten years to come, even if afterwards an extremely restricted group should bring together the rich input gathered until then.

The chapter advocates competition because neither of the two prerequisites that competition theorists unanimously ask for when they accept a 'natural'

Civil Code – The Way Forward (Cambridge, Cambridge University Press, 2008); and M. Hesselink (below, n. 6).

monopoly is met,[3] though clearly the structure of the ACFR/CFR was constructed on the part of the EC Commission and of its core academic players as a monopoly, designed in large part to exclude. These two prerequisites are not met because, first, the investment needed for the development of an optional European Code is not especially high, perhaps amounting to some 5, 10 or 20 million ; secondly, because we are far from an established product and procedure which only needs exploitation now – rather it is the product and procedure themselves which still need to be developed, and competition theory is unanimous that such a situation necessitates a strong input of competition. In other words: given these prerequisites, the current situation is perhaps even the polar opposite of one which might speak in favour of permitting a 'natural' monopoly.

Accordingly, the chapter deals with two questions: why we are far from an established product and procedure when a European Code is at stake (section II); and how competition could be structured (section III). In these sections, the chapter investigates possibilities for a truly competitive process in the development of a European contract law and its potential structures (while also examining why one should concentrate on contract law). It also asks the question which new trends need absolutely to be taken up for a modern contract law, and reflects on where input from other social sciences should, crucially, not be disregarded. Finally, it also considers the flaws of the overall structure of the DCFR and describes, at least in some instances, various alternatives to it.

One major flaw in the process so far should be remedied as rapidly as possible. If possible during 2008–09, but certainly in the next period of tenure, the EC Commission should be as frank as the European Parliament, and open a process explicitly aimed at a European Code. The lack of transparency which characterised at least some of the EC Commission's handling of the CFR process so far has not been helpful.

II. WHY COMPETITION?

1. Methods and Approaches Unclear

So far, two groups have principally been responsible for developing the ACFR, the Study Group probably still being the more prominent. The Study

---

3   For the natural monopoly (its prerequisites and its role as a rather rare exception) see, for instance, W. Sharkey, *The Theory of Natural Monopoly* (Cambridge: Cambridge University Press, 1982), chap. 15 and *passim*; see also R. Posner, *Natural Monopoly and its Regulation* (Washington, DC: Cato, 1999).

Group basically relied on a traditional comparative law method and comprised a large number of comparatists, with a scholar known in tort law, not contract law as initiator.[4] This group took as starting point the Principles of European Contract Law (PECL), also known as the Lando Principles.[5] These principles scarcely took into account the *acquis communautaire*, consumer contract law or even unfair contract terms law, although the *acquis* started to develop in contract law in the 1980s and unfair contract terms and consumer contract law, at least on the national level, as early as the 1970s. While this may have been understandable for a set of principles and, at an early stage, for a draft Code, after the turn of the century, so restricted an approach no longer seemed possible. The procedural response to this problem within the ACFR group was to add a second core group working on the *acquis communautaire*, then combining proposals from this group and the Study Group. Thus, the problem of integrating different approaches was postponed.

This development already shows how important the choice of method is: there is a *multitude of approaches* to choose from, but many were largely disregarded in the process so far. Should a traditional comparative law approach be adopted? Many would say that comparative law is restricted to a bird's eye view, which can only depict and follow what the core players in the national contract laws have developed and continue to develop. In other words, is comparative law and the input from the *acquis communautaire* enough? Is it sufficient if they are in the end combined, and not conceived as an integrated whole from the outset? More important, is it really convincing that one of the most important endeavours of European private law legislation, an endeavour where policy questions are paramount, should basically be approached without knowing what other social sciences think about the issues at stake: disregarding economic theory, behavioural sciences, organisational sciences, that are so important as regards long-term relationships, and also disregarding sociology? Can long-term relationships which have become so important in today's service society be thought about at all, without input from company law (which was not represented in the Study Group)? Or without any discussion of principal–agent theory, the problem of hold-up situations and many other relevant issues that might be mentioned? Likewise, a theory of

---

4   His major contribution to (quasi-)contract law was benevolent intervention into another's affairs which may explain the somehow astonishing prominence of this area of the law in the ACFR (occupying one book, like torts or the whole body of specific contract law): see C. von Bar, *Benevolent Intervention in Another's Affairs* (Munich: Sellier, 2006).
5   O. Lando and H. Beale (eds.), *Principles of European Contract Law* (Dordrecht et al.: Martinus Nijhoff), parts I (1996) and II (1999) and O. Lando, E. Clive, A. Prüm and R. Zimmermann (eds.), part III (The Hague et al.: Kluwer Law International, 2003).

consumer law without the rich insights derived from the last four decades of studies of information economy, as well behavioural economics, simply cannot appear firmly grounded.

Of course, one could say that economists looked at the results afterwards. But would it not be naïve to equate a thesis corrected by a professor with a book written by the professor himself? Having the chance to add some *ex post* modifications – accepted or rejected at the discretion of the ACFR group – is very far indeed from amounting to participation in the drafting process. Social sciences have been excluded from the process. Moreover, as regards most major countries, not even the core exponents of dogmatic thinking were included, and criticism drawn from their side as well is harsh und virtually unanimous. Is their input of so little value? Conceivably there are other approaches which are perhaps even more important, but which in any case have to be articulated *before* decisions are taken and designs are made – rather than appearing as little dots on a picture already painted. This is true with respect to the question of which role constitutional or EC Treaty values may occupy – a question which many view as related to that of 'Social Justice'.[6]

The answer delivered within the ACFR process was not only mechanical – adding a second group to cover the most blatant shortcoming – but to a large extent also exclusive. While it may perhaps be argued that at this stage of European legal science no more inclusive approach was possible, another procedure would of course allow for a more inclusive approach for the future. This would, first, give competition enough space, and then, when there are results, allow an informed decision on which elements should be incorporated – with decisions on inclusion or exclusion not turning on the judgement of one approach only. Is it really appropriate that, because one approach succeeded in finding support within the EC Commission, all the others must remain excluded, entering only as minor modifications, at the discretion of one drafting group? At least with respect to interdisciplinary research it is universally accepted that such a procedure cannot constitute an interdisciplinary work or product. Truly the question is whether the European Code should be a lawyer's Code only, or a societal and social sciences Code as well; whether it should be firmly grounded in dogmatic traditions, or rather be based on a bird's eye view (in the form of a summary, with many general clauses, and thus evading a host of hard questions).

The question of which approaches to include in a meaningful way (i.e. already when drafting starts) is not trivial; it is a core question and the answer can be given properly only as a result of competition.

---

6   The European Parliament even ordered an investigation: see M. Hesselink, *CFR & Social Justice* (Munich: Sellier, 2008). This contribution (and criticism made there) should be assessed against the background that M. Hesselink is a member of the Study Group.

In the end, in a *final drafting process*, of course, only an approach which integrates all the trends identified can produce satisfactory results. Such an *integrative approach* cannot manifest in a procedure where important approaches are used simply to confirm (perhaps slightly modify) what one or two approaches have established. This is not to criticise the endeavours undertaken so far – so long as integration, on the basis of results developed autonomously by all different approaches, is yet to come. Seen from this perspective, one or two approaches have now triggered the momentum for the real process – which is highly laudable, if it has not been intended to exclude the other steps suggested, and will not result in such exclusion. Ultimately, integration of the approaches may perhaps be even easier when results are first developed autonomously across individual approaches. However, it could also be the case that a group chooses an integrative approach right from the beginning.

2. Subject Matter Unclear

What is true for method, in relation to the ACFR, is true for subject matter as well. The subject matter is not clear: Should it be a grand old Civil Code, notwithstanding that family law, wills and estates, property law, and even torts and unjust enrichment, can easily be dissociated from contract law? And despite the fact that contract law has become so complex that finding a good contract law structure is a question of just enough complexity anyhow? The example of the Italian Code and the famous formulation of the alternative by Coase[7] show that the intersections between organisation (whether company, joint venture, or partnership) and contracts are even more meaningful. At least, this is the case if one takes the developments of the last decades seriously, and accepts that long-term relationships and networks of contracts are among the most powerful phenomena today (we are living in a network and in a services society, after all, and these are always based principally on these phenomena). The law of long-term relationships and networks draws at least as heavily on company law models as on contract law models – probably even more so. However, if it possesses limited expertise in this respect, a group will tend to disregard network and service society phenomena.

---

7   On the famous alternative of firm and market see R. Coase, 'The Theory of the Firm', 4 *Economica* 386 (1937); and nowadays for instance F. Easterbrook and D. Fischel, *The Economic Structure of Corporate Law* (Cambridge, Mass.: Harvard University Press, 1996), p. 8 et seq.; H. Eidenmüller, 'Kapitalgesellschaftsrecht im Lichte der ökonomischen Theorie', *Juristenzeitung (JZ)* 2001, 1041, at 1042; O. Hart, *Firms, Contracts, and Financial Structure* (Oxford: Clarendon, 1995), pp. 6–8, 15–55.

(a)   Including really all obligations and even more?
Both groups responsible for the ACFR, according to their name, are aimed at
European private or civil law in general – yet competition, company and capital market law would seem to be represented only marginally. The eight books
envisaged are intended to comprise contract law, a general law of obligations,
benevolent intervention, torts, unjust enrichment and (in the eighth book, until
now still missing) large parts of property law (or at least 'primarily' to
compare these areas (Article I.-I:101 paragraph 1), whatever this may mean in
terms of still further extensions). The books, their principal contents, and also
their order look very German[8] – yet this is not really the question. Rather, the
core question is whether even obligations is too abstract a category, and
whether torts, unjust enrichment and contracts have too little in common to be
grouped together. More precisely, is it not the case that even the links between
these three, formally 'similar' areas of the law, all dealing with obligations, are
not so strong that they cannot be dissociated without entailing shortcomings?
Such shortcomings are suggested by those who want the big Code and do not
content themselves with contracts. On the other hand, the existence of a law
of obligations in some countries does not yet speak in favour of the need for
such a law, and certainly not at European level. Contract is about autonomous
shaping of the parties' relations; torts is not. Finally, unjust enrichment neatly
falls into two main parts, one related to contracts, the other related to illegal
taking (often torts).

The ACFR, including all obligations pays a high price for little in return.
The structure of the ACFR becomes strange and complicated because of the
inclusion of obligations generally. The first three larger books contain: contract law (general part (book 2)); the law of obligations (general part (book 3));
then again, contract law (now specific contracts (book 4)). This formal disrup-
tion in the law of contracts is a high price to pay for rather little general law
of obligations within book 3. Most rules included in this book (which, according to its title, addresses 'obligations' generally) either can apply only to
contracts (about 40%) or, although theoretically they could apply to torts as
well, are of no material importance there (about 40%). The former is true for

---

8   This impression is further strengthened by the fact that benevolent intervention occupies a whole book (above n. 4), and even more by the fact that the concept of
'juridical act', which common law scholars and practitioners in particular have difficulty in understanding, was introduced with some prominence. For a common lawyer's
perspective see, for instance, R. Sefton-Green, n. 2 above. For the highly complicated
succession of books (2–4), jumping from contract to obligation (comprising, in part,
pure contract law) and then back to contract, see S. Grundmann, n. 2 above; and in
more detail S. Grundmann, 'Structural Elements in the Contract Law Parts of the
German Civil Code', in S. Grundmann and M. Schauer (eds.), *The Architecture of
European Codes and Contract Law* (Alphen: Kluwer International, 2006), 57.

such areas as rescission, price reduction, good faith (is there a tort 'in good faith'?), termination. The latter is true for such areas as performance (there are also rules on monetary obligations); most of plurality of debtors and creditors;[9] and also of transfer of rights and obligations and set-off and merger (see in more detail my contribution in footnote 2). A look at the contents of book 3 shows that little is left. Where rules apply to contracts only in any case, it is 'wrong' to include them in book 3; where they are in fact important only for contracts (though theoretically applicable also to torts), it would have been just as feasible to limit the rules to contracts, leaving it to case law to apply these rules by analogy to torts, if truly necessary, on a case by case basis. Rules which really matter for contracts and torts (and partly also unjust enrichment) are those on damages and on prescription.[10] I come back to some of this in a moment.

The second part of the price paid for the inclusion of all obligations is that formation of contracts makes appearances here and there, in book 2 with general concepts and again in book 3. The same is true for performance. A simple order following the life of contract, from formation via performance and breach to extinction, and then proceeding to extensions to third parties, becomes *impossible*. Moreover, it is no longer possible to have two separate pillars, although the importance of the phenomena would have called for this (for instance, negotiated contracts here and adhesion contracts there, or spot or exchange contracts here, and cooperation or long-term contracts there). There is too much complexity in the system (that is, of all 'obligations') to adopt such bifurcations in the ACFR. Conversely, concentrating on contracts would have left this option open. Contract, as it exists today, could have been depicted in a more realistic way, attaching weight to the phenomena and distinctions in line with what they possess in real life.

The third part of the price paid for the inclusion of all obligations is that where rules really matter for contracts and for torts (and partly also unjust enrichment), the authors of the ACFR seem to have put so much effort into generalisation, that they now no longer approach core questions of differentiation. Where rules apply to all obligations (which is not often the case), there is still the question whether they should apply in the same way for contracts,

---

9   Plurality of debtors is yet another example where the reason for having such plurality in torts differs radically from that in contracts. Therefore the prerequisites and the regime in one setting are not really helpful in the other.

10   Prescription (not considered further here) is the one area where largely parallel rules for contracts and torts would seem to be the more modern trend and, in principle, preferable. See on this area, for instance, R. Zimmermann, *Comparative Foundations of a European Law of Set-Off and Prescription* (Cambridge: Cambridge University Press, 2002), p. 62 et seq.

torts and unjust enrichment. This can be illustrated with respect to the second chance, immaterial damages and for 'restitutionary' remedies generally: with respect to (i) the second chance, the ACFR does not differentiate, but why not? Does the victim of a tort desire that the tort-feasor perform in kind? Does she want the tort-feasor, be it a car driver or even a doctor who has treated her poorly, to give her the necessary medical treatment? The answer would seem to be in the negative (indeed, in this sense section 249 paragraph 2 of the German Civil Code). No 'second chance' is the normal answer, while in contract law the contrary is true. The ACFR, in its longing for generalisation, does not differentiate. One can, of course, apply Article III.-3:203 lit. d, allowing the creditor to seek monetary compensation without setting an additional period of time whenever 'cure [in kind] would be inappropriate in the circumstances'. The question is, however, why the draft does not have the courage to decide typical cases, and instead postpones decisions and creates legal uncertainty by choosing a general clause ('inappropriate') for whole areas of the law (i.e. for the question: is there the right to a second chance in torts?). The picture is similar with respect to (ii) immaterial damages, regulated in Article III.-3:701 paragraph 3 ('Loss includes . . . non-economic loss . . . [which] includes pain and suffering and impairment of the quality of life'). This rule really leaves unanswered the core question: when should non-economic loss be compensated, beyond the (rather simple) cases of pain and suffering? This question is left open by awarding non-economic loss on the basis of 'impairment of the quality of life'. This criterion really begs the question:[11] it is much too open; alternatively, it does not help with the distinctions which need to be made. Is having to go to court over several years – potentially in a case which is existential for the contract partner concerned – not more of an 'impairment of the quality of life' than experiencing trouble in a journey? There are numerous cases in torts, in particular, in the areas of privacy, legal protection of personality, inroads into the lives of couples and, in addition, in cases in which immaterial loss can be awarded, because individual material loss is always difficult to prove, namely cases concerning environmental questions. A modern regulation of the law of torts would have to deal with these issues, but a modern contract law much less. In any event, the need, where it exists, would not be satisfied by the rule that has been selected. So even a good regime on torts would probably add little to the regime in contract law – and the regime chosen is of even less help, in either area. In contract, package travel, as the one disputed case,[12] could, for

---

[11]   In this sense (and far too open) see H. Eidenmüller, F. Faust, H. Grigoleit, N. Jansen, G. Wagner and R. Zimmermann, *Juristenzeitung* 2008, 529, at 539–541.

[12]   As is well known, the ECJ awarded damages for non-economic loss in case of considerable impairment of a package journey: Case C-168/00 *Simone Leitner/TUI* [2002] ECR I-2631.

instance, easily be understood as commercialisation of leisure time, and therefore as special. In fact, workers pay for their holidays by working in advance
and earning proportionately less while they work. The question is, however,
which type of inconvenience in contracts should really be compensated. In a
law on obligations, apparently, neither part – contracts or torts – acquires guidance on the truly controversial issues.

Finally, (iii) the law of restitution shows that, if the ACFR had limited itself to first drafting a convincing contract law, one could have approached the
old, unconvincing 'heritage' of the *Bürgerliches Recht* which concerns the
other important 'non-contractual' obligation, namely, unjust enrichment. This
is a heritage that, in Germany, both courts and scholars and, in 2002, the legislature as well have had to struggle with, all trying to bring contractual rules on
restitution and rules on restitution based on unjust enrichment closer to one
another.[13] Had one had the courage to think first of contracts, a coherent
system of restitution could have been designed where differences in dealing
with void contracts and with contracts avoided (for instance, via withdrawal
rights and contracts 'terminated' for breach of contract) could have been
discussed, to be upheld only where they are justified and made explicit. The
relevant rules would not have had to be split into two bodies of the law
(Articles III-3:511 et seq. and VII:1.101 et seq.) separated from one another by
about 400 rules. Careful coordination could have been achieved.

A fourth price is paid: Members of the Study Group have argued that a
remedy in tort often runs parallel to a contractual remedy, arguing, for
instance, that discrimination is also a tort. This argument, made to justify the
inclusion of the dual track, however backfires. Is it really intended to have a
highly detailed regime on anti-discrimination in the contractual arena (Article
II.-2:201 ff.) and then, if there is no remedy, have torts as a fall-back position?
Either tort is excluded, in which case the argument that torts have to be regulated as well falls away, or a remedy in tort is given, in which case Pandora's
box is opened, even if the legislature has founded a nuanced contractual
regime on whether and where it wanted to open it. In other words, though the
question of cumulative remedies (the only one in section 1 ('General') which
is important for the relationship to torts) of course must be decided, the question for contract law is whether it is exclusive or not.

---

[13]   See, in detail P. Sirena, 'The DCFR – Restitution, Unjust Enrichment and
Related Issues', above n. 2. Sirena raises the question why, if one includes benevolent
intervention, one excludes the no less puzzling phenomenon of malevolent intervention
into another's affairs.

(b)   Or rather dealing with contract law and clarifying the intersections?

From the above it follows that about half of the questions dealt with in Book 3, even in formal terms, cannot arise outside the realm of contracts. Most other questions, while potentially arising also in the realm of torts, in practice matter only for contracts, and they are mainly regulated in such a way that the regime for contracts applies by analogy to torts or other obligations. The remaining few questions where the relationship between contracts, on the one hand, and torts or other obligations, on the other, does matter are treated in a non-specific way in the DCFR, so that the advantages of creating a book on obligations appear to be rendered minimal. Conversely, considerable disadvantage have been identifed. Two would seem to be of particular importance: (i) regulating too much distracts attention from the few questions where the relationship between contracts and torts or other obligations does matter; (ii) the drafters are no longer free to follow a simple order which would have taken into consideration only the 'life' of a contract. Instead, they must split up general contract law into two books, in a rather artificial way. In addition, being unable to consider only the life of contract carries the consequence that the links between related issues in contract law, the value judgements, the differentiations within contract law, cannot be the sole concern. Therefore, these relationships cannot be developed in an optimal way, demonstrating that an optimal contract law has not been the prime aim.

The disadvantage identified first above is even more striking when we consider what has not been regulated in the book on obligations or, for that matter, elsewhere. Interestingly, some, perhaps even most, situations where the relationship between contract and tort is truly tricky are not dealt with, or at least not in detail. The ACFR lacks a section on networks of contracts, despite their high practical importance (see below section 3). Consequently, it remains very vague about the question of the role of direct claims between partners to the network who are not themselves linked by contract; in national laws, these claims are seen as based on torts, where they are accepted.[14] Direct claims, however, are a highly controversial issue and are a considerable obstacle to an optimal design of networks. Company law amply demonstrates that tort claims

---

[14]   Namely in France: see M. Fabre-Magnan, *Les obligations* (Paris: Presses Universitaires de France, 2004), pp. 465–472 and the slightly more restrictive leading decision of the Senate of the Cour de Cassation (Supreme Court), Bulletin Assemblée plénière, n° 5 = Dalloz 1991, 549; and on the European level: H. Beale and G. Howells, 'EC Harmonisation of Consumer Sales Law – a Missed Opportunity?' (1997) 12 *Journal of Contract Law* 21, 22–24; M. Bridge, in C.M. Bianca and S. Grundmann (eds.), *EU Sales Directive – Commentary* (Antwerp/Oxford: Intersentia, 2002), Art. 4 paras. 37–47; F. Gomez, 'Introduction' in ibid., para. 127 et seq.

within the organisation are considered in that microcosmos only in exceptional cases. A second field where torts and contracts are considered in parallel which is of high practical importance is liability of third parties involved in the negotiation process, namely representatives and intermediaries. Here the question is whether this third party is liable, although the contract is formed between the two partners to the contract. This issue arises, for instance, with respect to prospectus liability of intermediaries or liability for advice given, for example, in expert opinions. In many cases such opinion is given to one contract partner only, for instance, a bank which wants to place a mortgage on an immovable, and therefore has its value checked, but the valuation nevertheless interests the other contract partner, here the client of the bank, typically, the purchaser who borrows money. Again, the ACFR does not give advice on these questions, specifically, in the section devoted to the precontractual phase (Chapter 3 of Book II, Articles II-3:101 et seq.). There are not many intersections of similar importance between contracts and torts, but it is significant that the ACFR does not deal with them because it is too focused on generalising and transforming what is mainly contract law into a law of obligations. A good contract law would concentrate on an adequate structure for contract law, and then define and deal with the (few) intersections which really matter.

The alternative to the ACFR is a contract law including rules on restitution and, separately, a tort law including a part concerning restitutionary damages as well. If Europeanisation is not about dressing a monument, or a grand Code, it is advisable to go for a good and modern contract law and – perhaps one day in the future – a good tort law, where tort law is indeed market-related, or a good law of securities in movables or covered bonds. Too much energy is needed to create a good contract law to waste it on a general law of obligations (see below section 3). Accordingly, the alternative would be to regulate contracts completely, instead of designing abstract categories for all obligations (and, potentially, all traditional civil law matters). The latter project is the heritage of highly formal thinking, according to which all obligations have one characteristic in common: that they bind two parties (and even this, as will be seen, is questionable in contemporary life). Conversely, a convincing, modern contract law would be pragmatic in putting the structure of real markets in the forefront.

(c) Including all types of contract partners?

Even the question which types of contract partners should be included in a European (Contract) Code is sufficiently important to be decided in an open process, instead of just by one group. It may well be that the inclusion of all types of contract partners, as proposed by the ACFR, is preferable; I, for one, have much sympathy for this proposal. It may well be that only the basis of differentiation selected could be more meaningful – the reasons for differentiation could be more outspoken, more based on a solid theory that gives guidelines as to when markets really fail, and when market order by regulation is really needed.[15] But the central question is whether all approaches should have a say in this decision and a chance to advance their respective arguments.

The questions articulated in the two sections above are of such outstanding importance for the structure of the legislative instrument that, once the arguments have been advanced, it might well be appropriate for a democratically legitimised body to give the guidelines – *before* the structure is established by a drafting group, so that it is no longer open to real revision.

3.   Modern Questions Not Approached So Far

We come to a third area of concern. Comparing 1958 and today, undoubtedly contract law still today concerns the same 'eternal' problems which were also important half a century ago when the Community was founded. However, contemporary contract law must also deal with recently materialised phenomena and problems. This can be easily shown with reference to some core concepts, without serious responses to which no European Code can be envisaged. After all, a European Code must reach forward into the 21st Century and propose a system for contract law as it exists now and in the foreseeable future.

(a)   Important new phenomena in the era of European integration

Amongst such modern phenomena can be noted the following: (i) new distribution channels, and the vastly greater importance of information in the formation process; (ii) public regulation within contract law, consumer regulation being probably the most prominent branch today, though far from being the only one; (iii) the vastly increased importance of service contracts, bringing the law of long-term relationships onto the scene, as a second branch besides simple exchange contracts; (iv) standard contract terms which, though they are already an old phenomenon, appear in new dimensions; (v) new trends in performance and breach of contract; (vi) network contracts and third party effects of contracts. Further examples could be added.

The doctrine of formation of contract is influenced, on the one hand, by a thoroughly altered dimension of publicity and by the rise of completely new ways of marketing and distribution, starting from publicity in television and on the internet, via alternative channels of distribution, such as telephone

---

[15]   For greater detail on this concern see my contribution referred to in n. 2 above.

marketing, and ending with the whole area of new information technologies, mainly electronic commerce. More importantly still, the role of information in the formation of contract is nowadays viewed as being of greater prominence than it was 20 or 30 years ago. To put it bluntly, the *information society* became a reality only at the end of the 20th Century. Information is, today, the core question in the phase of formation, as well as later on.

Safeguards at the moment of formation of contract are needed today to a different extent and in other forms because mass transactions, and clients in such transactions, have become a much more important phenomenon than the lone individual non-professional partner, and because consumer protection associations are powerful players which could be integrated and used in the regulatory framework in a much more meaningful way. Consumer law is only one out of the plethora of fields and rules where the *public regulatory power* enters contract law, unfair competition (trade practices) and antitrust being others. Thinking of contract without market order, in the sense of Franz Böhm, and without modern regulation theory, is thinking of contract law in terms of 19th Century models.

The sheer number of specific contracts has exploded. This is characteristic across the whole area of services (financial services, to take just one example) but also true in areas such as contracts combining elements of custody (for the elderly or persons with disabilities) with housing, for instance. 'Modern' contract types[16] form part of the 'classic' corpus of contract law, which might be taken care of by mixing and stretching concepts developed for traditional contract types – but it can just as well be conceived as a fresh challenge. Business management and agency contracts have become equally, if not more, important than traditional exchange contracts. To be blunt, once again, the *services society* began to become a reality only at the end of the 20th Century. Accordingly, the model of long-term relationships has to become a second pillar in general contract law, and the latter can no longer be shaped exclusively on the model of exchange contracts.

Of core importance, too, for formation and content of contracts is the role of *standard contracts* (standard or unfair contract terms), despite the fact that standard terms were already developed in the first half of the 20th Century. What is new is the negotiation of such contracts between associations acting in the interests of both sides of the market. Although standard contract terms are thus an old phenomenon, increasingly, they are no longer seen as individual negotiation, a model traditionally applied in this area, but rather as a particular mode of (unilateral!) drafting and imposition of private law rules.

---

[16]   On which see a 'classic' in German Law: M. Martinek, *Moderne Vertragstypen*, 3 vols. (Munich: C.H.Beck, 1991–1993).

Moreover, in the time period considered here with respect to this last phenomenon, both the various antitrust implications and intersections between competition law and consumer law have been recognised, and the challenge of making both areas as coherent as possible has been addressed.

The phase of *performance* appears to be least affected by changes since 1958. Nevertheless, there are today more specific agreements on performance too, such as the just in time agreement. More important than this, though, are mass transactions, a phenomenon which has a powerful impact in this area as well.[17] It should further be added that this is a field where comparative law inquiries are particularly intense[18] and where, therefore, the processes of learning and convergence are too. Thus, even fundamental models such as '*Nachfrist*' and 'fundamental breach', and their impact on remedies still need to be brought into line.[19]

Finally, the question of *third party effects* of contracts now appears in a completely new light. By contrast with the middle of the 20th Century, contracts are no longer exclusively, and perhaps not even primarily, individual relationships between two parties (concept of privity). Instead, they frequently occur within networks and chains of contracts: in distribution chains, in the process of production, in the whole area of transfer of credits and other payment systems, for example. Within such chains, responsibilities can be allotted in a range of ways, and the results in one contract impact on other contracts (for instance, whenever there is a responsibility in the sale to the ultimate client: see Article 4 of the EC Sales Law Directive). This trend manifests itself in many legal systems. The German Supreme Court (BGH), for example,

---

[17]   Which is evident from the fact that for 80–90% of the sales contracts in mass transactions, the old Roman law model (contained also in the German Code before the reform) was substituted by a regime similar to that of the directive including repair and – in case this failed – replacement: see Bundesminister der Justiz (ed.), *Abschluß-bericht der Kommission zur Überarbeitung des Schuldrechts* (Cologne: Bundesanzeigerverlag, 1992), p. 25.

[18]   The comparative law inquiries on which the Convention is based go back to the year 1929: see communication in *RabelsZ* 3 (1929) 405; and E. Rabel, *Gesammelte Aufsätze*, vol. III, 'Rapport sur le droit comparé en matière de vente par "l'Institut für Ausländisches und Internationales Privatrecht" de Berlin' (1967), 381 ('Blue Report'). E. Rabel is seen as the 'master mind behind the draft Uniform International Sales Law': B. Grossfeld and P. Winship, 'The Law Professor refugee', 18 *Syracuse J. Int'l. L. & Com.* 3, 11 (1992). Of core importance is E. Rabel, *Das Recht des Warenkaufs – eine rechtsvergleichende Darstellung*, 2 vols. (Berlin: de Gruyter, 1957 and 1958). It is equally well known that the Hague Uniform Sales Law of 1964 needed a second try in order to receive rather far spread recognition among the (industrialised) states.

[19]   See some ideas in S. Grundmann, 'Regulating Breach of Contract – The Right to Reject Performance by the Party in Breach', (2007) 3 *European Review of Contract Law* 121.

has considerably relaxed the preconditions for third party effects (protection of third parties), no longer considering them as completely exceptional, and the UK legislature has recognised third party effects (protection of third parties) where case law had delivered the opposite outcome.[20]

(b)　The answers given by the ACFR

The ACFR's responses to these modern problems have been discussed in detail elsewhere (my contribution, see note 2). The main results were the following: (i) information rules play a significant role in the ACFR. Nonetheless, they constitute little more than a simple transcription of what could be found in the *acquis communautaire*. What is more, the three subject matters dealing with information in the phase of formation (information duties in the narrow sense, the regime on mistake and the regime on publicity) have not been coordinated: they are detached from one another, formally and in content, being split into three regimes that are separated by hundreds of paragraphs (Article II-3:101 et seq., II-7:201 et seq. and II-9:102 paragraph 4). (ii) Services is a topic in the specific part of contracts, but the general part remains modelled mainly on the simple exchange contract. In other words, the fact that long-term, relational contracts are different in many respects and, in today's service society, are conduits for approximately one half of gross net income has not led to a scheme in which contracts of exchange and contracts of cooperation form two pillars of at least largely similar weight in the general part. In terms of structure, we thus have a Code for the purely industrial society. (iii) Networks do not play a role in the Code, although economic organisation cannot now do without them (production chains, distribution chains, payment chains, joint endeavours). (iv) Regulation does not play a role where the *acquis comunautaire* had not already prepared the solution (for instance, anti-discrimination). So, for instance, unfair competition and its impact on the formation of contracts is largely a non-topic for the ACFR, despite the many helpful suggestions already to be found in the EC Trade Practices Directive.

　　The ACFR's design is based on a comparison of (old) contract laws which has not taken these trends into consideration or has done so only to a very limited extent. Society has changed radically over the last 20 to 30 years, in the wake of transition towards information and service society, globalisation and other trends. It would be astonishing if its core instrument of exchange and

---

20　German Private Law Supreme Court, Official Reports (*BGHZ*) 127, 378; 128, 168, 173; Contract (Rights of Third Parties) Act 1999; on this Act and tendencies in the case law which pointed in this direction already see, for instance, H. Collins, *The Law of Contract* (4th edn, London: LexisNexis/Butterworths, 2003), pp. 325–328; comparative law survey in V. Palmer, 'Contracts in Favour of Third Persons in Europe: First Steps Towards Tomorrow's Harmonization' [2003] *ERPL/REDC* 8.

cooperation, the contract, had not followed suit, and any general contract law must reflect this.

III.   WHICH WAY OF COMPETITION?

This chapter pleads for more competition. However, it is beyond the scope of the present chapter to establish its full design. Rather, it will identify the problem and key aspects of importance to that process.

1.   Monopolies and Their Trend to Eternalise

The ACFR has been developed in a setting with features of a monopoly. In 2001–2002, the situation was characterised by the following features. There was still not a longstanding discussion on European contract law – in fact, the term and the subject area really emerged only in the mid-1990s – and there was still no well established European academic discussion. This implied that there was not a large number of solutions in the arena of discussion, which remains the case today. In this scenario, the EC Commission took a decision which gave one group an overwhelming advantage over others. In addition to giving financial support to that group, by doing so, it also implicitly (others might say, in a rather outspoken way) pre-selected the group to serve as the blueprint for all future discussions, and thereby also pre-selected the method, construction of the subject matter, approach to modernity, etc. Later, this tendency was further accentuated by the fact that discussion with stakeholders was organised only around this proposal, and which most stakeholders deplored. The main concerns at this stage were that the procedure employed largely excluded alternative approaches and entailed time restraints that precluded substantial amendment.

The fact that other groups were free to do parallel work (which they did, in at least one case – of the so-called Code Gandolfi[21]) does not challenge this analysis. Clearly signalling a preference for one group or design may not stop *some* players from engaging in parallel work notwithstanding. The potential reasons, which relate to opportunity costs, are manifold: because the persons involved are over-optimistic or because they have already engaged substantially (high sunk costs) being just two amongst a range of possibilities. For those who have alternative opportunities to obtain academic prestige (such as the offer of an important textbook) and who are often those who would be

---

[21]   G. Gandolfi, Academie des privatistes européens (ed.), *Code Européen des Contrats – Avant projet* (Milan: Giuffrè, 2007).

among the strongest competitors and who in addition might make outstanding drafters, the signal given typically has different effects. For such individuals, often it will be rational not to engage in the process, as appears to have been the case so far as regards the European codification process – and again, due to opportunity costs. A strong signal is accordingly needed to reverse this trend.

In terms of monopolies, it is immaterial whether the groups involved in and favoured by the process prompted this procedure or only accepted it, happily, inadvertently or even with certain reservations. It is equally immaterial whether it was a matter of chance that the persons or only one person taking core decisions within the EC Commission earned an honorary degree within universities or one university highly involved in the organisation of the network of excellence. Anybody concerned with the process should in any case be aware of the fact that a monopoly, once established, has a tendency to persist, and that a strong political or administrative will is needed to return to a market characterised by competition.

A clear political signal, including the funding of other groups and the setting of a realistic timeframe would be paramount if competition were truly the objective.

2. Competition in Overall Solutions or Competition in Core Questions

There are many products with respect to which competition could take place. Two categories, however, immediately come to mind and, given the variety of possible approaches, topics and systems, a competitive process could include them both. The result would be a sufficiently structured competition which would, on the other hand, still leave space for creativity in the choice of product designs.

(a) Overall solutions

There could be a financing of competition at the level of contract law as a whole. Groups would need to submit designs and time schedules; four to five years would be a reasonable framework, given that the first steps are already visible, in the form of the different sets of principles and, of course, the ACFR, but also the horizontal directive (see note 1). This time period would also be needed if a social sciences or social values based approach were to have a chance to develop a (probably fundamentally divergent) set of rules. Indeed, at least one independent project each should be sponsored with a clear social sciences orientation, with strong emphasis on dogmatic thinking, and with a particular focus on principles and values and, if possible, one which seeks to adopt an integrative approach from the outset. For all approaches, two or more projects would be better still.

One would probably have to delineate the outer contours for such projects beforehand: Competition needs some order. It might therefore be helpful to gather the arguments in favour of a European Contract Code and those which speak for a broader design. Once again, this decision would have to be based on a competitive process. Deciding this question on the basis of one (comparative law) expert opinion given by one interested group (or one initiator of a group) is of course not acceptable. Furthermore, a list of questions – the basis for traditional consultations – would not seem to provide an ideal basis: competition is also about finding the best questions to which one wants answers. Despite this, the EC Commission might of course indicate some questions which it finds particularly intriguing.

(b)   Core questions

An alternative or additional approach to sponsorship would be to have groups decide which topics are of core importance. This might lead them to find out that formation of contract and the information regime, or a particular type of contract or a range of contracts such as long-term contracts, is worth investigating more thoroughly. Another approach would be to choose a phenomenon of contractual business organisation which is seen as particularly important for a modern Code, or for its style.

Competition about these questions will of course contribute to triggering many further interesting questions – perhaps of even greater interest than a chapter such as this might imagine. It could also be that the author of this chapter does not or did not want to disclose what, in his perspective, would be the most interesting question or set of questions to approach. As we all know, though designers of monopolies are keen to forget it, competition is simply the most powerful discovery device.[22] The beautiful aspect of a competition of ideas is that, before they are adopted by legislators, they cannot even have the negative external effects that normal competition can sometimes produce.

The path forward, in my view, should be to sponsor a combination of projects on overall solutions and on core questions, as the route with the best chances of delivering the best results. A valuable by-product would be an enormous increase in cross-border scientific networking (not just in one network or network of networks). In addition, such competition would give an enormous boost to the creation of a European private law academia. Indeed, because it would unite the core area of private law in which most private law scholars have expertise, it could give birth to an European private law academia proper.

---

[22]   See, in this respect, the Nobel prize-winning and today universally-accepted concept of v. Hayek, as stated, for instance in F. v. Hayek, 'Competition as a discovery procedure', in id., *New Studies in Philosophy, Politics, Economics and the History of Ideas* (Chicago: Chicago University Press, 1978), p. 179.

3.   Framework for Competition

One of the most challenging issues is that of the framework for the competition of ideas sketched so far.

In itself the question of *funding,* more specifically, its allocation, is a problem. In this respect, the ACFR could serve as a model, with overall proposals selected receiving a similar amount, irrespective of internal design: after all, the cost factor in relation to how aims are reached and products developed is a question to be left to the enterprise which makes the proposal. What, however, about the projects on core questions? What should be the response if there are many proposals for overall designs?

Yet this would only be the initial phase. Even more difficult might be the moment when sponsored projects produce results. What about the *choice among the proposals made*? Ideally, the market of observers would make an explicit enough choice. A body observing the market, such as the EC Commission or perhaps a European Law Institute, would probably need to check whether the expressions of opinion were largely undistorted, to avoid any cartels of 'opinion'. Ultimately, when trends are visible within the legal community and when the possibility of combinations has been tested, there must also be democratic legitimacy. This could take different forms. It could lead to the adoption of one proposal; it could just as well lead to appointing a commission taken from amongst groups advancing two or three proposals. Though a final commission, for the sake of coherence, would of course need to be small, it could nonetheless comprise members of a variety of profiles. Certainly, findings from the core questions would then need to be integrated into the most promising overall structure. Undoubtedly, the process as a whole would be a challenging one – and, as already has been stated, this type of competitive process would bring together European academia in a way as yet unparalleled.

IV.   A SHORT CONCLUSION

The issues outlined in the previous few lines could be thought to lead to the conclusion: 'Voi chi entrate lasciate ogni speranza' ('You who enter here, lose all hope'). Although in Italian, I would not label this an Italian solution, but rather a medieval one. A modern solution would be more optimistic: had Adam Smith given in to desperation, our world would be a very different place. However, despite all its problems, many of which he himself identified, he described competition as the source of the 'Wealth of Nations'. I am likewise convinced that competition presents us with the route to a better European Code.

4. The public/private divide in European law*

Norbert Reich

I. CAN WE TALK OF A 'EUROPEAN PRIVATE LAW'?

When discussing a 'divide' between 'public and private' in European law, we seem to suggest that there exists something like the classical division between 'public' and 'private law', the first referring to the relationship between citizens and the state, the second to those between (autonomous?) citizens. *'Publicum ius quod at statum rei Romanae spectat, privatum quod at singularum utilatem'*, as the Roman jurist Ulpian said.[1] This model is based on a separation between the state area where political prerogatives prevail, and the private sphere where autonomous persons interact according to their own preferences, a separation which permeates, at least in the continental tradition, the division of legal disciplines and court competences.

This classical model does not fit well with European, or more specifically EEC/EC/EU law. We may not know what the EEC/EC/EU 'is'– it may be a '*Staatenverbund*', in the terminology of the German Bundesverfassungsgericht,[2] a Union of States and Peoples[3] 'united in diversity', as the failed draft Constitution of 2004 formulated it, an institution *sui generis*, including certain

---

* My thanks go to Prof. Hans-W. Micklitz, EUI Florence, and to Prof. James Gordley, Tulane University Law School, LA, USA for critical comments on an earlier draft. Responsibility remains as usual with the author. An earlier draft was presented at the 14th General Meeting of the Common Core Group, Turin, 11 July 2008.
[1] Ulp. Dig. 1, 1, 1, 2, cited by Larenz and Wolf, *Allgemeiner Teil des Bürgerlichen Rechts*, 8.A., 1997, para 1 n. 20.
[2] BVerfGE 89, 155 at 188; English translation [1994] 1 CMLR 57. For a recent analysis see J.B. Cruz, 'The Legacy of the Maastricht-Urteil and the Pluralist Movement', [2008] ELJ 389. The most recent judgment of the German Constitutional Court of 30 June 2009 re Lisbon Treaty defines the European Union as 'an association of sovereign national states (Staatenverbund)', headnote 1 in the translation by the BVerfG.
[3] See W. v. Gerven, *The European Union – A Polity of States and Peoples* (2005).

'federal elements'[4] – but we do know that it is not a state. We also know it has legal personality (which will be extended by Article 47 of the Consolidated Version of the Treaty on EU to the Union once the Lisbon Treaty is ratified); that it is governed by a 'basic constitutional charter', as the ECJ has called it,[5] even though it does not have a 'Constitution'; that EEC/EC law takes supremacy and enjoys direct effect under certain circumstances (to which I return later); that this law is creeping into ever more areas of everyday life of citizens. Yet none of this actually explains whether talk of a 'public/private divide' makes any sense.

I would prefer to approach the topic from a more historical perspective, followed up by a functional analysis. Initially, EEC law was public international law in the classical sense, only later assuming a *sui generis* character, due to the intervention of the ECJ. It addressed *vertical relations* between state and citizens. Its impact was (leaving aside specific market regulations in agriculture and fishery matters) to increase citizens' mobility via fundamental freedoms and the anti-discrimination rules, and to 'free them' from restrictions imposed by states. Article 10 EC is the fundamental norm describing this new approach to public law: in their duty of loyal cooperation, Member States must allow the operation of these freedoms and protect citizens against discriminations based on nationality in their economic activities and (which came later) also in their civilian activities, for instance as students, retired persons, tourists. But this liberalising effect does not change the vertical structure of E(E)C law; it simply superimposes another layer of public law in the interest of free movement of citizens. This traditional approach might be called, with Christian Joerges,[6] a conflict of law-method: in regulating and modifying state jurisdiction in free movement matters, it transforms traditional public law from a country-of-activity to a country-of-origin principle. The *Cassis de Dijon* case,[7] well known to every EC lawyer, is the classical paradigm of this new approach and has been used ever since in ECJ decisions and secondary acts as the basis of the *mutual recognition* principle. Its importance for private law is still subject to controversy (a matter which will not be taken up here).

---

4 See J.H.H. Weiler, *The Constitution of Europe* (1999), 185–187 particularly with regard to international relations where he also talks of 'mixity'!

5 Case 294/83 *Les Verts v. European Parliament* [1986] ECR 1339 para 1365; *Opinion 1/91 on the European Economic Area* [1991] ECR I–6079.

6 Joerges and Rödl, 'Von der Entformalisierung europäischer Poltik und dem Formalismus europäischer Rechtsprechung im Umgang mit dem "sozialen Defizit" des Integrationsprojekts', ZERP (Bremen) DP 2/2008,7-11: 'Kollisionsrecht als Form europäischer Verfassung'.

7 Case 120/78 *Rewe Zentral v. Bundesmonopolverwaltung* [1979] ECR 649.

Private law does not exist in this context, as the very wording of Article 10 EC shows: only Member States (or, more recently, any public authority operating in a Member State) have this duty of cooperation and loyalty, not private parties. There is no obligation on private parties to support citizen mobility, only (via the theory of vertical direct effect of EC law) a right to be protected from unreasonable Member State restrictions on free movement or rules of discriminatory character, eventually paralleled by a secondary right of compensation under the *Francovich* doctrine.[8]

The only exception to this 'public law approach of European law' has been the competition rules, and Article 81(2) EC clearly shows their impact on contract law, implicitly guaranteeing freedom of contract as long as it does not contradict the competition rules.[9] Interestingly enough, the implementation of the competition rules was and still is built on public law enforcement, by the EC Commission, as its most powerful and prominent 'policeman' and, in parallel, as a recent development by national authorities under Regulation (EC) 1/2003.[10] Private enforcement was not regulated, or even mentioned, and it took the case law of the ECJ in matters like *SABAM*,[11] *Courage*[12] and *Manfredi*[13] to 'discover' private law remedies, which must be shaped by national law under the broad (and still rather unspecific) principles of 'effectiveness' and 'equivalence'[14] in the framework of their 'procedural autonomy'.[15] Of course, it is well known that an intense debate is under way on how, and in what direction, to intensify 'private enforcement' of the competition rules,[16] but this topic will not be taken up further here.

With regard to their private law side, the free movement and non-discrimination rules originally written into the EEC Treaty remained *leges imperfectae*. Citizens had to rely on national court or Commission procedures to enforce their rights; they could force neither their courts to make a reference

---

8   Cases C-6–9/90 *Francovich et al v. Republic of Italy* [1991] ECR I-5357.
9   Reich, *Understanding EU Law* (2nd edn, 2005), 274–277.
10   [2003] OL L1.
11   Case 127/73 *BRT v. Sabam* [1974] ECR 313.
12   Case C-453/99 *Courage v. Berhard Crehan* [2001] ECR I-6297.
13   Cases C-295–298/04 *Vicenzo Manfred et al v. Lloyd Adriatico Ass.* [2006] ECR I-6619.
14   Micklitz, Reich and Rott, *Understanding European Consumer Law* (2008), at paras 8.3–8.11.
15   Reich, 'Procedural autonomy of Member States vs. effective legal protection in recent Court practice – On the way to procedural plurality', Liber amicorum, Mikelenas, 2008, 271.
16   See Commission Green Paper of 19 December 2005 COM(2005)672; White paper of 8 April 2008 COM(2008)165; for an overview see Basedow (ed.), *Private Enforcement of EC Competition Law* (2007); a critique has been voiced by Editorial comments, 'A little more action please', *CMLRev* (2008), 609.

to the ECJ nor the Commission to take action in their behalf. *Francovich* liability as developed by the Court stepped into this gap, but did not change the basically vertical structure of EC law, because it is directed against Member States for actions of any public authority breaching EC law, not private parties. Elsewhere I have suggested extending these principles also to breaches by private parties beyond the competition rules.[17]

There has been no movement, so far, in this direction – with one important exception, worth mentioning here. In the famous *Defrenne II*[18] litigation it was for the first time declared that the non-discrimination rule of the then Article 119 EEC, now somewhat modified in Article 141 EC, is directly applicable in 'horizontal' relations. Perhaps unsurprisingly, the first step in positioning private relations autonomously in European law was taken in the field of labour and more generally employment law, in a development which has continued in important and controversial such *Bosman*,[19] *Angonese*,[20] *Viking*,[21] *Mangold*[22] and *Maruko*,[23] discussed further below. It may be useful to recall the central argument in *Defrenne II* with a view to developing here the theory of 'horizontal direct effect':

> the fact that certain provisions of the Treaty are formally addressed to the Member States does not prevent rights from being conferred at the same time on any individual who has an interest in the performance of the duties thus laid down. The very wording of Art. 119 shows that it imposes on States a duty to bring about a specific result to be mandatorily achieved within a fixed period. The effectiveness of this provision cannot be affected by the fact that the duty imposed by the Treaty has not been discharged by certain Member States and that the joint institutions have not reacted sufficiently energetically against this failure to act. To accept the contrary view would be to risk raising the violation of the right to the status of a principle of interpretation, a position the adoption of which would not be consistent with the task assigned to the Court by Art. 164 [now Art. 220, NR] ... [paragraphs 31–34].

A preliminary analysis of this contradictory state of EU law had been given by Ernst Steindorff in a seminal book, entitled *Community Law and Private*

---

[17] 'Horizontal liability in EC Law – "Hybridisation" of remedies for compensation in case of breaches of EC rights', *CMLRev* (2007), 705.

[18] Case 43/75 *G. Defrenne v. SABENA* [1976] ECR 455.

[19] Case C-415/93 *ASBL v. Bosman* [1995] ECR I-4921, paras 83–85.

[20] Case C-281/98 *R. Angonese v. Casa di Risparmio de Bolzano* [2000] ECR I-4139, paras 31–36.

[21] Case C-438/05 *International Transport Workers Federation (ITW) and Finnish Seamans Union (FSU) v. Viking Line* [2007] ECR I-10779.

[22] Case C-144/04 *Werner Mangold v. Rüdiger Helm* [2005] ECR I-9981.

[23] Case C-267/06 *Tadao Maruko v. Versorgungsanstalt der deutschen Bühnen* [2008] ECR I-1757.

Law.[24] The very limited impact of EEC/EC law on private law should not cause it to be forgotten that secondary legislation, in particular in labour, consumer, commercial agent, company and intellectual property law started to 'infect' national private law, lately transforming into more ambitious projects like the '*Acquis principles*' and the 'Draft Common frame of reference' (infra III 4). It suffices to refer to a paradox in EC law-making with regard to 'horizontal relations': even though ever more EC law is penetrating into this seemingly reserved area of Member State law under an 'internal market' or some other label (always of course subject to intense debates on competence which will not interest us here), the formal structure of the public/private divide has not changed. Directives, as we all know, do not have 'horizontal direct effect'; they cannot as such impose obligations on private individuals and thereby autonomously create rights of private persons; they may only be a basis of 'consistent', that is EC law conforming to interpretation within the limits of the *contra legem* principle.[25] This essentially 'vertical approach' of EC law to private law relations remains untouched, even if the 'vertical' avenue is somewhat strained in the case law of the ECJ, whereby relations governed in Member States by private law (e.g. employment relations with state participation) are 'relabelled' by the ECJ as 'vertical relations' where the theory of direct effect becomes applicable.[26]

What about the non-discrimination principle, one of the pillars of the citizenship concept, which has been extended to non-citizens who suffer from ethnic, sexual, age or some other sort of discrimination? Again labour law takes the lead, but scholars warn us not to extend the principle of non-discrimination too far into the area of private law, where autonomy should be the governing principle, thereby generously allowing for 'discrimination' or rather 'differentiated treatment' based on preferences, choices, and competition.[27]

Is it time to reconsider the traditional public/private law divide in European law? My answer will be a mixed one: yes and no! My concern will be directed at two elements of this divide:

- First, the formal structure of EC law, which more and more imposes itself on relations governed by private law (contract, tort, company law) by an ever extending theory of 'horizontal direct effect'.

---

[24]   Steindorff, *EG-Vertrag und Privatrecht* (1996) at 48–50 (possibility of – mandatory – private law norms to restrict free movement).
[25]   Most recently Case C-212/04 *K. Adeneler v. ELOG* [2006] ECR I-6057 para 110.
[26]   Craig and de Burca, *EU Law: Text, Cases and Materials* (4th edn, 2007), 282–287 referring to a 'broad concept of the state' at 284.
[27]   J. Basedow, 'Grundsatz der Nichtdiskriminierung', *Zeitschrift für Europäisches Privatrecht* (ZEuP) 2008, 230.

- Second, by an extensive non-discrimination principle which started in labour law and is now influencing (some authors would say 'invading') private law relations, where usually 'freedom of contract and association' are the leading paradigms.

II. RECONSIDERING THE DOCTRINE OF 'DIRECT EFFECT'

1. 'Horizontal Direct Effect' of Primary Law

The key to defining an autonomous role for private law within the EC legal context is the theory of *direct effect*. It is usually divided into 'vertical' and 'horizontal direct effect', both requiring at minimum a norm of EC law that is unconditional and sufficiently precise in conferring rights and imposing obligations. While the theory of 'vertical direct effect' marks the beginning of an autonomous EC legal order that had to get rid of its international public law origins, an extension to horizontal relations may help in identifying an adequate space for private law therein. Here I will examine some precedents which show the direction travelled albeit that they do not yet guarantee a coherent approach.

The traditional stand, as I mentioned before, regards the fundamental freedoms as directed against Member States. If they are violated by private entities, either the competition rules apply or the state has a duty to protect these freedoms against illegal private intervention, as the Court ruled in *Commission v. France*.[28]

It is not however necessary to take such a narrow interpretation, as is clear from the very wording and system of the Treaty.[29] The EC Treaty already in its earlier version takes a somewhat broader view, in aiming at the abolition of restrictions on freedom of movement 'between Member States', whatever their origin, per Article 3 (a), (c). The Court, in a series of cases, therefore extended the applicability of Articles 39, 43 and 49 EC also to privately imposed restrictions. This case law started with *Walrave*[30] in 1974, with respect to restrictions on free movement imposed by the by-laws of sporting

---

[28]   Case C-265/95 [1997] ECR I–6959; for an extension as general principle see Riesenhuber, *Europäisches Vertragsrecht* (2003) at 41–46; 'Schutzpflichten' instead of 'Drittwirkung'!

[29]   Peter-Christian Müller-Graff and Rudolf Streinz, 'Art. 49', in *EUV/EGV Kommentar*, 2003, margins 65–69.

[30]   Case 36/74, *Walrave v. Union Cycliste internationale* [1974] ECR 1405 paras 15–19.

associations. This decision takes a functional rather than formal approach to interpreting the fundamental freedoms, maintained in the well-known *Bosman* case.[31] This was concerned with free movement of workers, even though the Court also referred to services. Contrary to AG Lenz's suggestion, the Court did not discuss the applicability of the competition rules.[32] This precedent was confirmed and broadened in *Angonese*.[33] In the later *Wouters* case,[34] the Court summarised and confirmed its practice with regard to collective regulation by private entities:

> the abolition, as between Member States, of obstacles to freedom of movement for persons would be compromised if the abolition of State barriers could be neutralised by obstacles resulting from the exercise of their legal autonomy by associations or organisations not governed by public law.

While the earlier cases concerned relations determined by labour law, the *Wouters* case arose with regard to the autonomy of private associations to regulate the economic behaviour of their members which also fell under the competition rules. Even though, given the case before it, it must be regarded as an *obiter dictum*, the Court seemed to shape a general principle. It allowed exemption of private law relations from the free movement rules only insofar as they really trace back to the exercise of private autonomy. Where this effective individual autonomy in the sense of free choice is absent, the EC freedoms can be invoked, whether the origin of the restriction is state or privately imposed. The approach of the Court is a functional, not an institutional, one which can be extended to other areas where autonomy is distorted or simply absent. The fundamental freedoms thereby receive a constitutional dimension allowing their 'intrusion' into private law relations. This may remind the reader of the judgment of the German Constitutional Court of 19 October 1993[35] concerning the constitutionality of suretyships (*Bürgschaften*) imposed by banks on dependent family members, in which it was held that there is freedom of contract only where both parties avail of similar bargaining power, so that both parties act in a self-determined manner: freedom of contract, or party autonomy, is therefore absent where one party abuses the structural weakness of the other party.[36]

---

31   Above note 19.
32   See Reich, above note 17, at 707.
33   Above note 20.
34   Case C-309/99 *J. C. J. Wouters et al/Algemene Raad von de Nederlandse Ordre van Advocaaten* [2002] ECR, I-1577 para 120.
35   BVerfG 89, 214 = NJW 1994, 96; confirmed by later decisions of 5 August 1994, NJW 1994, 2749; 6 December 2005, WM 2006, 23.
36   For a detailed comment on this case law see P. Rott, 'German law on Family Suretyships: An Overrated System', in A. Colombi Ciacchi (ed.), *Protection of Non-Professional Sureties in Europe: Formal and Substantive Disparity* (2007), at 54–55.

That this 'intrusion' is most relevant in labour relations became evident in the later ECJ judgments concerning collective action by trade unions against the use of the fundamental freedoms by business. The *Viking*[37] and *Laval*[38] cases must be cited as the outstanding and controversial examples of this approach. *Viking* concerned a collective action in the first instance of the Finnish Seafarers Union, later combined with a supportive action taken by the International Federation of Transport Workers, a head association of trade unions in the shipping sector, which concerned the attempt of the Finnish Viking line, running its ferry *Rosella* between Helsinki and Tallinn at a loss, to outflag its operations from Finland to Estonia, in order to lower labour costs by attempting to pay Estonian wages to the crew. The London High Court, which had jurisdiction in the case, granted an injunction against these collective actions on the ground that they restricted the freedom of establishment of Viking. The English Court of Appeal however quashed this order and referred the case to the ECJ, which handed down its controversial judgment on 11 December 2007. In *Laval*, a Latvian construction company had won a contract in Sweden. When it started its operations with posted workers from Latvia, the Swedish construction worker's union *Bygnadds* insisted Laval pay wages according to Swedish law and practice, a demand eventually refused by Laval after it concluded a collective bargaining agreement with the Latvian construction workers' union. Following this refusal the building site was boycotted by *Bygnadds*, and Laval had to give up work and withdraw its workforce. The case, brought to the ECJ upon the reference of the Swedish Labour Court, mostly concerned the interpretation of the Posted Workers Directive 96/71/EEC, but also the 'horizontal applicability' of Article 49 EC on the freedom to provide services in favour of Laval and against the Swedish labour unions.

According to these judgments, the fundamental freedoms of Article 43 EC (*Viking*, paragraph 33) and Article 49 EC (*Laval* paragraph 98, less clearly) apply also in horizontal relations to 'rules of any other nature aimed at regulating in a collective manner gainful employment, self-employment and the provision of services'. In *Viking* (paragraph 34) this is justified by the fact that in some Member States working conditions are governed by law, in others by collective agreements; an exemption of the latter from the applicability the fundamental freedoms would 'risk inequality in its application'. In *Laval* (paragraph 98) a more functional argument, similar to that in *Wouters*, is used, namely that the abolition of 'obstacles to the freedom to provide services would be compromised if the abolition of State barriers could be neutralised

---

[37] Above note 21.
[38] Case C-341/05 *Laval & partneri v. Bygnadds* [2007] ECR I-11767.

by obstacles resulting from the exercise of their legal autonomy by associations and organisations not governed by public law'. Articles 43 (*Viking* paragraph 58) and 49 EC (*Laval* paragraph 97) therefore take direct effect and
confer rights on individuals whose freedoms are violated by trade union
collective action, as in our cases where the Finnish ship owner Viking Line
was prevented from re-flagging the vessel *Rosella*, and the Latvian construction company Laval suffered loss due to a boycott by the Swedish construction workers' union when posting its workers in Sweden. However (though
this cannot be discussed fully here) the argument of the Court in both cases
remains highly controversial because it limits the fundamental rights of labour
unions to take collective action, as guaranteed (in the limits of EC law, see
Viking paragraph 44, *Laval* paragraph 91!) in Article 28 of the Charter of
Fundamental Rights.

The judgments say nothing as regards the question whether similar principles
apply also to the free movement of goods rules under Articles 28/29 EC where,
according to the prevailing view among legal scholars, only the competition
rules are applicable to restrictions induced by associations under private law. Yet
it must be remembered that the monograph by Steindorff[39] already insisted that
the ECJ case law on 'exhaustion of intellectual property rights' once they have
been put on the internal market with the consent of the rightholder applies the
fundamental freedoms to relations governed by private law and forces them to
conform to the imperatives of free movement. There is no exemption of 'horizontal relations' between seemingly autonomous subjects of private law, namely
the rightholder on the one hand and the parallel importer on the other, the latter
being charged with violating the trade mark or patent of the first, but justified by
making use of the free movement provisions under Article 30, second sentence
with direct applicability in his favour. Even if the 'injection' of EC law takes the
formal route of a court order which could be subsumed under the loyalty obligation of Article 10 EC, obviously this does not leave private law relations unim-
paired by the requirements of their EC conformity.

In the opinion of this author, this process of extending 'horizontal direct
effect' of primary EC law is in principle open-ended: it is not limited to labour
law, to by-laws of private associations, or to the exercise of intellectual property rights. Commercial and consumer law are not devoid of 'collectively
imposed restrictions on free movement'. So long as the application of the
competition rules as *lex specialis* allows an adequate handling of these restrictions, we need not have recourse to the free movement rules, as we have
known since the seminal *Grundig* case.[40] But when non-economic entities

---

[39]   Above note 24 at 125, 143, 290, 299.
[40]   Cases 56 and 58/64 [1966] 299.

become subject to territorial restrictions or other indirect impediments on free movement (e.g. prohibitions on private reselling of products in standard form contracts or package leaflets, restrictions of use, unjustified price discriminations, national service clauses, economic disadvantages when leaving the citizen's country of origin imposed on them by standard terms of banks[41] and similar devices), the free movement rules may be invoked by consumers and other non-economic agents which are only inadequately protected by the competition rules. This principle might also be used to impose a special tort liability of undertakings segregating markets to the detriment of consumers, whether or not anti-competitive behaviour can be shown to exist.[42] Details of these principles however remain to be worked out and tested in court proceedings.

2. Limits to Horizontal Direct Effect of Regulations

EC regulations take direct effect, as can be seen from Article 249(2) EC itself. Due to a restrictive reading of the subsidiarity principle of Article 5(2) EC and the attached Protocol to the Amsterdam Treaty, Community institutions take the view that directives should be preferred to regulations, but only 'other things being equal' according to paragraph (6). I have criticised this view with regard to consumer law based on Article 153 EC. In my opinion, it would be perfectly compatible with rules on EC competence to 'codify' and consolidate the existing '*consumer acquis*' in a directly applicable regulation.[43]

In the area of transport services, based on Article 80 EC and not the internal market competence of Article 95, the Community has used its specific competence to create a set of regulations concerning air and rail passenger rights;[44]

---

41   See my discussion of so-called penalty clauses (*Vorfälligkeitsentschädigung*) in mortgage credits in the case of early repayment because of mobility requirements: Reich, 'Die vorzeitige Beendigung von Finanzierungen aus der Sicht des Kreditnehmers, insbesondere der Verbraucher', *Bankrechtstag* (1996), 43, 57.

42   See Micklitz, Reich and Rott, *Understanding*, supra note 14 at para 8.14.

43   Reich, 'A European Contract Law, or a European Contract Law Regulation for Consumers?', *Journal of Consumer Policy* (JCP) (2005), 383 at 398.

44   Regulation (EC) No 261/2004 of the European Parliament and of the Council of 11 February 2004 establishing common rules on compensation and assistance to passengers in the event of denied boarding and of cancellation or long delay of flights, and repealing Regulation (EEC) No 295/91, [2004] OJ L46/1. Concerning EU competence see Case C-344/04 *IATA and ELFAA v. Department for Transport* [2006] ECR I-403; a critical overview has been given by E. and M. Varney, 'Grounded? Air Passenger Rights in the EU', in Twigg-Flesner et al., *The Yearbook of Consumer Law 2008* (2007), 171. A similar Regulation (EC) 1371/2007 of 23 October 2007, [2007] OJ L315/14, concerns rail passengers' rights.

other areas will be subject to similar rules.[45] A recent case before the ECJ[46] concerned the defence of 'extraordinary circumstances' in case of technical problems in an aircraft which leads to the cancellation of a flight. The Court wrote, thus coming close to the traditional *force majeure* defence:

> Consequently, technical problems which come to light during maintenance of aircraft or on account of failure to carry out such maintenance cannot constitute, in themselves, 'extraordinary circumstances' . . . However, it cannot be ruled out that technical problems are covered by those exceptional circumstances to the extent that they stem from events which are not inherent in the normal exercise of the activity of the air carrier concerned and are beyond its actual control. That would be the case, for example, in the situation where it was revealed by the manufacturer of the aircraft comprising the fleet of the air carrier concerned, or by a competent authority, that those aircraft, although already in service, are affected by a hidden manufacturing defect which impinges on flight safety. The same would hold for damage to aircraft caused by acts of sabotage or terrorism [paragraphs 25–26].

Another area of limited private law effects of regulations is concerned with competition law. As will be recalled, under special authority the Commission enacted so-called 'exemption regulations' to avoid the negative effects of Article 81(2) for certain branches and to increase the competitiveness of European industry, in particular the car industry. These regulations, starting with Regulation (EC) 123/85,[47] continued with Regulation (EC) 1475/95[48] and concluded most recently with Regulation (EC) 1400/2002,[49] based on a 'more economic approach'. These regulations provide for detailed rules on contracting between the producer or importer of cars, and its distributors. In its early *Magne* case,[50] the Court refused any direct effect of the regulation on the contractual relationship between producers and dealers, because it only concerned the conditions of exemption. I have raised doubts with regard to this restrictive reading, in particular with regard to third party relations where a violation of one of the exemption conditions of the regulation may give rise to

---

[45]   See the detailed analysis of Karsten, 'European Passenger Law for Sea and Inland Waterway Transport', in Twigg-Flesner et al., *The Yearbook of Consumer Law 2008* (2007), at 201; ibid., 'Passenger, Consumers, and Travellers: The Rise of Passenger Rights in EC Transport Law and its Repercussion for Community Consumer Law and Policy', JCP (2007), 117.

[46]   C-549/07 *Friedrike Wallentin-Hermann v. Alitalia* [2008] ECR I-(22.12.2008).

[47]   [1985] OJ L15/16.

[48]   [1995] OJ L145/25.

[49]   [2002] OJ L203/30.

[50]   Case 10/86 *VAG Magne* [1986] ECR 4071 paras 12 and 16; confirmed by Case C-125/05 *VW-Audi Forhandlersforeningen v. Skandinavisk Motor Co A/S* [2006] ECR I-7637 para 56.

an action in compensation.[51] The recent *Skandinavisk* litigation concerned the question whether the substitution of Regulation (EC) 1475/95 by Regulation 1400/2002 was in itself sufficient grounds for a short termination period of one year, on the basis of the need to reorganise the distribution system in the sense of a *rebus sic stantibus* proviso, or whether the normal cancellation period of two years should apply. The Court answered this question by presenting detailed rules on how to interpret the interplay between the two regulations on the contractual relations which have to be determined either by a court of law or by an arbitrator. It said:

> in order for it to be 'necessary to reorganise the whole or a substantial part of the network' there must be a significant change, both substantively and geographically, to the distribution structures of the supplier concerned, which must be convincingly justified on grounds of economic effectiveness based on objective circumstances internal or external to the supplier's undertaking which, failing a swift reorganisation of the distribution network, would be liable, having regard to the competitive environment in which the supplier carries on business, to prejudice the effectiveness of the existing structures of the network. Any adverse economic consequences which would be liable to affect a supplier in the event that it were to terminate the distribution agreement with a two years' notice period are relevant in that regard.

It also commented on the burden of proof and on the formalities of the cancellation notice. This is of course a relatively specific area of contract and tort law, but it sustains my main argument that EC law is imposing itself in certain areas on national private law which must be directly applied by courts and arbitrators.[52]

3. Horizontal Direct Effect of Directives?

The conceptual approach taken by the ECJ in denying 'horizontal direct effect of directives' is well known and has been reaffirmed in several decisions since the *Dori* case:[53] if the Community wants to impose obligations on private parties, it must use the instrument of a regulation. But usually private law

---

[51] Reich, above note 17 at 721.

[52] See Case C-126/97 *ECO Swiss v. Benetton* [1999] ECR I-3055 paras 36–37, referring to the '*ordre public* quality' of the EC competition rules, which must be applied *ex officio* in recognition proceedings of an arbitration award similar to national law under the principle of equivalence.

[53] Cases C-91/92 [1994] ECR I-3325 paras 20–25; C-168/95 *Arcaro* [1996] ECR I-4705 paras 40, 42; C-397/01 *Pfeiffer* [2004] ECR I-8835 para 108; see the discussion by Arnull, *The European Union and its Court of Justice* (2nd edn, 2006), at 244–246. Similar principles apply to Commission decisions: see Case C-80/06 *Carp v. Econrad* [2007] ECR I-4473.

provisions take the shape of directives which are addressed to Member States, not to individuals. Member State legislation, under its specific constitutional provisions but respecting its obligations under Article 10/249 (3) EC, must transform these directives into 'obligation creating' instruments (e.g. for employers, suppliers of goods and services) paralleled for the 'other side' by subjective individual rights of employees, consumers or users.

Indeed, if the Community legislator wants to 'enact obligations for individuals with immediate effect', to use the *Dori* formula (paragraph 24), or avoid 'that a directive cannot of itself impose obligations on an individual and cannot therefore be relied upon as such against an individual' in the wording of *Pfeiffer* (paragraph 108), it must use an adequate instrument, and directives are not shaped for this purpose, even though they contain ever more detailed and specific provisions and leave Member States little room for autonomous adaptation. Indeed, Member States to some extent are degraded to notaries, simply rubber-stamping what has been decided in Brussels (a practice supported by the Court concerning the implementation duties of Member States under Article 10/249(3) EC). Nevertheless, in the doctrine of the Court obligations among private law subjects are either created autonomously by the parties themselves (this is the area of contract and company law) or by legislative or regulatory instruments under national, in certain exceptional cases also international, law (the area of tort law and civil liability in general[54]). This fundamental premise of private law has not been challenged by EU law even though it increasingly amounts to a fiction.

The problem lies in cases where Member States have not correctly fulfilled their obligations under a directive, or where they have not made any attempt to fulfil them at all – cases which have kept the Court busy in recent years! The debate therefore concerns how to remedy 'legislative failure', in some cases also 'administrative' or even 'judicial failure' in not correctly implementing or applying EC directives with spill-over effects on private law relations. The orthodox approach would simply be to refer to Article 10 EC: the Member State (including courts of law as 'Community courts') must either avoid or make good the loss which this failure puts on the shoulders of the individual. This is basically the approach of the ECJ and its followers by the remedies of:

---

[54]   For a different typology see Teubner, 'Societal Constitutionalism: Alternatives to State Centred Constitutional Theory?' in Joerges, Sand and Teubner (eds.), *Transnational Governance and Constitutionalism* (Oxford, 2004) at 18; Calliess, *Grenzüberschreitende Verbraucherverträge* (2006) at 196, relying on 'autonomous self-regulation' as a source of law; Michaels and Jansen, 'Private Law Beyond the State? Europeanisation, Globalisation, and Privatisation', *American J Comp L* (2006), 843; Basedow, 'The State's Private Law and the Economy – Commercial law as an Amalgam of Public and Private Rule-Making', *Am J Comp L* (2008), 703.

- consistent interpretation in the limits of the *no contra legem* principle;
- state liability;
- 'verticalising' private law relations, particularly in employment matters, between individual employees and state (controlled) entities as employers.[55]

Borderline cases have arisen before the ECJ where directives can be applied as at least allowing a 'negative horizontal direct effect'. The leading ECJ case had been *Unilever*.[56] This concerned the effect on a remedy for breach of contract because the product (virgin olive oil) did not conform to the recently amended Italian standards which, however, had not been notified to the Commission, in violation of the relevant Directive 83/189/EEC. The Court wrote, in referring to its earlier *CIA* judgment concerning the consequences of a non-notification of a technical regulation or standard under Directive 83/189/EEC on relations between private parties:[57]

> Thus, it follows from the case-law of the Court that the inapplicability of a technical regulation which has not been notified in accordance . . . can be invoked in proceedings between individuals .... Whilst it is true, that a directive cannot of itself impose obligations on an individual and cannot therefore be relied on as such against an individual ... that case-law does not apply where non-compliance with Article 8 or Article 9 of Directive 83/189, which constitutes a substantial procedural defect, renders a technical regulation adopted in breach of either of those articles inapplicable. In such circumstances, and unlike the case of non-transposition of directives, Directive 83/189 does not in any way define the substantive scope of the legal rule on the basis of which the national court must decide the case before it. It creates neither rights nor obligations for individuals [paragraphs 49–51].

The distinction drawn by the Court between non-implementation of a directive which cannot as such impose obligations, and non-notification in breach of a directive which may be directly held against private partics in an action for breach of contract, is not convincing. In both cases, non-compliance of a Member State with obligations contained in a directive – whether substantive

---

55   For an overview see Prechal, *Directives in EC Law* (2nd edn, 2005), at 255–261; v. Danwitz, 'Rechtswirkungen von Richtlinien in der neuen Rechtsprechung des EuGH', [2007] *Juristenzeitung (JZ)*, 697; Dashwood, 'From an Duyn to Mangold via Marshall: Reducing Direct Effect to Absurdity?' 9 *Cambridge Yearbook of European Legal Studies* (2006–2007), 81.
56   Case C-443/98 [2000] ECR I-7535; for a discussion see Craig and de Burca, *EU Law, Text, Cases and Materials* (4th edn, 2007), at 296–300 and Dashwood at 94 talk of 'incidental horizontal effect'; what is the difference from 'negative horizontal direct effect'?
57   Case C-194/94 *CIA Security v. Signalson and Securitel* [1996] ECR I-2201.

or procedural – has effects on private relations, at least in a 'negative way', that is, a remedy which one party would otherwise have had under national law if the directive had been applied or implemented correctly is excluded. The directive does not create obligations as such; it modifies them.

The distinction was further developed by AG Saggio in his opinion of 16 December 1999 in the *Oceano* case.[58] With regard to the legal effects of the Unfair Contract Term Directive 93/13/EC on a jurisdiction clause to the detriment of the consumer, he distinguished the effects of 'substitution' and 'elimination':

> It should further be noted that a solution of this kind, which distinguishes between the substitution effect and the exclusionary effect of a directive which has not been transposed within the prescribed period, already appears in embryo in the Court's case-law concerning the consequences of a declaration of failure to fulfil an obligation under the Treaty [paragraph 38].

While it is indeed the case that a directive cannot 'substitute' national law to create obligations as such, it may very well eliminate provisions of national law which restrict rights arising out of a directive, thereby merely 'extending' or modifying already existing but not 'enacting' or 'imposing' obligations on the other party.[59]

Consider, for example, the *Quelle* litigation, involving the question whether the Consumer Sales Directive 99/44/EC of 25 May 1999[60] allowed national law to impose a duty on the consumer who has received, but also used, the non-conforming product which was only later replaced by a conforming one, to pay compensation to the seller (*Nutzungsentschädigung*). Implementing German law was indeed interpreted by the referring Bundesgerichtshof as imposing such a duty on the consumer and as not allowing an interpretation of German law to the contrary. The Court interpreted Directive 99/44 straightforwardly as excluding such an obligation, in reliance both on the *travaux préparatoires* and on the protective ambit of the Directive. It stated:

---

58   Cases C-240–244/98 *Océano Group Ed. v. Rocio Murciano Quintero et al* [2000] ECR I-4941.

59   See Reich, Understanding at 23; Prechal at 268; a critique has been voiced by Rörig, *Die Direktwirkung von Richtlinien* (2001) at 56–63, discussing the relevant case law of the ECJ; Dashwood, above note 55 at 103; v. Danwitz at 703 referring to the problem of filling the gaps left by eliminating a provision which is contrary to a directive. This is however not a specific problem of directives but generally one of the principles of precedence of EC law as enunciated in *Simmenthal* (below note 65).

60   [1999] OJ L171/12; denying '*Nutzungsentschädigung*': Case C-404/06 *Quelle v. BVVZ* [2008] ECR I-2685.

If a seller delivers goods which are not in conformity, it fails correctly to perform the obligation which it accepted in the contract of sale and must therefore bear the consequences of that faulty performance. By receiving new goods to replace the goods not in conformity, the consumer – who, for his part, paid the selling price and therefore correctly performed his contractual obligation – is not unjustly enriched. He merely receives, belatedly, goods in conformity with the specifications of the contract, which he should have received at the outset [paragraph 41].

This seems a very convincing result. But how to implement it into national (German) law? The remedy of 'consistent interpretation' was first excluded by the referring court itself in the reference order (a view not upheld in the follow-up proceedings). The remedy of state liability does not help in representative proceedings, as was the case in *Quelle*, because the plaintiff, the German federation of consumer organisations, had not suffered any damage, except perhaps the costs of the proceedings themselves, which must anyway be settled by German law and allow a recovery of legal fees from the losing party, depending on the final decision of the Bundesgerichtshof (BGH). This creates a difficult situation for the plaintiff: she wins, but cannot use the judgment in favour of the person she is representing before a national court. Therefore the remedy of 'setting aside' conflicting national law would seem to be more appropriate.[61] This was indeed the result reached by the follow-up judgment of the BGH.[62]

It would seem that the ECJ took a similar (yet hardly further elaborated) direction in its controversial *Mangold* case,[63] involving *inter alia* the Framework Directive against discrimination 2000/78/EC.[64] The case concerned a German law which had allowed 'age discrimination' by lowering the age limit for fixed term contracts in employment relations within the time limit for implementation, weakening the situation of older employees. Formally, German law was not in violation of EC law because the time for implementation had not yet lapsed (Germany had been granted a delay of three years for implementation). But the Court took a more fundamental approach to the question: in its opinion, the prohibition of age discrimination is a general principle of EC law (a point discussed later in III 2) and therefore national legislators should not 'deteriorate' their law concerning employment relations

---

61   See W. van Gerven, 'On Rights, Remedies and Procedures', *CMLRev* (2000), 501 at 506–509.
62   BGH, judgment of 26.11.2008, Europäische Zeitschrift für Wirtschaftsrecht (EuZw 2009, 155), using the theory of 'directive conforming interpretation' for a 'Rechtsfortbildung' by way of a 'teleological reduction' of the scope of application of non-conforming national law.
63   Case C-144/04 *Werner Mangold v. Rüdiger Helm* [2005] ECR I-9981; critiqued in Reich, [2006] *Europäische Zeitschrift für Wirtschaftsrecht (EuZW)*, 21
64   [2000] OJ L303/16.

with older people, even during the implementation period of the directive. In the eyes of the Court, the German legislator violated its express and implicit obligations under Directive 2000/78, and the national court must set aside provisions of national law in opposition to this obligation. In what must be recognised as a somewhat confusing *dictum,* it held:

> Consequently, observance of the general principle of equal treatment, in particular in respect of age, cannot as such be conditional upon the expiry of the period allowed the Member States for the transposition of a directive intended to lay down a general framework for combating discrimination on the grounds of age, in particular so far as the organisation of appropriate legal remedies, the burden of proof, protection against victimisation, social dialogue, affirmative action and other specific measures to implement such a directive are concerned. In those circumstances it is the responsibility of the national court, hearing a dispute involving the principle of non-discrimination in respect of age, to provide, in a case within its jurisdiction, the legal protection which individuals derive from the rules of Community law and to ensure that those rules are fully effective, *setting aside any provision of national law which may conflict with that law.* [See, to that effect, Case 106/77 *Simmenthal* [1978] ECR 629, paragraph 21, and Case C-347/96 *Solred* [1998] ECR I-937, paragraph 30; emphasis added.]

These arguments are rather surprising given that Court referred to *Simmenthal* which concerned primary law.[65] The *Solred* case concerned a tax imposed in violation of an EC directive; it therefore concerns 'vertical' and not 'horizontal' direct effect. Are we to imply that the Court wanted to extend its case law, by allowing the 'negative horizontal effect' in employment relations (that is, relations governed by private law, as the parties of the case clearly demonstrate), thus restrictively interpreting or perhaps even overruling *Dori*? Or did it want to limit its *dictum* to a combined application of a 'general principle' (prohibition of age discrimination) and its expression in a specific directive (2000/78)? Later case law has not resolved the matter. According to the methodological critique and interpretation of AG Mazak in his opinion of 15 February 2007 in *Palacios de la Villa*[66] concerning the discriminatory effects of a strict age limit on employment:

> As I read the judgment, the Court did not therefore accept that Directive 2000/78 has horizontal direct effect; rather, it bypassed the lack of it by ascribing direct effect to the corresponding general principle of law [paragraph 132].

---

65   The case was concerned with the direct applicability of Art. 28 EC (then Art. 30 EEC) in conjunction with a specific EEC regulation in 'vertical' relations.
66   Case C-411/05, [2007] ECR I-8531; comment Reich [2007] *EuZW* 198.

I wonder, however, whether this reading of the *Mangold* case by AG Mazak is correct. In the paragraphs cited, the Court referred expressly to Directive 2000/78 when imposing the obligation on national courts to set aside national law contrary to the directive, similar to AG Saggio's earlier statement in the *Océano* case, though without citing him. In the follow-up to his opinion, AG Mazak expressly rejects the distinction between the 'substitution' and the 'exclusionary' direct effect of directives. The Court did not take up this discussion in its final judgment in the *Palacios* case, instead justifying the age limit on grounds of economic policy.[67] In *Adeneler*[68] the Court referred to *Mangold* only in the context of the obligations of the Member State during the implementation period, but not as regards the obligation to set aside a national provision in violation of a directive. Nevertheless, it broadened the principle of consistent interpretation with the following words:

> where a directive is transposed belatedly into a Member State's domestic law and the relevant provisions of the directive do not have direct effect, the national courts are bound to interpret domestic law so far as possible, once the period for transposition has expired, in the light of the wording and the purpose of the directive concerned with a view to achieving the results sought by the directive, favouring the interpretation of the national rules which is the *most consistent* [emphasis added] with that purpose in order thereby to achieve an outcome compatible with the provisions of the directive [paragraph 124].

From 'consistent' to '*most* consistent interpretation', taking us very close to what I would call 'negative horizontal direct effect'!

The *Maruko* case[69] concerned the discriminatory exclusion of a same-sex partner from a compulsory occupational pension scheme. The Court found non-justified discrimination. It did not discuss the question of 'horizontal direct effect', but seemed satisfied in characterising the contractual relationship between the employee, his surviving partner and the pension scheme managed by an autonomous public law institution (*Versorgungsanstalt*) as 'vertical'; this can be seen from the formulation 'that the combined provisions of Articles 1 and 2 of Directive 2000/78 preclude (such discriminatory) legislation' (paragraph 74). Mr. Maruko could therefore directly rely on the directive for a claim of his pension against the *Versorgungsanstalt*. Fortunately for him, the scheme was managed by a public law institution, rather than an insurance company or a group of companies. Should the result in the two cases really be different?

---

[67] Judgment of 16 Oct. 2007 at para 68, referring to the 'broad discretion of Member States in employment policy matters'; see comment by L. Waddington, *CMLRev* (2008), 895 at 904–905.

[68] Above note 25 at para 121.

[69] Above note 23.

In the more recent *Kükü̈devici* case,[70] which again concerned age discrimination under Dir. 2000/78, now fully implemented into German law, AG Bot convincingly discussed the ambiguities of the ECJ case law mentioned above and very openly favoured the theory of 'negative' or 'exclusionary horizontal direct effect' of a directive, first developed by AG Saggio. In a follow-up to *Mangold*, he insisted on the general Community law principle forbidding discrimination, including age discrimination.

This brief discussion shows that the case law of the ECJ excluding any direct horizontal effect of directives is unclear and contradictory. My preferred solution would be to allow exclusionary direct effect, eliminating any restrictions on claims by national law in violation of a directive,[71] particularly in consumer and employment relations which are characterised by an element of 'collective regulation', in a pension scheme, as in *Maruko,* or standard contracts as in *Quelle*, similar to the horizontal effect cases in primary law. Situations where the employer or supplier had a legitimate expectation of trusting the (incorrect) transposition of EC law by the directive should be resolved by limiting the retroactivity of the judgment, a remedy which the Court uses only hesitantly when two conditions have been fulfilled, namely, the risk of serious economic repercussions and the adaptation of practices not complying with Community law by reason of objective, significant uncertainty regarding the implications of EC provisions.[72] While in *Maruko* the ECJ denied the occurrence of such consequences, I would probably argue the contrary, because the additional element of 'serious economic repercussions' is difficult to prove and should not be required. In *Quelle*, however, there is no reason to deny the exclusionary effect of a rejection of the claim of the seller to compensation for the use of non-conforming goods by the consumer. There was ample critique in German legal literature against the legislative approach and its interpretation by the Bundesgerichtshof, so that *Quelle* could not reasonably rely on this (wrongful) interpretation of the directive.[73]

The opinion advanced here does not deny the need and importance of 'directive conforming' interpretation of national law where the remedy of 'negative direct horizontal effect' is not appropriate (which in any case should be the exception and not the rule). A good example is the recent *01051*

---

[70]　Case C-555/07 *Seda Kükü̈devici v. Sweden GmbH*, opinion of AG Bot of 7 July 2009, paras 80/85, not yet available in English.

[71]　See Reich, *Bürgerrechte in der EU* (1999), 105–108.

[72]　Case C-262/88 *Barber* [1990] ECR I–1889 para 41; Case C-292/04 *Meilicke* [2007] ECR I-1835, paras 36–37.

[73]　See the very thorough opinion of AG Trstenjak of 15 November 2007, citing extensively the controversies in German literature, para 38.

Telecom case.[74] It concerned a commercial transaction where the parties disagreed on the time from which the debtor had to pay interest for late payment. Should it be the date on which the debtor irrevocably instructed its bank to transfer the amount to the creditor, as the 'majority interpretation' (*herrschende Meinung*) of German law in implementing Directive 2000/35/EC on late payments[75] had argued? Or must it have 'reached' the creditor's bank, in line with the opinion of AG Poiares Maduro? Or is it the time when the amount was actually credited by the bank of the creditor that is relevant? The real question behind these perhaps apparently technical arguments was who has to take the risk of delays in the handling of a payment order within the banking system. The AG referred to the economic argument that the Directive aims to avoid 'procur[ing] the debtor with additional liquidity at the expense of the creditor' (paragraph 37). The Court, even going beyond the opinion of the AG, preferred the third, most 'creditor friendly' variant according to the wording of Article 3(1) lit c (ii), which reads:

> the creditor shall be entitled to interest for late payment to the extent that:
> (i)   he has fulfilled his contractual and legal obligations; and
> (ii)   he has not received the amount due on time, unless the debtor is not responsible for the delay.

In the opinion of the Court, 'received' in the different language versions means that,

> the decisive point for the assessment of whether, in a commercial transaction, payment by bank transfer may be regarded as having been made in time, thus excluding the possibility of the debt giving rise to the charging of interest for late payment within the meaning of that provision, is the date on which the sum due is credited to the account of the creditor [paragraph 28].

The Court, by contrast with the AG, did not discuss the question of 'direct effect' or 'consistent interpretation' in order to make national law conform to its interpretation of the Directive. Yet it should be kept in mind that the implementing German law concerned a default provision which the parties might modify, and its wording allowed different interpretations. Consequently the German court will have to accept an interpretation of the concept of *Leistung* in § 286 (3) of the BGB which conforms to the ruling of the ECJ, without being obliged to set aside any provision of national law to the contrary. This implies an important paradigm shift in the German law of obligations: from 'debtor' to 'creditor protection', which 'imposes' an 'additional' obligation on the debtor!

---

[74]   Case C-306/06 *01051 Telecom v. Deutsche Telecom* [2008] I-(3.4.2008).
[75]   [2000] OJ L200/35.

4.   'Horizontal Direct Effect' as a General Remedy under EC Law?

As a preliminary result of this discussion, it can be observed that the original 'public law' approach of the Community has gradually though not consistently been modified by a more functional concept of the public/private divide. The fundamental freedoms, including the free movement concept under citizenship premises can, under certain circumstances, have an effect on relations which are normally determined by private law, in particular in relation to organisations which enjoy power and regulatory competence somehow similar to that of states. Earlier examples included by-laws of associations relevant to the free movement of workers or self-employed persons, collective bargaining instruments enforced by collective action of trade unions, and standard form contracts; there may be a certain overlap with competition law. The somewhat problematic extension of this liberal *credo* of EC law, concerning actions of solidarity, in particular in labour disputes, which have suddenly become 'restrictions' of free movement, as can be seen in the recent *Viking* and *Laval* judgments,[76] could not however be discussed as such. The 'privatisation' of 'public relations' will not, therefore remain without conflict and critique.

Secondary law has entered into private law relations through an ever growing number of directives, and in recent times regulations too. The effect of these rather selective and specific instruments on private parties as such and private law in general, particularly in cases of non- or, more frequently, incomplete or faulty implementation by member countries is not yet clear. There is a certain discrepancy between a specific interpretation given in particular to a directive and the willingness of national courts to apply it straightforwardly in 'horizontal relations'. Since the basic idea of EC law amounts to an 'equal and effective protection' of all citizens, non-implementation should in principle be no defence in private law relations; otherwise a non-complying state could get a 'windfall profit' from non-compliance – a result in clear breach of Article 10 EC. Therefore, this contribution advocates a broader concept of a 'negative horizontal effect of directives' beyond existing remedies. This is particularly important in such socially sensitive areas as employment and consumer law.

The following section reflects on 'horizontal direct effect' beyond procedural aspects of EC private law, in particular, the substantive concept of non-discrimination.

---

76   Reich, 'Free Movement v. Social Rights in an Enlarged Union – the Laval and Viking Cases before the ECJ', [2008] *German Law Journal*, 125 at 160.

III. NON-DISCRIMINATION AND PRIVATE LAW

1. Is There a General Principle of Non-discrimination and Equality in Community Law?

The principle of non-discrimination plays an important role in Community law, and many cases decided by the ECJ refer to it as a general principle.[77] With regard to the economic law of the Community, market subjects should be treated as equals if they are in a similar situation. In many cases concerning regulated markets, the Court has repeatedly held that the principle of equality, namely that 'similar situations shall not be treated differently unless differentiation is objectively justified', is one of the general principles of Community law.[78] As an example, in *Codorniú*[79] the Court voided a Community regulation forbidding Spanish producers from using the traditional term *crémant*, reserved to French and Luxembourg producers of sparkling wine; Spanish producers were put on an unequal basis relative to other producers without justification.

But non-discrimination can take on a social dimension, for example with regard to discrimination based on gender, race, ethnic origin, age, disability or sexual orientation. This development is part of a more general trend concerned with fundamental rights. Therefore, Article 21 on 'Non-discrimination' of the Charter of Fundamental Rights, which will become formally part of EU law once the Lisbon treaty is ratified but which has already guided the ECJ in its interpretation and application of existing EC law,[80] reads:

1. Any discrimination based on any ground such as sex, race, colour, ethnic or social origin, genetic features, language, religion or belief, political or any other opinion, membership of a national minority, property, birth, disability, age or sexual orientation shall be prohibited.

---

[77]   Tridimas, *The General Principles of EU Law* (2nd edn, 2006), at 59–64; Reich, above note 9 at 190–191; Basedow, above note 27 at 232.

[78]   Cases 117/76 and 16/77 *Ruckdeschel* [1977] ECR 1753 para 7; C-15/95, *EARL de Kerlast v. Union régionale de coopératives agricoles (Unicopa) and Coopérative du Trieux* [1997] ECR I-1961 para 35.

[79]   Case C-309/89 *Codorniú SA v. Council* [1994] ECR I-1853.

[80]   See the recent judgments with private law importance in the *Laval* and *Viking* cases, above notes 23 and 38, and in Case C-272/06 *Productores de Música de Espana (Promusicae) v. Telefónica de Espana SAU* [2008] ECR I-271, paras 62–63: need to balance between the right to effective protection of property (copyright) and the right of protection of personal data, and hence of private life, in civil litigation between a rights management society and internet providers concerning disclosure of user data of copyrighted music.

2. Within the scope of application of the Treaty . . . and without prejudice to the special provisions . . . any discrimination on grounds of nationality shall be prohibited.

Those are obviously broad formulations which need to be transformed into legal 'rights' by Court practice. They are addressed to the Union/Community itself[81] and, within the general clause of Article 51 of the Charter, to Member States 'only when they are implementing Union law'. This corresponds to the existing case law of the ECJ.[82] Hence, they have a 'vertical direction' in relation to the Union or Member States – in the broad definition which we mentioned above, including any body or institution governed by public law. But what about private law relations?[83] Can the *Defrenne II* doctrine be extended to other relations governed by private law? The ECJ, in its seminal *Phil Collins* judgment,[84] insisted that the 'right to equal treatment . . . is conferred directly by Community law'; the national court must 'disapply the discriminatory provisions of a national law' (paragraph 34).

2.   Non-discrimination in Private Law Relations?

It is a hotly debated question whether the non-discrimination principle of EC law – whatever its scope and criteria – can also be applied to relations governed by private law, e.g. in employment, general contract, consumer, and company law. The principle of non-discrimination seems to contradict the fundamentals of private law relations, namely freedom of contract and party autonomy. To cite a recent article by a prominent German author, Jürgen Basedow:[85]

> *Der Gleichheitsgrundsatz oder das Verbot der Diskriminierung gehören nicht zu den tragenden Leitprinzipen des Privatrechts. Wer einen Vertrag schließt, tut dies im eigenen Interesse und nicht um Gerechtigkeit gegenüber anderen walten zu*

---

[81]   The ECJ had recognised the extension of the general principle of non-discrimination with regard to sex in its seminal Case C-25/02 *Katharina Rinke v. Ärztekammer Hamburg* [2003] ECR I-8349.

[82]   See Case 5/88 *Wachauf v. Bundesamt für Ernährung* [1989] ECR I-2609 para 19; a different opinion has been taken by Borowsky, in J. Meyer, *Kommentar zur Charta* (2005), Art. 51 para 14.

[83]   Basedow, above note 27 at 249 expressly rejects any horizontal direct effect of Art. 21 of the Charter.

[84]   Joined Cases C-92/92 and 326/92 [1993] ECR I-5145 concerning German copyright legislation which denied to authors and performers from other member countries the right to prohibit the marketing of phonograms manufactured without their consent where the performance was given outside its national territory.

[85]   Above note 27.

lassen. Wer unter mehreren Bewerbern einen Vertragspartner auswählen muss, hat nach der gängigen deutschen Redensart die 'Qual der Wahl', weil es im allge-meinen viele Auswahlkriterien gibt, über deren relatives Gewicht nur aufgrund subjektiver Wertschätzung befunden werden kann.

[The principles of equality or the prohibition of discrimination are not part of the fundamental principles of private law. He who concludes a contract does this in his own interest and not to make justice against others. She who has to choose a contract partner among several candidates has according to a German saying the 'pain of choice' because there exist usually several selection criteria, the relative value of which can only be assessed on subjective preferences.] [translation by author]

Basedow undertakes a detailed and critical analysis of primary and secondary EU law, as well as of the practice of the ECJ, and comes to the conclusion that 'there are only limited and selective prohibitions of discrimination, usually to balance situations of power, and not a general prohibition of discrimination in the conclusion of contracts'.[86]

A lively discussion arose in the context of employment law in the *Mangold* litigation.[87] As mentioned above, the main question was whether Germany, though not yet formally bound by the Framework Directive 2000/78 prohibit-ing under certain circumstances any discrimination based on age, violated a general principle of discrimination in lowering the age limit for fixed term contacts. In his opinion of 30 June 2005, AG Tizzano wrote:

It may also be recalled that, even before the adoption of Directive 2000/78 and the specific provisions it contains, the Court had recognised the existence of a general principle of equality which is binding on Member States 'when they implement Community rules' and which can therefore be used by the Court to review national rules which 'fall within the scope of Community law'. That principle requires that 'comparable situations must not be treated differently and different situations must not be treated in the same way unless such *treatment* is *objectively justified*' by the pursuit of a legitimate aim and provided that it 'is *appropriate and necessary* in order to achieve' that aim' [paragraph 82].

The Court largely adopted this argument, thereby *de facto* eliminating the special *délai de grace* afforded to Germany for implementation:

The principle of non-discrimination on grounds of age must thus be regarded as a general principle of Community law. Where national rules fall within the scope of Community law, . . . and reference is made to the Court for a preliminary ruling, the Court must provide all the criteria of interpretation needed by the national court to determine whether those rules are compatible with such a principle . . . Consequently, observance of the general principle of equal treatment, in particular

---

86 At 250.
87 Above note 22.

in respect of age, cannot as such be conditional upon the expiry of the period allowed the Member States for the transposition of a directive intended to lay down a general framework for combating discrimination on the grounds of age, in particular so far as the organisation of appropriate legal remedies, the burden of proof, protection against victimisation, social dialogue, affirmative action and other specific measures to implement such a directive are concerned [paragraphs 75–76].

This 'general principle' has drawn sharp criticism amongst legal scholars[88] (myself included[89]). It was also criticised in a later opinion by AG Mazak in *Palacios de la Villa*,[90] which notes that the international instruments and constitutional traditions referred to in *Mangold* enshrine the general principle of equal treatment, but that it was a bold proposition and a significant step to infer from that the existence of a specific principle prohibiting age discrimination. A general principle of equality *potentially* implies a prohibition of discrimination on any ground which may be deemed unacceptable, so that specific prohibitions constitute particular expressions of that general principle. However, it is a different matter to infer from the general principle of equality the existence of a prohibition of discrimination on a specific ground, and the reasons for doing so are far from compelling. Moreover, neither Article 13 EC nor Directive 2000/78 necessarily reflects an already existing prohibition of all the forms of discrimination to which they refer. Rather, the underlying intention was in both cases to leave it to the Community legislature and the Member States to take appropriate action to that effect. That is what the Court, too, seems to suggest in *Grant*[91] in which it concluded that Community law, as it stood, did not cover discrimination based on sexual orientation.

In her opinion of 22 May 2008 in *Bartsch*,[92] AG Sharpston gave a more nuanced explanation of *Mangold*, insisting on the historical dimension of this principle which had in the meantime been recognised, thereby justifying the special legislative power of the Community in Article 13 EC, which was the basis of the framework Directive 2000/78:

---

[88]   Basedow above note 27 at 242; further references in the opinion of AG Sharpston in Case C-427/06 [2008] *B. Bartsch v. Bosch and Siemens (BSH) Altersfürsorge*, ECR I-(23.9.2008) which concerned the compatibility of a so-called 'age-gap' clause in a pension scheme with primary (Art. 13) or secondary (Dir. 2000/78) Community law.

[89]   EuZW 2006, 21; 2007, 198.

[90]   Above note 66; Dashwood, above note 55 at 107.

[91]   Case C-249/96 *Lisa Jacqueline Grant v. South-West Trains* [1998] ECR I–621; the EU legislator reacted by way of Directive 2000/78; it is however not clear whether *Grant* would be decided differently: see Reich, above note 9 at 207.

[92]   Above note 88. Also in favour of *Mangold* the opinion of AG Bot of 7.7.2009 in Case C-555/07 *Küküdevici*, above note 70, paragraphs 77 and following.

For that reason, any argument to the effect that if a principle prohibiting discrimination on grounds of age had already existed, Article 13 EC or Directive 2000/78 would have been unnecessary is fundamentally misconceived. It is precisely because the general principle of equality has now been recognised also to include equality of treatment irrespective of age that an enabling legislative provision such as Article 13 EC *becomes* necessary and is duly used as the basis for detailed legislative intervention [paragraph 50].

This compromise might on the one hand explain the philosophical and political (or in the words of Basedow 'social' (*gesellschaftspolitisch*)[93]) basis of the prohibition on age discrimination, while at the same time restricting its scope and content to the legislative basis of Directive 2000/78, which is limited to employment relations and cannot be used as a general principle of private law. The same is true with regard to the other prohibitions on discrimination contained in the Directive, namely discrimination based on disability which, according to the Court in *Navas*,[94] only concerns a 'limitation which results in particular from physical, mental or psychological impairments and which hinders the participation of the person concerned in professional life', and therefore cannot be extended to disability by reason of sickness.

On the other hand, both primary and secondary EC law have extended the principle of non-discrimination also to private law situations under specific circumstances. This applies in particular with regard to the concept of *citizenship* of Article 17 EC, read together with the prohibition based on nationality 'within the scope of application of the Treaty' under Article 12 EC. Although there has as yet been no case concerning discrimination in private law relations, the arguments developed by the ECJ with regard to fundamental freedoms, namely the existence of a 'collective regulation', can also be used with regard to nationality clauses in standard contract forms or by-laws of private associations like boarding schools or private universities.[95] A recent case concerns a formally 'vertical' situation, with regard to the limited choice of surnames by mandatory rules of private international law, which was before the Court in the *Grunkin-Paul* case.[96] The litigation concerns a German couple

---

[93] Above note 27 at 236.

[94] See Case C-13/05 *Sonja Chacón Navas v. Eurest Colectividades* [2006] ECR I–6467 para 43; the Court insisted 'that a person who has been dismissed by his employer solely on account of sickness does not fall within the general framework laid down for combating discrimination on grounds of disability by Directive 2000/78' (para 47).

[95] Reich, above note 33 at 725.

[96] Case C-353/06; see the opinion of AG Jacobs of 30 June 2005 in the preceding Case C-96/04 [2006] ECR 3561 where the ECJ however regarded the reference as inadmissible. In his earlier opinion of 9 December 1992 in Case C-168/01 *Konstantinidis* [1191], argued before the enactment of the citizenship concept in EU

whose child was born in Denmark, where its name was determined according to the *ius soli*, which allowed it to take the last name of both its father and mother, while under the German *ius sanguinis* and *lex nationalitis* parents are forced to choose the last name of either the father or the mother; when the child settled in Germany it applied to maintain the Danish double name, but the request was refused under German law by the competent authority of the Amtsgericht. In her opinion of 24 April 2008, AG Sharpston referred to the earlier *Garcia Avello* case,[97] where the Court found discrimination occurred where children of a couple with double statehood were forced to assume a name according to the rules of the country of residence and cannot opt instead for those of the country of origin of one of the spouses. AG Sharpston insisted on the right of the child to choose its own name as a Union citizen:

> The question is not whether *parents* may be dissuaded from exercising their rights of movement and residence, or hindered in the exercise of those rights, by any rules which may apply in determining the surname of their children, born or unborn. It is whether a *child* whose birth has been lawfully registered under a particular name in accordance with the law of the Member State of the place of that birth – and who has not himself exercised any choice with regard to that registration – suffers inconvenience or hardship when exercising *his own rights* as a citizen of the Union if the Member State of his nationality refuses to recognise the name thus registered. The answer must be that he does [paragraphs 77–78].

In its judgment of 13 October 2008, the Court basically followed the opinion of AG Sharpston and regarded German legislation on names as an unjustified, non-proportional interference with the free movement rights of a Union citizen:

> None of the grounds put forward in support of the connecting factor of nationality for determination of a person's surname, however legitimate those grounds may be in themselves, warrants having such importance attached to it as to justify, in circumstances such as those of the case in the main proceedings, a refusal by the competent authorities of a Member State to recognise the surname of a child as already determined and registered in another Member State in which that child was born and has been resident since birth [paragraph 31].

---

law, AG Jacobs pointed to the fundamental right of a person to his name as part of European citizenship: '*civis Europeus sum*', at para 46; the Court argued with the somewhat artificial market aspects of distorting the spelling of a name which may create confusion with potential clients of Mr. Konstantinidis and therefore restrict non-proportionally his right to establishment.

[97]   Case C-148/02, [2003] ECR I-11613; for its importance on fundamental rights protection of economically inactive citizens see Elsmore and Starup, 'Union Citizenship – Background, Jurisprudence, and Perspective', [2007] *YEL*, 57 at 92.

This discrimination under the citizenship provisions is formally addressed 'vertically' to a Member State agency, namely the national court which determines questions of name, but in substance concerns the private law question of the name of a citizen which usually is determined by the rules of private international law which are not as such contested by the AG or the ECJ but which must still avoid any discrimination or unjustified restriction.

Secondary law has extended private law (beyond employment relations) discrimination prohibitions[98] to ethnic and racial origin by Artile 3 (1) (h) of Directive 2000/43/EC,[99] sex by Article 5 (1) of Directive 2004/113/EC,[100] and legal residents under Article 11 (1) (f) of the Long-term Resident Directive, 2003/109/EC.[101] The criteria are 'access to and supply of goods and services available to the public'. 'Housing' is mentioned only in Directive 2000/43, not in Directive 2004/113; Directive 2003/109 is limited to 'procedures for obtaining housing'. Therefore, not every differentiation in the selection of contract partners is a violation of EC law; there must already be an initial availability of certain goods and services to the public, e.g. via advertising or marketing.[102] Article 3 (2) of Directive 2004/113 and its recital 14 expressly guarantee the freedom to choose a contractual partner, so long as it is not based on the person's sex; special rules apply to insurance contracts.

But these limitations of the non-discrimination principle in private law matters do not mean that it remains 'an incomplete legal provision' (*unvollständiger Rechtsgrundsatz*), as Basedow suggests.[103] To the contrary: Member States are under an obligation to sanction non-justified discrimination in private law relations, whether or not they provide for private law remedies.

---

[98] For an overview see Schiek et al. (eds.), *Non-discrimnation Law* (2007), 11–14; Reich, above note 14 at 204–206. Basedow, above note 27 at 238 differentiates between a genuine 'prohibition of discrimination', which is not the formulation of the directives, and the need to 'combat discrimination', e.g. according to Art. 1 Dir. 2000/43; its Art. 2 (1) formulates that 'there shall be no direct or indirect discrimination based on race or ethnic origin'. Is the latter formula really a difference from a 'prohibition' *stricto sensu*? Otherwise the need for effective sanctions would not be understandable. Obviously, the Member States have a certain amount of discretion on how to implement this obligation.

[99] [2000] OJ L180/22

[100] [2004] OJ L373/37

[101] [2004] OJ L16/44; the latter has not been discussed by Basedow.

[102] Reich, above note 14 at 206; Schreier, 'Das Allgemeine Gleichbehandlungsgesetz – wirklich ein Eingriff in die Vertragsfreiheit?' [2007] *KritJ*, 278 at 285 referring to the somewhat misleading term in the implementing German legislation (AGG – *Allgemeines Gleichbehandlungsgesetz* 2006) *'Massengeschäft'* in contrast to 'individual transactions' where personal properties of the partner are important.

[103] At 240.

Private law, as already insisted by Steindorff,[104] has a *Sanktionsaufgabe* – the task of providing sanctions. They must be effective, as AG Poiares Maduro insisted in his opinion of 12 March 2008 in the Belgian *Feryn* case,[105] concerning ethnic discrimination by a producer of 'up-and-over doors', who publicly declared he did not employ immigrants (in the circumstance mostly persons of arabic origin) on the basis his clients would not accept this, for fear of theft:

> On the issue of sanctions, Article 15 of the Directive (2000/43, NR) provides that 'Member States shall lay down the rules on sanctions applicable to infringements of the national provisions adopted pursuant to this Directive and shall take all measures necessary to ensure that they are applied. The sanctions, which may comprise the payment of compensation to the victim, must be effective, proportionate and dissuasive . . .'. Moreover, as the Court held in *Von Colson and Kamann*, national courts have a duty to take all appropriate measures to ensure fulfilment of the Member States' obligation to achieve the result envisaged by the Directive. It is for the referring court to determine, in accordance with the relevant rules of domestic law, which remedy would be appropriate in the circumstances of the present case. However, in the main, purely token sanctions are not sufficiently dissuasive to enforce the prohibition of discrimination. Therefore, it would seem that a court order prohibiting such behaviour would constitute a more appropriate remedy. In sum, if the national court finds that there has been a breach of the principle of equal treatment, it must grant remedies that are effective, proportionate and dissuasive [paragraphs 27–29].

In its judgment of 10 July 2008, the Court largely followed AG Poiares Maduro's opinion, while allowing the employer to prove that in his actual recruitment policy he did not discriminate (a somewhat problematic defence, since it does not eliminate the deterrent effect of his public statements which were clearly discriminatory). With regard to remedies, the Court allowed the national jurisdiction a wide range of alternatives, provided the principles of effectiveness, proportionality and dissuasiveness were respected:

> If it appears appropriate to the situation at issue in the main proceedings, those sanctions may, where necessary, include a finding of discrimination by the court or the competent administrative authority in conjunction with an adequate level of publicity, the cost of which is to be borne by the defendant. They may also take the form of a prohibitory injunction, in accordance with the rules of national law, ordering the employer to cease the discriminatory practice, and, where appropriate, a fine. They may, moreover, take the form of the award of damages to the body bringing the proceedings [paragraph 39].

---

104 Above note 24 at 303 ff.
105 Case C-54/07; Reich, [2008] *EuZW*, 229.

On 2 July 2008, the Commission proposed to extend the principle of equal treatment between persons irrespective of religion or belief, disability, age or sexual orientation also to private law relations outside the labour market, in particular, consumer markets where 'access to and supply of goods and services available to the public, including housing' are concerned.[106] Albeit allowing some exceptions, the German *Allgemeine Gleichbehandlungsgesetz (AGG)* of 14 August 2006 already contains a similar provision in § 19.

3. Non-discrimination of Access to and Treatment in Services of General Interest and in Network Services

Services of general interest like communication, energy, transport have only recently come within the scope of Community law, in line with trends of deregulation and privatisation affecting these sectors. In the 'old days' these services were highly regulated by public law, where the principles of non-discrimination could be applied without dogmatic problems relating to party autonomy. The new regime is, by contrast, more concerned with competition and choice. Accordingly it has had to develop standards of its own, in particular by transposing (somewhat hesitantly) the idea of *solidarity* also to a more economic and competitive understanding of public services, thus including questions of consumer (or rather user) access and quality.[107] The EC Commission has proposed including these services in its work on consumer protection.[108] They are based on contract law, i.e. a 'horizontal' regime, even if substantially regulated by economic law.

The most important elements of this strategy have been, on one hand, the internal market approach, and on the other, the so-called 'universal service obligation' of providers.[109] Their impact is on free choice in access to services and in non-discriminatory treatment without distinguishing between consumers in the traditional sense and other users. Under the Universal Services Directive 2002/22/EC[110] and the revised Electricity Directive

---

[106]   COM(2008)426 final.

[107]   Ross, 'Promoting Solidarity: From Public Service to a European Model of Competition?', *CMLRev.* (2007), 1057 at 1070, insisting on the applicability of the general norm of Art. 16 EC.

[108]   Consumer Policy strategy, COM(2002) para 3.1.5; also COM(2007)99 at 12: EU Consumer Policy Strategy 2007–2013.

[109]   Rott, 'Consumers and Services of General Interest: Is EC Consumer Law the Future?', [2007] *JCP*, 53; Reich, 'Crisis of Future of European Consumer Law?', *Yearbook of Consumer Law 2008* (2009).

[110]   Dir. 2002/22/EC of the European Parliament and the Council of 2002 on universal service and users' rights relating to electronic communications, networks and services (Universal Services Directive) [2002] OJ L108/51.

2003/54/EC[111] 'household customers' should not be prevented from switching to another provider through direct or indirect impediments.[112]

The 'universal' or public service obligations concern access to services which should be open to anybody, with the detail to be regulated by Member States. It cannot easily be terminated; freedom of contract is suspended by mandatory rules in favour of non-professional users. These provisions are however rather weak at EU level: Member States are required only to ensure that there are 'adequate safeguards to protect vulnerable consumers, including appropriate measures to help them to avoid disconnection' under Article 3(5) of the Electricity Directive. Annex A gives consumers 'a right to a contract' with some basic information. They must be given notice 'of any increase of charges' and have a right to withdraw from contracts if they do not accept the new conditions, but there is no right to be informed about the calculation of the increase and a possible right to challenge it.

These principles are extended to other network services. Access rules are contained in the new Directive 2007/64/EC on payment services in the internal market.[113] Articles 19–22 contain detailed provisions protecting the 'recipient of services' against non-discrimination, and for providing assistance and detailed information on services covered by the Directive, not limited to the traditional consumer, but also including commercial clients. This right of 'access' to payment services without discrimination seems to transform payment systems in the EU, despite their heterogeneity, into a 'service of general economic interest' based on private law (without, however, a 'universal service obligation') and subject to special rules going beyond traditional concepts of private autonomy and freedom of contract.

In any case, the impact of this encroachment of regulation on private law has hardly been discussed so far. The non-discrimination principle has a special role to play in this context; it is surprising that Basedow's paper does not even mention it. This area seems to be, as Micklitz[114] correctly observes, a blind spot in the eyes of private law scholars, who believe that this highly regulated area still follows the principle of party autonomy. He writes:

---

[111]   Dir. 2003/54/EC of the European Parliament and the Council of 26 June 2003 concerning Common Rules for the Internal Market for Electricity [2003] OJ L176/32.

[112]   Rott at 56; Micklitz, 'The Concept of Competitive Contract Law', *Penn State* (2005), 549 at 576; Ch. Willett, 'General Clauses on Fairness and the Promotion of Values Important in Services of General Interest', in Twigg-Flesner et al. (eds.), *The Yearbook of Consumer Law 2007* (2008), 67 at 95–100.

[113]   [2007] OJ L319.

[114]   Micklitz, 'The Visible Hand of European Regulatory Private Law', EUI Working Papers Law 2008/14, at 16–18.

The network law develops, within the boundaries of universal services, concepts and devices whose reach must be tested with regard to their potential for general application beyond the narrow subject matter. Just one example may be mentioned: despite privatisation, network industries have to guarantee the accessibility and the affordability of their services. What is at stake here is the obligation to contract (Kontrahierungszwang) and the duty to continue delivery even in cases of late payment.

4. A Hypothesis as Conclusion: What is the Concept of Justice in EU 'Private' Law?

The foregoing discussion of the theory and practice of the 'horizontal direct effect' of both primary and secondary EC law, as well as the analysis of the concept of non-discrimination in private law, has shown the dividing line between 'public' and 'private' in European law to be ambiguous. The *instrumental character* of European 'private law' is obvious; it mostly contains mandatory and not just default rules. Critics fear that, eventually, it may abolish private autonomy, a fear that is in my opinion unfounded. EC law seeks to implement autonomy in the interest of free movement and non-discrimination. It is concerned with equality in private law relations that aims first at 'communitative justice' in the sense of 'fairness' in freely entertained transactions in markets of goods and services,[115] but which does not stop there, if we follow the scheme developed by Pakaluk on the basis of the Aristotelean *Nicomachean Ethics*:

> Aristotle thinks that there are there are three ways of producing an equality of divisible goods, and thus three forms of the virtue of justice. The first ('distributive') is for someone to distribute for individuals goods that are taken from a common stock . . . The second ('communitative') is for persons freely to exchange goods [on a market, NR] . . . The third ('corrective') is for a judge to correct for an inequality that is created by an act of injustice.[116]

EU law first steps in to secure freedom and fairness in contract relations which are impeded by unequal bargaining power where this denies free movement to one side and allows promises made by the stronger side to go unfulfilled. Because they eliminate socially unaccepted differentiations in contracting without otherwise restricting party autonomy, the rules on non-discrimination only partially go beyond this concept. *Communitative justice* is also the guiding principle with regard to services of general economic interest, where EU law insists on free choice and transparency which must be realised by the

---

[115] See Basedow, above note 27 at 246; Eidenmüller et al., above note 104 at 534; AG Sharpston in Bartsch, above note 88 at para 30.
[116] Pakaluk, *Aristotle's Nicomachean Ethics: An Introduction* (2005), at 195–196.

'universal service obligation' of certain providers, thus allowing equal access of potential users to network systems. *Distributive justice* comes into view in anti-discrimination provisions of employment law because these shift goods from one side (the employer) to others (certain groups of employees who must not be discriminated against, e.g. women, ethnic minorities). In services of general economic interest, in particular in cases of cut-offs, it is left to Member States to guarantee 'distributive justice' beyond free choice. '*Corrective justice*', finally, is at hand in the area of non-discrimination in employment, but also in general private law relations where 'goods and services available to the public' must not be marketed on discriminatory terms with regard to sex, ethnic origin, nationality, and other stigmatised characteristics. Here private law has to offer adequate remedies which must be, according to the case law of the ECJ, adequate, proportionate and dissuasive. This is the task of both contract and tort law, as far as private law is concerned.

Consequently it is incorrect to deny, as Basedow does, the 'specific operative importance of the general prohibition on discrimination in European law'.[117] The principle of equality certainly has a limited field of application insofar as it attaches to specific areas (e.g. sex, age, ethnic origin, disability, sexual orientation, but not sickness, income) and 'discrimination' can be reasonably distinguished from 'differentiation'. Within this field of application, however, it is without doubt a governing principle of private law. As a result it is to be welcomed that both Chapter 3 of the *Acquis* principles[118] and Chapter 2 of Book II of the Draft Common Frame of Reference[119] include provisions on discrimination, transferring into general (EU?) contract law the relevant EC directives.[120]

---

[117]   Basedow, above note 27: '*dem allgemeinen Diskriminierungsverbot (kommt) keine eigenständige operative Bedeutung im europäischen Privatrecht zu ... Seine Rolle ist die eines hermeneutischen Prinzips, welches das Verständnis des positiven Rechts erleichtert, weil es uns gestattet, einzelne Rechtsakte im Kontext zu sehen und auf ihre systematische Stimmigkeit zu prüfen. Ein eigener Regelungsgehalt kommt ihm nicht zu*'.

[118]   Acquis Group (ed.), *Principles of the Existing EC Contract Law (Acquis-Principles) – Contract I* (2008); for a comment see Leible, 'Non-Discrimination', in Schulze (ed.), *Common Frame of Reference and Existing EC Contract Law* (2008), 127.

[119]   Study Group on a European Civil Code (ed.), *Principles, Defintions and Model Rules of European Private Law (DCFR)* (2008) (similar in the Outline Edition 2009); a critique has been voiced by Eidenmüller et al., 'Der Gemeinsame Referenzrahmen für das Europäische Privatrecht', [2008] *JZ*, 529 at 535 suggesting the inclusion of the non-discrimination rules of EC law in public rather than private law provisions, thus misunderstanding the impact of non-discrimination on freedom of contract and choice and the *Sanktionsaufgabe* of private law as developed by Steindorff, above note 104.

[120]   Reich [2008] *JCP*, 369; Schulze and Wilhelmsson, 'From the Draft Common

What is true is that this imposition of EU/EC law principles on the private law of Member States shifts the focus away from an abstract concept of private autonomy to a more differentiated and multi-layered system of justice which may not previously have been present in Member State law, but which does not as such eliminate private autonomy.[121] Private law in the EU thereby assumes a public function.

ANNEX TO III/3

On 17 July 2009 the EP and the Council adopted Directive 2009/72/EC 'concerning common rules for the internal market of electricity and repealing Dir. 2003/54/EC'.[122] Art. 3(7) contains general obligations of Member States to protect final, in particular vulnerable consumers in markets with universal service obligations.

> In this context, each Member State shall determine the concept of vulnerable consumers which may refer to energy poverty and, inter alia, to the prohibition of disconnection of electricity to such consumers in critical times.

These provisions in no way improve the position of – in particular vulnerable – consumers against the old directive as mentioned above. They are too unspecific to take direct effect. Much more specific are the transparency requirements of Annex I concerning the contracting with the universal service supplier.

Frame of Reference towards European Contract Law Rules' [2008] *ERCL*, 154 at 168; reservations with regard to extending them to freedom of association have been voiced by Basedow p. 242.

[121] With regard to English law see the critical remarks by C. Twigg-Flesner, *The Europeanisation of Contract Law* (2008), at 133–138.

[122] [2009] OJ L 211/55.

5. The Draft Common Frame of Reference: how to improve it?

Jan M. Smits*

1. INTRODUCTION

The aim of this contribution is to discuss the view of law and lawmaking underlying the Draft Common Frame of Reference (DCFR).[1] It claims that the DCFR suffers from so-called *methodological nationalism* and therefore fails to adopt the right approach to dealing with private law in the European Union. The theoretical analysis is followed by some concrete suggestions on how to improve the DCFR so that it better meets its intended functions.

Section 2 offers a brief introduction to the DCFR. It is followed by an account of what is meant by 'methodological nationalism' and how this is applied in law (section 3). Sections 4, 5 and 6 subsequently offer an analysis of why the DCFR is to be qualified as an example of this methodology. This does not mean that the DCFR cannot fulfil a useful role in the present debate, but it may have to be a different role from that envisaged by the drafters. Sections 6 and 7 therefore offer an alternative and *differentiated* perspective on the way forward in European contract law.

2. THE DCFR: BACKGROUND AND PURPOSE

The presentation of the DCFR to the European Commission on 28 December 2007 was the result of four years of work by the *Study Group on a European Civil Code* and the *Research Group on the Existing EC Private Law* (the

* This chapter benefits from discussion at a workshop at the European University Institute (29 February–1 March 2008). It is a slightly amended and elaborated version of the paper presented at the SECOLA Conference on Fifty Years of European Contract Law (Barcelona, 6–7 June 2008).

[1] Von Bar, C., E. Clive and H. Schulte-Nölke (eds) (2008), *Principles, Definitions and Model Rules of European Private Law: Draft Common Frame of Reference, Interim Outline Edition*, Munich: Sellier.

'*acquis* group').[2] In its Communication on European Contract Law of 2004,[3] the European Commission indicated that 'definitions, principles and model rules' for a European contract law would have to be prepared in order to improve the quality and overall consistency of the existing *acquis* in this area. The present draft is the provisional result of this project and will be followed by a final version in 2008.

The DCFR consists of ten 'books', dealing with general provisions (Book I), contracts and other juridical acts (Book II), obligations and corresponding rights (Book III), specific contracts (Book IV), benevolent intervention in another's affairs (Book V), tort law (Book VI) and unjustified enrichment (Book VII). The books on acquisition and loss of ownership in movables (Book VIII), security rights in movables (Book IX) and trusts (Book X) are not yet published. The two annexes contain a list of definitions and rules on computation of time.

According to its drafters, the Common Frame of Reference has several purposes.[4] First (and foremost), it is a possible model for a 'political CFR': the current text is presented as an academic one and the European Commission has to decide whether it will use it as a building block when revising the present *acquis* or when drafting new rules. Second, the drafters regard the CFR as standing on its own as an academic text for legal science and teaching. They highlight that the DCFR will promote knowledge of private law in the jurisdictions of the European Union, and will in particular 'help to show how much national private laws resemble one another and have provided mutual stimulus for development and indeed how much those laws may be regarded as regional manifestations of an overall common European legacy'.[5] Third, in the same vein as the previously published Principles of European Contract Law, the CFR can be a source of inspiration for national courts, the European Court of Justice and national legislators. Finally, it may form the basis for an optional contract code.[6]

It should be reiterated that, in the view of the European Commission, the main aim of the final CFR is to serve as a 'tool box' for the European legislator:[7] it can, 'where appropriate',[8] make use of the CFR to draft new directives

---

[2]   These groups are the most important members of the *Joint Network on European Private Law* (CoPECL).
[3]   Communication on European Contract Law and the Revision of the *Acquis*: the Way Forward, COM(2004)651 final, OJ EC 2005, C 14/6.
[4]   *DCFR* (2008), 6 ff.
[5]   *DCFR* (2008), 6.
[6]   *DCFR* (2008), 37.
[7]   Communication (2004), 14.
[8]   Communication (2004), 3.

or to review the existing *acquis*. The instrument is not in any way binding upon the European legislator or the Member States,[9] but should derive its authority from the quality of its provisions.

When assessing the DCFR, we should keep in mind that the present text contains only the provisions and not the illustrations and comments that make the Principles of European Contract Law such a useful source of inspiration. However, much of the preparatory work can be found in the series *Principles of European Law*[10] as published by the *Study Group on a European Civil Code* and in the so-called *Acquis Principles* (ACQP),[11] which were designed to systematise the existing directives in the field of private law.

3.   METHODOLOGICAL NATIONALISM AND LAW

How to evaluate the DCFR? The Draft can be considered from the angle of different theoretical frameworks. The perspective chosen in this contribution is the angle of so-called methodological nationalism. This term was coined for the first time by the sociologist Herminio Martins.[12] It refers to the idea that the process of nation-state building fundamentally shaped our way of thinking, even to such an extent that the division of societies along the lines of nation-states is seen as the natural form of organising things.[13] Methodological nationalism can therefore be described as the assumption that the nation, state or national society is the natural social and political form of the modern world.[14] There are various modes of such methodological nationalism; one of them, in the words of Wimmer and Schiller, is to take 'national discourses, agendas, loyalties and histories for granted, without problematizing them or making them an object of an analysis in its own right'.[15]

---

[9]   Communication (2004), 6.
[10]   Published by Sellier Publishers (Munich) from 2006 onwards.
[11]   Research Group on the Existing EC Private Law (2007), *Principles of the Existing EC Contract Law* (*Acquis* Principles), *Vol. I: Contract: Pre-contractual Obligations, Conclusion of Contract, Unfair Terms*, Munich: Sellier, on which Jansen, N. and R. Zimmermann (2007), 'Grundregeln des bestehenden Gemeinschafts-privatrechts?', 62 *Juristenzeitung* 1113. *Vol. II* on *Performance, Non-Performance and Remedies* is announced for 2008.
[12]   Martins, H. (1974), 'Time and Theory in Sociology', in: J. Rex, *Approaches to Sociology*, London: Routledge & Kegan, 246, at 276.
[13]   See Wimmer, A. and N. Glick Schiller (2002), 'Methodological Nationalism and Beyond: Nation-State Building, Migration and the Social Sciences', 2 *Global Networks* 301, at 304.
[14]   See Wimmer and Schiller (2002), at 302.
[15]   Wimmer and Schiller (2002), at 304.

It is no surprise that the legal domain in particular has been largely affected by methodological nationalism. Nations and their products in the form of national legislation and case law are usually seen as the basic units of analysis in legal scholarship. The way we think about law, both as to its validity, enforcement and legitimation, is largely shaped by this method. At a very general level, even the mere distinction of national and international legal orders is an example of this way of thinking, as is the existence of the discipline of comparative law.[16] But at a more concrete level, methodological nationalism may prevent us from looking beyond traditional concepts.[17] Ulrich Beck is right when he says that increasing denationalisation and transnationalisation should lead us to a reconceptualisation of law within a new cosmopolitan framework, in order to avoid our discipline becoming 'a museum of antiquated ideas'.[18]

The point being made here is that when we think about law and the requirements it should meet, we (often implicitly) make use of concepts that were developed for law in the nation-state: our traditional way of thinking, developed for law in a national society, is then transplanted to the European or global level. The finding that this is wrong is clearly part of the debate in the field of European law[19] and, albeit to a lesser extent, in constitutional law,[20] but it is much less debated in other classical areas of law such as private law.[21] Often, the conceptual legal framework is transplanted to the European level without much deliberation of whether this is the proper approach. Also in drafting the CFR, this issue seems not to have been discussed: the structure and contents of the Draft are remarkably similar to those of a national civil

---

[16]   Cf. Joerges, C. (2004), 'The Challenges of Europeanization in the Realm of Private Law: A Plea For a New Legal Discipline', 14 *Duke J. Comp. Int. L.* 149, at 160.

[17]   Cf. Beck, U. (2003), 'Toward a New Critical Theory with a Cosmopolitan Intent', 10 *Constellations* 453, at 456: methodological nationalism prevents us from looking beyond the 'traditional conceptualisations of terms and the construction of borders between the "national" and the "international", domestic and foreign politics, or society and the state'.

[18]   Beck (2003), at 458.

[19]   I only need to refer to the elaborate discussion about the best way to characterise the European Union (not as a federation or as an international organisation, but as a *sui generis* type of entity).

[20]   Building on Habermas' concept of a 'postnational constellation' in which traditional democratic processes have to take on new forms: see Habermas, J. (2001), *The Postnational Constellation: Political Essays*, Cambridge, Mass: Harvard University Press.

[21]   Notable exceptions are Joerges, C. (2004), 149 ff., Michaels, R. (2005), 'Welche Globalisierung für das Recht? Welches Recht für die Globalisierung?', *RabelsZ*, 525 ff. and the contributions to Cafaggi, F. (ed.) (2006), *The Institutional Framework of European Private Law*, Oxford: OUP.

code, even though its function cannot in any way be compared to it, even in the view of the drafters.

In the following sections, I will discuss three features of the DCFR where this methodological nationalism comes to the surface. Implied in this qualification is that the DCFR takes too little into account that what is best at the *national* level may not be optimal at the *European* level.[22] The features I am interested in deal with the idea of a comprehensive codification of private law as such (section 4), the way in which the relevant rules are chosen (section 5) and the best way to represent law at a level other than that of the nation-state (section 6).

4.   COMPREHENSIVE CODIFICATION OR A MULTI-LAYERED EUROPEAN PRIVATE LAW?

The suggestion that the idea of codification is closely related to the nation-state needs little explaining: historically, codification of private law has been an expression of national identity. In the same vein, one needs little imagination to see that the ideal of a uniform private law laid down in one comprehensive text is closely related to two other goals: the quests for legal certainty and equality.[23] The question now is whether these goals are best attained at the supranational level by drafting a text that closely resembles the format of a national civil code, as is the case with the DCFR. Not only in terms of the topics addressed, but also with regard to its structure and the style of its provisions, the Draft looks like a national code. But can we really transplant the traditional features of a civil code into a text for the European Union?

The answer to this question can only be given if we realise that the function of the CFR is different from the traditional function of a national code. The drafters submit that the CFR will primarily be a 'toolbox' for new European legislation or a source of inspiration for national courts and legislators. Closest to our idea of a national code is that it may form the basis for an optional code. But if full harmonisation replacing national jurisdictions is *not* the aim of the CFR, this must mean something for the structure and substance of this instrument. Two things should be taken into account.

First, we should recognise that private law at the European level will continue to flow from various sources: there will be a continuous co-habitation

---

[22]   I have been critical about the entire project before: see Smits, J.M. (2006), 'European Private Law: a Plea for a Spontaneous Legal Order', in: D. Curtin, et al, *European Integration and Law*, Antwerp-Oxford: Intersentia.

[23]   Cf. Jansen, N. (2004), *Binnenmarkt, Privatrecht und europäische Identität*, Tübingen: Mohr Siebeck, 20.

of private law emanating from both national and European sources, which will also consist of private regulation.[24] This multi-layered structure of European private law prompts the question at which regulatory level issues are best regulated. The entire private law system can in any event no longer be governed by only one piece of legislation,[25] as this would be contrary to the allocation of normative powers between the Member States and the European Union.[26] The DCFR seems to shows little evidence of this insight. Thus, one could well argue that contract law is best regulated at the European level because of its close relationship to the European internal market, whereas e.g. the law of restitution, which serves the role of correcting and supplementing the existing law of obligations, best fulfils its function at the national level.[27] In Stephen Swann's phrase, we are 'constructing a castle in the air' wherever there are no common foundations beneath a European law of obligations.[28]

Second, any attempt to redraft present European private law should take into account the rules already in existence. Codification at the national level is often associated with starting afresh and abolishing the 'old' law, but this cannot be the case in the European Union. In this sense, it seems that the present DCFR is far removed from the (sector-specific and fragmentary) European *acquis*. The primary motivation for the project was the European Commission's desire to revise the existing European directives in the field of private law with a view to dealing with their fragmentary, inconsistent and less than fully effective character. If one judges the DCFR in terms of this objective, some of the proposed

---

[24] On private regulation at the European and supranational level see e.g. Cafaggi, F. (ed.) (2006), *Reframing Self-regulation in European Private Law*, The Hague: Kluwer; Schiek, D. (2007), 'Private Rule-making and European Governance: Issues of Legitimacy', *European Law Review* 443 and Zumbansen, P. (2007), *The Law of Society: Governance Through Contract*, CLPE Research Paper 2/2007.

[25] Cf. Cafaggi, F. (2006), 'Introduction', in: id. (ed), *The Institutional Framework of European Private Law*, Oxford: OUP, 1 and Cafaggi, F. (2008), 'The Making of European Private Law: Governance Design', in: F. Cafaggi, and H. Muir Watt, *Making European Private Law: Governance Design*, Cheltenham: Edward Elgar, 289.

[26] All traditional codifications were declared to be exclusive: they were the only source of law. See for a thorough analysis Van den Berg, P.A.J. (2007), *The Politics of European Codification: A History of the Unification of Law in France, Prussia, the Austrian Monarchy and the Netherlands*, Groningen: Europa Law Publishing.

[27] See Smits, J.M. (2008), 'A European Law on Unjustified Enrichment? A Critical View of the Law of Restitution in the Draft Common Frame of Reference', in: A. Vaquer (ed.), *European Private Law Beyond the Common Frame of Reference*, Groningen: Europa Law Publishing, 153.

[28] Swann, S. (2005), 'The Structure of Liability for Unjustified Enrichment: First Proposals of the Study Group on a European Civil Code', in: R. Zimmermann (ed.), *Grundstrukturen eines Europäischen Bereicherungsrecht*, Tübingen: Mohr Siebeck, 268.

provisions will indeed yield improvement (e.g. the draft deals with duties to provide information to the consumer, the effects of exercising the right of withdrawal and the creation of a uniform withdrawal period of 14 days). But most of the provisions do not relate to the existing *acquis* at all.[29] To be fair, the drafters do realise this by presenting their text as an 'academic CFR', a scholarly text which is not politically legitimised and which at best could provide the basis for a 'political CFR' to be drafted by the European Commission. But the Commission itself has already indicated that it will aim primarily at a revision of eight existing directives.[30] Provisions on the law of obligations in general (including *negotiotum gestio* and unjustified enrichment) and on some specific contracts (which are not covered by directives at all) do not fit this purpose. In this respect, it seems that part of the work done by the Study Group no longer reflects present reality.[31]

5.   CHOICE OF THE RELEVANT RULES

A second feature of national codifications is that there is usually little doubt about what the relevant rules should be and who should choose them. This is because at the national level there is usually a generally accepted criterion for deciding which rules are to be incorporated in the code, and because there is a generally accepted procedure for adopting such rules (in most cases this is a national democratic decision process). At the European level such consensus is lacking.[32] This makes it all the more important to employ a clear method when deciding which rules should be part of the CFR and who should adopt the final text.

According to the drafters of the CFR, its provisions are based on a comparative analysis of the law of the Member States and the applicable European law.[33] But this method is not very convincing if one does not know how this

---

[29]   Surprisingly, neither is the case law of the European Court of Justice codified in any way, whereas one would have expected a codification of the doctrine of state liability on the basis of *Francovich* and *Brasserie*.

[30]   Green paper on the revision of the *consumer acquis* of 8 February 2007, COM(2006)744 final. Also see Second progress report on the CFR of 25 July 2007, COM(2007)447 final.

[31]   The following remark (DCFR (2008), 10) is therefore surprising: '[w]hether particular rules might be used as a model for early legislation, for example, for the improvement of the internal coherence of the acquis communautaire ... is for others to decide'.

[32]   Cf., Study Group on Social Justice in European Private Law (2004), 'Social Justice in European Contract Law: a Manifesto', 10 *European Law Journal* 653.

[33]   *DCFR* (2008), 12.

comparative method was applied: did one look for the common denominator of the jurisdictions involved [34] or for the solution considered to be the 'better' one (and, if so, for what reason)? Discussion about the contents of the provisions is difficult if the drafters do not explain what motivated such choices. The following comment seems to indicate the approach adopted:[35]

> the model rules of course build on ... underlying principles ... . It would be possible to include in the DCFR a separate part which states these basic values and suggests factors that the legislator should bear in mind when seeking to strike a balance between them. For example, this part could be formulated as recitals, i.e. an introductory list of reasons for the essential substance of the following text ... . If this idea is thought to be useful, a fuller version could be developed at a later stage. It must be conceded, however, that, taken in isolation, such fundamental principles do not advance matters much at a practical level because of their high level of abstraction. Abstract principles tend to contradict one another. They always have to be weighed up against one another more exactly because only then are optimal outcomes assured.

This suggests that the underlying principles can be discussed *afterwards*, once the text has already been established. But how can choices already made be justified, if not on basis of (an internal debate about) the underlying values and of *how* these have to be weighed up against one another? Little help is available from an inventory of the 'core aims of European private law'[36] so long as the exact relationship between these aims is not made explicit.

6. HOW TO REPRESENT LAW BEYOND THE NATIONAL STATE?

In the nation-state, law is usually seen to consist of authoritative rules backed by coercive force which is exercised by legitimately constituted democratic institutions.[37] The way in which law is usually represented[38] matches these characteristics: describing law by way of rules pretends that these rules can

---

[34]   This is suggested in the *DCFR* (2008), 12, where it says that the CFR 'mediates' between diverging results in the various Member States.

[35]   *DCFR* (2008), 9.

[36]   The authors mention 'justice, freedom, protection of human rights, economic welfare, solidarity and social responsibility', to which they add for European regulation 'promotion of the internal market', 'preservation of cultural and linguistic plurality' and, specifically for the drafting of model rules, the goals of 'rationality, legal certainty, predictability and efficiency'. See *DCFR* (2008), 13.

[37]   Cf. Morgan, B. and K. Yeung (2007), *An Introduction to Law and Regulation*, Cambridge: CUP, 303–304.

[38]   On the very idea of representing law see Roberts, S.A. (2005), 'After Government? On Representing Law Without the State', 68 *Modern Law Review* 1.

create the necessary legal certainty and equality needed to guide those affected by them. In this sense, our understanding of rules is closely related to what these rules can *do*[39] at the national level: they organise society, presuming that the rules came into being in a democratic process and can therefore be enforced by the state institutions. It is thus the national democratic process that enables policy trade-offs to be made transparently and authoritatively.[40]

The question is whether law beyond the national state should be represented in the same way, in particular when, as is the case with the CFR, the aim of the provisions is not directly to influence the conduct of private parties and to be enforced, but primarily to be a source of inspiration. If a text is proposed as an 'academic CFR', should this not influence the way in which the provisions are drafted? The answer must be affirmative: in my view the presentation of legal texts should depend largely on their function. A national civil code needs to be presented in a different way from a set of rules the aim of which is to help improve the existing *acquis*, or to inspire legislators and courts across Europe or to play a role in legal science and teaching.

It seems to me that this insight has not been sufficiently taken into account in the drafting of the CFR. The authors regard the fact that they were able to distil common rules as evidence of how much national private laws may be regarded as 'regional manifestations of an overall common European legacy'.[41] I am also convinced that, in the field of private law, European Member States have a lot in common. But it seems wrong to conclude this merely from being able to draft common rules. Whether jurisdictions resemble one another becomes clear only if all relevant factors are taken into consideration. It may be more important to find uniformity in the use of similar arguments[42] than in common rules or case decisions: a common *text* will necessarily be interpreted in different ways in different countries.

This pleads for a differentiated way of representing European private law, depending on whether its function is to create binding rules, offer a source of inspiration or form the first step towards the creation of an optional contract code.[43]

---

[39]   Cf. Twining, W. and D.R. Miers (1999), *How To Do Things With Rules*, 4th edn, Cambridge: CUP.
[40]   Morgan and Yeung (2007), 305.
[41]   *DCFR* (2008), 6.
[42]   See e.g. Smits, J.M. (2008), 'The German Schuldrechtsmodernisierung and the New Dutch Civil Code: a Study in Parallel', in: O. Remien (ed.), *Schuldrechtsmodernisierung und Europäisches Vertragsrecht*, Tübingen: Mohr Siebeck, 117ff.
[43]   Micklitz, H.-W. (2008), *The Visible Hand of European Regulatory Private Law: The Transformation of European Private Law from Autonomy to Functionalism in Competition and Regulation*, EUI Working Paper 2008/14.

When it comes to revising the existing *acquis*, the right approach is to build directly upon the existing directives, making them more coherent and adding some concrete definitions.[44] This part of the European private law system will resemble national provisions the most. But in the absence of a single European private law society in which there is a common understanding of the meaning of specific provisions, it is too early to draft provisions in other areas of private law. There, Europeanisation should start with the emergence of a common European legal tradition, for which teaching and legal scholarship are far more important than the drafting of specific rules. Such teaching and scholarship should indeed focus on finding common *arguments* in European jurisdictions, thus allowing for a competition of legal ideas.[45] Finally, when creating an optional contract code yet a third perspective is to be adopted. As such codes will have to compete with national jurisdictions, their provisions should certainly not be common denominators of existing national legal systems; instead, they should contain the rules that make this code a good competitor on the market of legal rules. The DCFR, with its many open-ended provisions and unclear policy choices,[46] is clearly not such a competitor. Again, it is the function of the rules in question that decides how they should be drafted.

7. THE WAY FORWARD: SUGGESTIONS FOR IMPROVEMENT

The above discussion of the DCFR is a critical one. Its main point is that it is wrong to draft rules for the CFR in the way we are familiar with at the national level, as if these are rules to be applied in a national legal community. Challenging the regulatory monopoly of states must mean something for the structure and substance of the European rules being put into place. The way forward should therefore consist of a differentiated approach: it depends on the function of the rules in question (revision of the *acquis*, offering a source of inspiration or creating an optional code) and how they should be presented.

---

[44]   With much less generalisation of the existing rules than advocated by the *acquis* group: cf. Jansen and Zimmermann (2007), 1120 ff.

[45]   Cf. Wilhelmsson, T. (2002), 'The Legal, the Cultural and the Political: Conclusions from Different Perspectives on Harmonisation of European Contract Law', *European Business Law Review* 551 and Smits, J.M. (1998), 'A European Private Law as a Mixed Legal System', 5 *Maastricht Journal of European and Comparative Law* 328.

[46]   See now also Eidenmüller, H., F. Faust, H.C. Grigoleit, N. Jansen, G. Wagner and R. Zimmermann (2008), 'Der Gemeinsame Referenzrahmen für das Europäische Privatrecht', 63 *JuristenZeitung* 529.

Concrete suggestions for the improvement of the DCFR follow directly from this functional approach. If we take the present text as a starting point, the following points should be taken into account in adapting it to the real 'toolbox' envisaged by the European Commission:

- the DCFR should make clear how its provisions relate to the existing *acquis*. As already indicated in section 4, the Commission aims primarily at a revision of the existing directives. This calls for an articulate analysis of this *acquis*: the DCFR should make abundantly clear which provisions are in line with it and which are not. If provisions of existing directives are not part of the DCFR, it should explain extensively why this is the case.
- in so far as the provisions of the DCFR do not relate to the existing *acquis*, they should be presented in a more discursive way. Any instrument for scholarship and teaching should be presented as a source of legal ideas, meaning that various options are put forward. In other words: an academic CFR should not make any choices itself, but should offer an inventory of the various solutions. The publication of the present text – without any comments on how choices were made – is useless and can only be seen as an attempt to monopolise the debate.
- if the present DCFR is also to serve as a draft for an optional contract code, it should explain which provisions will be part of such a code. Moreover, it should indicate what criterion is used to select these rules (thus explaining why the optional code is a good competitor compared to national jurisdictions).

6. The empirical missing links in the Draft Common Frame of Reference*

Fernando Gomez

1. INTRODUCTION

The Principles, Definitions and Model Rules of European Private Law, known as the Draft Common Frame of Reference ('DCFR')[1] constitute the impressive output of an important academic and legal endeavour in the field of private law and, in particular, of contract law,[2] in the European context. Although largely academic in inspiration and spirit, and almost entirely in manufacture, the DCFR is not the typical academic product: it is not a commentary, treatise, collection of essays or papers devoted to European contract law or to contract law generally. It is a body of proposed model rules, accompanied[3] by a set of standard terms, or definitions, to facilitate comprehension, use and application, which may eventually govern real-world behaviour of individuals or firms or, at least, influence real-world law-makers in the drafting of rules which will directly govern the behaviour of economic agents in society.

Law, understood as the set of social institutions ruling behaviour in organised and purposeful ways, and not as an academic discipline or field for intellectual scrutiny, and private law in particular, are essentially practical or

* I am grateful to participants at a workshop on the DCFR at the European University Institute for helpful discussions of the ideas reflected in the chapter, to the Spanish Ministry of Innovation and Science for financial support, under grants SEJ2007-60503 and SEJ2006-10041, and to Marian Gili for excellent research assistantship.

[1] All references will be made to the Interim Outline Edition of the DCFR, published by Sellier, Munich (2008).

[2] Although the DFCR covers ground beyond contract law, and emphatically defends the choice of broad coverage (see pp. 19 ff. of the Introduction to the DCFR), the fact is that both quantitatively and qualitatively the bulk of the DCFR is contract law, and thus I will essentially devote my observations to contract law in the DCFR.

[3] The model rules and the definitions should be considered inextricably linked, according to the drafters of the DCFR.

pragmatic in nature. Law tries to regulate the behaviour of the agents under its rule so as to be conducive to a recognisable social goal – in the best scenario, the promotion of social welfare in the relevant society. Thus, how the actual addressees of proposed legal rules respond to them is a crucial element of the whole enterprise.

This makes empirical knowledge in the relevant field particularly valuable to inform the design, drafting and implementation of rules which, immediately or through the intermediation of other bodies or rules, pursue the regulation of behaviour in society. The preceding statement does not imply that theoretical knowledge in its various forms – normative as to the desirable goals, histori-cal as to the origin of existing arrangements, analytical in terms of how to craft the best framework to elucidate real-world behaviour, and so forth – plays no role in the exercise. On the contrary, without that theoretical knowledge it is difficult not only to understand, but also to improve and operate social institu-tions such as the legal system. Although the theoretical background upon which the understanding of contracting behaviour and contract law that prevails throughout the DCFR could raise some criticism, I will not pursue the issue here.[4] Given the practical purpose of the legal enterprise, and that, conse-quently, our knowledge about how the real world in which the legal system is to be part, and how the agents are expected to interact with it seems of partic-ular relevance, I will concentrate on the level and kind of empirical knowledge involved in the DCFR process.

According to the words of the drafters themselves, the DCFR is mainly the product of comparative studies of EU law and the laws of the Member States.[5] These studies, as long as they are not – and I take them, or at any rate I assume them, not to be – mere reflection of the law in the books, but of how the law in the Member States is currently applied to regulate behaviour of individuals and firms, constitute empirical knowledge or evidence. In a broad – and, I believe, correct – sense, empirical knowledge covers the information concern-ing the outside world and is based upon observation, experience or experiment carried on in an organised, purposeful way.[6]

Part of this collection of empirical knowledge is what one could call – at least under the prevalent criteria, or fashion, if one prefers, in the social sciences – the most sophisticated or fancy one, contained in studies using large

---

     4   I have already raised some criticisms concerning the lack of a clear behav-ioural starting point in the DCFR process: see Fernando Gomez, 'The Harmonization of Contract Law in Europe: A Law and Economics Perspective', 4 *European Review of Contract Law* (2008) 89.
     5   See p. 12 of the Introduction to the DCFR.
     6   See Lee Epstein and Gary King, 'The Rules of Inference', 69 *U. Chi. L. Rev.* (2002), 2.

amounts of data and subject to state-of-the-art statistical analyses. But this kind of evidence – quantitative and statistical – though part of our empirical knowledge about a given field, does not exhaust the available empirical evidence. Also qualitative studies based on organised and informed observation, if adequately performed, usefully increase our empirical knowledge of the set of real world phenomena that may be of interest. Thus, comparative legal analyses can provide us with extremely helpful data about what legal rules are actually governing behaviour and the problems that their application encounters, thus allowing those in possession of such knowledge, under certain conditions, to draw inferences for future rules and future behaviour.

It is clear, though, that legal-comparative analyses of EU law and of the law of the Member States, however accurate, exhaustive and thoughtful they may be, do not exhaust the entire repository of empirical knowledge at our disposal concerning contract law, and contracting behaviour more generally. It is indeed the portion that is more quantitative in spirit, and makes use of the standard techniques of statistical analysis, the one that is outside the scope of the traditional legal-comparative analysis, which, in turn, lies at the core of the DCFR. Accordingly, one could conclude that the empirical knowledge upon which the DCFR is based, and without any positive nor pejorative connotations, is the 'traditional' one – inside legal academia – based upon the qualitative observation by legal experts of what rules are in place in a given jurisdiction, and what are the successes and failures of the actual rules applied. The less traditional and more modern – again, no praise or blame attached – knowledge about contracting and contract law, based upon quantitative and statistical analyses, has been essentially overlooked by the DCFR. The result of this oversight is that the proposed rules in the DCFR may be, at least in certain areas covered by its scope, flawed by the absence of adequate empirical support of the hypothesis or conjectures about the expected behaviour of the agents subject to the rules and the likely effects of these on the future situation of individuals and firms. It may be true that the amount of quantitative empirical literature statistically testing a precise hypothesis about content of general rules in contract law is still relatively scarce,[7] but there is a large body of quantitative evidence that sheds light on contracting behaviour – in the broad but also in the narrow sense: behaviour subject to contract law rules – and the likely effects on the reactions of individuals and firms of rules such as those proposed in one or the other Book of the DCFR.[8]

---

[7]   This is the claim by Russell Korobkin, 'Empirical Scholarship in Contract Law: Possibilities and Pitfalls', *U. Ill. L. Rev.* (2002) 1036.

[8]   See, on this claim in the broader perspective, ibid., at 1035–1036; George Geis, 'Automating Contract Law', 83 *N. Y. U. L. Rev.* (2008) 452.

The DCFR contains model rules for both B2B and B2C transactions. I will explore my claim in two areas that are particularly relevant for one and the other kind of transactions. In section 2 I will present how the existing knowledge concerning consumer behaviour in markets does not seem to have informed the model rules on consumer protection and the role of consumers in contracting. In section 3 I will present how the quantitative evidence on long-term contracts in distribution chains has not been duly considered in Book IV, Part E, dealing with commercial agency, franchising and distributorship, a central area of B2B contractual relationships. Finally, section 4 briefly draws some implications for the future steps in the process of building European contract law.

2.   THE EMPIRICAL EVIDENCE CONCERNING CONSUMER BEHAVIOUR IN CONSUMER TRANSACTIONS

In the past quarter of a century psychologists and economists have been systematically exploring how human beings in actual situations depart in their actions and choices from the requirements of rational calculation, will-power and self-interest which characterise a rational-based approach to understanding human behaviour. Given the typically high – though not always insurmountable – obstacles to observing real-world behaviour in many circumstances by a sufficient number of individuals similarly situated, these studies have heavily relied on experimental methodologies. Thus, most of this literature is grounded on the statistical analysis of data concerning actual behaviour by individuals in very diverse sets of circumstances through the use of experiments designed by researchers to confirm or refute a given hypothesis about human behaviour. A non-trivial part of this knowledge can be relevant for understanding how individuals, essentially consumers, behave in a wide variety of circumstances similar to those that they may encounter in consumer markets.[9]

In laboratory settings it has been well documented that some phenomena[10] repeatedly appear in observed individual behaviour. People seem to show

---

[9]   See, for a useful survey of this literature and of its applications to the law – also beyond consumer and contract law – Colin Camerer and Eric Talley, 'Experimental Study of the Law', in A. M. Polinsky and S. Shavell, *Handbook of Law and Economics*, Vol. II, North Holland, Amsterdam (2007), p. 1619.

[10]   See, among many surveys helpful for legal audiences, Cass Sunstein (ed.), *Behavioral Law and Economics*, Cambridge University Press, Cambridge (2000); Christine Jolls and Cass Sunstein, 'Debiasing through Law', 35 *Journal of Legal Studies* (2006) 199.

bounded rationality, that is, limited capacity to acquire and process information, as revealed by the use of cognitive heuristics that can lead to errors in judgement and decision-making. For instance, the hindsight heuristic – which attaches over-dimensioned likelihoods to events that have actually occurred with respect to the true or actual likelihood – may lead to decisions *ex post facto* that do not correspond with the best course before the events happened. Or the availability heuristic, which relies excessively on easily available data or information, thus leading to reactions that follow too closely, and may be mistakenly, the limited amounts of information that are not hard to recall with immediacy, particularly if it has been widely publicised or the object of media attention. The representative heuristic – excessive representativeness of small samples – may lead people to judge events and courses of action too quickly based on how those events externally resemble a typical or representative example within the category we are operating. Agents have also been consistently shown to behave with clear over-optimism when facing less than certain events, that is, overtly to underestimate probabilities of bad outcomes affecting them.

Psychologists and economists have also uncovered and experimentally confirmed other important expressions of bounded rationality – as departure from pure or perfect rationality is commonly labelled. Individuals have been shown to suffer from inconsistencies in the valuation of outcomes that are time related, due to hyperbolic discounting – too little weight is attached to future and uncertain outcomes in decisions made presently, and excessive weight to immediate or present outcomes. Other sources of departure in observed behavioural responses from the axioms of expected utility in the neoclassical sense have been identified: individuals tend to show loss aversion, that is, they give special weight and importance to what is presented to them, or is perceived by them to be losses with respect to a given benchmark, than the importance they attach to missed opportunities to gain measured against the same baseline. Moreover, an endowment effect – valuation of an asset not as it really is, but depending on the set of entitlements owned by the agent over the asset – implies that individuals would ask higher amounts to depart from something they consider their own, than to acquire the same thing from someone else. And a *status quo* bias – reticence to alter the existing state of the world due to attaching some unidentified intrinsic value to it – makes existing situations particularly sticky and likely to persist, even if agents can introduce changes at low cost.

These findings should not lead us to think that all individuals, in all situations, are subject to these shortcomings or departures from rational behaviour. Even if we disregard individuals integrated in large organisations that have incentives to overcome such biases, such as firms,[11] it would be unfounded to

---

[11]   See Chip Heath, Richard Larrick, and Joshua Klayman, 'Cognitive Repairs:

assume that every consumer in all potential consumer markets will be afflicted by those observed regularities of 'irrational' behaviour.

The first reason lies in the fact that it has been well documented that the presence and incidence of those cognitive and behavioural biases are not identical between individuals. Cognitive abilities, education, experience, and context that may have some debiasing properties do play a role, even if they do not make those mistakes or departures from rationality disappear completely.[12]

Moreover, even if one takes the magnitude and relevance of the experimental findings relative to those behavioural biases for granted, as I do, an assumption of consumer misperception and mistake does not hold universally, due to problems in generalising the findings of experimental psychology and experimental economics: it is one thing to identify some bias in a laboratory setting, even repeatedly, but a very different one to test the statistical significance of such bias on real-world markets using rigorous empirical techniques.[13] And even if the empirical tests do not confirm that economic agents (consumers, for instance) behave rationally, this by itself is not an empirical confirmation as such of the presence and magnitude of the behavioural biases, given that the data may be influenced by some other unobserved variable.

Several empirical studies have tested implications of bounded rationality models of consumer behaviour in different settings, and have not found support for the hypothesis based on the pervasive presence of behavioural biases in consumer markets.[14] In credit card markets, studies have tested (i) evidence that high-borrowing consumers pay higher interest rates, once attracted by low introductory teaser rates;[15] (ii) the true causal factors behind

---

How Organizational Practices Can Compensate for Individual Shortcomings', 20 *Research in Organizational Behavior* (1998) 1; Jeffrey Rachlinski, 'The Uncertain Psychological Case for Paternalism', 97 *Northwestern U. L. Rev.* (2003) 1214.

    [12]   See for a summary of this evidence Jeffrey Rachlinski, 'Cognitive Errors, Individual Differences, and Paternalism', 73 *U. Chi. L. Rev.* (2006) 216.

    [13]   The issue of the general validity of the findings in the laboratory for the real world phenomena that one is trying to analyse is not exclusive of experimental psychology or experimental economics; also the natural sciences encounter this epistemological matter. It is true, however, that due to the nature of the underlying subject matter – human behaviour and choice – one is particularly aware of the need to justify why the environment in the laboratory is sufficiently similar to the outside world to provide a basis to make inferences about the latter based on the former: see Richard Posner, *Frontiers of Legal Theory*, Harvard University Press, Cambridge, Mass., London (2001), p. 263.

    [14]   A good summary of such studies is in Joshua Wright, 'Behavioral Law and Economics, Paternalism and Consumer Contracts: An Empirical Perspective', *New York University Journal of Law & Liberty* (2007) 470.

    [15]   See Tom Brown and Lacey Plache, 'Paying with Plastic: Maybe Not so Crazy', 73 *U. Chi. L. Rev.* (2006) 77, finding no evidence of hyperbolic discounting.

the correlation between credit card debt and filings for personal bankruptcy;[16] (iii) the factors explaining the 'Borrow High Lend Low' puzzle.[17] Also with respect to allocation of shelf space in supermarkets, it has been tested whether this is a result of manipulation by retailers of cognitive biases afflicting consumers, or a response to manufacturer margins for different lines of products.[18] Choice of calling plans when different pricing options are introduced has also been investigated.[19]

There are on the other hand studies showing how behaviour in a given consumer market supports the presence of a certain behavioural bias as an important factor behind observed patterns. These include evidence with respect to: (i) credit card markets and hyperbolic discounting;[20] (ii) fitness club markets and time-inconsistent preferences with unsophisticated consumers who are not aware of their own time inconsistency;[21] (iii) internet purchases of computer equipment using price search engines and consumer myopia concerning hidden terms and attributes.[22]

---

[16]　See Todd Zywicki, *Bankruptcy and Personal Responsibility: Bankruptcy Law and Policy in the Twenty-First Century*, Yale University Press, New Haven, Conn. (2007).

[17]　The puzzle refers to the observation that many people borrow on their credit cards – at high interest rate – while holding positive balances on their accounts, yielding no or little interest: David Gross and Nicholas Souleles, 'Do Liquidity Constraints and Interest Rates Matter for Consumer Behavior? Evidence from Credit Card Data', 117 *Quarterly Journal of Economics* (2002) 149; Nadia Massoud, Anthony Saunders, and Barry Scholnick, 'Who Makes Credit Card Mistakes?' University of Alberta and NYU Working Paper (2006), available at www.philadelphiafed.org/econ/conf/consumer creditandpayments2007/papers/Scholnick_Who_Makes_Credit_Card_Mistakes.pdf, find that traditional demographic (age, educational level, country of origin if immigrant) and economic variables (income) seem to be the major factors explaining the puzzle, and not so much the various cognitive and behavioural biases that afflict human choice.

[18]　See Benjamin Klein and Joshua Wright, 'The Economics of Slotting Contracts', 50 *Journal of Law and Economics* (2007) 421.

[19]　See Eugenio Miravete, 'Choosing the Wrong Calling Plan? Ignorance and Learning', 93 *American Economic Review* (2003) 297.

[20]　See David Gross and Nicholas Souleles, 'Do Liquidity Constraints and Interest Rates Matter for Consumer Behavior? Evidence from Credit Card Data', 117 *Quarterly Journal of Economics* (2002) 149; Haiyan Shui and Lawrence Ausubel, 'Time Inconsistency in the Credit Card Market', Working Paper, University of Maryland (2004); Stephan Meier and Charles Sprenger, 'Impatience and Credit Behavior: Evidence from a Field Experiment', Working Paper, Federal Reserve Bank of Boston (2006).

[21]　See Stefano Della Vigna and Ulrike Malmendier, 'Paying not to Go to the Gym', 96 *American Economic Review* (2006) 694.

[22]　See Glenn Ellison and Sara Ellison, 'Search, Obfuscation, and Price Elasticities on the Internet', MIT Department of Economics Working Paper 04-27 (2004), available at http://ssrn.com/abstract=564742.

The sensible response to this apparently conflicting evidence is not to weigh it in a quantitative fashion, but to conclude, tentatively, that the evidence is still inconclusive regarding the real world impact in consumer markets of many of the behavioural biases present in laboratory settings. Arguably, it should lead us to consider that there is no single empirically satisfactory answer for the entire range of biases and for the entire set of circumstances and markets in which consumers may exhibit those biases.

There is an additional factor, however, that seems important for the actual behaviour of consumers in real world markets – and thus for the design of the legal rules governing such markets – even if one assumes the universal presence of cognitive and behavioural biases in consumers. That factor is learning. People may learn from prior mistakes, at least when they possess good feedback mechanisms that allow them to become aware of the consequences of mistakes, and induce them to avoid the same errors in later rounds of trade or future market interactions. Given that their own pockets – sometimes, their own life and limb – are at stake, the incentives to draw lessons from past mistakes and to improve performance in later transactions are powerful and often effective.[23] The likelihood that learning takes place and is effective in eliminating the negative consequences of bounded rationality is greater the more standardised the product or service (thus allowing learning not only from one's own past experience, but also from that of other consumers) and the higher the routine nature of the transaction. Learning by consumers is important, not just in empirical studies of behavioural biases in consumer markets, but also for their normative consequences: if learning is expected, the benefits of a regulatory or legal intervention in the relevant market are lower for a given initial level of biased behaviour among consumers. Although conceptually different from learning, other kinds of consumer reactions to biases, such as developing personal rules to guide behaviour precisely to counteract the former, may also lead to results that resemble those of learning.[24]

There is substantial empirical evidence showing that consumers learn from mistakes and improve their behaviour in a wide range of consumer markets:

---

[23]   See Richard Epstein, 'Behavioral Economics: Human Errors and Market Corrections', 73 *U. Chi.. L. Rev.* (2006) 111; Richard Epstein, 'The Neoclassical Economics of Consumer Contracts' 93 *Minnesota L. Rev.* (2008) 803.

[24]   See Roland Benabou and Jean Tirole, 'Willpower and Personal Rules', 112 *Journal of Political Economy* (2004) 848; Dilip Soman and Amar Cheema, 'When Goals are Counterproductive: The Effects of Violation of a Behavioral Goal on Subsequent Performance', 31 *Journal of Consumer Research* (2004) 52.

credit card markets,[25] video rental markets,[26] and telephone markets,[27] for instance. Still, of course, learning may take time and may be costly, so consumer learning is not a magic formula that always restores markets to the level of functioning which full rationality and full information would characterise. In fact, it is clear that firms can interfere with learning processes of consumers through various means, do so when this is in their interest, and that the market environment can sustain such shrouding behaviour by firms. For instance, firms can hide or make less accessible the elements of the transaction on which consumers are more easily misled; they can create artificial non-standardisation and product multi-dimensionality to retard and increase learning costs; they can engage in bundling to discourage learning and comparison shopping; they can engage in loss-leader tactics. Even in a non-bounded rationality environment firms may engage in some of these tactics to increase consumer search costs, but behavioural biases and the possibility of learning may provide them with additional reasons for such tactics.[28]

In sum, consumer learning does not eliminate the relevance of behavioural biases for consumer markets, but may recommend a more parsimonious attitude in assessing their magnitude and effects, while also pointing to the importance, for a full understanding of real world consumer markets, of the context and conditions of the market required to make consumer learning possible or to make firm tactics opposing learning feasible.

Cumulatively, the above issues and especially the empirical evidence reviewed suggest it would not be wise – at least at this moment in time – to make the model of consumer behaviour arising from the experimental literature

---

[25] See Sumit Agarwal, Souphala Chomsisengphet, Chunlin Liu, and Nicholas Souleles, 'Do Consumers Choose the Right Credit Contracts?', Working Paper, Federal Reserve Bank of Chicago (2006), available at http://ssrn.com/abstract=943524; Sumit Agarwal, John Driscoll, Xavier Gabaix, David Laibson, 'Learning in the Credit Card Market', National Bureau of Economic Research Working Paper (2008), available at http://ssrn.com/abstract=1091623.

[26] See Peter Fishman and Devin Pope, 'The Long-Run Effects of Penalizing Customers: Evidence from the Video-Rental Market', University of California at Berkeley Department of Economics Working Paper (2007) available at www.econ.berkeley.edu/users/webfac/koszegi/e218_f07/Fishman_Job_Market_Paper.pdf.

[27] See Eugenio Miravete, 'Choosing the Wrong Calling Plan? Ignorance and Learning', 93 *American Economic Review* (2003) 297.

[28] See, for additional factors why learning by consumers may not be feasible substantially to make up for initial consumer mistakes, and why sellers do not have incentives to provide learning opportunities or even to correct the mistakes by their actions, Oren Bar-Gill, 'Informing Consumers About Themselves', Law & Economics Research Paper Series, New York University School of Law, NYU Center for Law and Economics, WP no. 07-44, available at http://ssrn.com/abstract=1056381, p. 9.

in behavioural psychology, behavioural economics, and behavioural law and economics the cornerstone of consumer policy and rules in consumer law and contract law dealing with B2C transactions. Thus, one should not criticise the DCFR for failing to embrace the behavioural account of consumer choice and decision-making as the starting point for regulation of consumer transactions, or for not rewriting consumer law and contract law in that light.

But cautious treatment is different from total disregard. Policy-making – and certainly the DCFR is making policy in consumer and other markets – cannot turn its back on evidence from the outside world that policy measures are trying to influence in pursuit of one or other normative goal. This implies that the experimental literature, together with the rest of the empirical evidence – based on data on real-world contracting behaviour – is not irrelevant for the design of the optimal legal toolkit, in the present European context, for 21st century consumer markets. Policy-makers ignore empirical evidence at their peril, and this shortcoming can be detected in the approach taken by the DCFR.

The model rules could have been better tailored to what seem to be the major informational and behavioural obstacles to the adequate functioning of consumer markets (and those that are more resistant to improvement as an effect of improved competition or available information on products and services) that empirical studies have uncovered: consumer misperception of non-salient features and elements of the transaction as a whole (and not just of the product or service, or of the firm providing them); consumer misevaluation of patterns of future use or utility from the product due to hyperbolic discounting of the future, over-optimism or self-serving biases; consumer misperception of features that are probabilistic in their outcomes, especially where these lie far ahead in the future (which suggests a need for greater caution with long-term B2C contracts than with spot transactions); the importance of obstacles (such as product differentiation, bundling and other 'de-standardising' strategies) preventing the operation of instruments (such as learning from past experience, comparison shopping, and seller's branding and reputation) which have 'debiasing' or equivalent effects for consumers.

When one looks at model rules proposed in the DCFR to deal with the imbalance of information between contracting parties, one still clearly perceives an emphasis on physical and other attributes of the product or service, identity of the seller or provider, contract terms, and legal means of redress: Articles II.-3: 102 (2) and II.-3: 103 DCFR. It is true that in this field the DCFR also contains some general formulations, such as 'information that the other person can reasonably expect' in Article II.-3: 101, or 'material information as the average consumer needs in a given context to take an informed decision on whether to conclude a contract' in Article II.-3: 102 (1), or 'all the relevant information' in Article II.-3: 102 (2). But once again these are either implicitly or explicitly centred on attributes of the product or service, or do not realise that part of the problem lies in the fact that consumers – and human beings more generally – under certain conditions, which are the ones more troublesome for the functioning of consumer markets, may need a little help, in terms of specific information, learning or other tools, to make them actually reasonable and rational.

One can contrast this approach in the DCFR with recent proposals by empirically informed scholars who, despite varying degrees of sympathy for the actual relevance for real-world markets of experimental findings, agree that disclosure rules should be crafted to tackle consumer biases concerning their own uses of goods and services, and thus including, when feasible, information on actual average features of use,[29] and even, where this is insufficient, past information on individual use by that same consumer.[30] For instance, the efficiency of the personal credit market could be improved, it is suggested, by encouraging or even mandating more personalised information (already in the possession of lenders) which may improve the way in which consumers make credit choices.[31]

Similarly, a closer look at the empirical evidence could have saved the model rules proposed in the DCFR from the time and trouble of trying to solve

---

[29]   See Alan Schwartz, 'How Much Irrationality Does the Market Permit?', 37 *Journal of Legal Studies* (2008) 131; Oren Bar-Gill, 'Informing Consumers About Themselves', Law & Economics Research Paper Series, New York University School of Law, NYU Center for Law and Economics, WP no. 07-44, available at http://ssrn.com/abstract=1056381, p. 53; Oren Bar-Gill, 'The Behavioral Economics of Consumer Contracts', 93 *Minnesota L. Rev.* (2008) 797.

[30]   See Oren Bar-Gill, 'Informing Consumers About Themselves', Law & Economics Research Paper Series, New York University School of Law, NYU Center for Law and Economics, WP no. 07-44, available at http://ssrn.com/abstract=1056381, p. 57. It is true, however, that the DCFR contains general rules of contract law and it is not specific regulation of a given consumer market, the realm in which this kind of individualised information disclosure could be more adequately imposed eventually: Christine Jolls and Cass Sunstein, 'Debiasing through Law', 35 *Journal of Legal Studies* (2006) 209.

[31]   For instance, the recent Directive 2008/48/EC (OJ L133, 22.5.2008, pp. 66–92), on credit agreements for consumers does not require such kind of information on average use – e.g. of credit card borrowing, of penalties incurred for late payment, and so forth – much less on past use by the individual consumer affected. In the US, the Bankruptcy Abuse Prevention and Consumer Protection Act of 2005 forces lenders personally to inform consumers how much increased interest they would pay and how much longer would it take to repay the debt if they chose the minimum monthly payment. It is true, however, that the 2008 Directive improves upon Directive 87/102/EEC (the old consumer credit Directive) on other features that empirical literature has highlighted, such as interest payable for late payments or penalties for default.

irresoluble problems and, perhaps, not so relevant problems in the field of consumer contracting.

The DCFR still places emphasis on the opportunity of the contracting party (not only the consumer, but the issue of standard form contracting and e-transactions may be considered more important in the consumer context) to be informed and to read the contract terms that will govern the transaction as a result of the binding force of the agreed contract. Article II.-3:105, on formation of contract by electronic means, imposes upon businesses the duty to supply to the other party, before that party consents to an offer or makes an offer, the contract terms in text form. In turn, Article II.-9:103, on terms not individually negotiated, makes those terms enforceable against the non-drafting party (the consumer, always, but also a business party) if the latter party was aware of them, or if the drafter took steps to draw attention to the contract terms before or when the contract was concluded.

There is evidence of various kinds that consumers, in e-transactions and in other forms of contracting relying on standard terms, do not commonly read contract terms before entering into the contract, do not have the capacity or the willingness to read and understand the implications of standard contract terms, and do not value the opportunity to read the terms prior to contract, nor do they typically value the more advantageous contract terms they may hypothetically be able to find if they read standard contract terms in advance and shop around for more favourable ones.[32] Moreover, there is evidence that the opportunity

---

[32]   See, for a summary of evidence of consumers not reading the terms, Robert Hillman and Jeffrey Rachlinski, 'Standard-Form Contracting in the Electronic Age', 77 *N. Y. U. L. Rev.* (2002) 429; Robert Hillman, 'Online Boilerplate: Would Mandatory Web Site Disclosure of e-Standard Terms Backfire?', in O. Ben-Shahar (ed.), *Boilerplate. The Foundation of Market Contracts*, Cambridge University Press, Cambridge (2007), p. 83. For an excellent discussion of the factors that make reading the standard terms an unattractive – and hopeless – course of action for consumers see Omri Ben-Shahar, 'The Myth of the Opportunity to Read in Contract Law', University of Chicago Law School, John M. Olin Law & Economics Working Paper No. 415 (2008), available at http://ssrn.com/abstract=1162922, p. 7.

On the potential valuation by consumers of the opportunity to read and of favourable terms in the set of standard terms, using a large sample of real-world contracts (End User Licence Agreements in online transactions on software products), it has been found that the absence of presumptively unfavourable – for the consumer, that is, pro-seller – choice of law and choice of forum clauses does not affect the price consumers pay for the goods: Florencia Marotta-Wurgler, '"Unfair" Dispute Resolution Clauses: Much Ado About Nothing?', in O. Ben-Shahar (ed.), *Boilerplate. The Foundation of Market Contracts*, Cambridge University Press, Cambridge (2007), p. 45. Additionally, this study does not reveal any statistically significant difference between consumers and business buyers of the same software goods. Using the same database of online software contracts, and after constructing a comprehensive index of the 'quality' in

to read standard terms before signing the contract does not change the substantive content of the contract terms as regards the rights and obligations of consumers. An empirical analysis of more than 500 types of contracts, in the context of online software transactions, found that standard terms that were not made available to the consumer prior to the transaction but were sent together with the product to the consumer after the contract was binding,[33] were no worse, in terms of consumer friendliness across all dimensions of the transaction, than standard terms made available to consumers prior to the purchase decision.[34] Rather the size of the firm and the number of years the seller has been in operation seem to be the main drivers for the quality of standard terms.[35]

---

terms of consumer friendliness of the set of standard terms (covering aspects as the acceptance of the licence, the scope of the licence, the transfer of the licence, warranties and warranty disclaimers, limitations of liabilities, maintenance and support, and conflict resolution) it has been found that there is no evidence that consumers of a given type of product are willing to pay higher prices in order to get more favourable contract terms of a standard nature: Florencia Marotta-Wurgler, 'Competition and Quality of Standard Form Contracts: An Empirical Analysis of Software License Agreements', New York University School of Law, Law and Economics Research Paper Series, Working Paper No. 05-11 (2005), p. 23 (available at http://ssrn.com/abstract=799274 (forthcoming in the *Journal of Empirical Legal Studies* (2008)). As with the study previously cited on dispute resolution clauses, a third related study (Florencia Marotta-Wurgler, 'Are "Pay Now, Terms Later" Contracts Worse for Buyers? Evidence from Software License Agreements', New York University School of Law, Law and Economics Research Paper Series, Working Paper No. 05-10 (2005), p. 23 (available at http://ssrn.com/abstract=799282 (forthcoming in the *Journal of Legal Studies* (2008)) shows no perceptible difference in the overall buyer-friendliness of the terms between consumer and business buyers, nor between products typically oriented to consumers and more business-like types of products.

[33] Two relevant decisions by the Federal US Court of Appeals, 7th Circuit (*ProCD v. Zeidenberg* 86 F.3d 1447 (7th Cir. 1996), and *Hill v. Gateway 2000 Inc.*, 105 F.3d 1147 (7th Cir. 1997)) confirmed the validity and binding effect of the terms in these transactions, commonly known as 'Pay Now, Terms Later', or rolling contracts.

[34] See Florencia Marotta-Wurgler, 'Are "Pay Now, Terms Later" Contracts Worse for Buyers? Evidence from Software License Agreements', New York University School of Law, Law and Economics Research Paper Series, Working Paper No. 05-10 (2005), p. 21 (available at http://ssrn.com/abstract=799282 (forthcoming in the *Journal of Legal Studies* (2008)).

[35] See ibid. The market structure (whether there is less or more competition in the relevant product market does not seem to play a role either in the forces leading to more or less consumer-friendliness of the standard terms: Florencia Marotta-Wurgler, 'Competition and Quality of Standard Form Contracts: An Empirical Analysis of Software License Agreements', New York University School of Law, Law and Economics Research Paper Series, Working Paper No. 05-11 (2005), p. 29 (available at http://ssrn.com/abstract=799274 (forthcoming in the *Journal of Empirical Legal Studies* (2008)).

So, available empirical evidence does not clearly show that imposing duties to disclose standard contract terms and provide consumers with opportunities to read them, as proposed in the model rules of the DCFR, actually improves the material situation of consumers, in terms of the welfare they obtain from the transaction.[36]

3.   EMPIRICAL EVIDENCE ON LONG-TERM DISTRIBUTION CONTRACTS

The DCFR's relative disregard for empirical evidence on contracting and contract law in the real world (that is, in addition to the legal-comparative study of EU and Member States' law) extends beyond the realm of consumer behaviour and contracting. With regard to distribution contracts, understood in the economic sense, and so including commercial agency, franchising, and distributorship contracts, there are also empirical deficits in the DCFR.

Economic theory[37] has for some time cogently argued as the crucial aspect of long-term distribution contracts their essentially incomplete nature, while also highlighting the primary relevance of breaches of contractual duties by the distributor that are unverifiable to an outside adjudicator such as a court or arbitrator. The open-ended character of the relationship and the disciplining force of termination by the principal give these considerations remarkable salience. The preservation of the conditions for termination at will in long-term distribution contracts that is substantially unconstrained by legal requirements concerning good cause, or the imposition of compensation *ex post* thus seem, from an economic perspective, important with regard to an efficient legal regime in this area of contracting for B2B transactions.

---

[36]   Some even argue that concentrating effort on disclosure duties may actually be harmful for consumers, if these 'procedural' sorts of protections associated with the opportunity to read are negatively correlated with the willingness of courts to strike down individual clauses – and not the entire set of standard terms – for substantive reasons, or adopt more effective means to prevent those clauses that are actually detrimental to consumer welfare: Robert Hillman, 'Online Boilerplate: Would Mandatory Web Site Disclosure of e-Standard Terms Backfire?', in O. Ben-Shahar (ed.), *Boilerplate. The Foundation of Market Contracts*, Cambridge University Press, Cambridge (2007), p. 89; Omri Ben-Shahar, 'The Myth of the Opportunity to Read in Contract Law', University of Chicago Law School, John M. Olin Law & Economics Working Paper No. 415 (2008), available at http://ssrn.com/abstract=1162922, p. 25.

[37]   George Mathewson and Ralph Winter, 'The Economics of Franchise Contracts', 28 *Journal of Law & Economics* (1985) 503; Benjamin Klein, 'The Economics of Franchise Contracts', 2 *Journal of Corporate Finance* (1995) 9.

This view seems to be supported by available empirical evidence concerning effects on the behaviour of contracting parties of the legal rules that restrict or impose legal conditions to terminate the contract on the initiative of the principal or manufacturer.[38] This evidence refers to franchising,[39] but there does not seem to be a powerful reason to doubt that its main findings would not be applicable to other contractual arrangements in distribution chains which share issues of controlling opportunism by distributors (and, as we will see in a moment, also by manufacturers).

The first and best-known piece of empirical evidence concerning termination of long-term distribution contracts is Brickley, Dark, and Weisbach's.[40] They hypothesised that laws restricting franchisor termination rights would lead to less franchising. This was on the basis that if, for instance, cheating franchisees received compensation after the franchisor terminated, the benefits from cheating increased, and so the extent of breaches by franchisees. This would lead to less profitable franchising, making other arrangements (such as franchisors running the units directly) more profitable by comparison. Interestingly, because franchisees are assumed to be able to generate higher revenue in the operation of units than are franchisors, the reduction of franchised units also leads to an aggregate reduction of units: while the franchisor will, after laws restricting termination, find it profitable to run some of the units it would have franchised were the franchisee able to commit not to cheat, there will be some marginal units that are no longer profitable to run or to franchise.

---

[38] See James Brickley, Frederick Dark, and Michael Weisbach, 'The Economic Effects of Franchise Termination Laws', 34 *Journal of Law & Economics* (1991) 101; John Beales III and Timothy Muris, 'The Foundations of Franchise Regulation: Issues and Evidence', 2 *Journal of Corporate Finance* (1995) 157; Darrell Williams, 'Franchise Contract Terminations: Is There Evidence of Franchisor Abuse?', *10th Annual Proceedings of the Society of Franchising*, Lincoln, International Center for Economic Franchise Studies, College of Business Administration, University of Nebraska (1996); Francine Lafontaine and Kathryn Shaw, 'Targeting Managerial Control: Evidence from Franchising', 36 *RAND Journal of Economics* (2005) 131; James Brickley, Sanjog Misra, and Lawrence Van Horn, 'Contract Duration: Evidence from Franchising', 49 *Journal of Law & Economics* (2006) 173; Jonathan Klick, Bruce Kobayashi, and Larry Ribstein, 'The Effect of Contract Regulation: The Case of Franchising', George Mason Law and Economics Research Paper 07-03 (2007), available at http://ssrn.com/abstract=951464.

[39] The reason for this lies in the fact that the studies are based on the US experience, where state legislation interfering with termination at will has concentrated on franchise contracts. Moreover, it seems that franchising plays a somewhat larger role in US distribution compared with the European context.

[40] See James Brickley, Frederick Dark, and Michael Weisbach, 'The Economic Effects of Franchise Termination Laws', 34 *Journal of Law & Economics* (1991) 101.

Brickley, Dark, and Weisbach also consider that unconstrained termination can be used by the franchisor not only to discipline non-cooperative behaviour by franchisees, but also to exploit and abuse franchisees by trying to own those units that, through franchisees' sales effort or their market discovery, turn out to be particularly profitable, instead of sharing the profit from those lucrative units with the franchisee.[41] But if this is the case, and franchisors use their termination rights to expropriate franchisees of their specific investments, and franchisees do not correctly estimate the expected cost of this opportunistic behaviour by franchisors, there will be too much franchising as some franchisees pay, as franchise fees, more than the true reservation prices for their units. Laws restricting termination by franchisors would also decrease franchising in this scenario.

Brickley, Dark, and Weisbach however rule out this second possibility by focusing their analysis on differences between industries. Specifically, they argue that if termination primarily serves to discipline franchisees' non-cooperative behaviour, the effect of termination laws on the rate of franchising will be most pronounced in industries with substantially non-repeating business. In areas or sectors with significant repeat business, disciplining franchisees is less important since the self-enforcement mechanisms induce better behaviour from the franchisee: otherwise, it will lose repeat business and suffer revenue loss. In industries without much repeat business, there is less potential for self-enforcement, making termination more important as a policing tool. On the other hand, if termination clauses primarily allow the franchisor to exploit the franchisee, no such cross-industry relation would appear, and no systematic difference in the change in franchising across industries would be found. Brickley, Dark, and Weisbach's data show that the effect of legislation conditioning termination of franchise agreements is greater (and, in statistical terms, significantly so) in industries they classify as particularly subject to non-repeating customers (restaurants, hotels, and auto rental agencies) than in other sectors.

---

[41]   Both explanations of termination by the franchisor (or by the manufacturer, or principal, more generally), the benevolent (discipline on non-verifiable breach by the other party) and the sinister (expropriation of value from specific investments by the 'weaker' party) are consistent with the brutal factual observation that it is principals, and not the other parties, who typically terminate the relationship. In a Spanish survey carried out by a business daily newspaper (*Expansión*, 9 December 1996), in 88% of the cases termination is decided by the principal, in 8% by the distributor, and in 4% it is a joint decision (I have taken these figures from Cándido Paz-Ares, 'La terminación de los contratos de distribución', 8 *Advocatus* (2003) 32). Also, a look at litigated cases points in the direction of the principal or manufacturer being the party behind most disputed cases of termination. In view of this, it seems that we need some more elaborated empirical analysis to test which theoretical explanation is empirically corroborated by facts.

In turn, Beales and Muris[42] look at whether data on franchise terminations and non-renewals support the efficiency or the opportunistic explanation for terminations. What they label an efficient termination is one in which the franchisor detects a breach of quality provision duties by a franchisee. Opportunistic termination is defined as any non-efficient termination, presumably driven by the exploitative reasons mentioned earlier. Beales and Muris collected data on terminations (by both franchisor and franchisee) in 13 industries over eight years. Their independent variables included: growth in number of outlets (which should increase breaches); growth in sales per outlet (should decrease breaches); and proxies for appropriable rent (which should increase opportunistic terminations). Their results neither support nor present cause to reject the opportunism hypothesis: the estimated coefficients are often of the wrong sign or statistically insignificant. However, they did obtain a robust, significant, and negative coefficient on the 'growth in outlets' variable. This suggests that, if opportunism or expropriation by the franchisor is a factor, its effect is diluted by the franchisor's interest in maintaining its reputation in order to attract additional quality franchisees.

Williams also examined termination rates of franchise contracts, in a sample of over 1,000 contracts through a four-year period, and found no evidence of termination being influenced by a franchisor appropriating for himself those units which, whether through franchisees' sales effort or for other reasons, turned out to be particularly profitable.[43] In fact, the main factors driving termination rates appeared to be a desire to transfer the unit (frequently by the franchisee herself) and to close units underperforming due to poor franchisee performance or a disadvantageous location.

Klick, Kobayashi and Ribstein[44] also used data on franchising chains to assess the relative importance for termination of the disciplining and expropriation stories. They examined state laws limiting franchisor termination rights to identify the effect of termination at will on both the decision to franchise and franchisor expansion generally. In their first set of empirical tests, using firm-level data on franchising in the fast food industry, their regressions showed that constraining termination led to a reduction in franchising and to a

---

[42] See John Beales III and Timothy Muris, 'The Foundations of Franchise Regulation: Issues and Evidence', 2 *Journal of Corporate Finance* (1995) 157.

[43] See Darrell Williams, 'Franchise Contract Terminations: Is There Evidence of Franchisor Abuse?', *10th Annual Proceedings of the Society of Franchising*, Lincoln, International Center for Economic Franchise Studies, College of Business Administration, University of Nebraska (1996).

[44] See Jonathan Klick, Bruce Kobayashi, and Larry Ribstein, 'The Effect of Contract Regulation: The Case of Franchising', George Mason Law and Economics Research Paper 07-03 (2007), available at http://ssrn.com/abstract=951464.

smaller increase in franchisor-operated units. With their second data set they sought to connect changes in laws conditioning termination with state employment in industries characterised by a high degree of franchising. There they found that restrictions on termination at will are correlated with a decrease in franchised industries' employment rates relative to employment rates in industries with little franchising. Both tests, thus, tend to support the view that the disciplining effect of termination on franchisees' non-cooperative behaviour seems to outweigh opportunities for franchisor abuse and expropriation of value which termination at will may allow.

Lafontaine and Shaw[45] have investigated whether data sustain the proposition that franchisor opportunism is an important factor behind the rate of termination. If this were true, so they claimed, and franchisors were disproportionately acquiring, through unwarranted termination, the more profitable franchise units, one would expect that more established franchising chains would demonstrate increasing company ownership (that is, franchisor's ownership) over time. Lafontaine and Shaw's findings were not consistent with that prediction.

Brickley, Misra, and Van Horn[46] sought to assess the 'exploitation' theory of franchising (i.e., powerful franchisors are able to impose contract terms on weaker franchisees), concentrating on clauses regulating contract duration which are typically crucial for the chances that franchisees recover relation-specific investments (those which lose all, or a substantial fraction, of value outside the contract) made in contemplation of the contract being in place for some period of time. Specific investments make the franchisee vulnerable, because the termination of the contract will not allow the franchisee to recover the specific, and thus non-salvageable, investment. The longer the contract term, the higher are the chances of complete recovery of investment by the franchisee.

Using a large sample of franchising firms, Brickley, Misra, and Van Horn analysed the effects on contract duration clauses of several factors: the number of years the franchisor has been in operation; the number of sites the franchising network comprises (that is, the franchisor's size); the average total initial investment of a franchisee entering the franchise network; the number of weeks of off-site training of a franchisee's personnel. The first two factors relate to the power, experience and contractual strength of the franchisor; the second two are good proxies for the level of specific investments made by the franchisee. If the exploited franchisee view were correct, we would expect that

---

[45]   See Francine Lafontaine and Kathryn Shaw, 'Targeting Managerial Control: Evidence from Franchising', 36 *RAND Journal of Economics* (2005) 131.
[46]   See James Brickley, Sanjog Misra, and Lawrence Van Horn, 'Contract Duration: Evidence from Franchising', 49 *Journal of Law & Economics* (2006) 173.

the larger and more sophisticated the franchisor, the more exploitative the contract terms and the shorter the contract duration will be. Again, if the naïve franchisee image were correct, the level of specific investments would not raise contract duration, given that exploitative franchisors would try to appropriate the value of the non-amortised specific investments incurred by the franchisee.

Empirical results show that the four factors are positively and significantly correlated with the length of the contract term: both the level of the investments by the franchisee and the size and the experience of the franchisor tend to increase contract duration,[47] contrary to the prediction of the 'exploitation' hypothesis. And these results hold irrespective of the fixed effects of the particular industry in which the franchisor operates. There is thus evidence to indicate that franchisors are responsive to the level of specific investments by franchisees, and are more responsive as they become bigger and better established. Such results furthermore provide indirect evidence that the threat posed by opportunistic and exploitative behaviour on the part of franchisors is not in reality a particularly worrisome problem[48] or, at least, is sufficiently marginal so as not to show up in the data.

A further striking feature emerges from results produced by the empirical studies just summarised. It can be observed that legislation restricting termination at will increases, rather than decreases, the number of terminations; that is, when the law sets some conditions for terminating a franchise contract (such as financial compensation or showing good cause for termination) franchisors terminate more and not less often, as might be expected.

The explanation advanced by some commentators for this counterintuitive empirical finding runs along the following lines:[49] unconstrained termination at will induces franchisors to be more forgiving of minor (even if verifiable) instances of breach by the franchisee. To be forgiving at the beginning, is not

---

[47]   See Roger Blair and Francine Lafontaine, *The Economics of Franchising*, Cambridge University Press, New York–Cambridge (2005), pp. 259–260, who also find that larger franchisors tend to offer longer contracts on average than smaller ones.

[48]   It is true, however, that Brickley and his co-authors also find a positive effect of legal restrictions on franchise termination (in the state where the franchisor has its headquarters) on contract duration clauses: Brickley, Misra, and Van Horn, 'Contract Duration: Evidence from Franchising', 49 *Journal of Law & Economics* (2006) 185. They hypothesise that this effect is due to the increased bargaining power such legislation gives franchisees upon termination of the contract, thus reducing the value of short term contracts for the franchisor.

[49]   See John Beales III and Timothy Muris, 'The Foundations of Franchise Regulation: Issues and Evidence', 2 *Journal of Corporate Finance* (1995) 169; Cándido Paz-Ares, 'La terminación de los contratos de distribución', 8 *Advocatus* (2003) 52.

too costly for a franchisor, given that she always retains the ability to terminate without any restriction, financial or otherwise, as soon as she observes that her benevolence has not been repaid with cooperative behaviour by the franchisee. On the contrary, if the decision to terminate is legally constrained, the franchisor will terminate on the first occasion she can, with regard to severance or compensation payment to the franchisee, legally and costlessly do so. The franchisor (or the principal, more generally) will not be inclined to act forgivingly in front of a first minor breach if there is sufficient evidence that termination would be deemed an acceptable punishment of franchisee's breach. This would lead, then, to more terminations, rather than fewer, following legislation which makes termination more difficult and/or costly for the franchisor.

In sum, the empirical evidence on long-term distribution contracts clearly indicates that one should be prima facie sceptical of rules that interfere in such extended incomplete commercial relationships with the aim of restricting the ability of principals to use termination of the distribution contract as an effective means to improve the efficiency of performance of agents, franchisees and other firms down the distribution chain, in other comparable arrangements in the contract networks which, in the end, deliver goods and services to consumers.

Returning to the DCFR, one can legitimately ask whether this substantial body of knowledge about the effects on real-world distribution markets of the rules of contract law that govern relevant relationships has been duly taken into consideration in the DCFR's proposed model rules.

The DCFR seems to have been drafted with close attention to the regime introduced for commercial agents by the Commercial Agency Directive, even if the proposed model rules, it must be acknowledged, do simplify and clarify the complicated regime contained in Directive 86/653/EEC (OJ L382, 31.12.1986, pp. 17–21). As a general rule for long-term distribution contracts (encompassing not just commercial agency, but also franchising and distribution), the DCFR provides for several important conditions and legal duties that restrict the disciplining use of termination by principals and manufacturers along distribution networks.

Firstly, the DCFR (Article IV.E.2:303, probably inspired by the general principle in Article 17.2(c) of the Commercial Agency Directive) imposes a general duty (that is, applicable to all kinds of contractual arrangements) to pay damages for termination with inadequate notice, in an attempt to try to ensure that an agent obtains the benefit she would have enjoyed had the notice period been complied with. The average benefit of the previous three years is taken as the benchmark to assess that benefit.

Secondly, Article IV.E.2:305 contemplates an indemnity for goodwill which broadly (though not in every detail) corresponds with Article 17.2(a) of the Commercial Agency Directive. This later indemnity is not mandatory (except for commercial agency, under the complex regime proposed in Article IV.E.3:312, in turn inspired by Article 17.2(b) of the Directive) but it would, unless otherwise agreed by the parties, be applicable also in favour of the agent, franchisee or distributor party who had breached the contract, even fundamentally.

Moreover, Article IV.E.2:304 prohibits all clauses which allow one party to terminate for any other than a fundamental breach, thus precluding the use of termination of the contract to sanction instances of non-verifiable breach, a common occurrence in long-term, incomplete, and poorly specified contractual relationships, as are those prevailing in the area of distribution.

Such solutions contained in the proposed model rules, all of which have the effect of restricting termination by the principal in this field of contracting which, it must again be emphasised, is not B2C, but B2B, seem difficult to reconcile with the important empirical evidence concerning the real-world consequences of legal restrictions on termination in distribution networks, which points strongly to the efficiency costs which may ensue from such legal restrictions which are also to the detriment of distributors and potential distributors. A closer look at this evidence would likely have encouraged a more parsimonious view of the beneficial effects of ad hoc, contract-specific rules which, in a commercial setting, aim from the start to favour one of the contracting parties. At minimum, closer consideration of relevant empirical studies would have counselled adoption of a less deferential attitude towards the highly controversial solutions contained in the Commercial Agency Directive, and a critical stance with regard to its extension to other contractual arrangements in distribution chains.

4.   CONCLUSION

In general, the law, both as an academic endeavour and as social institution designed to influence individual and social conduct, concerns real human beings, situations and phenomena – the real world. This is, of course, no less true of contract law. With due respect to purely theoretical and normative analyses – these are also necessary to the law as an intellectual discipline, and to legal systems – this essential feature of the law ought to place empirical knowledge at the forefront of legal interest.

In this chapter, I have tried to show that, while the DCFR has accomplished an important task, it has not made use of the entire range of empirical knowledge that was at its disposal. Beyond empirical evidence concerning the rules in place in EU law and in the legal systems of the Member States, there is a substantial and rich body of knowledge relating to real-world contracting behaviour of real-world people which has been developed using widely accepted techniques in the social sciences – experimental and statistical, but also qualitative.

I have illustrated this general point about the insufficient use of empirical evidence in the DCFR with two specific applications concerning two distinct areas of contracting falling within the scope of the DCFR: consumer behaviour and contracting, and long-term distribution contracts. In both areas, current empirical knowledge is far from complete. Nonetheless, the fact remains that to be able to understand and to anticipate, albeit imperfectly, the potential effects of legal rules on the functioning of markets for goods and services and on the behaviour of contracting parties one needs empirical information. It would have been preferable then, both in epistemological and policy-making terms, to rely on imperfect data and knowledge, rather than, as has the DCFR, almost entirely to renounce the use of data at all.

7. A spontaneous order for Europe? Why Hayek's libertarianism is not the right way forward for European private law

Martijn W. Hesselink

1. INTRODUCTION

With the recent publication of the draft Common Frame of Reference,[1] the process of revising the Consumer Acquis under way,[2] and the idea of an optional European code of contract law under consideration,[3] today the Europeanisation of private law is at a defining stage where crucial choices will have to be made. Some of the main issues include regulatory legitimacy (who should bring about the revised *acquis*, the CFR and any optional code of contract law: scholars, courts, or parliament?), the level and scope of mandatory rules for the protection of weaker parties such as consumers and SMEs,

---

[1]   Von Bar et al. (eds.), *Principles, Definitions and Model Rules of European Private Law; Draft Common Frame of Reference (DCFR) Interim Outline Edition* (Munich: Sellier, 2008).

[2]   *Green Paper on the Review of the Consumer Acquis*, Brussels, 8 Feb. 2007, COM(2007)744.

[3]   See *A More Coherent European Contract Law, an Action Plan*, Brussels, 12 Feb. 2003, COM(2003)68 final. See also: *European Contract Law and the Revision of the Acquis: the Way Forward*, 11 Oct. 2004, COM(2004)651 final. Today, the idea of an optional code of contracts seems to be lower on the political agenda than it was in 2003 when the Commission launched its ambitious Action Plan (see the *First Annual Progress Report on The Common Frame of Reference*, 23 Sept. 2005, COM(2005)456 final, 5; *Second Progress Report on The Common Frame of Reference*, 25 July 2007, COM(2007)447 final. In the words of Diana Wallis MEP, 'it is hardly the time to be seen to be moving towards anything that remotely resembles a European Civil Code; if the voters of Europe did not want a constitution it is hardly the moment to force a civil code, even just a contract code on them. The political moment, the political context is not right; however, as with the constitution, the practical arguments in favour of greater harmonisation will remain': Diana Wallis, 'European Contract Law – The Way Forward: Political Context, Parliament's Preoccupations and Process', in: *ERA-Forum Special Issue on European Contract Law – Developing the Principles for a 'Common Frame of Reference' for European Contract Law* (Trier: 2006), 8 at 8.

the ideological character of the rules of general private law (neoliberal, social-ist or something in between?), and the values that should underlie a CFR and/or an optional instrument and should guide its interpretation.[4]

It has been suggested recently that the ideas of Friedrich von Hayek should play a prominent role in shaping the future of European private law. The most outspoken Hayek supporter has been Jan Smits who launched a plea for European private law as a spontaneous legal order. In response to a manifesto on social justice in European contract law which had been published the year before by a group of scholars which was concerned about the CFR process as it had been announced by the European Commission,[5] Smits wrote:[6] 'What constitutes the best rules for Europe cannot, in my view, be decided by an almighty legislator that has the power to change the existing distribution of power and riches – if this is what one wants to do at all. The present legal system is the result of a long process of *trial* and *error* through which a partly spontaneous order has come into being. ... To me, law is not primarily the result of conscious choice, but of spontaneous development. In this respect, I am influenced by the work of Nobel Prize winner Friedrich Hayek.' Others also have taken Hayek as a source of inspiration for European private law. For example, Stefan Grundmann regards the integration of consumer and commer-cial relationships into general private law as a 'powerful discovery procedure' in the sense of Hayek.[7]

---

[4]   On the issues see Martijn W. Hesselink, *CFR & Social Justice. A short study for the European Parliament on the values underlying the draft Common Frame of Reference for European private law: what roles for fairness and social justice?* (Munich: Sellier, 2008).

[5]   Study Group on Social Justice, 'Social Justice in European Contract Law: a Manifesto', 16 *European Law Journal* (2004) 653.

[6]   Jan M. Smits, 'European Private Law: a Plea for a Spontaneous Legal Order', in: Deirdre M. Curtin, Jan M. Smits, André Klip and Joseph McCahery, *European Integration and Law* (Antwerp and Oxford: Intersentia, 2006), 85. See also Jan M. Smits, 'The Harmonisation of Private Law in Europe: Some Insights from Evolutionary Theory', 31 *Georgia Journal of International and Comparative Law* (2002) 79; Jan Smits, *The Good Samaritan in European Private Law. On the Perils of Principles without a Programme and a Programme for the Future* (Deventer: Kluwer, 2000).

[7]   See e.g. Wolfgang Kerber and Stefan Grundmann, 'An Optional European Contract Law Code: Advantages and Disadvantages', 21 *Eur J Law & Econ.* (2006) 215; Stefan Grundmann, 'Europäisches Vertragsrecht – Quo Vadis?', *JZ* (2005) 860; Stefan Grundmann, 'The Structure of European Company Law: From Crisis to Boom', 5 *EBOL Rev* (2004) 601; Stefan Grundmann, 'Consumer Law, Commercial Law, Private Law: How can the Sales Directive and the Sales Convention be so Similar?', *EBLR* (2003) 237; Stefan Grundmann and Wolfgang Kerber, 'Information Intermediaries and Party Autonomy – The Example of Securities and Insurance Markets', in: Stefan Grundmann, Wolfgang Kerber, Stephen Weatherill (eds.), *Party*

Friedrich von Hayek was born in 1899 in Vienna where he grew up and was educated in law and political sciences. In 1931 he became a professor of economics at the London School of Economics; in 1950 he moved to Chicago and in 1962 to Freiburg. His most famous book is *The Road to Serfdom*, published during the Second World War (also in an abridged form in the *Reader's Digest*), in which he warned that plans for a socialist planned economy after the war would bring Britain into the hands of the same demon that they were fighting at the time, i.e. totalitarianism.[8] Hayek was admired by members of the Chicago School, especially Milton Friedman.[9] And British Prime Minister Margaret Thatcher in a cabinet meeting once famously slapped Hayek's *The Constitution of Liberty* on the table and said: 'This is what we believe in.'[10] In 1974 Hayek was awarded the Nobel Prize for economics. He died in 1992.

Hayek wrote extensively, not only on economics, political science and psychology, but also on law. His style is crystal clear and cogent and his rhetoric superb. But is he convincing? In particular, should his ideas play an important role in the current debate concerning the future of private law in Europe? Should European private law indeed become a spontaneous order? And what does Hayek's theory of law have to offer for the choices that are currently on the table concerning European contract law? These questions will be examined in this chapter.

II. HAYEK'S THEORY OF LAW

Before we can assess the relevance of Hayek's thinking for the European private law debate we first need to know more about Hayek's view of the nature of law in general and of private law in particular. Hayek set out his theory of law in three books: *Rules and Order* (1973), *The Mirage of Social Justice* (1976), and *The Political Order of a Free People* (1979). They were published together in one volume in 1982 as *Law, Legislation and Liberty*.[11]

Autonomy and the Role of Information in the Internal Market (Berlin and New York: Walter de Gruyter, 2001).

[8] Friedrich.A. Hayek, *The Road to Serfdom* (first edition 1944) (London and New York: Routledge Classics, 2005). See also his *The Constitution of Liberty* (Chicago: University of Chicago Press, 1978) and *The Fatal Conceit; The Errors of Socialism* (London: Routledge, 1988).

[9] See Milton and Rose D. Friedman, *Two Lucky People: Memoirs* (Chicago: University of Chicago Press, 1998), 333.

[10] Alan Ebenstein, *Friedrich Hayek: A Biography* (Chicago: University of Chicago Press, 2001), 292.

[11] Friedrich A. Hayek, *Law, Legislation and Liberty; A New Statement of the*

A.   Spontaneous Order, no Planning

The basic idea underlying Hayek's theory of law is that of what he called 'a spontaneous order'.[12] Hayek contrasted two kinds of social order: a spontaneous order and an order which is based on the rational design (planning) by government. In a spontaneous order individuals are free to pursue their own interests or, as Hayek put it, to make use of their information for their purposes. The resulting order is neither designed nor intended by anybody but is the mere result of spontaneous and evolutionary development. In contrast, in a planned order (an organisation) individuals have to do what the government tells them to do: they have to follow its commands.

According to Hayek, a spontaneous order is superior for two reasons. First, it is the only order that guarantees individual liberty because a planned order necessary leads to ever more planning and ultimately to the total abolition of individual freedom; second, because no planner will ever possess all the information necessary to take the right decisions. Information is dispersed among individuals. Therefore, by definition, a planner when making a decision will disregard all the facts of which he is not aware. Hayek spoke of the 'incurable ignorance of everyone'.[13] The only way of dealing with this problem in a society as complex as our own is through the mechanism of a market in which individuals are allowed to use their own knowledge for their own purposes.[14] In a 'Great or Open Society'[15] market prices function as signals for individuals for what they should do: '[c]ompetition operates as a discovery procedure not only by giving anyone who has the opportunity to exploit special circumstances the possibility to do so profitably, but also by conveying to the other parties the information that there is some such opportunity. It is by this conveying of information in coded form that the competitive efforts of the market game secure the utilization of widely dispersed knowledge.'[16] This anonymous mechanism (Adam Smith's 'invisible hand') leads to a spreading of information that no planner, not even the most representative and well informed government, could ever achieve.

Liberal Principles of Justice and Political Economy (London and New York: Routledge, 2003). Volume I: *Rules and Order*; Volume II: *The Mirage of Social Justice*; Volume III: *The Political Order of a Free People*.

[12]   The idea was already present in his *The Road to Serfdom*, above note 8, 17.
[13]   *Rules and Order*, above note 11, 13.
[14]   Ibid., 55.
[15]   The concept of a great society refers to Adam Smith, the concept of an open society to Karl Popper. See Adam Smith, *The Wealth of Nations* (first edition 1776) (London: Penguin Books 1999) and Karl Popper, *The Open Society and Its Enemies* (first edition 1945) (London: Routledge Classics 2006) respectively.
[16]   *The Mirage of Social Justice*, above note 11, 117.

B.   The Crucial Role of Private Law

In a spontaneous order a key role is played by 'rules of just conduct'. These
are the rules of private law (including criminal law), as opposed to the rules of
public law (especially administrative law) which belong to the realm of planning. Ideally, these rules of just conduct develop organically, through natural
selection, as a custom, which can be found by the courts when they have to
resolve a dispute. Not surprisingly, Hayek was much taken by the common law
tradition and, within the civil law tradition, by the evolutionary approach of
Von Savigny's Historical School.[17] However, Hayek acknowledged that often,
especially in modern society, custom develops too slowly to provide answers
to all questions that may arise. In order to fill these gaps legislation may be
needed.[18]

Although, therefore, Hayek preferred private law to develop organically,
through custom rather than to be designed by a legislator, it is important to
emphasise that in Hayek's view private (including criminal) law is the *only* area
where the legislator, properly understood (see below), should play a role. The
only way in which the legislator is allowed to limit the freedom of individuals
is through rules of just conduct, i.e. the rules of property, tort and contract.[19]
These private law rules must be 'of universal application', i.e. they have to
apply equally to all individuals ('formal justice').[20] Moreover, they are almost
always 'negative rules': they forbid certain kinds of actions but they do not tell
individuals what they should do. This idea is rather similar to the ordoliberal
idea of a 'private law society'.[21] Although Hayek regarded the ordoliberals as
his allies fighting for the same cause (i.e. the battle against socialism),[22] he did
not consider himself to be an ordoliberal (nor a conservative, for that matter).

---

17   *Rules and Order*, above note 11, 22 and 74
18   *The Political Order of a Free People*, above note 11, 37 and 124.
19   *The Mirage of Social Justice*, above note 11, 109.
20   Ibid., 148.
21   See generally Franz Böhm, 'Privatrechtsgesellschaft und Marktwirtschaft', 17
Ordo (1966), 75. On ordoliberalism and European integration see Miguel Maduro, *We,
the Court; The European Court of Justice & the European Economic Constitution*
(Oxford: Hart Publishing, 1998), 126–131. On ordoliberalism and contract law see
Brigitta Lurger, *Grundfragen der Vereinheitlichung des Vertragsrechts in der
Europäischen Union* (Vienna and New York: Springer, 2002), 396–400. On ordoliberalism and European private law see Alessandro Somma, 'Social Justice and the Market
in European Contract Law', 2 *ERCL* (2006) 181, 182.
22   With regard to the ordoliberal expression 'social market economy', which he
regarded as a pleonasm – and which incidentally has now been explicitly adopted by
the European Union in the Lisbon Treaty (in Article 3, Section 3) – Hayek said: 'I
regret this usage though by means of it some of my friends in Germany (and more
recently also in England) have apparently succeeded in making palatable to wider

The main difference between them seems to be that Hayek did not regard market power as a problem per se, and therefore saw a smaller scope for competition law.[23]

C.   The Mirage of Social Justice

According to Hayek the concept of social justice is empty and meaningless because a society cannot be just or unjust.[24] Justice is an attribute of individual conduct: it determines what can be expected from individuals. In practically all cases these individual rules are negative: they tell us to refrain from certain conduct (the kind of conduct we would want others to refrain from demonstrating towards us (Kant)) with a view to preserving everybody's liberty.[25] Society cannot have any (positive) obligations towards individuals.

In particular, there is no obligation for a society to assure a just distribution of welfare among its members. In other words, Hayek explicitly rejected the notion of distributive justice: 'no particular distribution of incomes can be meaningfully described as more just than another'.[26] The reason is that the distribution cannot meaningfully be said to have been brought about by anyone. 'It has of course to be admitted' he said, 'that the manner in which the benefits and burdens are apportioned by the market mechanism would in many instances have to be regarded as very unjust *if* it were the result of a deliberate allocation to particular people. But this is not the case. Those shares are the outcome of a process the effect of which on particular people was neither intended nor foreseen by anyone . . . To demand justice from such a process is clearly absurd, and to single out some people in such a society as entitled to a particular share evidently unjust.'[27]

Moreover, the concept of social justice is not merely meaningless but also dangerous. Indeed, it is the greatest enemy of individual liberty: '[w]hat we have to deal with in the case of "social justice" is simply a quasi-religious superstition of the kind which we should respectfully leave in peace so long as it merely makes those happy who hold it, but which we must fight when it becomes the pretext of coercing other men. And the prevailing belief in "social justice" is at present probably the gravest threat to most other values of a free

circles the sort of social order for which I am pleading' (*The Mirage of Social Justice*, above note 11, 180 (note 26)).
23   *The Political Order of a Free People*, above note 11, Ch. 15.
24   *The Mirage of Social Justice*, above note 11, 69.
25   Ibid., 36.
26   Ibid., 142.
27   Ibid., 65 (emphasis in the original).

civilization.'[28] According to Hayek social justice equals socialism,[29] and socialism is society's greatest enemy because it leads to the abolition of individual freedom, to the substitution of private law by public law,[30] and ultimately to totalitarianism. Hayek felt very strongly about the dangers of social justice. He insistently warned that '[i]t is not enough to recognize that "social justice" is an empty phrase without determinable content. It has become a powerful incantation which serves to support deep-seated emotions that are threatening to destroy the Great Society.'[31] As said, the spectre is that of totalitarianism: '[i]t is indeed the concept of "social justice" which has been the Trojan Horse through which totalitarianism has entered'.[32]

Hayek did not deny that the market mechanism makes some people better off than others. On the contrary, he fully acknowledged that the operation of the market can lead to hardship. But that is inevitable: without this negative feedback the market could not fulfil its signalling function which is the solution to our fundamental ignorance and the basis for the prosperity of our society. As he put it, 'It is only because countless others constantly submit to disappointments of their reasonable expectations that every one has as high an income as he has; and it is therefore only fair that he accept the unfavourable turn of events when they go against him.'[33]

Hayek also acknowledged that the chances of individuals depend not only on future events but also on their initial position. He even admitted that there may be a case in justice for correcting positions which have been determined by earlier unjust acts or institutions. However, he added, it will generally be impracticable to correct this by general rules.[34]

D. Welfare Economics is Childish

Hayek consistently rejected all conceptions of social justice including utilitarianism, i.e. the idea that society should strive for the greatest happiness for the largest number, which is the basis for welfare economics and for most of today's law and economics. Moreover, he was particularly critical of welfare economics for another reason as well: its solution to the problem of justice begs the question. We need rules of justice only because of our fundamental

---

[28]   Ibid., 67.
[29]   Ibid., 65.
[30]   Ibid., 87.
[31]   Ibid., 133.
[32]   Ibid., 136.
[33]   Ibid., 128.
[34]   Ibid., 131. In *The Road to Serfdom*, above note 8, 106, Hayek still believed that there was a strong case for reducing inequality of opportunity.

ignorance with regard to the ends and opportunities that different individuals have. Therefore, a theory that bases justice entirely on knowledge concerning exactly those same facts is pointless. If we really knew everything that the utilitarians need to know in order to decide whether a certain rule is just (in particular, the 'preferences' of everyone concerned and their relative importance) we would not need the concept of justice in the first place.[35] Hayek put it this way: 'It has indeed always amazed me how serious and intelligent men, as the utilitarians undoubtedly were, could have failed to take seriously this crucial fact of our necessary ignorance of most of the particular facts, and could have proposed a theory which presupposes a knowledge of the particular effects of our individual actions when in fact the whole existence of the phenomenon they set out to explain, namely of a system of rules of conduct, was due to the impossibility of such knowledge.' As a consequence, welfare economics and, by implication, the economic analysis of law[36] are equally pointless:[37] '[t]he childish attempts to provide a basis for "just" action by measuring the relative utilities or satisfactions of different persons simply cannot be taken seriously. To show that these efforts are just so much nonsense would require entering into somewhat abstruse argument for which this is not the place. But most economists begin to see that the whole of the so-called "welfare economics", which pretends to base its argument on inter-personal comparisons of ascertainable utilities, lacks all scientific foundation. The fact that most of us believe that they can judge which of the several needs of two or more known persons are more important, does not prove either that there is any objective basis for this, nor that we can form such conceptions about people whom we do not know individually. The idea of basing coercive actions by government on such fantasies is clearly an absurdity.'

E.   Legal Positivism is a Socialist Ideology

One of the greatest enemies of freedom is legal positivism which, according to Hayek, is also closely related to socialism. Legal positivism is based on the mistaken idea that all law is deliberately made. That idea is historically wrong because law is older than legislation.[38] It is also morally wrong because it risks turning the spontaneous order into an organisation and private law into public law. In particular, in relation to private law legal positivism makes no sense: '[i]t is evident that so far as legal rules of just conduct, and particularly the private law, are concerned, the assertion of legal positivism that their content

---

35   *The Mirage of Social Justice*, above note 11, 20.
36   *The Political Order of a Free People*, above note 11, 159.
37   Ibid., 201–202 (note 35).
38   *Rules and Order*, above note 11, 72

is always an expression of the will of the legislator is simply false.'[39] The root of the problem is that jurisprudence has been taken over by public lawyers who are almost without exception socialists,[40] the worst example being Hans Kelsen. Indeed, legal positivism and socialism are intimately related: 'Legal positivism is . . . simply the ideology of socialism . . . and of the omnipotence of the legislative power. It is an ideology born out of the desire to achieve complete control over the social order, and the belief that it is in our power to determine deliberately in any manner we like, every aspect of this social order.'[41] Moreover, legal positivism has also become the chief ideological support of unlimited democracy.[42]

F. Against Unlimited Democracy

In view of Hayek's constant warning against totalitarianism it seems somewhat surprising, at first, that he was so sceptical of the achievements of democracy. Hayek speaks of 'the miscarriage of the democratic ideal'.[43] He even went as far as to say that 'I must frankly admit that *if* democracy is taken to mean government by the unrestricted will of the majority I am not a democrat, and even regard such government as pernicious and in the long run unworkable.'[44] The two main problems with democracy as it exists today are unlimited democracy and the confusion of legislation with government.

The problem with our current democratic institutions is that they produce, through bargaining, an outcome that is not wanted in its entirety by anyone and that very often is contradictory.[45] Hayek exclaimed: [46] 'Is there really no other way for people to maintain a democratic government than by handing over unlimited power to a group of elected representatives whose decisions must be guided by the exigencies of a bargaining process in which they bribe a sufficient number of voters to support an organized group of themselves numerous enough to outvote the rest?' This a rhetorical question because in Hayek's view there is a solution: limited government.[47]

Moreover, Hayek wanted to draw a sharp distinction between government (essentially decisions concerning the spending of tax revenue) and legislation

---

39 *The Mirage of Social Justice*, above note 11, 46.
40 *Rules and Order*, above note 11, 134.
41 *The Mirage of Social Justice*, above note 11, 53.
42 Ibid., 53.
43 *The Political Order of a Free People*, above note 11, 98.
44 Ibid., 39 (emphasis in the original).
45 Ibid., 6.
46 Ibid., 4–5.
47 Ibid., 11.

(i.e. enacting 'rules of just conduct', i.e. mainly private law), and the bodies responsible for it.[48] Both should be elected democratically, the latter, which concerns us here, in a rather peculiar way which Hayek described in quite some detail in his outline for a model constitution.[49] What is needed is an 'assembly of men and women elected at a relatively mature age for fairly long periods, such as fifteen years'. The members of this 'assembly of representatives' should consist of 'persons who already had made their reputation in the ordinary pursuits of life'. They should not be re-eligible but should be assured of continued public employment e.g. as a lay judge. The election should take place by asking each group of people of the same age once in their lives (e.g. in the calendar year of their 45th birthday) to select from their midst representatives to serve for 15 years. This senate would not be a very busy body. In contrast to such a legislative body, our current legislature, which is organised along party lines which in turn represent vested interests, is very well equipped for 'government' (i.e. notably the administration of public resources) but is completely unfit to enact what Hayek regarded as true legislation, i.e. 'rules of just conduct', which include notably the rules of private law.

G.   No Third Way

A crucial element in Hayek's theory is that he rejected any kind of compromise between libertarianism and socialism. The reason is that any interference with the spontaneous order necessarily leads straight to socialism. Indeed, '[t]he strongest support of the trend towards socialism comes today from those who claim that they want neither capitalism nor socialism but a "middle way", or a "third world". To follow them is a certain path to socialism, because once we give licence to the politicians to interfere in the spontaneous order of the market for the benefit of particular groups, they cannot deny such concessions to any group on which their support depends.' Therefore it is all or nothing: '[w]e face an inescapable choice between two irreconcilable principles, and however far we may always remain from fully realizing either, there can be no stable compromise.'[50] This is essentially the same message, delivered in 1979, as in *The Road to Serfdom* in 1944.

---

[48]   Ibid., 38.
[49]   Ibid., 113–115.
[50]   Ibid., 151. In the same sense see *The Road to Serfdom*, above note 8, 43.

III.   WHAT CONTRACT LAW?

A.   Contracts and Contract Law

Contract law is the main subject of European private law, not only of Community legislation in the area of private law, but also of the debate on the future of European private law. So, if Hayek's theory is to be relevant for European private law then it must have something to say on what contract law should look like. What is Hayek's theory of contract law? In *Law, Legislation and Liberty* he mentioned contracts on many occasions, albeit most of the time merely vicariously.[51] For example, he said that individuals should have no positive obligations except those voluntarily assumed (without, however, giving any explanation as to why promises should be enforceable in law – see below[52]). As to contract law, he repeatedly cited the freedom and the binding force of contract as the foundations of an open and free society. Moreover, he made clear that the rules of just conduct – the only ones allowed in a free society – are the rules of private law which include, of course, contract law. Therefore, everything that Hayek had to say on the rules of just conduct applies to contract law. However, Hayek never expressed himself more specifically about what contract law (or indeed any other part of private law) should look like.

In a theory of law which proclaims contract law as the cornerstone of society (together with property law) one would expect some more detailed developments with regard to the type of contract law that a free and open society needs. The binding force and freedom of contract come in many different varieties, and their generic endorsement can hardly be regarded as distinctive for any theory of law. Indeed, without much exaggeration one could define contract law, and the theories pertaining to it, as the law that is concerned exclusively with the question when, to what extent and in what ways contracts should be binding. There are many fundamental questions: when is a binding contract concluded? Can a party withdraw from a contract if his agreement was based on a mistake? Should immoral contracts be unenforceable? What should determine the interpretation of a contract, the common intention of the parties or its objective meaning? Do supervening events justify relief from the contractual bond? What should be the remedies in the case of a breach of contract? Can third parties have a right under a contract? Hayek had nothing to say about these questions.

---

[51]   Cf. e.g. *The Mirage of Social Justice*, above note 11, 36–37, 124 and 146; *The Political Order of a Free People*, above note 11, 150.

[52]   *The Mirage of Social Justice*, above note 11, 36.

B.   The Binding Force of Contract

Indeed, even with regard to the general problem of the binding force of contracts Hayek had little to offer. The enforcement of a contract by state authorities is a major interference with the freedom of any individual who does not (or no longer) want to perform a contract that he concluded. There may be utilitarian (law and economics), or positivistic (Kelsen, Hart), or other justifications for enforcing contracts, but Hayek flatly rejected, and indeed ridiculed, all social justice theories and also legal positivism.[53] This leaves us with the question why, when and to what extent should contracts be legally binding in a free and open society as advocated by Hayek.[54]

Clearly, for its proper functioning a market economy depends entirely on contracts and hence on the expectation that contracts will be performed, and therefore at least partially on the expectation that a party who refuses to perform his side of the contract will be forced by the state to perform the contract or to compensate the damage that the other party sustains. This may go as far as allowing the unpaid seller publicly to sell the buyer's property in order to satisfy his claim. However, this does not justify per se that in a spontaneous order a free person should be forced by the public authorities to perform his contract and, ultimately, to give up his property. There is nothing free or spontaneous about contract enforcement. Why should commutative justice be enforced in a spontaneous order? Why not leave it to the parties themselves and leave any problems to be solved entirely by the free market, e.g. through business reputation?[55]

The answer that enforcing freely concluded contracts is in the best interest of all (i.e. it increases social welfare) would be clearly utilitarian. Hayek said: 'Our only moral title to what the market gives us we have earned by submitting to those rules which makes the formation of the market order possible. These rules imply that nobody is under an obligation to supply us with a particular income unless he has specifically contracted to do so.' But Hayek did not explain why these rules which make the formation of the market order

---

53   A Kantian (or similar) individualistic theory of moral obligation may explain the morally binding character of promises, but not their enforceability in law. See Immanuel Kant, *Metaphysik der Sitten* (first edition 1797–1798) (Frankfurt am Main: Suhrkamp, 1977), 219. Cf. Ernst-Joachim Mestmäcker, *Legal Theory without Law; Posner v. Hayek on Economic Analysis of Law* (Tübingen: Mohr Siebeck, 2007), 53.

54   Ibid., who endorses Hayek and rejects Kelsen, does not answer the question either, even where (on p. 55) he explicitly rejects a positivistic explanation for the binding force of contract.

55   Cf. Stewart Macaulay, 'Non-Contractual Relations in Business: A Preliminary Study', 28 *American Sociological Review* (1963) 55; Hugh Collins, *Regulating Contracts* (Oxford: Oxford University Press, 1999), Ch. 5.

possible should be morally and indeed *legally* binding and why contracts should be so. It seems that Hayek implicitly relied on some utilitarian notion. Indeed, he often referred to the 'general interest' as the basis of the market order and its 'rules of just conduct'.[56] However, as we saw, Hayek explicitly rejected utilitarianism, chiefly on the ground of the incommensurability of the ends ('preferences') that individuals have and the impossibility of obtaining the necessary information with regard to these ends.

If the answer is: to avoid (violent and anarchic) self-help, then this clearly implies a limit to freedom on account of a (not individual but) social value: peace. This raises the question what social values other than the stability of society should be allowed to determine the enforceability of contracts. If the answer is none, the question becomes what contract law should look like if the enforceability of contracts is to be limited merely to the level that avoids violence (especially since individuals differ in their tendency to be violent while Hayek accepted only abstract rules). It is far from clear what this means in terms of rules on formation, validity, interpretation and remedies. Indeed, the best thing to go on would probably be the prevailing ideas of social justice, including possibly some sentiments with regard to the fairness of (certain) prices.

C.   Unfair Prices

One of the few subjects of contract law that Hayek addressed explicitly, albeit rather summarily, is the idea of unfair prices. Hayek explicitly rejected unfair price rules.[57] However, under Hayek's definition, there is no reason why the 'rules of just conduct' could not include a rule to the effect that one should refrain from charging an unfair price (just as one should refrain from fraud). This is not a question of distributive justice. An unfair price rule would be an 'abstract rule' which, at least in theory, could protect a millionaire against a poor seller.[58] Hayek's point against social justice is that private law is concerned with the just conduct of individuals *vis-à-vis* each other. The rules of private law should tell individuals what conduct is expected from them, and what they can claim *from each other* (not from society – tax and transfer) in the case of a failure to comply with these rules of just conduct. Therefore, an unfair price rule seems perfectly compatible both with Hayek's rejection of social justice (an unfair price rule is a matter of commutative, not of distributive justice) and with his notion of spontaneous order (Hayek's legislative

---

[56]   *The Mirage of Social Justice*, above note 11, 73.

[57]   Ibid., 38. See also *The Road to Serfdom*, above note 8, 38 and 115.

[58]   Hayek seems to assume that an unfair price rule could not be a generic rule of universal application. Cf. *The Mirage of Social Justice*, above note 11, 128–129.

body could adopt it just as much as a common law judge could do). So, he needs an additional explanation for his rejection of unfair price rules. In sum, this is another example where Hayek's theory fails to explain even the features of contract law that he explicitly addresses.

D. Market Totalitarianism

Hayek's rejection of social justice is also much more radical than his advocates within the European private law debate seem to realise. Not only did he reject all notions of social justice including, in particular, utilitarianism, but he was also totally against any mix between spontaneous order and social justice concerns. In his view, those proposing a middle ground between free markets and distributive justice are the worst. In his libertarian legal order there was no place for anything but rules that apply equally to individuals. So, when Smits underlines that he 'certainly [does] not deny that the legislator sometimes needs to intervene to protect the interests of weaker parties',[59] this is completely incompatible with Hayek's idea of a spontaneous order that Smits is endorsing in that same paragraph. As we saw, Hayek rejected any mixed approaches in the strongest possible terms, because, in his view, they will necessarily lead to socialism and then, equally necessarily, to totalitarianism. In Hayek's terms, Smits' idea that the legislator sometimes needs to intervene to protect the interests of weaker parties is exactly the kind of redistribution that Hayek rejects: mere socialism and therefore out of the question. Similarly, when Grundmann quotes 'Hayek's knowledge problem' in defence of his proposal to integrate consumer and commercial relationships in Europe into general private law as a 'powerful discovery procedure' in the sense of Hayek,[60] because thus the legislator 'is much more forced each time to name the difference in fact which justifies a particular rule' which 'reduces the risk of consumer law hypertrophy or commercial law privilege',[61] that would

---

[59]   Smits 2006, above note 6, 85.

[60]   He refers to the paper 'Competition as Discovery Procedure', in: Friedrich A. Hayek, *New Studies in Philosophy, Economics and the History of Ideas* (London and Henley: Routledge & Kegan Paul, 1978), Ch. 12, which was published in German as 'Der Wettbewerb als Entdeckungsverfahren', *Kieler Vorträge* Vol. 56 (Kiel: 1968), and was republished in Friedrich A. Hayek, *Freiburger Studien; Gesammelte Aufsätze* (Tübingen: Mohr Siebeck 1994), 249, as well as later also being included in *Law, Legislation and Liberty*, Vol. 3 (*The Political Order of a Free People*), above note 11, Ch. 15.

[61]   See e.g. Stefan Grundmann and Wolfgang Kerber, 'Information Intermediaries and Party Autonomy – The Example of Securities and Insurance Markets', in: Stefan Grundmann, Wolfgang Kerber, Stephen Weatherill (eds.), *Party Autonomy and the Role of Information in the Internal Market* (Berlin and New York: Walter de Gruyter, 2001); Stefan Grundmann, 'Die Struktur des Europäischen

certainly not go far enough for Hayek: the whole idea of considering consumers or professionals differently brings us on the slippery slope to totalitarianism.[62]

Hayek repeatedly and firmly rejected any compromise between a spontaneous order and legislation which is guided by considerations of social justice. Following Hayek, even consumer protection would lead straight to socialism, and from there to totalitarianism. Clearly, if regulatory and distributive elements were indeed to lead directly and necessarily to a totalitarian society where individual freedom is completely abolished, that would certainly be a very strong (if not decisive) argument against any such elements in our economy and, by the same token, against any social justice considerations in European private law.

However, Hayek's apocalyptic scenario has been completely disproved by the facts. His essentially empirical claim is demonstrably false, and it was so even at the time when he made it. The welfare state as it was developed in Western Europe in the second half of the 20th century may be rightly criticised for a number of reasons, but nowhere has it led to a totalitarian state. Each country has struck a different balance between individual freedom and social solidarity. And most have gradually revised that balance after abandoning the excessive faith in central planning in the 1970s. But no country can seriously be said to have come even close to the abolition of individual freedom in a way similar to that of the totalitarian regimes of Nazism and communism. On the other hand, Hayek's analysis also fails to take into account the possibility, and the reality, that in functioning welfare states individuals actually enjoy greater freedom (in the substantive sense of capabilities to live the lives they want to live) than in many crudely capitalist countries.[63] Indeed, there is no evidence of any positive link between unrestricted capitalism and personal freedom. As Kymlycka put it, with regard to Hayek, 'this defence of market freedom must also be a contingent one, for history does not reveal any invariable link

---

Gesellschaftsrechts von der Krise zum Boom', *ZIP* (2004) 2402; Stefan Grundmann, 'The Structure of European Company Law: From Crisis to Boom', 5 *EBOL Rev* (2004) 601; Stefan Grundmann, 'Europäisches Vertragsrecht – Quo Vadis?', *JZ* (2005) 860; Wolfgang Kerber and Stefan Grundmann, 'An Optional European Contract Law Code: Advantages and Disadvantages', 21 *Eur J Law & Econ* (2006) 215; Stefan Grundmann, 'Verbraucherrecht, Unternehmensrecht, Privatrecht – warum sind sich UN-Kaufrecht und EU-Kaufrechts-Richtlinie so ähnlich?', 202 *AcP* (2002) 40; Stefan Grundmann, 'Consumer Law, Commercial Law, Private Law: How can the Sales Directive and the Sales Convention be so Similar?', *EBLR* (2003) 237.

[62]   This quite apart from the fact that markets are of only limited use as a discovery device because they usually fail to reflect the effects on parties other than the contracting parties (externalities). Cf. e.g. Jürgen Habermas, *Die postnationale Konstellation; Politische Essays* (Frankfurt am Main: Suhrkamp, 1998), 143.

[63]   See e.g. Amartya Sen, *Development as Freedom* (Oxford: OUP, 1999).

between capitalism and civil liberties. Countries with essentially unrestricted capitalism have sometimes had poor human rights records (e.g. military dictatorships in capitalist Chile or Argentina; McCarthyism in the United States), while countries with a extensive welfare state have sometimes had excellent records in defending civil and political rights (e.g. Sweden).'[64]

The trouble with Hayek is that his obsession with totalitarianism made his analysis too black or white, all or nothing: either a completely spontaneous order or totalitarianism.[65] It is hard to think of a political theory as absolute and deterministic as Hayek's, apart from Marx perhaps. This all or nothing – in other words: totalitarian – character of Hayek's theory and its Cold War rhetoric make it not only difficult to accept but also largely irrelevant to most contemporary debates, including the one on the future of European private law, for the simple reason that all existing systems are mixed and do contain consumer law – not least EC contract law, where precisely the consumer *acquis* is currently under revision, and the draft CFR, that contains consumer protection rules also beyond the scope of the *acquis*. All existing economies are mixed economies and the key question that we have to answer is: what is the right mix? For private law this means: how much freedom of contract? What to do with unbalanced contracts? How much strict liability in tort? What limits to property rights and to the rights of shareholders? On these questions and on the more general question of what role distributive and other social justice elements could play in contract law Hayek has nothing to say. Richard Posner (hardly a socialist himself!) remarks: 'A mixed system is what we and our peer nations have; what help Hayek's thought offers to someone trying to evaluate such a system is unclear.'[66]

---

[64]   Will Kymlicka, *Contemporary Political Philosophy: An Introduction* (Oxford: OUP, 2001), 102. See also Naomi Klein, *Shock Therapy; The Rise of Disaster Capitalism* (New York: Metropolitan Books, 2007), who argues that market fundamentalism of the Chicago School brand (remember that Milton Friedman was inspired by Hayek) cannot be introduced except in an authoritarian and violent way. She reports (on p. 84) that Hayek travelled to Pinochet's Chile several times to admire the free market laboratory, and (on p. 131) that he wrote a letter to Margaret Thatcher to urge her to use Pinochet's model for transforming Britain's Keynesian economy.

[65]   See, specifically with regard to Hayek's categorical rejection of the need to protect expectations outside contract, Patrick S. Atiyah, *Essays on Contract* (Oxford: OUP, 1986), 91.

[66]   Richard A. Posner, 'Hayek, Law, and Cognition', *New York University Journal of Law & Liberty* (2005) 161.

IV. EUROPEANISATION

A. Against Nationalism

Hayek repeatedly warned against nationalism. In his view, nationalism was one of the two greatest threats to our civilisation (the other is, of course, socialism).[67] In spite of his enthusiasm for an international legal order, he was nevertheless also very cautious. In 1976 he wrote: 'While I look forward, as an ultimate ideal, to a state of affairs in which national boundaries have ceased to be obstacles to the free movement of men, I believe that within any period with which we can now be concerned, any attempt to realize it would lead to a revival of strong nationalist sentiments and a retreat from positions already achieved.'[68] On this point, 30 years later it can be seen that he was right: as a result of both further Europeanisation and globalisation neo-nationalism is on the rise, especially in some countries, like the Netherlands, that stood out in the past for their internationalism.

In view of his anti-nationalism it seems likely that Hayek would have approved of a large internal market. Hayek wrote that 'It is only by extending the rules of just conduct to the relations with all other men, and at the same time depriving of their obligatory character those rules which cannot be universally applied, that we can approach a universal order of peace which might integrate all mankind into a single society.'[69] This raises the question of how such a market with common rules of just conduct could be introduced other than by the legislator. The paradox is, of course, that such a world private law – or European private law to start with – might be better but will not come about spontaneously. A legislative intervention of some sort is necessary.

B. A Centralised Private Law

Hayek – just like Austrian economics more generally – is usually associated with decentralisation. This is correct as far as government is concerned, especially the provision of government services (which in any case should be limited to public goods). The reason is of course the problem of dispersed information: the further the government is removed from the citizens who are affected by its decisions (notably tax spending) the less likely it is to possess the right information for taking the ends and opportunities of everyone concerned into account. However, in Hayek's view the same reasoning does

---

[67] *The Mirage of Social Justice*, above note 11, 111: 'the two greatest threats to a free civilization: nationalism and socialism'.

[68] Ibid., 58.

[69] Ibid., 144.

not apply to legislation, including, in particular, private law legislation.[70] When discussing centralisation and decentralisation, Hayek says that it is 'desirable that the legislative power should extend over a larger territory than the governmental one' and that '[i]t would probably be desirable to restrict federal arrangements to government proper and to have a single legislative assembly for the whole federation'.[71] The EU is of course not a federation. However, the same idea seems to imply, *mutatis mutandis*, to the EU today: legislation (i.e. essentially private law legislation) should take place at the European rather than the national level.

Indeed, it seems that in the view of Hayek the enactment of rules of private law would be the first task of international and supranational organisations such as the EU.[72] However, it is unclear how this idea fits with Hayek's idea that the legislator should only fill the gaps in the organically developed (judge-made) private law. In an international context what is the existing private law that the legislator should revise? This is exactly the main question which is now on the table in Europe. It is essentially the problem of the construction of an internal market. Spontaneous orders (markets) work better to the extent that they are larger, but national borders can only be removed effectively through legislation. Indeed, the most effective way of removing national borders in private law would probably be a European civil code.

The implication seems to be that Hayek would have looked favourably upon the abolition of national borders, and of the internal market, and of private law legislation on the European rather than the national level. Maybe even a European civil code could fit with Hayek's spontaneous order, especially if it were an optional one.[73] In itself, this is, of course, not necessarily a decisive argument for a common European private law, especially if one rejects the idea of a spontaneous order for Europe (see below). Nevertheless, it is a strong argument against those economists who claim that private law legislation should take place on the national level because this is more efficient than on the European level.[74] Indeed, such theories seem to be biased by nationalism.[75]

---

[70]   See e.g. *The Political Order of a Free People*, above note 11, 103.
[71]   *The Political Order of a Free People*, above note 11, 132.
[72]   Ibid., 108–109.
[73]   Smits 2006, above note 6, is also in favour of an optional code.
[74]   See e.g. Roger Van den Bergh, 'Forced Harmonization of Contract law in Europe: Not to be Continued', in: Stefan Grundmann and Jules Stuyck (eds.), *An Academic Green Paper on European Contract Law* (The Hague: Kluwer Law International, 2002), 249.
[75]   Martijn W. Hesselink, 'The European Commission's Action Plan: Towards a More Coherent European Contract Law', 10 *European Review of Private Law* (2004) 397, 417.

V. PRIVATE LAW: SPONTANEOUS ORDER OR DEMOCRATIC DESIGN?

A. Legislation and its Discontent

How should a system of private law come about? Who, if anybody, has the right and the task to make it? Should private law rules be developed by the courts on a case by case basis, be decided upon by a majority vote and political compromise, or be designed by experts? Although traditions differ (the paradigms being the German professor, the French legislator and the English judge[76]), today in all Member States of the European Union the answer is nevertheless: all of the above. In all Member States today private law is a mix of judge-made law and legislation, and almost everywhere private law legislation is drafted, in one way or the other, with the assistance of academic legal experts. Having said that, very different mixes of expert drafting, democratic decision making, and judicial law-making are possible and do indeed exist in the different Member States.

With the publication by the European Commission in 2003 of its Action Plan on European contract law all of a sudden this question became acute.[77] In that plan the Commission announced that it envisaged adopting a Common Frame of Reference which was meant to serve multiple purposes including, in particular, providing the basis for a possible optional European code of contract law, and that this CFR would be designed by a group of academic experts. A group of scholars was alarmed and published a manifesto in which it raised the issue of legitimacy and called for a more democratic procedure.[78] It was in reaction to this manifesto that Jan Smits, in his turn, wrote, invoked by Hayek, 'that law is not primarily the result of conscious choice, but of spontaneous development'.[79] However, it is doubtful whether Hayek's theory of law, and in particular his concept of a spontaneous order, can be of any assistance for answering the question how private law in Europe should come about. The reason is that Hayek's theory of law is far from clear on the role that the democratically elected legislator should play in the area of private law.

---

[76] R.C. Van Caeneghem, *Judges, Legislators & Professors; Chapters on European Legal History* (Cambridge: CUP, 1987), especially ch. 2.
[77] *Action Plan*, above note 3.
[78] *Social Justice in European Contract Law: a Manifesto*, above note 5. Specifically on the need for a democratic procedure see also Martijn W. Hesselink, 'The Politics of a European Civil Code', 10 *European Law Journal* (2004) 675.
[79] See the passage quoted in the Introduction.

B.   The Paradox of Enforcing a Spontaneous Order

In *Law, Legislation and Liberty*, Hayek explained at great length how custom ('rules of just conduct') develops: it is not the result of rational design by anyone but rather the (unintended) outcome of an organic process of natural selection. Thus, in the way it develops and is learned by individuals it is very similar to language. Convincing as this may be, with this point Hayek had not yet explained how custom must be turned into law. It is one thing to say that there is a customary rule that one should keep his promises. It is quite another that contracts are legally enforceable.

Surprisingly, Hayek's theory is far from clear concerning this central question of how standards of just conduct (custom) should be turned into law. At first, in the first volume (*Rules and Order*), Hayek rather naïvely claimed that the common law judge should find the relevant customs on a case by case basis.[80] This notion is obviously problematic for a number of reasons.[81] First, the organic development of the law by the courts, on a case by case basis, may sound nice as an ideal, but in real life the parties to a dispute will often present the court with different views concerning the existing customs and then the court will have to decide which party's claim and argument will prevail. Hayek failed to acknowledge that the development of the common law (and of the increasingly case law-oriented civil law) is in fact not spontaneous but directed by courts which make choices.[82] In other words, Hayek's metaphors of spontaneous order and natural selection are imprecise, to say the least, because actually the order is designed, and the selection is made, not by nature but by judges. Secondly, judges suffer from the same fundamental ignorance as everyone else. Even if one agrees with Hayek that no public authority can ever obtain the information that a spontaneous order would yield, *to the extent that* members of an open society which is based on a spontaneous order rely on courts for the resolution of their dispute, what information do judges possess with regard to the merits of the claims made by the respective parties? As Collins put it, 'Hayek is right to insist that the regulation of markets is an extremely complex task which stretches the capacity of human institutions to the limits. It is then astonishing, however, that he should seek to vest this task in the ordinary courts exclusively, when this institution has such deep flaws in

---

80   *Rules and Order*, above note 11, 78.
81   For a defence of Hayek's position, on his own terms, see Todd J. Zywicki and Anthony B. Sanders, 'Posner, Hayek and the Economic Analysis of Law', 93 *Iowa L. Rev.* (2008) 559.
82   Cf. Brian Z. Tamanaha, *On the Rule of Law: History, Politics, Theory* (Cambridge: CUP, 2004), 70: 'Hayek's characterization of the common law resounds of the old Medieval view that the law is discovered, not made'.

its capacity to acquire and process information about its environment.'[83] Moreover, if whatever the judge acknowledges as a custom must be accepted as a rule of just conduct, as Hayek seemed to suggest, and if there is no external standard for judging it, then Hayek's idea of the common law judge leads directly to positivism, albeit not of Kelsen's legislation-centred type but of the case law-oriented kind. Finally, some existing customs are not (or no longer) desirable,[84] for example, because they are inefficient (think only of externalities and market failures): they may harm the functioning of the market rather than supporting it. According to Posner, 'Hayek goes too far in promoting custom as a source of law, neglecting the fact that inefficient customs are inevitable given the process by which customs are formed.'[85]

This last point is actually acknowledged by Hayek and it is here (and only here) that Hayek sees a task for the legislator. However, this raises the question of what the role and limits of private law legislation should be once it is admitted in principle. The way in which Hayek elaborated the legislator's task in the third volume of the book (*The Political Order of a Free People*) is not only far from convincing (why should laws be made exclusively by middle-aged men and women?) but also hardly compatible with a spontaneous order as he had outlined in the first volume. As said, the task of the legislative body is the revision of the body of private law, because private law 'will need continual development and revision as new and unforeseen problems arise with which the judiciary cannot deal adequately'.[86] It is not clear, however, how this legislative body must determine when there is a need for revision. Frankly, it is difficult to see, as a practical matter, how private law legislation, once it is admitted in principle, can be limited in a meaningful way to updating the judge-made law when this is needed and how it can be assured that the members of the legislative body will try to formulate existing customs rather than following their own ideas of justice.

In final analysis, the same criticism applies to Hayek's spontaneous order that he addressed to the concept of social justice: it is devoid of any meaning. To the extent that the spontaneous order relies on the law for enforcing existing custom, choices will have to be made, even by courts, between the alternatives subjected

---

[83]   Collins 1999, above note 55, 82.
[84]   See Gunther Teubner, *Recht als autopoietisches System* (Frankfurt am Main: Suhrkamp, 1989), 73, who points out that Hayek's theory *'führt zu einer grotesken Überwertung von Gewohnheitsrecht und ähnlich "spontan" gebildeten Ordnungen und zu einer Abwertung von politischen Normierungen als konstruktivistisch'*: Posner 2005, above note 66, 151: 'he is insufficiently critical of the limitations of custom as a normative order'.
[85]   Richard A. Posner, 'Law and Economics in Common-Law, Civil-Law, and Developing Nations', 17 *Ratio Iuris* (2004) 66, 77.
[86]   *The Political Order of a Free People*, above note 11, 124.

to their enforceable decision. These decisions are just as arbitrary and just as centralised (at least in a pyramid-like court system) with the same ensuing informational problems as the legal positivism that Hayek rejected.[87] The only difference is that courts are not democratically elected. Moreover, as we saw, Hayek actually wanted the democratically elected legislator to play an important role in the further development of private law. Indeed, filling the gaps in the existing private law and updating it should be the main task of parliament. In fulfilling this task, the legislator should try to determine what the existing custom is. Presumably, they should try to do so without being biased by their personal ideas and preference but, in practice, of course, every MP would simply have complete discretion. In other words, private law in Hayek's spontaneous order would be essentially positivistic. This leads us to the surprising conclusion that in the area where he regarded positivism as most inappropriate, i.e. private law, Hayek himself was actually a positivist.

C.   European Private Law as a Mixed System

So, should European private law be the result of natural selection, expert design, majority decision or something somewhere in between? It is not at all clear how Hayek would answer this question. The inherent tension within Hayek's theory of law (or between different stages in its development), together with his anti-nationalism and his idea that private law legislation should be centralised, makes it very difficult to determine what Hayek would have found the best way forward for European private law. As said, he might even have supported a European civil code especially if it were an optional one.

However, the question that concerns us here is not whether Hayek would have been critical of the European Commission's Action Plan or of the draft CFR that was recently presented jointly by the Study Group on a European Civil Code and the Research Group on EC Private Law (*Acquis* Group).[88] The real question is what we can learn from Hayek that is important for the future of European private law. Hayek regarded law, in particular private law, as 'the product not of any rational design but of a process of evolution and natural selection'.[89] He said that '[a] legislator, in trying to maintain a going spontaneous order, cannot pick and choose any rules he likes to confer validity upon

---

[87]   Or worse, because judges are smaller in number than MPs and in many countries still tend to be recruited from a limited section of society and have access to a limited section of potentially relevant information with regard to the possible implications of their decisions for individuals.

[88]   *DCFR*, above note 1.

[89]   *The Mirage of Social Justice*, above note 11, 59.

them, if he wants to achieve his aim'.[90] He also wrote that '[n]o system of law has ever been designed as a whole, and even the various attempts at codification could do no more than systematize an existing body of law and in doing so supplement it or eliminate inconsistencies'.[91] These are important points.

Although the democratically elected legislator should not be limited by the past where it can make real progress, the opposite idea of a clean slate, where the legislator would start from scratch without having any regard to existing experience, would not only be unwise but, as a destruction of cultural patrimony, even immoral. The merit of Hayek's theory is that it underlines that our private law is the outcome of organic development and that it cannot be reduced pragmatically to a certain functionality that is rationally ascribed to it. Of course, that same argument has been made by scholars in the tradition of the Historical School, today's followers of Savigny like Zimmermann and Jansen having pointed to the experience contained in legal concepts,[92] and, in a very different way, also by Teubner who describes the law as an autopoietic system which continuously regenerates itself[93] (the advantage of the latter analysis compared to both Hayek's theory and neopandectism being frankly that in Teubner's analysis legislation retains its natural place).

Does this mean that there should be more attention to tradition? Of course, what exactly is the right mix for European private law between legal tradition, expert design, and democracy is difficult to say in the abstract. However, within the CFR process so far the consideration devoted to tradition has been considerable. The experts have produced a draft CFR that was inspired mainly by the national traditions in the different Members States, the developing international tradition in the area of contract law (CISG, Unidroit Principles, PECL) and the admittedly fairly recent Community tradition (*acquis communautaire*).[94] On the detailed level of specific rules the CFR certainly contains a number of innovations. However, on the whole it is best characterised as an attempt to codify existing law rather than as an attempt to design an entirely new private law from scratch. What is actually missing so far is any democratic input. Although in this respect the CFR process is in line with the tradition and the current practice in many Member States, an attempt to involve the European Parliament at a much earlier stage of the drafting should have been made.[95]

---

[90]   Ibid., 61.

[91]   *Rules and Order*, above note 11, 100.

[92]   See most recently Nils Jansen and Reinhard Zimmermann, 'Restating the Acquis communautaire? A critical Examination of the "Principles of the Existing EC Contract Law"', 71(4) *MLR* (2008) 505.

[93]   See Teubner 1989, above note 84.

[94]   'Introduction', *DCFR*, above note 1, 21.

[95]   Hesselink 2004, above note 78.

VI. CONCLUSION

What can we learn from Hayek for the further development of European contract law? What we should retain from Hayek is his rejection of extreme positivism. Law is a contingent phenomenon, historically grown in response to needs of a specific society. This also means that we should be suspicious of universalism and strong functionalism (related to strong pragmatism). Whatever the future of European contract law should look like, it would be totally wrong to think that we could start designing it with a clean slate. Therefore, the drafters of the CFR have been rightly inspired by the existing national, European and international traditions. One of the most fundamental insights from Hayek's work (already centrally present in *The Road to Serfdom*) is that of our incurable ignorance and its implications for the limits of central planning. This insight certainly also affects private law, although not necessarily in the ways suggested by some of his followers. Also, Hayek's warnings against nationalism are still most relevant today. Finally, he rightly reminds us that we should not be unduly impressed by the scientism of the economic analysis of law which is based on the illusion that welfare consequences for individuals of legal rules, including those of the consumer *acquis* or the CFR, can be measured and compared.

What we should certainly reject is Hayek's totalitarianism. His all or nothing approach has no empirical basis; it is completely detached from reality. The implication is dramatic. If the only argument for a spontaneous order is that it will save us from totalitarianism then there is little reason to adopt Hayek's spontaneous order. A mixed economy of the kind that we are familiar with in Europe is much more attractive. As Ole Lando put it, 'Experience seems to show that societies, which build on a market economy combined with solidarity, fairness and loyalty, fare better than those where the law of the jungle governs'.[96] However, unfortunately on the crucial question of what would be the right mix Hayek had hardly anything to say, and he also uttered precious little on the kind of contract law (how much freedom?) such an economy would need. Therefore, a democratically designed contract law drawn up by a legislator inspired by the private laws in Europe as they have grown organically, but making its own choices on the issues that it deems socially most important, seems to be a much better way forward for Europe than a spontaneous order.

---

[96]   Ole Lando, 'The Structure and the Legal Values of the Common Frame of Reference (CFR)', 3 *European Review of Contract Law* (2007) 245, 251.

8. The authority of an academic 'Draft Common Frame of Reference'

Nils Jansen

I. INTRODUCTION

The idea of a *Common Frame of Reference* for European contract law (CFR) is highly political. It is not only a controversial project in itself,[1] but moreover it is essentially open-ended. Political actors, especially in the European Commission, have been reluctant to formulate clear aims or visions with regard to the form, the legal nature or the date for such an instrument to come into being.[2] Indeed, different papers published by the Commission and by the Parliament have presented rather different ideas.[3] These days, even the

---

[1]   See Jansen (2004), 1 ff.; Jansen/Zimmermann (2008), 506 ff.; Eidenmüller/Faust/Grigoleit/Jansen/Wagner/Zimmermann (2008), 529 ff.

[2]   See Jansen (2006a), 540 f.

[3]   Thus, in 2002 the European Parliament had proposed an extremely ambitious timescale for the enactment of a European Civil Code by the year 2010 (Resolution of the European Parliament on the approximation of the civil and commercial law of the Member States [2002] OJ C140E/538). However, in a Communication entitled 'A More Coherent European Contract Law: An Action Plan', the European Commission relegated the idea of a Code to a secondary position; and in a later Communication the idea of a European Contract Code was explicitly rejected: Communication from the Commission to the European Parliament and the Council, 'European Contract Law and the revision of the *acquis*: the way forward', COM(2004)651 final (11 October 2004). Likewise, the Council has 'welcomed' 'the Commission's repeated reassurance that it does not intend to propose a "European Civil Code" which would harmonise contract laws of Member States and that Member States' differing legal traditions will be fully taken into account': press release of 28/29 November 2005 – 14155/05 (press 287), 28. In the course of these developments, the intriguing term of a 'common frame of reference' had been created as the official label for an instrument which is not supposed to be enacted as a piece of legislation but which, nonetheless, will have to be endorsed by the European legislators in some way or other and will, therefore, become a determining factor in the development of European contract law: Communication 'an action plan', above. But whereas this instrument was originally meant to cover large areas of contract law, the focus has more recently been placed on the consumer *acquis*: COM(2005)456 final (23 September 2005).

Commission seems no longer to put much emphasis on the original CFR process. In a 'Green Paper on the Review of the Consumer Acquis' of February 2007, a second project was announced, besides the CFR process,[4] to review eight directives in the field of consumer contract law.[5] At present, this second and parallel project even enjoys 'priority'.[6] Hence, a 'political' CFR was not published by the Barroso Commission before 2009, as had originally been envisaged.

Nevertheless, the *Study Group on a European Civil Code*[7] and the *Research Group on EC Private Law (Acquis Group)*,[8] the main academic actors within the CFR process, have published an 'Interim Outline Edition' of their academic 'Draft Common Frame of Reference' (DCFR[outl.]).[9] A final version of this 'academic' Draft CFR (DCFR) was published at the beginning of 2009. The scope of this DCFR is highly ambitious.[10] Apart from general rules on contract law, the DCFR[outl.] covered not only specific rules on diverse contracts, such as sales, lease of movable goods, services (with the exclusion of labour law), mandate, commercial agency, franchise and distributorship, and on personal securities, but also on non-contractual obligations, such as 'benevolent intervention in another's affairs',[11] the law of delicts and unjust enrichment. Other fields, such as loans, trusts, and also movable property law have been included in the final version of the DCFR.[12] Even if a political CFR might be enacted at some point, it cannot be expected to cover such a broad field. On the contrary, since the Commission presently appears to be focussed on consumer law,[13] a future CFR will most likely be limited to the general principles of contract law and, eventually, some specific contracts.

---

[4]   Compare also the Communication from the Commission to the Council, the European Parliament and the European Economic and Social Committee, 'EU Consumer Policy strategy 2007–2013', COM(2007)99 final (13 March 2007) at p. 9.

[5]   COM(2006)744 final (8 February 2007).

[6]   Second Progress Report on the Common Frame of Reference: COM(2007)447 final (25 July 2007).

[7]   On that Group see v. Bar (2000), 1 ff.; Wurmnest (2003), 732 ff.

[8]   www.acquis-group.org. The Group was founded in 2002; in 2008 it published the first part of its *Acquis Principles* (ACQP): The Research Group on the Existing EC Private Law (Acquis Group) (2007). For more detail on these Principles see Jansen/Zimmermann (2008).

[9]   v. Bar/Clive/Schulte-Nölke (2008a).

[10]   v. Bar/Clive/Schulte-Nölke (2008b), n. 67.

[11]   On these rules see Jansen (2007), 962 ff.

[12]   v. Bar/Clive/Schulte-Nölke (2008b), nn. 37 ff. For a leading participant's critique of this broad approach and a plea for a focus on contract and business law see Schulze (2008b), 10 ff.

[13]   COM(2005)456 final (23 September 2005).

Thus, the legal community of Europe has been confronted with a text which very much looks like a modern codification but lacks the political authority of a state or state-like legislator. Evidently neither the Study Group nor the *Acquis* Group can claim any political or 'democratic' legitimacy for their Principles. Both Groups were the result of private initiatives, and they have co-opted new members from within the groups. At the same time, even if the DCFR formally appears to be written as an academic draft for a political instrument, it does not present itself as an internal paper written for commissions and bureaucrats only. On the contrary, the Interim Outline Edition was already published as a book which was addressed to the whole community of European (private) lawyers: it was sold very cheaply (for 9.90) as it should be easily accessible also for students. What is more, its broad scope means that it cannot reasonably be understood as a draft for a political CFR only.[14] Apparently, its authors intend this text to become a part of, and a reference text[15] for, the discourse on private law in Europe.[16] Thus, for the DCFR's *raison d'être* and legal existence, the political process in Brussels appears to be largely irrelevant.

This shows that the DCFR is not just an academic draft for a political instrument, but must be seen in the tradition of the Lando Commission's *Principles of European Contract Law* (PECL),[17] on which, indeed, the text is based.[18] Of course, these Principles cannot claim to be 'valid law' in the same sense of a state's codification or a directive of the European Union.[19] Nevertheless, the PECL have achieved a remarkably high degree of academic and even legal authority; they can be seen as the basis of a genuine European contract law.[20] They have been taken as authoritative by European legislators;[21] they have

---

[14]   Cf., critically, Schulze (2008b), 15.
[15]   On the idea of a reference text for European private law see Jansen (2006a), 540 ff.
[16]   Schulte-Nölke (2008), 50.
[17]   Lando/Beale (1995); Lando/Beale (2000); Lando/Clive/Prüm/Zimmermann (2003); on the PECL see Zimmermann (2006a), 111 ff.; Zimmermann (2006b), 560 ff.
[18]   The DCFR includes most of the PECL rules, though in a different order and often with different wording; v. Bar/Clive/Schulte-Nölke (2008b), nn. 50 ff. Not all of what was changed can be regarded as improvements. This is especially so because such changes were piecemeal, rather than stemming from the thorough critical revision of the PECL that is needed; see Eidenmüller/Faust/Grigoleit/Jansen/ Wagner/Zimmermann (2008), 541 ff., 546 f.
[19]   Michaels (1998), 590 ff., 610 ff.
[20]   Zimmermann (2006b), 563.
[21]   Cf. for Germany, where the legislator has regarded international codifications, like the CISG, but also the PECL, as highly authoritative reference texts during the discussions with regard to the *Schuldrechtsreform* (reform of the law of obligations) in 2001/2002. This was even more remarkable, as the PECL had been published only two

been used by European courts;[22] and they are understood, even by traditional national lawyers, as a 'source of law'.[23] Yet, although the DCFR is not backed, in the same way as the PECL, by the authority of leading European comparative lawyers,[24] the force of the DCFR may become even greater than that of the PECL. There are three factors which may contribute to such a development. First, the DCFR includes not only the traditional *acquis commun* as restated by the PECL, but also parts of the *acquis communautaire* as reformulated by the *Acquis* Group's *Acquis Principles* (ACQP).[25] It may thus be regarded as a more complete reformulation of European private law. Second the political context of the DCFR: it might be (mis-)understood as resulting from an intense discussion on the future of European private law; and it is supported substantially by the European Commission – both in financial and political terms.[26] Finally it will be much more easily accessible for most lawyers than the PECL or the ACQP, which are expensive and not easily available in bookshops. The extent to which the DCFR could and perhaps should become a text of legal authority for the present and future European private law is therefore a vital question.

---

years before, and as the rules on prescription, which were taken as the model for the legislator, were not even officially published; see *BT-Drucksache* 14/6040 (14 May 2001), 80, 86, 89, 92 f., 131, 133 ff., 177, 179, 181 f., 186, 188, 196, 209, 212, 217 f., 220, 223, 238, 240, 244, 268 (CISG), 92, 103, 129, 131, 164 f., 214 (PECL); *BT-Drucksache* 14/7052 (9 October 2001), 174 f. (CISG), 178 (PECL). Before, influential authors had introduced these Principles into the critical discussion of the first draft of the reform as supra-national reference texts: see Huber (2001), 31 ff.

[22]   Zimmermann (2003a), 49 ff., further references within. Remarkable developments, in this respect, are reported from Spain, where the PECL are used by the *Tribunal Supremo* and also by lower courts as a driver for change and as a reference text in a process of modernising contract law: see Vendrell Cervantes (2008), 534 ff. analysing 12 decisions of the *Tribunal Supremo* and nine decisions of other courts, all but one between 2005 and 2007. For the Netherlands, where the PECL are likewise beginning to influence actual practice, see Busch (2008), 549 ff.

[23]   See, e.g., Canaris (2000a), 13 ff., 29 ff.: 'Rechtsgewinnungsquelle'; Canaris uses the UNIDROIT Principles and the PECL as a basis for introducing a contractual claim for profits that is not acknowledged by the German BGB.

[24]   In fact, whereas in the Lando Commission the major work has been done by a group of leading professors who represented their respective jurisdictions and could thus guarantee a solid comparative basis for their Principles, the Study Group and also the *Acquis* Group delegated the work to young scholars, who usually did their comparative and drafting work while preparing their PhD theses; cf. v. Bar/Clive/Schulte-Nölke (2008a), 41 ff. What is more, these working groups were too small to represent all relevant national legal systems; often they consisted only of four to six young scholars.

[25]   On the *Acquis* Group and the *Acquis* Principles, see above n. 8.

[26]   Cf. Schulte-Nölke (2008), 50: 'it is somewhat unrealistic and idealistic that a broad agreement of lawyers . . . on a CFR will emerge . . . Therefore it was very helpful that the Commission has supported the process by its Communications and some funds from its research programmes.'

II. UNDERSTANDING THE CFR PROCESS

1. Private Law, Codifications, and the State[27]

Yet, to ask such a question may at first sight appear rather strange for traditional European jurists, who have long worked on the assumption that the validity of all law ultimately derives exclusively from the state.[28] Nearly all private disputes discussed in academic literature had been, or could have been, brought before the state's courts, which applied, as a matter of course, a national state's law. For most lawyers, this was neither a problem nor in any sense peculiar: was it not obvious that *all* law's validity depended on the state? In fact, when Hans Kelsen and Herbert Hart described the positive law's validity and identity as conceptually depending on a basic norm or a rule of recognition,[29] and thus presupposing a sovereign's authority,[30] they gave expression to a common understanding. How, then, could a merely academic text gain legal, quasi-legislative authority?

However, it is generally known that this connection between the law and the state is of rather recent origin and cannot, therefore, be included in the concept of law. The state is a modern concept, at least as it is understood today as an abstract legal entity or juristic person dominating a people in a specific geographic part of the world.[31] In this sense it describes neither the Roman Republic nor ancient and medieval empires, nor even the early monarchies in Sicily, England, France, and Spain. In fact, the concept was coined only after the religious conflicts of the 16th and 17th centuries, when the traditional monarchies were transformed into European nation states.[32] It was not until then that the state was seen as an abstract entity independent of the Emperor's person, that it developed an extensive, complex administration monopolising the exercise of power, and that it gained immediate control of its citizens.[33]

---

[27] This part of the chapter is substantially based on Jansen/Michaels (2007), 345 ff.; see also Michaels/Jansen (2006), 843 ff. and the contributions to Jansen/Michaels (2008).

[28] See Ehrlich (1906), 425: '*[j]etzt ist es selbstverständlich nur der Staat, der bestimmt, welches Recht in seinen Gemarkungen gelten solle*'. See also Michaels (2005), 1245 f.

[29] Kelsen (1960), 196 ff.; Kelsen (1967), 193 ff.; Hart (1994), 100 ff.

[30] Hart (1994), 50 ff.

[31] Cf. Jellinek (1914), 174 ff., 180 ff.; v. Crefeld (1999), 1; cf. also Reinhard (2002), 15 ff. In substance, this conception of the state goes back to Hobbes; today it is widely acknowledged.

[32] Cf. Harding (2002), 295 ff., 307 ff.; v. Crefeld (1999), esp. 124 ff.; Möllers (2000), 215 ff., further references within.

[33] Before, central domination had typically been mediated by independent powers: see Reinhard (2002), 196 ff., 212 ff.

True, attempts to control and administer private law publicly can be observed long before these modern states appeared, under the Roman Emperors, by the Popes of the Catholic Church after the reforms of Gregory VII, and by the administrations of the quickly growing European cities from the 11th century onwards.[34] Yet, it was not before the modern states appeared on the scene that the idea of some sort of a sovereign's full public control of private law was conceivable. Nevertheless, the idea that the law is based on a nation state is taken to be implied within the concept of law by most jurists today.[35]

This idea of the sovereign state's control of the law was connected with the ideal of a codification from an early stage.[36] It may thus appear evident to explain codifications historically as an expression of the states' control of private law[37] on the one hand, and of the private law's validity being grounded on the state on the other. Indeed, codifications were initiated by governmental administrations and thus originated in the political sphere of the state. And they were, interestingly, successful only in strong states.[38] The CFR project can easily be understood from such a perspective: the European Union would be conceived of as a political, quasi-state authority; the CFR process would be seen as the European Union taking full control over large parts of private law; and the European Union would replace the national states as the ultimate foundation of the validity of private law. For many lawyers, this would be a rather comfortable analysis. As it will probably not be possible to formulate a final political CFR in the near future, discussions on the DCFR would be discussions about a possible future law of little practical relevance.

---

[34]   Cf. Donahue (2008), 541 ff.

[35]   For a non-representative sample of authors from various traditions see Röhl (2001), 184 ff., 186, 282 ff.; Grimm (1991), 40 ff., 41: 'Produkt staatlicher Entscheidung'; Braun (2001), 216 ff.; (critically) Esser (1990), 337: '*der rechtstheoretische Solipsismus der etatistischen Haltung entspricht völlig dem Ausschließlichkeitsanspruch des politischen Positivismus*'; Unger (1975), 281–284. For a succinct summary, see Bodenheimer (1940), 52 ff.

[36]   See, for Hermann Conring's arguments in favour of a codification of German private law, Luig (1983), 378. On earlier, humanistic arguments for a codification of the law cf. Caroni (1978), 911 f.; Coing (1977), 798 ff., 805 ff.; Mohnhaupt (1998), 103 ff.

[37]   As an expression of a 'strong state', the codifications have been seen by Meder (2006), 477 ff.; Caroni (2003), 39 ff.; Wieacker (1967), 324, 333: 'Staatskunstwerk'; Wieacker (1954), 41; Reinhard (2002), 301 ff.; Varga (1991), 71 ff., 334 ff.: 'codification is nothing but a means for the state to assert its domination by shaping and controlling the law'.

[38]   Thus, private law was codified in 1734 in Sweden, in 1756 in Bavaria, in 1794 in Prussia, in 1804 in France, in 1811 in Austria, but only in 1896/1900 in the German *Reich*.

Yet such an understanding may be a misleading and possibly dangerous misconception. Not everybody would fully agree with a historical explanation of the European codification movement as a process of the state taking control over private law;[39] indeed, such an explanation may be the result of a one-sided focus on the development of states. Codifications have also been described, from an internal legal perspective, as 'a specific historical phenomenon that originated in . . . legal science'.[40] In fact, it is remarkable that common law systems proved so resistant to codification movements.[41]

There are many factors which help to explain why codifications were more successful in civilian states. The law in these systems was based on a complex multi-layered system of written and unwritten legal sources of different kinds of authority;[42] it was therefore perceived as highly unsecure and arbitrary. More important, however, was probably the fact that the normative status of Roman law as a source of positive law had become untenably awkward. In the increasingly rationalistic world of the 18th century, Roman law had lost its previous status as legal *ratio scripta*. It was therefore felt that the whole legal system was in need of fundamental reform and a unified legislative foundation. In the course of these developments, codifications had become a central element of enlightened natural-law thinking which proved highly influential in 18th century continental Europe. Codifications were regarded as necessary for rationally reordering and systematising private law, an idea which was deeply entrenched in the civilian concept of law. Thus, the codification movement cannot be fully understood without taking these purely internal, genuinely legal aspects into account. In the same way, it is remarkable that the CFR process today does not originate in the political sphere alone, but is mainly supported by academic lawyers who are based in civilian systems. Again, it is felt that the present plural state of the law in Europe is unsatisfactory; and again, the idea of a uniform European system of private law constitutes a strong motive for drafting a (D)CFR.

---

[39] For the following text see in more detail Jansen/Michaels (2007), 379 ff.

[40] Zimmermann (1995), 98; see also Mohnhaupt (1998), 104.

[41] For more detail see Jansen/Michaels (2007), 384 ff., and the further references within. Indeed, the codification debate in England is as old as that on the European continent, and from the 19th century onwards, the discussions in common law countries were no less intense than those in civilian systems. They resulted only exceptionally in civil codes, though. Instead, there are different, specifically American outcomes of the codification debate, namely the Restatements and the UCC, both of which have created a substantial degree of national uniformity and systematisation of the law.

[42] Oestmann (2002). For the medieval times similarly Berman (1983), 10 ff., 199–519; Grossi (1996), 223 ff.

2.   The Authority of Legal Sources and the Concept of Law

In the 19th and 20th centuries, the two democratic ideals that the law could be found in a publicly accessible legislative text and that it could be seen as an expression of a people's political will became key arguments within the codification movements. These ideals presuppose a concept of law that describes legal rules as resulting from and being determined by the political process. However, as is widely known, none of these ideals have ever been achieved.[43] Codifications have never made the law accessible to laymen: even if it is true that a Frenchman used to carry his *Code civil* with him, it is unlikely he understood it. Second, codifications have never been written by legislators in Parliament and often not even by administrations, but by commissions of scholars and other legal experts. A democratic legitimisation of the codification idea may therefore be regarded as artificial.[44] In fact, even the more reformatory codifications did not fundamentally change the law but mainly restated the law in a more simple form.[45] Accordingly, courts have generally continued earlier lines of jurisprudence on the one hand,[46] and codifications have never prevented later legal change by academic argument and judicial activity on the other hand.[47] This must be taken as a clear indication of the fact that legal systems may retain large parts of their autonomy even if they are codified.

However, the autonomy of legal systems, and especially of private law, does not only consist in the fact that judges determine the content of a codification; the legal elites also determine which texts may be applied as sources of law. From the perspective of systems theory, this is an evident truism: if social systems define their boundaries from within, the law's boundaries and

---

43   More detailed Jansen/Michaels (2007), 380 ff., with further references.

44   But see, for a defence of the democratic-legitimisation idea, Rödl (2008).

45   Zweigert/Kötz (1996), 78 ff., 84 ff. (for France), 137 ff., 142 ff.; Koschaker (1966), 205 (for Germany). See also, for the new Dutch Code, Hondius (1991), 378 ff., 381 ff., 386 ff.: The new code was primarily meant to update the old codification both substantially and systematically. It does contain material changes, of course, but these are probably less important than the systematic revision; what is more, many of these changes are restatements of judge-made law. The code was discussed in the parliament, and although these discussions had an impact on the final outcome, they did not amount to more than peripheral corrections on the original academic draft. On the methodological debate see Mertens (2004), 18 ff., 33 ff., 51 ff., with further references.

46   Zimmermann (2003 b), n. 17; see also the contributions to Falk/Mohnhaupt (2000); for France Zweigert/Kötz (1996), 88 ff., 93 ff.; Gordley (1994), 459 ff.; cf. also Kelly (1987), 319 ff.

47   For Germany, this can be seen in nearly all commentaries to Schmoeckel/ Rückert/Zimmermann (2003); cf. also vol. II (2007). See Zimmermann (2003 b), n. 17 (in vol. I), and, as an example, Haferkamp's commentary to § 242 (*Treu und Glauben*) (in vol. II); a summary is given in n. 88.

thus its textual basis can only be determined from the internal perspective of the law and those participating in legal discourse.[48] Historical evidence confirms this rather theoretical assumption: the applicability and thus the validity and authority of legal texts have always been determined from within a legal system. Thus, the *Corpus iuris civilis* did not become the legal basis for the *ius commune* because an Emperor had declared it binding, but for the only reason that it had become the object of academic legal education in Italy and then in most other European countries.[49] True, at the end of the 15th century it had been argued that the use of the recently found Digest had been prescribed by Emperor Lothar III of Supplinburg in 1137.[50] But this story, an *ex post* invention that served to legitimise the use of Roman law, was not only wrong as a matter of historical fact: more importantly, it was simply irrelevant for the law. The Lothar legend was part of the political discourse, where the applicability of Roman law had become controversial. It was a political myth, not an answer to a legal problem. Until the 17th century, lawyers saw no need to explain or justify the applicability of Roman law: they simply applied it.[51] And when the legal profession realised that there was – in terms of the constitutional doctrine of their time – no basis at all to apply Roman law, they nevertheless continued to do so.[52]

Likewise, the *Sachsenspiegel* became a widely acknowledged textual basis for the law in Saxonia – and later also in other parts of Germany – although it had not been enacted as a formal legislative act. To the contrary, it was a private compilation restating the law of the Saxons (but enriched by some more innovative elements). It was laid down by a private nobleman, who had, perhaps, been put in charge of the project by a local Prince;[53] in this respect the *Sachsenspiegel* bears remarkable similarities with the DCFR.[54] When the *Sachsenspiegel* was regarded as legally binding and was thus treated, until the 20th century,[55] as the legal basis of positive Saxonian law, this cannot be

---

48   Luhmann (1995), 15: '*[d]as Recht bestimmt, was die Grenzen des Rechts sind, bestimmt also, was zum Recht gehört und was nicht*', 98 ff.; Teubner (1989), 1 ff.

49   See Jansen (2008), 164 ff., 168 ff., with further references.

50   Cf. Wieacker (1967), 145; Luig (1983), 355, 357 f., 372 f.

51   Jansen (2008), 177 ff.

52   Cf. Thibaut (1814), 11 (§ 13): '*[d]aß der Grund der recipirten Rechte jetzt wegfalle, oder unsre Lage zweckmäßigere Gesetze erheische, steht* juristisch *der Anwendung derselben nicht entgegen*'.

53   See Wieacker (1967), 106 f.; Pahlmann/Schröder (1996), 123 ff.; Kannowski (2006), 503 ff.

54   See, for this parallel, Hähnchen (2008).

55   RGZ (decisions of the Empire's Supreme Court in matters of private law) (of 9 July 1932) 137, 324, 343 f.

explained with an external political source of legal validity, but only with the fact that it was treated as valid law by the participants in legal discourse.[56]

It might be argued, though, that all this is merely history, and that the examples are chosen, moreover, from times when no states existed which had monopolised the power and the competence to make the law. Is it not true that there are legislators today which can and do determine the statutes and codifications that must be applied by the courts? Again, however, it is doubtful whether such an argument is based on a full understanding of the legal process. Thus, during the 19th century, Prussian judges continued to decide cases on the basis of Justinian's *Corpus iuris civilis* although they could (and probably should) have relied on the Prussian civil code (*Allgemeines Landrecht*, ALR) instead.[57] The strong Prussian state could apparently not make them change their practices. In fact, the ALR had never achieved a legal status comparable to that of the later *Bürgerliches Gesetzbuch* (BGB) of the German *Reich*: instead of becoming a main subject within the academic curriculum, the many German territorial codes had long been relegated to the practical, non-academic part of legal education; they had not received much attention in legal literature;[58] and they were increasingly interpreted and taught from the perspective of the Roman common law (*Gemeines Recht / ius commune*).[59]

Indeed, during much of the 19th century, private law had been understood as largely autonomous against the states' political sphere.[60] It was not until the enactment of the BGB that German private lawyers – both in academia and in the judiciary – shifted their perspective on private law from the Roman sources to the new state's legislation. This remarkable shift of perspective made the BGB the main basis of positive German private law. This is apparent from the extraordinary amount of exegetic literature on the BGB already in existence before 1900.[61] This body of work cannot simply be explained with a parliament's legislative act; rather, it resulted ultimately from the decision of the German academic profession in 1896 to replace the *Corpus iuris* with the BGB as the normative basis of academic teaching and doctrinal

---

56   See also Kannowski (2006), 516 ff.
57   Kiefer (1989), 191 ff., 225 ff., further references within.
58   Friedberg (1896), 7 ff.
59   See, for the ALR, v. Savigny (1824), 6 f.
60   See Haferkamp (2008), 669 ff., 672 f., 675 ff.
61   See Zimmermann (2003 b), n. 14, further references within. In 1899, a bibliography contained about 4,000 titles of this kind; this was probably more than all the literature ever published on the ALR. Even more remarkably, whereas the literature on the ALR had normally contained references to the *Gemeines Recht*, this was less the case for the new literature: The BGB was, from early on, understood as an autonomous source of the law.

research.[62] True, this decision may in turn be understood as resulting from a shift in perspective of German lawyers and judges on the state's political will and legislation after 1871.[63] Yet, again, this was a development which can only be understood from within the legal system, as the result of legal discourse; it would be misleading to interpret it as an act of the state taking control of private law.

Likewise the constitutionalisation of European private law during the second half of the 20th century has not been mandated by written constitutions like the German *Grundgesetz* (GG). Indeed, it had originally been axiomatic that the fundamental constitutional rights protected the citizens (only) against the state.[64] In the new German constitution's first article it was therefore laid down that these rights 'are binding upon the legislator, the administration and the judiciary as immediately applicable law' (Article 1 III GG). It followed that they were not binding, normally, between fellow citizens.[65] Accordingly, the 'indirect horizontal effect' of constitutional rights, and thus the constitutionalisation of private law rested on the conviction of academic lawyers[66] and judges[67] that these rights express values which, under the social and economic

---

[62]   Friedberg (1896), 5 ff., 16 ff.; see Zimmermann (2003 b), n. 15.

[63]   Haferkamp (2008), 679 ff.

[64]   v. Mangoldt (1949), 5: '*[i]n den Grundrechten sollte also das Verhältnis des Einzelnen zum Staate geregelt werden, damit der Mensch in seiner Würde wieder anerkannt werde*'. This was in accord with the commonly held view of the Constitution of Weimar: cf. Anschütz (1933), Art. 117, n. 1; 118, n. 556. What was new in 1949 was the decision to make the constitutional rights binding also on the parliament: cf. v. Mangoldt (1949), 7.

[65]   There are only few exceptions, where the opposite has explicitly been laid down; cf. Arts. 9 III 2, 20 IV, 48 II GG. Accordingly, in the first edition of one of the leading earlier commentaries on the *Grundgesetz*, von Mangoldt, who had taken a leading part in the formulation of the *Grundgesetz* (above n. 64), did not even discuss the problem of an indirect effect for fundamental rights; instead he emphasised that the intention of Art. 1 III GG was to clarify that constitutional rights were binding also on the legislator: v. Mangoldt (1953), Art. 1, n. 4. The problem of an (indirect) effect of constitutional rights between private citizens can only be found in the second edition by Friedrich von Klein which responds to the discussions after 1948: v. Mangoldt/v. Klein (1957), 61 ff. (Vorbemerkungen A II 4), and further references within.

[66]   Leading authors in this process were (in Germany) Nipperdey (1950), 121 ff.; (1961), 12 ff.; Enneccerus/Nipperdey (1959), 91 ff. (§ 15 II.4. and 5.); Dürig (1956), 176 ff.

[67]   See BAGE (decisions of the Federal Court of Labour Law) 1, 185, 191 ff., 193 (3 December 1954; this judgment was apparently strongly influenced by Nipperdey [see above n. 66], who was the first President of the Court); BVerfGE (decisions of the Federal Constitutional Court) 7, 198, 203 ff. (15 Jan. 1958 – *Lüth*) arguing that the constitution's fundamental rights constituted an objective normative order ('*objektive Wertordnung*') and that they would therefore also be binding on the courts that decided in matters of private law. On the later development of the relevant case law see Classen (1997), 65 ff.

conditions of the 20th century,[68] should also become relevant within the private-law relations of citizens.[69]

All this shows that it is the legal process itself and not the political system of the government that ultimately determines the sources of the law, and thus decides the question of which normative texts must or may be applied when deciding a case and are valid in this sense. The same is true for what is here referred to as the 'authority' of a legal source, i.e. the formal weight of a normative text in legal argumentation. Norms may be understood as arguments that must be taken in consideration, or they can be understood as binding commands. Norms may be given preponderance over other norms on the one hand, and they may be applicable only subsidiarily on the other. And where norms are applicable only subsidiarily, judges may interpret the norms of primary application narrowly in order to be able to apply the 'better', subsidiary norm. Thus, the concept of the authority of a norm is so ambiguous that it is difficult for a parliament to legislate on this issue. Again, the authority of a norm is determined by the legal system, from within the legal process.

Of course, all this does not mean that the law is not influenced by political decisions, nor that lawyers disregard the legislator. Law is responsive to the political process; the decision of the German legal profession to make the state's codification the reference of private law discourse is a clear example of this. But it would be misleading to understand the law simply as an expression of the will of political actors or as a function of the political system. The applicability (or validity) of a legal source and its authority are ultimately determined from within the legal process. Thus, in Germany at the turn of the 20th century the concept of private law changed when the BGB replaced the *Corpus iuris* as the main point of reference of legal discourse, and changed again when it was later 'constitutionalised'. Likewise, the concept of modern private law is in flux as supranational and European legal acts on the one hand and private lawmaking on the other begin to influence the development of private law. In more theoretical terms, this entails that the 'rule of recognition' or *Grundnorm* of modern private law can no longer be identified with the national state or another political sovereign; instead we are observing a process of fragmentation and pluralisation of different rules of recognition.[70]

---

[68]   Accordingly, most authors and courts have explained the indirect horizontal effect of constitutional rights as a 'new doctrine' (Nipperdey (1961), 15: *'neue Lehre'*) which expressed a change of meaning and function of the constitutional rights: Nipperdey (1961), 15 ff.; BVerfGE 7, 198, 205 (n. 67).

[69]   On the debate see Stern (1988), 1515 ff.; cf. also Ruffert (2001), 8 ff.; Papier (2006), 1331 ff., nn. 2 ff.

[70]   See Wendehorst (2008), 590 ff.

3. Private Codifications and the Law

These observations help to explain the present CFR process: it must be seen both as an attempt by politicians in the European Union to unify and control private law, and at the same time as a continuation of the Lando process of privately unifying private law by means of private codifications.[71] The success of the *Principles of European Contract Law* which have widely been well received and which have substantial legal authority in many national discourses[72] may be taken as an indication that there are many lawyers who feel a need for a European civil code or a comparable, quasi-legislative law-book. As legislators want to draft statutes in a way that matches the 'European state of the art', they may be prepared to accept principles of European law as a model. This has happened already in the context of the German *Schuldrechtsreform*,[73] and it is apparently happening again in the present reform of the French *Code civil*. Now, such legislation has been reconstructed, convincingly, as part of the legal discourse: as the formulation of national legislative acts is increasingly guided by constitutional, European or indeed supranational law, modern legislation presupposes the application of law and thus becomes part of the internal legal process.[74] In such complex legal dynamics, privately carried-out codifications may gain the status of authoritative texts as well. In constitutional terms, there are fewer restrictions on legislators than on judges about which texts to treat as authoritative. Furthermore, private lawmaking has become a normal phenomenon of modern law, especially on the supranational level; and private codifications, like the PECL, very much look like an official legislative act. They are drafted in the form of a modern code; and they do not purport to be a convincing argument about the content of future law, but a valid expression of positive European law.[75] They are not formulated to convince a participant in legal discourse, but to be applied by their addressees. Indeed, these principles usually offer no reasons for the position taken, but comments that are meant to explain the provisions' meanings.

---

[71]   On the concept of a private codification (*Privatkodifikation*) see Michaels (1998), 590 f.

[72]   See above nn. 20 ff. with further references.

[73]   Above n. 21.

[74]   See Wendehorst (2008), 569 ff., completing the internal perspective of the judge as a participant in the legal system and the external perspective of the comparatist as an outside observer with the sovereign perspective of the legislator (and its advisors) as the creator of the law and the subordinate perspective of the citizens (and their lawyers) as the subjects of the law.

[75]   See Art. 1:101 (1) PECL: '[t]hese Principles are intended to be applied as general rules of contract law in the European Union'.

It is not surprising that such principles are likewise used by national academic lawyers[76] and also by judges.[77] On the one hand, there is a growing feeling that the nationalised state of private law in Europe is unsatisfactory. True, private law rests on political decisions, and the modern codifications have been conceived of as an expression of a people's identity.[78] But in contract law, many of the differences between the national European systems cannot be explained on the basis of diverging political values or as expressing national identities: often, they can only be explained as the result of historical accident. Private codifications may be used as a means of overcoming this type of difference: to treat European principles as authoritative may lead to a slow convergence of the national legal systems. On the other hand, during the 19th and 20th centuries, codifications have become 'prison cells' of private law. In many countries, the rules of a national codification are today regarded, by the legal community, as unsatisfactory, and yet they are the basis of private law. Lawyers may look for other sources of the law to overcome the traditional limitations of their codifications. It is not surprising that they have recourse to European principles as soft law, if these principles look attractive and if they have been assigned sufficient authority in European legal discourse.[79]

All in all, the authority of a private codification of European private law may quickly increase as a result of mutually stabilising processes of recognition that are supported by the developments of Europeanisation and privatisation of private law. It is apparent that the Study Group and the *Acquis* Group, the authors of the DCFR[outl.] and DCFR intend and support such a process of recognition by making the DCFR[outl.] publicly accessible[80] and by promoting the Principles at conferences.[81] Both Groups can count on the fact that there is no legal competence for the European Union to legislate comprehensively in matters of private law,[82] and that the DCFR will, most probably, remain for the

---

[76]   Above n. 23.
[77]   Above n. 22.
[78]   Jansen (2004), 19, further references within.
[79]   This is apparently what actually happens in Spanish contract law: Vendrell Cervantes (2008).
[80]   Above at 149.
[81]   It is probably no coincidence that the two main conferences on the DCFR[outl.] were held in Osnabrück (17 to 19 April 2008) and Münster (3 and 4 July 2008), where the Study Group and *Acquis* Group or leading members of the Groups are based. Other large conferences, open to the general public, were held at Trier (6 and 7 March 2008) and Barcelona (6 and 7 June).
[82]   For more detail see Hähnchen (2008), *passim*, with a discussion of different possible bases of competence and different legal forms (such as directives, regulations etc.) for the CFR. On the one hand, there is no legal basis for a binding European instrument comprehensively codifying or restating European private law, yet, on the

time being the only private codification of the European law of obligations.[83] All this does not mean, however, that the DCFR will in fact achieve such status. It will only then become an authoritative legal text, if it is recognised as such within the community of European private lawyers. It is therefore for *us*, the participants in legal discourse, not for *others*, such as politicians or the members of the European administration, to determine the future status of the DCFR.

III.   A REFERENCE TEXT FOR EUROPEAN PRIVATE LAW?

The mechanisms of recognising quasi-legislative texts and private codifications have usually not involved conscious decisions. Thus, there is remarkably little literature on the virtues and deficiencies of single rules or specific proposals in the PECL. Nevertheless, European lawyers should be aware of the consequences of their legal behaviour; they should have an idea of the quality of the texts they are treating as authoritative. Now, a detailed analysis of the different rules of the DCFR is neither possible nor necessary here. Instead, since the authority of a comprehensive text on European private law cannot depend on the deficiencies of some arbitrarily chosen rules, the text will be assessed from a more abstract perspective.[84] It will be argued that the DCFR does not formulate adequate principles of European law and should therefore not be regarded as authoritative for three reasons: first, the DCFR is not a coherent set of norms, but a compilation of nine 'text masses' independently prepared by different actors, and these text masses do not harmonise well with each other. Second, the DCFR is not based on a clear and coherent normative foundation or on a clear vision about its function and aim; at the same time, the DCFR entails unacceptably severe infringements on the traditionally central value of the individuals' private autonomy. Third, whereas a codification should decide legal questions and leave, as far as possible, questions of doctrine to the legal discourse, the DCFR takes the opposite approach and leaves vital questions of law to the judge instead of deciding them itself; it can thus not add to a unification of private law in Europe. At the same time

---

other hand, it does not appear politically wise for European politicians to discuss further competences for the European Union.

[83]   But see the Principles of European Tort Law which have been prepared by the European Group on Tort Law (2005); on these Principles see Jansen (2006a); Schmidt-Kessel (2006).

[84]   This part of the chapter largely relies on the study of a group of German lawyers of which the author is a member: see Eidenmüller/Faust/Grigoleit/Jansen/Wagner/Zimmermann (2008); see also Jansen (2009).

it unnecessarily and often unconvincingly dogmatises private law. If taken as authoritative, it would thus become an obstacle for the law's future development.

(1) The DCFR is based on nine different text masses that have been prepared and formulated independently of each other.[85] The first of these text masses were the PECL of the Lando Commission, which finished its work after completing the third part of its Principles in 2003. These Principles were developed as a restatement of the *acquis commun*, i.e. the European contract law, to the extent that it can be reconstructed by the methods of legal comparison, from the national legal systems of Europe. A characteristic feature of the PECL consists in the fact that they do not take Europe's new law, the *acquis communautaire*, into account: when the Lando Commission started its work in the early 1980s, such an *acquis* did not yet exist, and later this focus on the traditional law existing in the national legal systems was maintained.[86] Nevertheless, as these Principles have gained substantial quasi-legal authority, they have been made, in a revised form, the basis of the DCFR.[87]

The second group of texts was prepared by seven different working teams within the Study Group. These working teams were based at different European universities, namely at Amsterdam (two groups, one for mandate, the other for commercial agency, franchise and distribution contracts), Bergen (lease of goods), Hamburg (personal security), Osnabrück (non-contractual obligations), Tilburg (service contracts) and Utrecht (sale). These teams usually consisted of a small group of young researchers under the supervision of a more senior scholar; and they were advised by an international team of experts. All these groups have published or are preparing separate publications of their principles. They have chosen remarkably divergent methods and did not consistently adopt the Lando Commission's approach of a comparative restatement. Thus, the Principles on the law of sales are largely based on the CISG and on the European directive on the sale of consumer goods;[88] they thus offer a rather traditional view on the law of sales.[89] In contrast, the Tilburg working team on service contracts has chosen a more innovative

---

[85]   Eidenmüller/Faust/Grigoleit/Jansen/Wagner/Zimmermann (2008), 532 f.; cf. also Schulze (2008b), 5 ff.
[86]   Jansen/Zimmermann (2008), 509, further references within.
[87]   v. Bar/Clive/Schulte-Nölke (2008b), nn. 50 ff. See above n. 18.
[88]   Directive 1999/44/EC of the European Parliament and of the Council of 25 May 1999 on certain aspects of the sale of consumer goods and associated guarantees [1999] OJ L171/99, 12.
[89]   Study Group on a European Civil Code, Hondius/Heutger/Jeloschek/ Sivesand/Wiewiorowska (2008).

approach:[90] the group has developed a 'general part' of service contracts and has structured the wide field of services by devising a wholly new system of rather abstract basic types of services. Most European lawyers would find it difficult to apply these rules, for which there are no corresponding rules in national legal systems.[91] It should be clear that such different approaches do not easily fit in well with each other. This becomes even more problematic as the – rather central – service contract of 'mandate' has not been included in the Principles on service contracts, but has been treated separately by another team. However this is not the only strained internal relationship: even more severe tensions result from the fact that the rules of mandate on the one hand and on representation (taken from the PECL) on the other do not harmonise with each other.[92]

The final ninth 'text mass' is the *Acquis* Principles as formulated by the *Acquis* Group.[93] This group formulated its principles not on the basis of a comparison of national legal systems, but reconstructed general principles from the European *acquis communautaire* alone. Debating whether it is possible to formulate general principles of contract law on the basis of the consumer *acquis* and whether the method of generalising from rather specific rules, found in different directives, to general principles can be pursued without 'political' decisions is beyond present purposes.[94] Yet it should be clear that such principles are necessarily informed by different values from the Principles of the Lando Commission and the Study Group.[95] One example is the scope of the content-control of contracts: whereas the Study Group wishes to introduce general supervision of all terms in consumer contracts, the *Acquis* Group wants to restrict such control to terms that have not been individually negotiated.[96]

(2) This leads to the second point of critique, namely that the DCFR has not been formulated on the basis of a clear and coherent normative foundation or a clear vision about its function and aims.[97] There has been no research as to

---

[90] Study Group on a European Civil Code, Barendrecht/Jansen/Loos/ Pinna/Cascao/van Gulijk (2006); on these principles see Wendehorst (2006), 290 ff.; Cashin Ritaine (2008), 563 ff.

[91] Cf. Eidenmüller/Faust/Grigoleit/Jansen/Wagner/Zimmermann (2008), 531.

[92] The point is argued in more detail in Eidenmüller/Faust/Grigoleit/ Jansen/Wagner/Zimmermann (2008), 542 f.

[93] Above n. 8.

[94] For a critical account see Jansen/Zimmermann (2008).

[95] For an analysis of the values underlying the *acquis* see Micklitz (2008), 26 ff., 38 ff.

[96] See Art. II.- 9:404: Meaning of 'unfair' in contracts between a business and a consumer DCFR and v. Bar/Clive/Schulte-Nölke (2008b), n. 79.

[97] The point is argued in more detail in Jansen (2009).

whether and in which way Europe's old and new law, the *acquis commun* and the *acquis communautaire*, can be integrated into a coherent body of private law rules. What is more, the authors of the DCFR have apparently failed to integrate relevant developments in private law theory convincingly. For instance, the recent discussion on the normative foundations of private law, initiated by the economic analysis of private law,[98] the European Union's use of private law as a means of economic regulation,[99] and the loudly voiced postulate of more concern for (distributive) justice in private law,[100] have all been subsumed into the DCFR simply by the declaration that all such values and policies are relevant. Thus, the authors of the DCFR have formulated a long list of relevant values and policies[101] without giving an indication of how to decide in cases of conflict.[102] This lack of a clear conception of the normative foundation and substance of private law is perhaps the main reason for the severe infringement of the individuals' private autonomy, although this principle has traditionally been understood as the foundation of private law, and especially of contract law, in Europe. True, during the 20th century, a 'materialisation' of private law has become a common direction in European private law.[103] Yet the DCFR goes far beyond such developments and thus threatens the normative heritage of European private law.[104] What is more, some of these values, like efficiency, have found their way into the formulation of some of the DCFR's provisions, but not into others, although the normative questions addressed by these provisions are clearly similar.[105] Yet, the most urgent problem consists in the fact that all of these values could be relevant when applying the numerous general clauses and the normatively open concepts, such as 'reasonable'. As a result, the DCFR presents itself, in normative terms, as extremely vague. It does not really unify the substance of private law, but leaves most difficult normative questions to the judges.

---

[98]   Posner (2003); for Germany Eidenmüller (2005); Schäfer/Ott (2005).
[99]   Micklitz (2008), *passim*.
[100]   See Study Group on Social Justice in European Private Law (2004).
[101]   v. Bar/Clive/Schulte-Nölke (2008b), nn. 22 ff.; the list contains traditional private-law values, such as rationality, legal certainty, predictability, efficiency, good faith, justice, freedom, e.g. freedom of contract, protection of human rights, and economic welfare, but also solidarity and social responsibility, the promotion of the internal market, and even the preservation of cultural and linguistic plurality. Not all of these values have a generally agreed meaning; 'freedom' and 'justice' are clear examples of ambiguous 'values'.
[102]   Eidenmüller/Faust/Grigoleit/Jansen/Wagner/Zimmermann (2008), 534 ff.
[103]   See, for Germany, Canaris (2000b), 273 ff.
[104]   Eidenmüller/Faust/Grigoleit/Jansen/Wagner/Zimmermann (2008), 537 ff.
[105]   Ibid., 535 f.

(3) This leads to the third fundamental problem of the DCFR, namely the imbalance between doctrinal petrification and normative vagueness. On the one hand, the DCFR is full of definitions (many of which are misleading or not consistently followed by the text[106]); it compresses the traditional *negotiorum gestio* into the narrow conceptual structure of 'benevolent intervention in another's affairs', although such an institute is acknowledged in no European legal system;[107] and it devises a totally new doctrinal structure and another special 'general part' for the law of services.[108] On the other hand, the DCFR has introduced into nearly every article a general clause, like 'good faith', or normatively vague terms, like 'reasonable'; it thus delegates the substantive questions of law to the decision of judges.[109] Thus, the law of extra-contractual liability does not set any 'bright line' limit against an arbitrary *extension* of liability; at the same time it introduces a *reduction* clause which makes it possible for the judge to reduce liability, 'where it is fair and reasonable'.[110]

Accordingly, even if the DCFR were to be accepted as an authoritative text, European private law would not necessarily be more unified in terms of the substance of law. On the one hand, judges could easily continue their national traditions under the new provisions of a DCFR. It is not difficult to imagine that a German judge would regard only an interest protected under § 823 I BGB[111] as an 'interest worthy of legal protection' (Article VI.-2:101: Meaning of legally relevant damage (1) (c)) and thus grant no compensation for pure economic losses, whereas a French judge would not hesitate to include purely financial interests under this general clause. On the other hand, the decision of private-law disputes would increasingly become a matter of the judges' arbitrary discretion. Citizens could no longer rely on private law; instead they would have to hope for – or fear – a judge's individual moral sentiments.

This shows that the main focus of the DCFR is on doctrine, rather than on the substance of legal rules. But this is the wrong approach both for a legislative text and for a private codification. A codification is expected to lay down legal rules and thus to decide substantive questions of law, not to lecture on doctrinal problems. Doctrine can only develop over time; it is the result of self-referential and reflexive processes in which doctrinal 'theories' or proposals are

---

106 Ibid., 547 ff.
107 See Jansen (2007).
108 DCFR, Book IV, Part C.
109 Eidenmüller/Faust/Grigoleit/Jansen/Wagner/Zimmermann (2008), 537 ff.
110 Art. VI.-6:202: Reduction of liability DCFR see Eidenmüller/Faust/Grigoleit/Jansen/Wagner/Zimmermann (2008), 539 ff.
111 Namely 'life, body, health, freedom, property or another right'; cf. also Lawson (1977), 185 ff., 190.

developed, analysed, criticised, modified and acknowledged by legal actors and stabilised by the legal practice. Doctrine is formulated descriptively and purports to be correct, not to be valid (as would be a legislative command):[112] accordingly, all over Europe, doctrinal statements are authoritative *imperio rationis*, not *ratione imperii*. It has never been heard of that a new doctrinal system has been – successfully – mandated only by a legislator.[113] Doctrine must be the result of legal discourse, not of legislative activity. Of course, legislators had often to presuppose certain doctrinal assumptions when formulating a legal norm. But such doctrinal assumptions are a means for the legislator to express him- or herself; they are not an end in themselves. What is more, legislators could mostly rely on the doctrinal state of the art prevailing in their time; they have not seen their task in developing new models. Of course, this would not be possible, for a European text, as far as the national legal orders have developed into different doctrinal systems. Yet, the first thing to be done under such conditions is to develop comparative restatements of the law, as it stands in the different legal systems of Europe; at the same time, new doctrinal approaches could be proposed as an academic contribution to the legal discourse. Such proposals should be based on arguments; they should not be devised as an authoritative text. But the attempt authoritatively to lay down a totally new doctrinal system without giving arguments is not helpful for the future of European private law.

V.   CONCLUSION

This analysis of the CFR process has shown that it is not at all unlikely that private codifications will become authoritative reference texts for European private law and will determine the future development of the law. Such inner-legal authority would not depend on a political act from outside the legal system, but on the community of European private lawyers acknowledging such (a) text(s) as authoritative. The DCFR is a candidate for such a text. It is a highly important question, therefore, whether the DCFR should be elevated to such a status. The answer must be a clear 'no'. The DCFR is not a homogenous text, but a – normatively and systematically – incoherent compilation of

---

[112]   See, in more detail, Jansen (2005), 753 ff.

[113]   In fact, from the 16th century onwards, legislation often included doctrinal explanations; yet, this was never meant to introduce doctrinal innovations, but to make the law more easily accessible; cf. Schröder (1989), 41 ff. However, such doctrinal explanations in the law have never been helpful, but only petrified the law; this has been a good reason for an increasing legislative self-restraint in the codifications from the 19th century onwards.

nine 'text masses'; it cannot be understood as a fair restatement of European private law; and it leaves decisive questions of the law to the judge instead of deciding them itself; at the same time, it unnecessarily and arguably unconvincingly dogmatises private law.

This is not to say, however, that the work done by the Study Group and by the *Acquis* Group was useless or that it should be ignored; far from it. Both groups have done important research; and they are publishing, in a series of independent books, proposals for restatements or new doctrinal systems of parts of European private law. Even if the DCFR should not be treated as an authoritative text, these volumes should be discussed as important academic contributions to the emerging discourse of European private law. This discourse about the doctrinal, normative and conceptual shape of European private law should not be interrupted before a constructive exchange of arguments has taken place. At present, the discourse of European private law is not mature enough, though, to be restated within an authoritative reference text.[114]

REFERENCES

Anschütz, G. (1933), *Die Verfassung des Deutschen Reiches vom 11. August 1919*, 14th edition, reprint 1966, Darmstadt.

v. Bar, C. (2000), 'Die Study Group on a European Civil Code', in Gottwald (ed.), *Festschrift für Dieter Henrich*, Bielefeld, 1.

v. Bar, C., E. Clive and H. Schulte-Nölke (eds) (2008a), *Principles, Definitions and Model Rules of European Private Law: Draft Common Frame of Reference (DCFR)*: Interim Outline Edition, Munich.

v. Bar, C., E. Clive and H. Schulte-Nölke (2008b), 'Introduction', in C. v. Bar, E. Clive and H. Schulte-Nölke (2008a), 1.

Barendrecht, M., C. Jansen, M. Loos, A. Pinna, R. Cascao and S. van Gulijk (eds) (2006), *Principles of Euopean Law. Service Contracts*, Munich.

Berman, H.J. (1983), *Law and Revolution. The Formation of the Western Legal Tradition*, Cambridge, Mass.

Bodenheimer, E. (1940), *Jurisprudence*, Cambridge, Mass.

Braun, J. (2001), *Einführung in die Rechtswissenschaft*, 2nd edition, Tübingen.

Busch, D. (2008), 'The Principles of European Contract Law before the Supreme Court of the Netherlands. On the Influence of the PECL in Dutch Legal Practice', *Zeitschrift für Europäisches Privatrecht*, 16, 549.

---

[114]   In particular, it lacks the institutional support of a – politically and academically – independent body. The most convincing approach would be to establish a European Law Institute, modelled on the American Law Institute. Such an institute could take the responsibility for the future development of European private law by structuring and institutionalising the present debates. See, for similar proposals, Ebke (1999), 189 ff.; Schmid (2001), 680 ff., most recently Ernst (2008), 280 ff.; Eidenmüller/Faust/Grigoleit/Jansen/Wagner/Zimmermann (2008), 550; Zekoll (2008).

Canaris, C.-W. (2000a), 'Die Stellung der "UNIDROIT Principles" und der "Principles of European Contract Law" im System der Rechtsquellen', in Basedow (ed.), *Europäische Vertragsrechtsvereinheitlichung und deutsches Recht*, Tübingen, 5.
Canaris, C.-W. (2000b), 'Wandlungen des Schuldvertragsrechts – Tendenzen zu seiner Materialisierung', *Archiv für die civilistische Praxis*, 200, 273.
Caroni, P. (1978), 'Kodifikation', in A. Erler and E. Kaufmann (eds), *Handwörterbuch zur deutschen Rechtsgeschichte*, vol. II, Berlin, col. 907.
Caroni, P. (2003), *Gesetz und Gesetzbuch. Beiträge zu einer Kodifikationsgeschichte*, Basel.
Cashin Ritaine, E. (2008), 'The Common Frame of Reference (CFR) and the Principles of European Law on Commercial Agency, Franchise and Distribution Contracts', *ERA-Forum*, 8, 563.
Classen, C.D. (1997), 'Die Drittwirkung der Grundrechte in der Rechtsprechung des Bundesverfassungsgerichts', *Archiv für öffentliches Recht*, 122, 65.
Coing, H. (1977), 'Zur Vorgeschichte der Kodifikation: Die Diskussion um die Kodifikation im 17. und 18. Jahrhundert', in B. Paradisi (ed.), *La formazione storica del diritto moderno in Europa*, Florence, 797.
v. Crefeld, M. (1999), *The Rise and Decline of the State*, Cambridge.
Donahue, C. (2008), 'Private Law Without the State and During its Formation', *American Journal of Comparative Law*, 56, 541.
Dürig, G. (1956), 'Grundrechte und Zivilrechtsprechung', in T. Maunz (ed.), *Vom Bonner Grundgesetz zur gesamtdeutschen Verfassung. Festschrift zum 75. Geburtstag von Hans Nawiasky*, Munich, 175.
Ebke, W.F. (1999), 'Unternehmensrechtsangleichung in der Europäischen Union: Brauchen wir ein European Law Institute', in U. Hübner (ed.), *Festschrift für Bernhard Großfeld*, Heidelberg, 189.
Ehrlich, E. (1906), 'Internationales Privatrecht', *Deutsche Rundschau*, 126, 419.
Eidenmüller, H. (2005), *Effizienz als Rechtsprinzip*, 3rd edition, Tübingen.
Eidenmüller, H., F. Faust, H.-C. Grigoleit, N. Jansen, G. Wagner and R. Zimmermann (2008), 'Der Gemeinsame Referenzrahmen für das Europäische Privatrecht – Wertungsfragen und Kodifikationsprobleme', *Juristenzeitung*, 63, 529.
Enneccerus, L. and H.C. Nipperdey (1959), *Allgemeiner Teil des Bürgerlichen Rechts*, 15th edition, vol. I, Tübingen.
Ernst, W. (2008), 'Der "Common Frame of Reference" aus juristischer Sicht', *Archiv für die civilistische Praxis*, 208, 248.
Esser, J. (1990), *Grundsatz und Norm in der richterlichen Fortbildung des Privatrechts*, 4th edition, Tübingen.
European Group on Tort Law (2005), *Principles of European Tort Law*, Vienna.
Falk, U. and H. Mohnhaupt (eds) (2000), *Das Bürgerliche Gesetzbuch und seine Richter. Fallstudien zur Reaktion der Rechtspraxis auf die Kodifikation des deutschen Privatrechts*, Frankfurt am Main.
Friedberg, E. (1896), *Die künftige Gestaltung des deutschen Rechtsstudiums nach den Beschlüssen der Eisenacher Konferenz*, Leipzig.
Gordley, J. (1994), 'Myths of the French Civil Code', *American Journal of Comparative Law*, 42, 459.
Grimm, D. (1991), 'Rechtsentstehung', in D. Grimm (ed.), *Einführung in das Recht*, 2nd edition, Heidelberg.
Grossi, P. (1996), *L'ordine giuridico medievale*, Rome–Bari.
Hähnchen, S. (2008), 'Die Rechtsform des CFR und die Frage nach der Kompetenz', in M. Schmidt-Kessel (ed.), *Der gemeinsame Referenzrahmen. Entstehung, Inhalte, Anwendung*, 141.

Haferkamp, H.-P. (2008), 'The Science of Private Law and the State in Nineteenth Century Germany', *American Journal of Comparative Law*, 56, 667.

Harding, A. (2002), *Medieval Law and the Foundations of the State*, Oxford.

Hart, H.L.A. (1994), *The Concept of Law*, 2nd edition, Oxford.

Hondius, E. (1991), 'Das neue Niederländische Gesetzbuch. Allgemeiner Teil', *Archiv für die civilistische Praxis*, 191, 378.

Hondius, E., V. Heutger, C. Jeloschek, H. Sivesand and A. Wiewiorowska (eds) (2008), *Principles of European Law. Sales*, Munich.

Huber, U. (2001), 'Das geplante Recht der Leistungsstörungen', in W. Ernst and R. Zimmermann (eds), *Zivilrechtswissenschaft und Schuldrechtsreform*, Tübingen, 31.

Jansen, N. (2004), *Binnenmarkt, Privatrecht und europäische Identität*, Tübingen.

Jansen, N. (2005), 'Dogmatik, Erkenntnis und Theorie im europäischen Privatrecht', *Zeitschrift für Europäisches Privatrecht*, 13, 750.

Jansen, N. (2006a), 'Traditionsbegründung im europäischen Privatrecht', *Juristenzeitung*, 61, 536.

Jansen, N. (2006b), 'Principles of European Tort Law? Grundwertungen und Systembildung im europäischen Haftungsrecht', *Rabels Zeitschrift für ausländisches und internationales Privatrecht*, 70, 732.

Jansen, N. (2007), 'Negotiorum Gestio and Benevolent Intervention in Another's Affairs: Principles of European Law?', *Zeitschrift für Europäisches Privatrecht*, 15, 962.

Jansen, N. (2008), 'Das gelehrte Recht und der Staat', in R. Zimmermann *et al.* (eds), *Globalisierung und Entstaatlichung des Rechts*, vol. II: *Nichtstaatliches Privatrecht – Geltung und Genese*, Tübingen, 159.

Jansen, N. (2009), 'Doctrinal Definition, Policy, and Legitimacy. Some Critical Remarks on the Draft Common Frame of Reference', *Revue Trimestrielle des Contrats*, 814.

Jansen, N. and R. Michaels (2007), 'Private Law and the State. Comparative Perceptions and Historical Observations', *Rabels Zeitschrift für ausländisches und internationales Privatrecht*, 71, 345.

Jansen, N. and R. Michaels (2008), 'Beyond the State? Rethinking Private Law', *American Journal of Comparative Law*, 56, 526.

Jansen, N. and R. Zimmermann (2008), 'Restating the Acquis Communautaire? A Critical Examination of the "Principles of the Existing EC Contract Law"', *Modern Law Review*, 71, 505.

Jellinek G. (1914), *Allgemeine Staatslehre*, 3rd edition, Kronberg.

Kannowski, B. (2006), 'Der Sachsenspiegel und die Buch'sche Glosse – Begegnung deutschrechtlichen und romanistischen Denkens?', in G. Dilcher and E.-M. Distler (eds), *Leges – Gentes – Regna. Zur Rolle von germanischen Rechtsgewohnheiten und lateinischer Schrifttradition bei der Ausbildung der frühmittelalterlichen Rechtskultur*, Berlin, 503.

Kelly, D.R. (1987), 'Ancient Verses on New Ideas: Legal Tradition and the French Historical School', *History and Theory*, 26, 319.

Kelsen, H. (1960), *Reine Rechtslehre*, 2nd edition, Vienna.

Kelsen, H. (1967), *Pure Theory of Law*, Vienna.

Kiefer, T. (1989), *Die Aquilische Haftung im "Allgemeinen Landrecht für die Preussischen Staaten" von 1784*, Pfaffenweiler.

Koschaker, P. (1966), *Europa und das römische Recht*, 4th edition, Munich.

Lando, O. and H. Beale (eds) (1995), *Principles of European Contract Law, Part I*, The Hague.

Lando, O. and H. Beale (eds) (2000), *Principles of European Contract Law, Parts I and II*, The Hague.

Lando, O., E. Clive, A. Prüm and R. Zimmermann (eds) (2003), *Principles of European Contract Law, Part III*, The Hague.

Lawson, F.H. (1977), '"Das subjektive Recht" in the English Law of Torts', in F.H. Lawson (ed), *Many Laws*, Oxford, 176.

Luhmann, N. (1995), *Das Recht der Gesellschaft*, Frankfurt am Main.

Luig, K. (1983), 'Conring, das deutsche Recht und die Rechtsgeschichte', in M. Stolleis (ed.), *H. Conring (1606–1681). Beiträge zu Leben und Werk*, Berlin, 355.

v. Mangoldt, H. (1949), 'Schriftlicher Bericht des Abgeordneten Dr. von Mangoldt über den Abschnitt I. Die Grundrechte', in Parlamentarischer Rat Bonn 1948/49, *Schriftlicher Bericht zum Entwurf des Grundgesetzes für die Bundesrepublik Deutschland* (= Anlage zum stenographischen Bericht der Sitzung des Parlamentarischen Rates am 6. Mai 1949), Bonn.

v. Mangoldt (1953), *Das Bonner Grundgesetz*, Frankfurt am Main.

v. Mangoldt, H. and F. v. Klein (1957), *Das Bonner Grundgesetz*, 2nd edition, Frankfurt am Main.

Meder, S. (2006), 'Die Krise des Nationalstaates und ihre Folgen für das Kodifikationsprinzip', *Juristenzeitung*, 58, 477.

Mertens, B. (2004), *Gesetzgebungskunst im Zeitalter der Kodifikation*, Tübingen.

Michaels, R. (1998), 'Privatautonomie und Privatrechtskodifikation. Zu Anwendbarkeit und Geltung allgemeiner Vertragsrechtsprinzipien', *Rabels Zeitschrift für ausländisches und internationales Privatrecht*, 62, 580.

Michaels, R. (2005), 'The Re-State-Ment of Non-State Law. The State, Choice of Law, and the Challenge from Global Legal Pluralism', *Wayne Law Review*, 51, 1209.

Michaels, R. and N. Jansen (2006), 'Private Law Beyond the State? Europeanization, Globalization, Privatization', *American Journal of Comparative Law*, 54, 843.

Micklitz, H.-W. (2008), *The Visible Hand of European Regulatory Private Law. The Transformation of European Private Law from Autonomy to Functionalism in Competition and Regulation*, EUI Working Papers Law 2008/14.

Möllers, C. (2000), *Staat als Argument*, Munich.

Mohnhaupt, H. (1998), 'Gesetzgebung des Reichs und Recht im Reich vom 16. bis 18. Jahrhundert', in B. Dölemeyer and D. Klippel (eds), *Gesetz und Gesetzgebung im Europa der Frühen Neuzeit*, Berlin, 83.

Nipperdey, H.C. (1950), 'Gleicher Lohn der Frau für gleiche Leistung', *Recht der Arbeit*, 121.

Nipperdey, H.C. (1961), *Grundrechte und Privatrecht*, Krefeld.

Oestmann, P. (2002), *Rechtsvielfalt vor Gericht*, Frankfurt am Main.

Pahlmann, B. and J. Schröder (1996), 'Eike von Repgow', in G. Kleinheyer and J. Schröder (eds), *Deutsche und Europäische Juristen aus neun Jahrhunderten*, 4th edition, Heidelberg, 123.

Papier, H.-J. (2006), 'Drittwirkung der Grundrechte', in D. Mertens and H.-J. Papier (eds), *Handbuch der Grundrechte in Deutschland und Europa*, vol. II, Heidelberg, 1331.

Posner, R.A. (2003), *Economic Analyis of Law*, 6th edition, New York.

Reinhard, W. (2002), *Geschichte der Staatsgewalt. Eine vergleichende Verfassungsgeschichte Europas von den Anfängen bis zur Gegenwart*, 3rd edition, Munich.

The Research Group on the Existing EC Private Law (Acquis Group) (ed.) (2007), *Principles of the Existing EC Contract Law (Acquis Principles). Contract I. Pre-contractual Obligations, Conclusion of Contract, Unfair Terms*, Munich.

Rödl, F. (2008), 'Law Beyond the Democratic Order? On the Legitimatory Problem of Private Law 'Beyond the State'', *American Journal of Comparative Law*, 56, 743.

Röhl, K.F. (2001), *Allgemeine Rechtslehre*, 2nd edition, Cologne.

Ruffert, M. (2001), *Vorrang der Verfassung und Eigenständigkeit des Privatrechts*, Tübingen.

v. Savigny, F.C. (1824), *Landrechtsvorlesung 1824*, edited by Wollschläger, C. (1994), *Landrechtsvorlesung 1824. Drei Nachschriften*, vol. I, Frankfurt am Main.

Schäfer, H.-B. and C. Ott (2005), *Lehrbuch der ökonomischen Analyse des Zivilrechts*, 4th edition, Berlin.

Schmid, C. (2001), 'Legitimitätsbedingungen eines Europäischen Zivilgesetzbuchs', *Juristenzeitung*, 56, 674.

Schmidt-Kessel, M. (2006), *Reform des Schadenersatzrechts*, vol. I: *Europäische Vorgaben und Vorbilder*, Vienna.

Schmoeckel, M., J. Rückert and R. Zimmermann (eds), *Historisch-kritischer Kommentar zum BGB (HKK)*, vol. I (2003), vol. II (2007), Tübingen.

Schröder, J. (1989), 'Das Verhältnis von Rechtsdogmatik und Gesetzgebung in der neuzeitlichen Rechtsgeschichte (am Beispiel des Privatrechts)', in O. Behrends and W. Henckel (eds), *Gesetzgebung und Dogmatik*, Göttingen, 36.

Schulte-Nölke, H. (2008), 'Contract Law or Law of Obligations? – The Draft Common Frame of Reference (DCFR) as a Multifunctional Tool', in Schulze (2008a), 47.

Schulze, R. (ed.) (2008a), *Common Frame of Reference and Existing EC Contract Law*, Munich.

Schulze, R. (2008b), 'The Academic Draft of the CFR and the EC Contract Law', in Schulze (2008a), 3.

Stern, K. (1988), *Das Staatsrecht der Bundesrepublik Deutschland*, vol. III/1, Munich.

Study Group on Social Justice in European Private Law (2004), 'Social Justice in European Contract Law: a Manifesto', *European Law Journal*, 10, 653.

Teubner, G. (1989), *Recht als autopoietisches System*, Frankfurt am Main.

Thibaut, A.F.J. (1814), *System des Pandekten-Rechts*, vol. I, 4th edition, Jena.

Unger, R.M. (1975), *Knowledge and Politics*, New York.

Varga, C. (1991), *Codification as a Socio-Historical Phenomenon*, Budapest.

Vendrell Cervantes, C. (2008), 'The Application of the Principles of European Contract Law by Spanish Courts', *Zeitschrift für Europäisches Privatrecht*, 16, 534.

Wendehorst, C. (2006), 'Das Vertragsrecht der Dienstleistungen im deutschen und künftigen europäischen Recht', *Archiv für die civilistische Praxis*, 206, 205.

Wendehorst, C. (2008), 'The State as a Foundation of Private Law Reasoning', *American Journal of Comparative Law*, 56, 567.

Wieacker, F. (1954), 'Aufstieg, Blüte und Krisis der Kodifikationsidee', in *Festschrift für Gustav Boehmer*, Bonn, 34.

Wieacker, F. (1967), *Privatrechtsgeschichte der Neuzeit*, 2nd edition, Göttingen.

Wurmnest, W. (2003), 'Common Core, Kodifikationsentwürfe, Acquis-Grundsätze – Ansätze von internationalen Wissenschaftlergruppen zur Privatrechtsvereinheitlichung in Europa', *Zeitschrift für Europäisches Privatrecht*, 11, 714.

Zekoll, J. (2008), 'Das American Law Institute – ein Vorbild für Europa?', in R. Zimmermann et al. (eds),. *Globalisierung und Entstaatlichung des Rechts*, vol. II: *Nichtstaatliches Privatrecht – Geltung und Genese*, Tübingen, 101.

Zimmermann, R. (1995), 'Codification: History and Present Significance of an Idea', *European Review of Private Law*, 3, 95.

Zimmermann, R. (2003a), *Die Principles of European Contract Law als Ausdruck und Gegenstand Europäischer Rechtswissenschaft*, Bonn.

Zimmermann, R. (2003b), 'Das Bürgerliche Gesetzbuch und die Entwicklung des Bürgerlichen Rechts', in Schmoeckel, Rückert and Zimmermann (2003).

Zimmermann, R. (2006a), 'The Principles of European Contract Law: Contemporary Manifestation of the Old, and Possible Foundation for a New, European Scholarship of Private Law', in F. Faust and G. Thüsing (eds), *Beyond Borders: Perspectives on International and Comparative Law – Essays in Honour of Hein Kötz*, Cologne, 111.

Zimmermann, R. (2006b), 'Comparative Law and the Europeanization of Private Law', in M. Reimann and R. Zimmermann (eds), *The Oxford Handbook of Comparative Law*, Oxford, 539.

Zweigert, K. and H. Kötz (1996), *Einführung in die Rechtsvergleichung*, 3rd edition, Tübingen.

9. Legal innovation in European contract law: within and beyond the (Draft) Common Frame of Reference

Florian Möslein

I. DYNAMICS OF CHANGE AND LEGAL INNOVATION: A NEVER-ENDING PROCESS

The plea for a *modern* legislative framework for European contract law is on almost everyone's lips, articulated by supporters of the Common Frame of Reference (CFR) as well as its critics.[1] If one important function of contract law is to reduce transaction costs, the need to mirror actual market reality seems indeed rather obvious.[2] In this perspective, modern types of contracts, modern governance instruments of contractual relationships as well as modern drafting techniques should promptly be reflected in the contract law provided by the legislator. Responsiveness to actual market developments seems particularly relevant on the European level: due to the allocation of competences, European contract law must effectively contribute to the establishment and the proper functioning of the Internal Market,[3] for instance by reducing negotiating costs of international transactions.[4] Moreover, the legislative project of the CFR is explicitly linked to the so-called Lisbon agenda with its strategic goal to make the EU 'the most competitive and dynamic knowledge-based economy in the world'.[5] A modern approach seems paramount for a future

---

[1]   On the one hand, for instance: COM(2007)447 final, at p. 11 ('coherent modern rules of contract law'); on the other: Grundmann (2008), p. 246.

[2]   For general discussions of the relationship between default rules and hypothetical consent see Ayres/Gertner (1989), pp. 89–93; Coleman/Heckathorn/Maser (1989); Posner/Rosenfield (1977), p. 89.

[3]   In much more detail see Hesselink/Rutgers/de Booys (2008); Ziller (2006), pp. 92–99; see also Hesselink (2005), pp. 76 ff.; Rutgers (2005), p. 143.

[4]   In this direction see COM(2003)68 final, at pp. 10 ff. See also Gomez (2008), pp. 95–98.

[5]   European Council, Presidency Conclusions, 23–24 March 2000 (Lisbon), SN 100/00 (sub 5.), available at www.consilium.europa.eu. For the linkage with the CFR

European contract law. All that remains controversial is the evaluation of the CFR against this yardstick. As long as the final ('political') CFR is not published, academic discussion is based on the Draft Common Frame of Reference (DCFR),[6] which raises serious doubts whether a future European contract law promises to be modern, whether in its method of elaboration, its general policy choices or its substantive approach.[7]

The question is not only whether the (D)CFR is modern in 2009 or 2010, but whether such an instrument remains open for legal innovation in the years to come: what is modern today may be outdated tomorrow. Market reality changes on a perpetual basis. An effective contract law must primarily be adaptive.[8] Whether or not they were modern by 19th century standards, the codifications of that period would never have survived without their implicit capacity to respond to the fundamental social, political, technological and economic changes of the 20th century.[9] A truly modern legislative framework needs to be forward-looking in its own approach, but also requires an underlying, equally forward-looking legal methodology.[10] It must be able to respond to the dynamics of change: responsiveness, flexibility and openness to legal innovation are key features of a modern contract law.[11] Of course, legislators need to take fundamental values like legal certainty, fairness and social justice into account. These values play a central role for the quality of contract law. But markets, products and transactions are changing rapidly, and this dynamic is nonetheless relevant for the design and assessment of the legislative framework.[12] The responsiveness to change seems particularly relevant when a contract law instrument is not primarily designed as a directly applicable legal text, but as an instrument for law-making. Legislation at a more or less distant stage can produce modern rules only if supported by adaptive instruments.

Hence, this contribution is not primarily concerned with the substance of the (D)CFR, but with the process of legal innovation that it may trigger. The hypothesis is that the adoption of this instrument will have some impact on the future development of European contract law. Its nature and likely effects will

---

see COM(2003)68 final, at p. 16 ('This frame of reference should meet the needs and expectations of the economic operators in an internal market which envisages becoming the world's most dynamic economy').

6   v. Bar/Clive/Schulte-Nölke (2008).
7   See, for example: Grundmann, in this volume, Chapter 3, at pp. 48–52.
8   Hadfield (2004), pp. 194–199; in general: van Alstine (2002), pp. 790–815.
9   Stürner (1996), p. 742; in a comparative perspective see Melin (2005), p. 45.
10   For an extensive discussion see Hesselink (2009).
11   Pistor et al. (2003), p. 679 is similar (for a different area of law); see also Gomez (2008), p. 106.
12   In the context of corporate law, a much stronger proposition is advocated by Pistor et al. (2003), p. 678 ('The capacity of legal systems to innovate is more important than the level of protection a legal system may afford').

depend on the dynamics which the CFR triggers. The question is, will it provide a dynamic framework for legal innovation?

By contrast with the rich literature on innovation theory within the management discipline,[13] research on legal innovation is surprisingly scarce.[14] Concerning US-American case law, one of the few articles on legal innovation recently stated:

> Despite the omnipresent recognition of legal change, only a few scholars have devoted substantial attention to the processes by which legal precedents develop and change over a substantial period of time. The existing scholarly treatments of legal change are invariably primitive. Legal change is treated as if it is something that just happens – that follows inexorably from the emergence of social needs and changed social conditions.[15]

Legal change and evolution have at least been subjects of some research from the perspective of institutional and evolutionary economic theory.[16] Legal innovation, however, implies more than the reaction of the legal system to changes in social values and economic conditions. Legal innovation requires some new, creative element which was not formerly part of the relevant legal framework. It requires some sort of intellectual advance relative to the current state of the law.[17] As regards contract law, such intellectual advances can originate in the creativity of private parties, their lawyers, the business community at large, national or supranational legislators, the courts or legal academia. Legal innovation can literally occur at any level of the legal hierarchy.[18] Yet both the process and likelihood of legal innovation depend on the institutional framework in which these actors operate.[19]

---

[13]   Comprehensively, for instance: Tidd/Bessant/Pavitt (2009); v. Hippel (1994); Van de Ven/Angle/Scott Poole (2000); see also Erdmann (1993).

[14]   See, however, Duffy (2007); Romano (2006); Ulen/Garoupa (2008); with respect to legal scholarship see Cheffins (2004); Siems (2008b).

[15]   Duffy (2007), p. 3.

[16]   Recently, for instance, see Eckardt (2008); Kerber (2008b); see also: Lampe (1987); Okruch (1999); Stein (1981); Teubner (1986); v. Wangenheim (1995); and already Sinzheimer (1948).

[17]   Duffy (2007), p. 3; similar for legal scholarship see Ulen/Garoupa (2008), pp. 1564 ff.

[18]   Duffy (2007), pp. 3 ff.

[19]   For instance, innovation patterns certainly differ in common and civil law systems, even though it seems highly speculative to claim in general that common law provides for a more efficient form of legal innovation. See, however, Priest (1977); Rubin (1977); and the contributions in Rubin (2007).

II.   THE (D)CFR AS AN INSTRUMENT OF LEGAL INNOVATION

A new instrument for lawmaking will change the framework. An evaluation of the CFR's impact on legal innovation needs to draw primarily on its key features. Functions, elements and purposes of this instrument are of key importance, but they are far from precisely defined.[20] Recent political discussion and the academic DCFR give at least some intimation of the direction in which the CFR is likely to develop.

Whereas, in 2001, the European Commission's *Communication on European Contract Law* set out four different options,[21] the 2003 *Action Plan* favoured essentially a combination of two avenues by proposing to improve the existing *acquis communautaire* and to draft future legislation by using a Common Frame of Reference.[22] This was specified by the 2004 Communication, suggesting the CFR contain common fundamental principles of contract law, definitions and some model rules.[23] The academic DCFR has been elaborated along these lines.[24]

1.   Functions: Toolbox, Optional Instrument – and Exclusive Codification?

The impact of the CFR on legal innovation depends, above all, on its functions. A binding European Civil Code would provide a much tighter framework than mere recommendations. However, even the drafters of the DCFR were puzzled in this respect.[25] While two potential functions are explicitly attributed to the CFR,[26] there has been much speculation about a third one.

According to the Commission, the CFR is primarily designed as an instrument for future law-making: '[t]he main goal of the CFR is to serve as a tool box for the Commission when preparing proposals, both for reviewing the existing *acquis* and for new instruments'.[27] However, as the notion of a tool box does not fit easily into the classical categories of legal instruments, this

---

[20]   The role of the final CFR in European contract law is therefore still unclear: see, for instance: Hesselink (2008), p. 249.

[21]   COM(2001)398 final (no action, promotion of common contract law principles, improvement of existing legislation, adoption of new comprehensive legislation).

[22]   COM(2003)68 final.

[23]   COM(2004)651 final.

[24]   For a more extensive account of these developments see Beale (2005).

[25]   Beale (2007), p. 259 ('We have had to work this out as we have gone along, trying to think what legislators would find helpful'); see also: Ernst (2008), p. 257.

[26]   See, for instance: Schmidt-Räntsch (2008), pp. 19–21.

[27]   COM(2004)651 final, p. 14; see also: COM(2005)184 final, p. 11.

expression has been paraphrased in various ways. For instance, the CFR is described as a 'reservoir' of concepts, terms and definitions;[28] as a 'translating tool' for analysing different laws and for discussing similarities and differences;[29] or as a 'co-ordination device' allowing national and European legislators to make informed decisions.[30] One of the most accurate descriptions is its comparison to a handbook that lawmakers can use to revise existing legislation and prepare new legislation in the area of contract law.[31] Accordingly, its draftsmen have conceptualised the DCFR as a framework set of rules, which lawmakers 'can refer to when in search for a commonly acceptable solution to a given problem'.[32] The CFR is intended to be a source of inspiration, for the legislator, but also for other actors.[33] In fact, the DCFR already plays a role in the current revision of the Consumer *Acquis*,[34] even though the link between the two projects is not entirely clear.[35] The proposal for a new Directive on Consumer Contractual Rights did not really clarify how the Commission makes use of the CFR as a legislative toolbox. The question still arises whether legal reform based on a toolbox follows substantially different patterns than legal innovation from scratch.[36]

In addition to its prime function as a toolbox,[37] the (D)CFR may, at a later stage, also be used as a basis for an optional instrument.[38] Two conceptually distinct mechanisms can be deployed to make contracts subject to CFR rules. Parties can either incorporate the CFR in the contract as a set of standard terms (subject to the mandatory rules of the invariably applicable national law) or they can select it as the applicable law (substituting for the national legal order that would otherwise apply).[39] Whereas parties are free to choose the first

---

[28] Lando (2007), p. 246.

[29] Beale (2007), p. 276.

[30] Schulte-Nölke (2007), p. 348.

[31] COM(2007)447 final, p. 10; Beale (2007), p. 269 ('draftsman's handbook') is similar.

[32] v. Bar (2007), p. 350.

[33] See, for instance, Smits (2008), p. 272. See in greater detail section III.1 below.

[34] Green Paper on the Review of the Consumer Acquis, COM(2006)744 final. On the potential influence of the CFR see COM(2007)447 final, at p. 10 and Hesselink (2008), p. 249. No reference to the DCFR has now been made, however, in the Proposal for a Directive on consumer rights, COM(2008)614 final.

[35] Rutgers/Sefton-Green (2008), p. 430.

[36] For a detailed discussion see below, III.2 and 3.

[37] Beale (2006), p. 313; Hesselink (2008), p. 249 (idea of an optional code of contracts 'seems to be lower on the [current] political agenda').

[38] COM(2004)651 final, at p. 5; see also Jansen (2006), p. 355; Schmidt-Räntsch (2008), pp. 32–38.

alternative,[40] the second track would require legislative intervention at the European level. Currently, neither the Convention on the law applicable to contractual obligations (the so-called Rome Convention) nor the Rome-I Regulation, applicable since 17 December 2009, provide for the possiblity of choosing the CFR as applicable law.[41] While the desirability of such an optional instrument is heavily disputed,[42] it would certainly allow for vertical regulatory competition. Competition of this kind might also trigger a 'discovery procedure' for legal innovation.[43] However, economic theory does not yet provide any model sufficiently sophisticated to predict such an effect.[44] In any event, an optional instrument would have a different impact on legal innovation from a legislative toolbox, and it would also require a fundamentally different substantive approach, for instance, in terms of coverage and level of abstraction.[45] Until the European institutions finally decide the matter, both possibilities need to be kept in mind, but the focus should be on the more realistic toolbox alternative.

In turn, a third functional possibility seems to be clearly excluded. The CFR does not aim at replacing existing national contract laws, and it is not designed as a uniform European Civil Code.[46] Though such a code might remain a long-term aim of academics and politicians,[47] for now there is no concrete plan to enact the CFR as an exclusive binding instrument.[48] Legal and functional

---

[39]   In much more detail see Ernst (2008), pp. 263–266; see also v. Bar (2007), p. 350.

[40]   For instance by pushing a 'blue button': Schulte-Nölke (2007), pp. 348 ff.

[41]   See recitals 13 and 14 of the Regulation (EC) No 593/2008 of the European Parliament and of the Council on the law applicable to contractual obligations (Rome I) of 17 June 2008, OJ 2008 L 177/6; see also: Martiny (2007), pp. 217 ff.

[42]   On the one hand: Beale (2007), p. 270 (reduction of cross-border transaction costs); on the other: Ernst (2008), pp. 270–273 (unfit to solve problems going beyond the privity of contract).

[43]   Hayek (1968).

[44]   In some depth (with respect to company law) see Heine/Röpke (2005); see also id. (2006); van den Bergh (2007), pp. 117–124; Kerber (2008a), pp. 89–91; Kerber/Grundmann (2006), pp. 218–223; Gomez (2008), p. 100 (esp. n. 7).

[45]   The draftsmen of the DCFR were aware of these tensions: Beale (2006), pp. 305 ff.; see also the conclusion drawn by Smits (2008), p. 279: '[t]his pleads for a differentiated way of representing European private law, dependent on whether its function is to create binding rules, offer a source of inspiration or form the first step towards the creation of an optional contract code'.

[46]   See, for instance: v. Bar (2007), pp. 352 ff.

[47]   v. Bar (2002); Gandolfi (2002); Lando (2002). As to the level of political support (mainly by the European Parliament), see Eidenmüller *et al.* (2008) p. 530.

[48]   The European Council has even explicitly welcomed 'the Commission's repeated reassurance that it does not intend to propose a "European Civil Code" which

analysis of the (D)CFR should therefore be extremely cautious in relying on such a hypothesis.[49] Much better, the instrument should be conceptualised as what it (probably) is – 'soft law', which might at a later stage be backed or, at most, be formally adopted by European institutions.[50] While the (D)CFR may foster convergence and thereby facilitate a future unification of European contract law,[51] such convergence will be the result – and certainly not the starting point – of legal evolution triggered by this instrument.

2. Elements: Comparative Law, Acquis Communautaire – and Social Sciences?

The main elements of the DCFR figure in the Commission's initial worksheet and are also rooted in the institutional setting of the project. The task was to take into account 'national contract laws (both case law and established practice), the EC *acquis* and relevant international instruments'.[52] It has been jointly carried out by the Study Group on a European Civil Code, drawing on the comparative work of the Lando Commission, the Principles of European Contract Law (PECL) and the Research Group on EC Private Law (*Acquis* Group).[53] Against this background, it cannot come as a surprise that comparative law and the *acquis communautaire* are the central building blocks of the DCFR.

The comparative approach[54] based on national legal orders[55] seems intuitively plausible. European contract law has always been, and to some extent needs to be, based on comparative legal research. Harmonisation requires a certain effort of comparison.[56] More generally, legal innovation is often inspired by comparative legal research, also at national level.[57] Legislative and

---

would harmonise contract laws of Member States': see Press Release of 28–29 November 2005 to the 2694th Council Meeting 'Competitiveness (Internal Market, Industry and Research), 14155/05 (Presse 287), p. 26 (Council conclusion n. 10).

[49] See, however Grundmann (2008), p. 227 ('Let's do as if it was a Code!').

[50] Lando (2007) p. 256; Mekki/Kloepfer-Pelèse (2008), p. 339.

[51] Many observers indeed believe that the CFR will ultimately lead to a fully fledged European Civil Code: see Hondius (2004), p. 13 ('pre-code'); Collins (2004), p. 124 ('just call it a Code'); see also Beale (2006), pp. 306 ff.

[52] COM(2004)651 final, at p. 11.

[53] See, for instance, Schulze (2008), pp. 5–7.

[54] In more detail see Kerameus (2008).

[55] Staudenmayer (2003), p. 123.

[56] Schwartze (2006), pp. 10–14; see also: Mansel (1991), p. 531; Micklitz (1998), pp. 273 ff.; Schulze (1993), pp. 464 ff.

[57] In general see Zimmermann (2006), pp. 10 ff.; Zweigert/Kötz (1996), pp. 14–16; with respect to the courts: Möslein (2006).

judicial lawmaking often starts with the 'moving of a rule or a system of law from one country to another'.[58] Perhaps 'most changes in most systems are the result of borrowing'.[59] In any event, legal transplants are reckoned as a fertile source of legal change,[60] and as a driving force for the convergence of legal regimes.[61] Consequently, the potential impact on future legal innovation is not so much based on the comparative approach as such, but on the presentation of comparative solutions by the (D)CFR. The instrument does not, at least not in its body, present the full panoply of comparative solutions, but rather tries to define common denominators or 'best solutions'.[62] This brings us to the purposes of the (D)CFR.[63]

The second building block of the DCFR, the existing *acquis communautaire*, is not surprising either. Legal change never starts from scratch, but needs to take the existing, politically legitimised legal framework into account. At the European level, however, the *acquis* led a rather shadowy existence while it was believed to be too narrow and piecemeal as a starting point.[64] Once harmonisation started to go beyond market regulation to address parts of facilitative law,[65] and the process of system building in European contract law gathered momentum,[66] the *acquis* gained influence.[67] The crucial question is then whether the (D)CFR should (or does) produce a 'true-to-life' picture of existing rules, or whether it should go beyond that point, either by choosing between different existing options or even by proposing new approaches.[68] Again, this takes us back to the question of its purposes.

A potential third element – social experience, often an inspiration for legal change – has been deliberately left out. Established contractual practices are

---

58   Watson (1974), p. 21.
59   Ibid, p. 95; and more extensively see Ewald (1995).
60   Mattei (1997), p. 124; for a recent survey on the controversial discussion see Rehm (2008), pp. 3–10.
61   For contract law see Lurger (2002), pp. 28–34; Smits (2002), pp. 62 ff.; for corporate law see Siems (2008a), pp. 256–258.
62   Cf. the references above at n. 55 and below at n. 85.
63   See below, section II.3.
64   Lando (2007), p. 246; Schulte-Nölke (2007); see also, for instance: Steindorff (1996), p. 52 (*'Stückwerk'*); Taupitz (1993), p. 535 (*'pointillistisch'*).
65   On this paradigmatic change see Grundmann (2002), paras. 19–25; see also id. (2003).
66   Riesenhuber (2003); see in general Grundmann (2000).
67   COM(2001)398 final, p. 8; COM(2003)68 final, pp. 7–21. For a plea in favour of this approach see Grundmann (2004).
68   See Jansen/Zimmermann (2008); Eidenmüller *et al.* (2008), pp. 533 and 544 ff.; Ernst (2008), pp. 253 ff. (*'Modernisierungsmotor'*); Gomez (2008), p. 104 ('acquis not sacred').

the only empirical element that is included, ranking among the comparative references,[69] whereas other empirical evidence of market behaviour in combination with insights from the economic and social sciences are excluded. This is unfortunate, as these extra-legal elements might have provided valuable information about the actual behaviour of market participants. Recent laboratory and empirical studies by economists, psychologists and other social scientists on human interaction in contracting environments might have inspired new and especially creative solutions.[70] Though it might have triggered true legal innovation, for better or worse, such an approach has never been part of the DCFR project.

3.　Purposes: Clarification, Unification – and Innovation?

The DCFR has been characterised as a 'multi-purpose tool'.[71] Assessing its potential impact on legal change clearly requires identification of its various purposes.[72] These are based on both elements of the DCFR, and closely interact with its potential functions.

The first, and most plausible, purpose is clarification. As a toolbox for the legislator, the (D)CFR provides information on whether, and how, to legislate on the European level.[73] For that purpose, the text primarily needs to disclose similarities and differences between various national solutions but also within the *acquis*.[74] The diversity of national laws is not only a condition for legislative intervention on the European level, but also provides for different potential solutions. A toolbox might be expected to present the full range of possibilities rather than single, uniform solutions, because only a variety of tools would seem to make it a helpful and flexible assistant for legal change. Indeed, the DCFR has been described as a 'dictionary'[75] and 'translating tool',[76] designed to create a common basis of understanding.[77] One of the draftsmen even made it clear that the 'CFR should not try to hide differences', and instead 'present the legislator with options'.[78]

---

[69]　See the reference in n. 52.
[70]　In much more detail see Gomez in this volume, Chapter 6, pp. 101 ff.
[71]　Schulte-Nölke (2007), p. 348.
[72]　Ernst (2008), pp. 257 ff.
[73]　Beale (2008), pp. 319 ff.
[74]　Similar Beale (2007), p. 276.
[75]　v. Bar (2007), pp. 352 and 357 ff.
[76]　Beale (2007), p. 276.
[77]　In this sense Schulte-Nölke (2007), p. 340.
[78]　Beale (2007), 257, at 268.

In this perspective unification, as a second purpose,[79] sounds inconsistent. Unification inevitably reduces the range of possible solutions to choose from. Nonetheless, the CFR has been explicitly assigned the task 'to find possible common denominators, to develop common principles and, where appropriate, to identify best solutions'.[80] Of course, a coherent framework requires some degree of unification, at least with respect to terminology.[81] Some additional reduction of legal and cultural diversity is due to the fact that the DCFR has been drafted in English, unlike most national laws and, in principle, the *acquis communautaire*.[82] Diversity is further reduced because the DCFR is a snap-shot in time, suppressing any later, divergent change.[83] But the DCFR goes far beyond what would have been necessary: the text does not propose any different options or alternative solutions, beyond a single, seemingly accidental, exception.[84] Diversity is only reflected in the notes which have been published at a later stage (in October 2009).[85]

This so-called best-solution approach is vulnerable to strong criticism. Picking uniform best solutions requires choices which often have policy implications and which should therefore be left to the legislator (lack of legitimacy).[86] Moreover, the relevant criteria have not been defined, either by the legislator or the academics (lack of objectivity),[87] at least so far.[88] Unfortunate as this unification might be for the toolbox function, it is unavoidable for the CFR's second function as an optional instrument. As well as a code, an optional instrument has to provide unambigous rules.[89] Otherwise, it could neither fulfil normative functions nor reduce transactions costs, given that parties would have to negotiate and agree to pick single options. Thus the multi-functionality of the (D)CFR creates an obvious conflict between its goals. A toolbox requires as much diversity as possible; an optional code as

---

[79]   Even further see Oderkerk (2007), p. 320 ('ultimate goal').
[80]   COM(2003)68 final, at p. 17; Staudenmayer (2003), p. 123 is similar. See also: Beale (2006), p. 312; Smits (2008), p. 277.
[81]   Schulte-Nölke (2007), p. 342; see also v. Bar *et al.* (2008), Intr., para. 64.
[82]   For more detail see Sefton-Green (2008); see also Ernst (2008), p. 256.
[83]   With respect to the *Acquis* see Ernst (2008), pp. 255–257.
[84]   See DCFR II.-9:404 (where a uniform solution could not be agreed upon); v. Bar et al. (2008), Intr., para. 79.
[85]   v. Bar et al. (2008), Intr., para. 14; see also: Beale (2008), pp. 319 ff.
[86]   Study Group on Social Justice in European Private Law (2004); see also: Canivet/Muir Watt (2005); Lurger (2005); Rutgers (2006); Wilhelmsson (2004).
[87]   Oderkerk (2007), pp. 316 and 321 ff.
[88]   The comments, to be published at a later stage in the full edition, 'will elucidate each rule': see v. Bar *et al.* (2008), Intr., para. 14. See also Beale (2008), p. 331 ('flag up' policy choices).
[89]   Beale (2006), p. 306.

much unification as possible.[90] That unification has been strongly favoured will have an impact on future legal change in European contract law.[91]

Whether innovation constitutes a third purpose of the DCFR is controversial: simultaneously the instrument is being heavily criticised for inventing too much and too little.[92] Innovation goes even beyond unification. It requires not only the selection of a single best solution from a given set, but the creation of additional, new approaches.[93] Even though the Commission deliberately announced an improved, 'modern' set of rules,[94] it never required the draftsmen to invent new solutions. Instead, the explicit aim was to identify best solutions, taking into account the elements of existing (national) contract laws and the EC *acquis*.[95] While the relevance of other *existing* material was specifically authorised, the creation of new solutions received no mention.[96] According to this official mission of the DCFR, innovation is necessarily restricted to questions where none of the existing elements provides an answer. As a result, innovative solutions are presented either at the detailed level of specific rules[97] or in areas that are not well covered by the existing legal frameworks (like service contracts).[98] The official mission simply left no wider scope for legal innovation.[99] This constraint is inevitably at odds with the explicit claim to provide for a modern legislative framework.

III. THE (D)CFR'S IMPACT ON LEGAL INNOVATION

Even if legal innovation was not given prominence in the DCFR itself, the instrument could nonetheless change the pattern of future legal change in

---

90 Beale (2006), pp. 305 ff.; Ernst (2008), pp. 257 ff. are similar.
91 See below, section III.3.
92 On the one hand: Eidenmüller *et al.* (2008), pp. 544–547; Grundmann (2008), pp. 246 ff.; implicitly Gomez (2008), pp. 104 ff.; on the other hand: Smits (2008), pp. 276 ff. With respect to the *acquis* see Ernst (2008), p. 254 ('*Modernisierungsmotor*') and Jansen/Zimmermann (2008).
93 See the references in n. 17.
94 COM(2003)68 final, at p. 19 ('modernising'), COM(2004)651, at p. 3 (purpose to 'improve the quality and coherence of the existing acquis and future legal instruments in the area of contract law'); COM(2007)447 final, at p. 11 ('coherent modern rules of contract law').
95 COM(2004)651, at p. 11.
96 See, once again: COM(2004)651, at p. 11.
97 Hesselink (2008), p. 255.
98 Eidenmüller *et al.* (2008), p. 531; Ernst (2008), n. 101.
99 Similar Hesselink (2008), p. 255: the DCFR is 'best characterised as an attempt to codify existing law rather than as an attempt to design an entirely new private law from scratch'.

European contract law. Yet the effect of a non-binding instrument might be thought insignificant. Moreover, its main elements, comparative experience and pre-existing rules have always inspired legal innovation.[100] Will a condensed compendium of these sources, a 'reservoir of existing legal rules',[101] have any impact on legal innovation at all?[102]

1.   Actors of Legal Innovation

This question calls for clarification with respect to the potential agents of legal innovation. According to the Commission, the CFR may be used by the European lawmaker, but also by national legislators, legal practitioners and the courts.[103] Legal innovation can occur at all these levels of the legal hierarchy. It has, moreover, two dimensions, within and beyond the system of the DCFR.

First, as regards private actors, their degree of private autonomy determines legal innovation within a given system. Legal regimes with highly mandatory rules generally exhibit less innovation than regimes with a more enabling approach.[104] Private actors play a greater role in default-oriented frameworks where they can experiment with innovative solutions. As 'legal laboratories', they operate at comparatively limited exposure to risk, and their behaviour indicates demand for legal change:[105] '[p]ut differently, a highly enabling law provides a fertile ground for legal innovation'.[106] Should the (D)CFR reduce private autonomy, as many suspect,[107] legal innovation within the system may indeed be at stake. But private autonomy can ultimately only be restricted by a binding instrument.[108] By contrast, a toolbox or optional instrument full of mandatory solutions may still increase legal innovation, though beyond its own system. An optional instrument can foster legal innovation at the national level by increasing regulatory competition.[109] A toolbox can provide ready-

---

[100]   See above, section II.2.
[101]   Ernst (2008), p. 277 ('*Normspeicher*').
[102]   For a general functional analysis of non-binding instruments in European private law see Schwartze (2007).
[103]   COM(2004)651 final, at p. 5.
[104]   Pistor *et al.* (2003), p. 678.
[105]   For a more detailed analysis see Bachmann (2006), pp. 50–55.
[106]   Pistor *et al.* (2003), p. 681.
[107]   For instance: Eidenmüller *et al.* (2008), pp. 537 ff.; see also Lando (2007), pp. 251–256.
[108]   Smits (2008), p. 278 (no direct influence on the conduct of private parties) is similar.
[109]   See, with respect to European contract law: Kerber/Grundmann (2006), pp. 221 ff.

made solutions which private parties can 'rationally anticipate',[110] but also adjust to their specific needs.[111] Moreover, the CFR may influence long-term legal innovation by setting the agenda for future academic discussion and legal teaching.[112] In any event, the impact on private legal innovation depends not primarily on the substance of the (D)CFR, but on its potential functions.

The same is true, secondly, for legal innovation by the courts. Within the CFR, a more open textured style might provoke a more creative interpretive strategy.[113] General principles need to be shaped by case law, which allows for judicial innovation, but risks reducing legal certainty and might put the ECJ to the test.[114] However, these concerns would seem to be less important if parties deliberately opt for this instrument; and a toolbox can at most inspire judicial interpretation of effectively applicable legal rules (judicial innovation beyond the CFR). When courts need to decide between different interpretations of national or European rules, they might tend to choose the alternative certified as the 'best solution' by the (D)CFR;[115] such a choice might even be compulsory once future rules are explicitly based on the CFR.[116] As a toolbox, the CFR would rather restrict the margin of judicial interpretation, thereby reducing scope for legal innovation.

The most significant impact on legal innovation is to be expected at the level of the (European) legislator. As a toolbox, the CFR primarily addresses this actor, providing it with a substantive framework for future lawmaking.[117] Even if not binding,[118] the CFR is likely to change the way that European contract law is created and designed. This procedural change is in itself an innovation, and the degree of novelty seems much higher than on the substantive side.[119] Innovation theory, focussing more generally on the process of generating, selecting and developing ideas, would probably qualify the CFR

---

[110] Hesselink (2008), pp. 250 ff.; see also above, section II.1.
[111] Ernst (2008), p. 266.
[112] v. Bar *et al.* (2008), Intr., para. 7; see also v. Bar (2007), p. 351; Hesselink (2008), p. 250; Smits (2008), p. 272.
[113] Gomez (2008), p. 106. For examples of such rules see Eidenmüller *et al.* (2008), pp. 536, 539 ff. and 547–549.
[114] Eidenmüller *et al.* (2008), p. 537.
[115] Hirsch (2007), pp. 941 ff.; Gomez (2008), p. 91; Ernst (2008), pp. 260 ff.; Smits (2008), p. 272. See, however, Riesenhuber (2008), pp. 201–206 (no requirement of systematic interpretation).
[116] Beale (2007), p. 263; Hesselink (2008), p. 250, and extensively Riesenhuber (2008), pp. 208–214.
[117] COM(2004)651 final, pp. 2–5 ('main role').
[118] For its potential legal form (regulation, recommendation or interinstitutional agreement), see COM(2004)651 final, p. 19; Ernst (2008), pp. 260–262; Riesenhuber (2008), pp. 190–200.
[119] Cf above, section II.3.

as a 'process innovation'.[120] The analysis of this process innovation should focus on the European legislator. Legal innovations of other actors[121] may well follow a similar pattern,[122] but the toolbox has been primarily designed for the process of lawmaking at the European level, and it should be analysed accordingly.

2.   Costs of Lawmaking

Lawmaking comes at a cost. Apart from costs of communicating and administering legal change, the lawmaker incurs analytical costs:[123] reliable data on factual circumstances is required to justify the effective necessity to legislate. Moreover, the lawmaker needs information on possible regulatory strategies and their implementation. This information will allow the drafters to elaborate, formulate and assess a range of alternative solutions. Lawmaking requires not only a theoretical and empirical impact analysis, but first and foremost research on existing solutions. In order to generate new ideas for solving an identified regulatory problem, drafters need to be aware of legislative experience, be it in a comparative or in a historical perspective. This is why both elements of the DCFR, comparative research and pre-existing legal rules, have always inspired legal innovation. However, a condensed knowledge resource makes information on both comparative law and the existing *acquis* available at lower cost.[124] Instead of launching a specific comparative research for every single legislative project, the legislator simply has to consult the CFR. The toolbox will reduce the specific research cost that any legislative change requires; the investment was already previously made when the CFR project was launched. Thus, the legislator faces a sunk-cost phenomenon which is likely to have two implications for future patterns of legal innovation.[125]

On the one hand, legal change will probably occur earlier, more frequently and at quicker pace. New legislation will take less effort to prepare, absent the

---

[120]   See, for instance, Davenport (1993); Hage/Meeus (2006); for the seminal distinction of product and process innovation see Schumpeter (1912).

[121]   Including national legislators see Beale (2007), p. 263; Ernst (2008), p. 261; even further (legislators in third countries) see v. Bar (2007), p. 351.

[122]   The same might be true for the transposition of the acadamic DCFR into the political CFR: v. Bar *et al.* (2008), Intr., para. 6 ('a possible model'); Smits (2008), pp. 271 ff. is similar.

[123]   More extensively on these costs see van Alstine (2002), esp. pp. 816–822; Davis (2006), pp. 156–158; Gomez (2008), p. 98.

[124]   Schulte-Nölke (2007), p. 348 ('a coordination device which permits national and EC legislation an informed decision') is similar.

[125]   Generally on this phenomenon in European law-making see Kirchner (2006), p. 319.

requirement for specific research in advance. Lower research costs create an incentive to legislate at an earlier point in time.[126] Moreover, new legislation is easier to justify and communicate if a large stock of comparative precedents is already at lawmakers' fingertips.[127] Similar considerations apply to other actors. The ECJ, for instance, will be more inclined to develop general principles in contract law once it can rely on the CFR.[128] From a quantitative perspective, legal change in European contract law will probably gain momentum after adoption of the CFR.

On the other hand, the quality and direction of legal change may also alter. Whenever specific information is available at comparatively low cost, legislative decision makers will be inclined to base their decisions on this information.[129] The DCFR reduces the cost of information on comparative law and the *acquis*, but the costs of empirical evidence and the insights of the social sciences will remain stable.[130] In all likelihood, the European lawmaker will tend to avoid the more cost-intensive information and rely on comparative experience, rather than develop original, indigenous solutions.[131] Moreover, the lawmaker will probably discriminate against specific comparative experience: information on the 'best solution' is cheaper than information on second-best solutions, hidden in the notes and more costly to process.[132] Yet more expensive is comparative information not covered by the CFR, that is, information on legal systems outside the EU,[133] and also information on the latest developments in EU countries. The DCFR is no more than a snap-shot, which is unlikely to be updated, either through technical revision or by judicial interpretation.[134] Consequently its comparative information is at risk of quickly becoming out of date. Lawmaking on such a basis is unlikely to be dynamic and forward-looking.[135] Instead of fostering legal innovation, the CFR risks exacerbating petrification and obsolescence

---

[126]   In more detail (and on the application of investment theory to law-making in general) see Parisi/Fon/Ghei (2004).

[127]   Romano (2006), p. 213 is similar with respect to the Model Business Corporation Act in the US.

[128]   Kraus (2008); for the general tendency see Skouris (2007), p. 66.

[129]   Calvert (1985), p. 545; in general see Birchler/Butler (2007); Macho-Stadler/Perez-Castrillo (2001).

[130]   See above, section II.2.

[131]   For an economic analysis of these two forms of legal innovation see Grajzl/Dimitrova-Grajzl (2008).

[132]   See the references in n. 85; Beale (2007), p. 264 is different.

[133]   Oderkerk (2007), p. 321.

[134]   See the reference in n. 83 and accompanying text.

[135]   For an opposite view (on the assumption that national laws will converge) see COM(2003)68 final, p. 16.

in European contract law.[136] Furthermore, legal change based on comparative experience generally harbours the risk of distorting, rather than improving, the pre-existing legal framework, as the focus on transplantation often implies an under-investment in the institutions that are necessary to implement legal transplants.[137] This interdependence is particularly relevant at the European level, where such institutions exist only in part.[138]

3. Framing the Innovation Process

Legal innovation in European contract law will also be influenced by the 'architecture' of the DCFR: by its coverage, its systematic approach and its structure.[139] As a framework for the innovation process, the instrument is likely to channel the discourse about future developments of European contract law, but also to exclude inconsistent, perhaps particularly innovative approaches. Social sciences largely agree on the importance of framing effects, which inevitably exert an influence on our selective perception of possible options, and ultimately on our decisions. A large body of research in sociology, communication theory and cognitive neuroscience demonstrates how frames influence social interaction and human decision making.[140] This research has shown how frames also influence collective problem-solving: groups that begin with a predetermined menu of options tend to narrow their frame of reference, so that later attempts to define problems more broadly will be constrained by the initial definitions used. In contrast, groups starting with a broader search are significantly less constrained and consider a much wider range of possible solutions.[141] Menus tend to anticipate the results of the innovation process.[142]

The DCFR frames the future innovation process at various levels. One framing effect concerns the scope of application, for instance, with respect to consumer and tort law,[143] but also with respect to the integration of rules on

---

[136]   Nottage (2004), pp. 241 ff.; in general on these phenomena see Parisi (2010); Parisi/Carbonara (2008), pp. 348–350; Schmidt (1991), p. 58.

[137]   Berkowitz/Pistor/Richard (2003); see also Pistor *et al.* (2003), p. 681.

[138]   Gaps in the European framework can be compensated at the national level, however. One example is general clauses in a system where background rules are missing: Grundmann (2006), pp. 158–160.

[139]   In general see Grundmann/Schauer (2006).

[140]   See, respectively: Goffman (1974); Snow *et al.* (1986); Johnson-Cartee (2005); Kahneman/Tversky (2000); De Martino *et al.* (2006).

[141]   van de Ven (2007), p. 157, referring to a large series of experiments carried out by Maier (1970).

[142]   Ayres (2006) is similar with regard to contractual behaviour.

[143]   v. Bar (2007), pp. 355–357; Grundmann (2008), pp. 227–238.

information and the formation of contracts[144] and, on the other hand, with respect to the (current) exclusion of property law,[145] regulated markets,[146] important parts of the negotiation process (unfair competition law),[147] and protective devices for specific weaker parties like employees and tenants.[148] Framing is also relevant with respect to system-building within the DCFR, for instance, with regard to boundaries and intersections of the different areas included, like contracts and torts,[149] and classifications of different instruments and types of contracts.[150] Service contracts[151] are just one example: many national contract laws have different categories, and there has been no prototype in European contract law so far.[152] Nonetheless, future discussions will probably focus on specific rules of service contracts rather than on the systematic category itself.[153] A third possible framing effect concerns the technical structure of the entire system: the numbering and order of rules, their subdivisions and grouping, and the relationship between general and specific rules.[154]

Given the potential functions of the (D)CFR, this structure has an additional, important implication: it determines the scope of elements which may, at a later stage, be transformed into black-letter law. The DCFR as a whole may even deter the legislator from picking any specific parts, out of fear that the system 'will collapse, like a house of cards, as soon as one dares to touch a single rule contained therein'.[155] However, this bias concerns not only framing effects, but the well-known phenomenon that rules operate differently depending on the system in which they are placed. Just as legal transplants can

---

[144] Grundmann (2008), pp. 238–241; Fages (2008), pp. 305–315; Schulte-Nölke (2007), pp. 333–337.

[145] Van Erp (2008); v. Bar/Drobnig (2004), pp. 317 ff.

[146] Micklitz (2008), pp. 16 ff.

[147] Grundmann (2008), pp. 240 ff.

[148] Hesselink (2008), p. 266; for further exclusions see Micklitz (2008), pp. 15–22.

[149] Grundmann (2008), pp. 234 ff.

[150] This classification does, of course, not preclude the possibility mixing contracts: DCFR II – 1:108; Ernst (2008), p. 251. For a different classification see Grundmann (2008), pp. 241–244 (exchange, pooling of interest, trusteeship); for further issues of classifications see Eidenmüller *et al.* (2008), pp. 542 ff.; Sirena (2008); Langenbucher (2008).

[151] DCFR IV.C.-1:101 ff.; see the references in n. 98.

[152] Both the freedom of services and the Services Directive do not define the category. For an extensive discussion see Wendehorst (2006).

[153] See, however, Baldus (2008).

[154] More extensively on the structure see v. Bar (2007), pp. 358 ff.; Lando (2007), pp. 249–251.

[155] Hesselink (2008), p. 255; v. Bar (2007), p. 357 is similar.

transform into legal irritants,[156] specific rules may 'run riot' once singled out of the common framework. Adjusting CFR rules to the existing framework of European (contract) law seems to be the real challenge.[157] Without any indication as to which elements operate separately, the reluctance to sever parts of the (D)CFR looks like an entirely rational strategy.

4. Setting Virtual Defaults

On a more detailed level, the DCFR made plenty of substantive choices, in particular due to its best-solution approach. These determine general principles, specific rules, definitions and even the drafting style.[158] To what extent do these choices also determine future European lawmaking and legal innovation? Given that the legislator has to take a positive decision to transform the rules of the DCFR into formal law, one could argue that its choice remains entirely unbiased. In this perspective, everything depends on the 'force of argument': DCFR solutions will be adopted only if they convince the legislator.[159] As a non-binding instrument, the (D)CFR cannot prevent the European legislator from deviating from it. Formally, DCFR rules do not even have the force of default rules or presumptions which are applicable as long as there is no explicit opt-out.[160] Instead, each single DCFR rule requires formal adoption: '[l]egislators will have absolute control over whatever goes into any new or revised instrument at the time it is passed'.[161]

There are, however, political, economic and behavioural reasons to think that DCFR rules will possess a significant measure of 'stickiness', transforming them into virtual defaults for the legislator.[162] On the political level, the DCFR is the 'model from which to start the negotiations'.[163] Compared to alternative solutions, its rules are in 'pole position'.[164] Referring to the DCFR is also a route by which the Commission can justify the whole project in retrospect. *Vice versa*, proposals based on DCFR rules are easier to justify, given that they are based on comparative research and on important, yet not univer-

---

[156]   Teubner (2001); Legrand (1997); see also Watson (2006) and the references in nn. 58–61.
[157]   See nn. 137 ff.
[158]   In more detail, for instance, see Beale (2007), pp. 262–264 (definitions and level of abstraction); v. Bar (2007), p. 354 (drafting style).
[159]   v. Bar (2007), p. 360; Ernst (2008), p. 278.
[160]   However, Beale (2007), p. 263 pleads for a partially stronger instrument.
[161]   Beale (2007), p. 269.
[162]   In general, see Ben-Shahar/Pottow (2006); Johnston (1990); Korobkin (1998a); Korobkin (1998b).
[163]   Beale (2008), p. 330.
[164]   Ernst (2008), p. 278.

sal, academic support. Moreover, the implicit arguments on which this support was based can hardly be tested *ex post facto*.[165] From an economic perspective, the sunk cost phenomenon favours the adoption of DCFR choices rather than the development of alternative solutions.[166] Behavioural scientists would argue with reference to anchoring effects that human choice is heavily influenced by the option presented first, which becomes a reference point ('anchor') for the appreciation and valuation of alternative solutions.[167] This effect is particularly strong where information is incomplete or very complex, as is as likely to be the case with respect to the Europeanisation of contract law. Despite procedural safeguards, legislative decisions are as likely to be driven by similar cognitive effects as any other human decision, given that they are ultimately taken collectively by human beings.[168] The choices of the DCFR will therefore probably become anchors and virtual defaults for future European lawmaking.

IV. LEGAL INNOVATION IN A MULTI-LAYERED SYSTEM OF CONTRACT LAWS

With its basis on pre-existing solutions, the DCFR does not propose many new, innovative solutions previously unseen in the national or European legal framework. Moreover, the instrument is unlikely to trigger future legal innovation, given that it strongly frames legal discussion. The DCFR's rather 'traditional' solutions will be almost as sticky as default rules. The best-solution approach is likely to slow down the driving forces of legal innovation at the European level, replacing the Schumpeterian process of 'creative destruction' with an additional layer of path dependency.[169]

If legal innovation at the European level is likely to diminish this does not, however, necessarily paralyse the entire system of European contract law. Multi-layered legal systems provide a broader institutional framework for legal innovation,[170] so that analysis based on the European layer alone is inadequate.

---

[165] Smits (2008), pp. 277 ff.

[166] Above, section III.2.

[167] Sunstein/Thaler (2006), pp. 246 ff.; Tversky/Kahnemann (1974) is groundbreaking.

[168] See, for instance: Glaeser (2006); Rachlinski/Farina (2002).

[169] Figuratively, see Grundmann (2008), pp. 246 ff.; Pistor (2002), p. 98 is similar with respect to IMF's non-binding standards. See also: Roe (1996), pp. 643–645 (integrating theoretical insights of chaos theory, path dependency and the theory of punctuated equilibrium).

[170] With respect to corporate law, for instance, see Romano (2006); Heine/Kerber (2002).

National legislators and private parties might even be better suited as laboratories of legal innovation: Testing new legal solutions at a lower level mitigates the risk and affects fewer people.[171] The innovation procedure might also promise better results at a level where the needs of market participants are more homogeneous and easier to identify. Greater homogeneity also raises the chances of legal innovations being widely accepted.[172] One could even argue that legal innovation at the European level is at odds with the aim of contributing to the Internal Market, because transaction costs decrease only if the (default) contract law rules are applied by a majority of market actors across Europe.[173] Likewise, an optional instrument promises to be more succesful if expressing majoritarian rather than innovative rules.[174] All these factors may speak in favour of European contract law representing the common denominator, rather than the modern, innovative cutting edge. Yet there are countervailing effects.[175]

This preliminary discussion demonstrates that legal innovations do not necessarily need to be tested and developed at the central, European level. In a multi-layered system, national legislators could effectively take the lead in legal innovation. However, it is crucial to allow for legal innovations to be tested at the lower level, and to provide for a dynamic mechanism at the central level which ensures that successful, widely accepted innovations are taken over.[176] This requires both an ongoing European screening process for future best solutions and a substantial playing field for national legislators, be it on the basis of a well-designed optional regime or on the basis of minimum harmonisation.

The CFR may not itself need to be modern. But in order to avoid petrification of the entire system of European contract law, it is essential to specify the functions of the political CFR, and to discuss and develop a multi-layered order of legal and institutional innovation.[177] In a competitive environment of constant dynamic change, creative destruction must have its place in European contract law, at least somewhere in the multi-layered system.

---

[171] Romano (2006) (with respect to US corporate law).
[172] On this interplay see Parisi/v. Wangenheim (2006).
[173] Gomez (2008), p. 102; Hesselink (2006), pp. 77 ff. are similar.
[174] Smits (2008), pp. 279 ff. gives the opposite view; for a general discussion see Kerber/Grundmann (2006), p. 227.
[175] From an economic perspective see Sah (1991) and Sah/Stiglitz (1985).
[176] Kerber/Heine (2002), p. 185.
[177] Smits (2008), pp. 279 ff. is similar.

REFERENCES

Ayres, Ian (2006), 'Menus Matter', *U. Chi. L. Rev.* 73, 3.

Ayres, Ian and Robert Gertner (1989), 'Filling Gaps in Incomplete Contracts: An Economic Theory of Default Rules', *Yale L. J.* 99, 87.

Bachmann, Gregor (2006), *Private Ordnung – Grundlagen ziviler Regelsetzung*, Tübingen: Mohr Siebeck.

Baldus, Christian (2008), 'Biens et services, goods and services: analytisch, systematisch oder gar nichts?', *Zeitschrift für Gemeinschaftsprivatrecht* 1.

v. Bar, Christian (2002), 'Paving the Way Forward with Principles of European Private Law', in Stefan Grundmann and Jules Stuyck (eds), *An Academic Green Paper on European Contract Law*, The Hague/London/New York: Kluwer, 137.

v. Bar, Christian (2007), 'Coverage and Structure of the Academic Common Frame of Reference', *ERCL* 350.

v. Bar, Christian, Eric Clive and Hans Schulte-Nölke (eds) (2008), *Draft Common Frame of Reference (DCFR) – Interim Outline Edition*, Munich: Sellier European Law Publishers.

v. Bar, Christian and Ulrich Drobnig (2004), *The Interaction of Contract Law and Tort and Property Law in Europe*, Munich: Sellier European Law Publishers.

Beale, Hugh (2005), 'The Development of a European Private Law and the European Commission's Action Plan on Contract Law', *Juridica International* 1, 4.

Beale, Hugh (2006), 'The European Commission's Common Frame of Reference Project: A Progress Report', *ERCL* 303.

Beale, Hugh (2007), 'The Future of the Common Frame of Reference', *ERCL* 257.

Beale, Hugh (2008), 'The Draft Common Frame of Reference: Mistake and Duties of Disclosure', *ERCL* 317.

Ben-Shahar, Omri and John Pottow (2006), 'On the Stickiness of Default Rules', *Florida State University Law Review* 33, 651.

Berkowitz, Daniel, Katharina Pistor, and Jean-François Richard (2003), 'Economic Development, Legality, and the Transplant Effect', *European Economic Review* 47 (1), 165.

Birchler, Urs and Monica Butler (2007), *Information Economics*, London: Routledge.

Calvert, Randall (1985), 'The Value of Biased Information: A Rational Choice Model of Political Advice', *The Journal of Politics* 47 (2), 530.

Canivet, Guy and Horatia Muir Watt (2005), 'Européanisation du droit privé en justice sociale', *Zeitschrift für Europäisches Privatrecht (ZEuP)* 13, 517.

Cheffins, Brian (2004), 'The Trajectory of (Corporate Law) Scholarship', *Cambridge Law Journal* 63, 456.

Coleman, Jules, Douglas Heckathorn and Steven Maser (1989), 'A Bargaining Theory Approach to Default Provisions and Disclosure Rules in Contract Law', *Harvard Journal of Law and Public Policy* 12, 639.

Collins, Hugh (2004), 'The "Common Frame of Reference" for EC Contract Law: a Common Lawyer's Perspective', in Melisa Meli and Maria Rosaria Maugeri (eds), *L'armonizzazione del diritto private europeo*, Giuffrè: Milan, 107.

Craswell, Richard (1992), 'Efficiency and Rational Bargaining in Contractual Settings', *Harvard Journal of Law and Public Policy* 15, 805.

Davenport, Tom (1993), *Process Innovation*, Harvard Business School Press: Boston.

Davis, Kevin E. (2006), 'Lawmaking in Small Jurisdictions', *University of Toronto Law Journal* 56, 151.

De Martino, Benedetto, Dharshan Kumaran, Ben Seymour and Raymond J. Dolan

(2006), 'Frames, Biases, and Rational Decision-making in the Human Brain', *Science* 313, 684.

Duffy, John F. (2007), 'Inventing Innovation: A Case Study of Legal Innovation', *Tex. L. Rev.* 86, 1.

Eckardt, Martina (2008), 'Explaining Legal Change from an Evolutionary Economics Perspective', *German L. J.* 9, 437.

Eidenmüller, Horst, Florian Faust, Hans Christoph Grigoleit, Nils Jansen, Gerhard Wagner and Reinhard Zimmermann (2008), 'Der Gemeinsame Referenzrahmen für das Europäische Privatrecht – Wertungsfragen und Kodifikationsprobleme', *Juristenzeitung (JZ)* 529.

Erdmann, Georg (1993), *Elemente einer evolutorischen Innovationstheorie*, Tübingen: Mohr Siebeck.

Ernst, Wolfgang (2008), 'Der 'Common Frame of Reference' aus juristischer Sicht', *Archiv für die civilistische Praxis* 208, 248.

Ewald, William (1995), 'The Logic of Legal Transplants', *Am. J. Comp. Law* 43, 489.

Fages, Bertrand (2008), 'Pre-contractual Duties in the Draft Common Frame of Reference – What Relevance for the Negotiation of Commercial Contracts?', *ERCL* 304.

Gandolfi, Giuseppe (2002), 'Un Code Européen des Contrats: Pourquoi et Comment', in Stefan Grundmann and Jules Stuyck (eds), *An Academic Green Paper on European Contract Law*, The Hague/London/New York: Kluwer, 193.

Glaeser, Edward L. (2006), 'Paternalism and Psychology', *U.Chi.L.Rev.* 73, 133.

Goffman, Erving (1974), *Frame Analysis – An Essay on the Organization of Experience*, Northeastern Univ. Press: Boston.

Gomez, Fernando (2008), 'The Harmonization of Contract Law through European Rules: a Law and Economics Perspective', *ERCL* 89.

Grajzl, Peter and Valentina Dimitrova-Grajzl (2008), 'The Choice in the Lawmaking Process: Legal Transplants vs. Indigenous Law', Working Paper, www.ssrn.com (abstract-id: 1130124), 20 July.

Grundmann, Stefan (ed.) (2000), *Systembildung und Systemlücken in Kerngebieten des Europäischen Privatrechts – Gesellschaftsrecht, Arbeitsrecht, Schuldvertragsrecht*, Tübingen: Mohr Siebeck.

Grundmann, Stefan (2002), 'Introduction', in Massimo Bianca and Stefan Grundmann (eds), *EU Sales Directive – Commentary*, Antwerp/Oxford/New York: Intersentia.

Grundmann, Stefan (2003), 'Consumer Law, Commercial Law, Private Law – How Can the Sales Directive and the Sales Convention be so similar?', *EBLR* 14, 237.

Grundmann, Stefan (2004), 'The Optional European Code on the Basis of the Acquis Communautaire – Starting Point and Trends', *ELJ* 698.

Grundmann, Stefan (2006), 'The General Clause or Standard in EC Contract Law Directives – A Survey on Some Important Legal Measures and Aspects in EC Law', in Stefan Grundmann and Dennis Mazeaud (eds), *General Clauses and Standards in European Contract Law*, The Hague/London/New York: Kluwer, 141.

Grundmann, Stefan (2008), 'The Structure of the DCFR – Which Approach for Today's Contract Law?', *ERCL* 225.

Grundmann, Stefan and Martin Schauer (eds) (2006), *The Architecture of European Codes and Contract Law*, The Hague/London/New York: Kluwer.

Hadfield, Gillian K. (2004), 'The Many Legal Institutions That Support Contractual Commitments', in Claude Menard and Mary M. Shirley (eds), *Handbook of New Institutional Economics*, New York/Dordrecht: Springer, 175.

Hage, Jerald and Marius Meeus (eds) (2006), *Innovation, Science and Institutional Change: A Research Handbook*, New York/Oxford: Oxford University Press.

v. Hayek, Friedrich A. (1968), 'Competition as a Discovery Procedure', reprinted in: *Quarterly Journal of Austrian Economics* 5:3, 9.

Heine, Klaus and Wolfgang Kerber (2002), 'European Corporate Laws, Regulatory Competition and Path Dependence', *European Journal of Law and Economics* 13, 47.

Heine, Klaus and Katarina Röpke (2005), 'Vertikaler Regulierungswettbewerb und europäischer Binnenmarkt – die Europäische Aktiengesellschaft als supranationales Rechtsangebot', *ORDO* 56, 1575.

Heine, Klaus and Katarina Röpke (2006), 'Zentralität und Dezentralität im europäischen Zivilrecht', in Klaus Heine and Wolfgang Kerber (eds), *Zentralität und Dezentralität von Regulierung in Europa*, 155.

Hesselink, Martijn W. (2005), 'Non-Mandatory Rules in European Contract Law', *ERCL* 44.

Hesselink, Martijn W. (2008), 'Common Frame of Reference and Social Justice', *ERCL* 248.

Hesselink, Martijn W. (2009), 'A European Legal Method? On European Private Law and Scientific Method', *European Law Journal* 15, 20.

Hesselink, Martijn W., Jacobien Rutgers and Tim de Booys (2008), 'The Legal Basis for an Optional Instrument on European Contract Law', Working Paper, www.ssrn.com (abstract-id=1091119), 20 July.

v. Hippel, Eric (1994), *The Sources of Innovation*, New York/Oxford: Oxford University Press.

Hirsch, Günter, 'Erwartungen der gerichtlichen Praxis an einen Gemeinsamen Referenzrahmen für ein Europäisches Vertragsrecht', *Zeitschrift für Wirtschaftsrecht (ZIP)* 937.

Hondius, Ewoud (2004), 'Towards a European Civil Code', in Arthur Hartkamp *et al.* (eds), *Towards a European Civil Code*, The Hague/London/New York: Kluwer (3rd edn), 3.

Jansen, Nils (2006), 'European Civil Code', in Jan Smits (ed.), *Elgar Encyclopedia of Comparative Law*, Cheltenham, UK and Northampton, Mass.: Edward Elgar, 247.

Jansen, Nils and Reinhard Zimmermann (2008), 'Restating the Acquis Communautaire? A Critical Examination of the "Principles of the Existing EC Contract Law"', *Modern Law Review* 71, 505.

Johnson-Cartee, Karen S. (2005), *News Narrative and News Framing: Constructing Political Reality*, Lanham, Mld.: Rowman and Littlefield Publishers.

Johnston, Jason S. (1990), 'Strategic Bargaining and the Economic Theory of Default Rules', *Yale L.J.* 100, 615.

Kahneman, Daniel and Amos Tversky (eds) (2000), *Choices, Values, and Frames*, New York/Cambridge: Cambridge University Press.

Kerameus, Konstantinos D. (2008), 'Comparative Law and the CFR', in Reiner Schulze (ed.), *Common Frame of Reference and Existing EC Contract Law*, Munich: Sellier European Law Publishers, 25.

Kerber, Wolfgang (2008a), 'European Systems of Private Laws: An Economic Perspective', in Fabrizio Cafaggi and Horatia Muir Watt (eds), *Making European Private Law: Governance Design*, Cheltenham, UK and Northampton, Mass., US: Edward Elgar, 64.

Kerber, Wolfgang (2008b), 'Institutional Change in Globalization: Transnational Commercial Law from an Evolutionary Economics Perspective', *German L. J.* 9, 411.

Kerber, Wolfgang and Stefan Grundmann, 'An Optional European Contract Law Code: Advantages and Disadvantages', *European Journal of Law and Economics* 21, 215.

Kerber, Wolfgang and Klaus Heine (2002), 'Zur Gestaltung von Mehrebenen-Rechtssystemen aus ökonomischer Sicht', in Claus Ott and Hans-Bernd Schäfer (eds), *Vereinheitlichung und Diversität des Zivilrechts in transnationalen Wirtschaftsräumen*, Tübingen: Mohr Siebeck, 167.

Kirchner, Christian (2006), 'The Development of European Community Law in the Light of New Institutional Economics', in Ulrich Bindseil, Justus Haucap and Christian Wey (eds.), *Institutions in Perspective – Festschrift in Honor of Rudolf Richter*, Tübingen: Mohr Siebeck, 309.

Korobkin, Russell (1998a), 'The Status Quo Bias and Contract Default Rules', *Cornell L. Rev.* 83, 608.

Korobkin, Russell (1998b), 'Inertia and Preference in Contract Negotiation: The Psychological Power of Default Rules and Form Terms', *Vand. L. Rev.* 51, 1583.

Kraus, Dieter (2008), 'Die Anwendung allgemeiner Grundsätze des Gemeinschafts-rechts in Privatrechtsbeziehungen', in Karl Riesenhuber (ed.), *Entwicklungen nicht-legislatorischer Rechtsangleichung im Europäischen Privatrecht*, Berlin: de Gruyter, 39.

Lampe, Ernst J. (1987), *Genetische Rechtstheorie: Recht, Evolution und Geschichte*, Freiburg (Breisgau): Alber.

Lando, Ole (2002), 'Why Does Europe Need a Civil Code', in Stefan Grundmann and Jules Stuyck (eds), *An Academic Green Paper on European Contract Law*, The Hague/London/New York: Kluwer, 207.

Lando, Ole (2007), 'The Structure and the Legal Values of the Common Frame of Reference (CFR)', *ERCL* 245.

Langenbucher, Katja (2008), 'The Draft Common Frame of Reference: Agency Authority and Its Scope', *ERCL* 375.

Legrand, Pierre, 'The Impossibility of Legal Transplants', *Maastricht Journal of European and Comparative Law* 4, 111.

Lurger, Brigitta (2002), *Grundfragen der Vereinheitlichung des Vertragsrechts in der Europäischen Union*, Vienna/New York: Springer.

Lurger, Brigitta (2005), 'The Future of European Contract Law between Freedom of Contract, Social Justice, and Market Rationality', *ERCL* 442.

Macho-Stadler, Inés and J. David Pérez-Castrillo (2001), *An Introduction to the Economics of Information – Incentives and Contracts*, New York/Oxford: Oxford University Press (2nd edn).

Maier, Norman (1970), *Problem Solving and Creativity in Individuals and Groups*, Belmont, Cal.: Brooks-Cole Pub. Co.

Mansel, Heinz-Peter (1991), 'Rechtsvergleichung und europäische Rechtseinheit', *Juristenzeitung (JZ)* 529.

Martiny, Dieter (2007), 'CFR und internationales Vertragsrecht', *Zeitschrift für Europäisches Privatrecht (ZEuP)* 212.

Mattei, Ugo (1997), *Comparative Law and Economics*, Ann Arbor, Mich: University of Michigan Press.

Mekki, Mustapha and Martine Kloepfer-Pelèse (2008), 'Good Faith and Fair Dealing in the DCFR', *ERCL* 338.

Melin, Patrick (2005), *Gesetzesauslegung in den USA und in Deutschland*, Tübingen: Mohr Siebeck.

Micklitz, Hans-W. (1998), 'Perspektiven eines europäischen Privatrechts – Ius Commune Praeter Legem?', *Zeitschrift für Europäisches Privatrecht (ZEuP)* 253.

Micklitz, Hans-W. (2008), 'The Visible Hand of European Regulatory Private Law', EUI Working Paper 2008/14, www.cadmus.iue.it, 20 July.

Möslein, Florian (2006), 'Rechtsangleichung durch Richterrecht', in Karl Riesenhuber and Kanako Takayama (eds), *Rechtsangleichung – Grundlagen, Methoden und Inhalte*, Berlin: de Gruyter, 279.

Nottage, Luke (2004), 'Convergence, Divergence, and the Middle Way in Unifying or Harmonizing Private Law', *Annual of German and European Law* 1, 166.

Oderkerk, Marieke (2007), 'The CFR and the Method(s) of Comparative Legal Research', *ERCL* 315.

Okruch, Stefan (1999), *Innovation und Diffusion von Normen: Grundlagen und Elemente einer evolutorischen Theorie des Institutionenwandels*, Berlin: Duncker & Humblot.

Parisi, Francesco (2010), 'Harmonization of European Private Law: An Economic Analysis', in Mauro Bussani and Franz Werro (eds), *European Private Law – A Handbook – Vol. 2*, Bern: Stämpfli, Durham, NC: Carolina Academic Press and Brussels: Bruylant (forthcoming).

Parisi, Francesco and Emanuela Carbonara (2008), 'Harmonizing European Law: Bargaining, Competition and Legal Obsolescence', in Thomas Eger *et al.* (eds), *Internationalization of the Law and its Economic Analysis – Festschrift for Hans-Bernd Schäfer*, Wiesbaden: Gabler, p. 339.

Parisi, Francesco, Vincy Fon and Nita Ghei (2004), 'The Value of Waiting in Lawmaking', *European Journal of Law and Economics* 18, 131.

Parisi, Francesco and Georg v. Wangenheim (2006), 'Legislation and Countervailing Effects from Social Norms', in Christian Schubert and Georg v. Wangenheim (eds), *The Evolution and Design of Institutions*, London: Routledge, 25.

Pistor, Katharina (2002), 'The Standardization of Law and Its Effect on Developing Economies', *Am. J. Comp. Law* 50, 97.

Pistor, Katharina, Yoram Keinan, Jan Kleinheisterkamp and Mark D. West (2003), 'Innovation in Corporate Law', *Journal of Comparative Economics* 31, 676.

Posner, Richard A. and Andrew M. Rosenfield (1977), 'Impossibility and Related Doctrines in Contract Law: An Economic Analysis', *Journal of Legal Studies* 6, 83.

Priest, George L. (1977), 'The Common Law Process and the Selection of Efficient Rules', *Journal of Legal Studies* 6, 65.

Rachlinski, Jeffrey J. and Cynthia R. Farina (2002), 'Cognitive Psychology and Optimal Government Design', *Cornell L. Rev.* 87, 549.

Rehm, Gebhard M. (2008), 'Rechtstransplantate als Instrument der Rechtsreform und transplantation', *RabelsZ* 72, 1.

Riesenhuber, Karl (2003), *System und Prinzipien des Europäischen Vertragsrechts* Berlin: de Gruyter.

Riesenhuber, Karl (2008), 'Systembildung durch den CFR – Wirkungen auf die systematische Auslegung des Gemeinschaftsrechts', in Martin Schmidt-Kessel (ed.), *Der Gemeinsame Referenzrahmen*, Munich: Sellier European Law Publishers, pp. 174–216.

Roe, Mark J. (1996), 'Chaos and Evolution in Law and Economics', *Harv. L. Rev.* 109, 641.

Romano, Roberta (2006), 'The States as Laboratory: Legal Innovation and State Competition for Corporate Charters', *Yale J. on Reg.* 23, 2097.

Rubin, Paul H. (1977), 'Why is the Common Law Efficient?', *Journal of Legal Studies* 6, 51.

Rubin, Paul H. (ed.) (2007), *The Evolution of Efficient Common Law*, Cheltenham, UK and Northampton, Mass.: Edward Elgar.

Rutgers, Jacobien (2005), 'The Rule of Reason and Private Law or the Limits of

Harmonization', in Annette Schrauwen (ed.), *Rule of Reason: Rethinking Another Classic of EC Legal Doctrine*, Groningen: Europa Law Publishing, 143.

Rutgers, Jacobien (2006), 'An Optional Instrument and Social Dumping', *ERCL* 199.

Rutgers, Jacobien and Ruth Sefton-Green (2008), 'Revising the Consumer Acquis: (Half) Opening the Doors of the Trojan Horse', *ERPL* 427.

Sah, Raaj K. (1991), 'Fallibility in Human Organizations and Political Systems', *Journal of Economic Perspectives* 5, 67.

Sah, Raaj K. and Joseph A. Stiglitz (1985), 'Human Fallibility and Economic Organizations', *The American Economic Review* 75, 292.

Schmidt, Hartmut (1991), 'Economic Analysis of the Allocation of Regulatory Competence in the European Communities', in Richard M. Buxbaum *et al.* (eds.), *European Business Law*, Berlin: de Gruyter, 51.

Schmidt-Räntsch, Jürgen (2008), 'Per Knopfdruck nach Europa und per Mausklick zum Europäischen Vertragsrecht für Verbraucher? – Zwischenbilanz zum Europäischen Vertragsrecht', in Karl Riesenhuber (ed.), *Entwicklungen nicht-legislatorischer Rechtsangleichung im Europäischen Privatrecht*, Berlin: de Gruyter, 1.

Schulte-Nölke, Hans (2007), 'EC Law on the Formation of Contract – from the Common Frame of Reference to the "Blue Button"', *ERCL* 332.

Schulze, Reiner (1993), 'Allgemeine Rechtsgrundsätze und Europäisches Privatrecht', *Zeitschrift für Europäisches Privatrecht (ZEuP)* 442.

Schulze, Reiner (2008), 'The Academic Draft of the CFR and the EC Contract Law', in Reiner Schulze (ed.), *Common Frame of Reference and Existing EC Contract Law*, Munich: Sellier European Law Publishers, 3.

Schumpeter, Joseph (1912), *Theorie der wirtschaftlichen Entwicklung*, Leipzig: Duncker & Humblot.

Schwartze, Andreas (2006), 'Die Rechtsvergleichung', in Karl Riesenhuber (ed.), *Europäische Methodenlehre – Handbuch für Ausbildung und Praxis*, Berlin: de Gruyter, 75.

Schwartze, Andreas (2007), 'Europäisierung des Zivilrechts durch "soft law" – Zu den Wirkungen von Restatements, Principles, Modellgesetzen und anderen nicht verbindlichen Instrumenten', in Thomas Eger and Hans-Bernd Schäfer (eds), *Ökonomische Analyse der Europäischen Zivilrechtsentwicklung*, Tübingen: Mohr Siebeck, 130.

Sefton-Green, Ruth (2008), 'Sense and Sensibilities: The DCFR and the Preservation of Cultural and Linguistic Plurality', *ERCL* 281.

Siems, Mathias M. (2008a), *Convergence in Shareholder Law*, New York/Cambridge: Cambridge University Press.

Siems, Mathias M. (2008b) 'Legal Originality', *Oxford Journal of Legal Studies* 28, 147.

Sinzheimer, Hugo (1948), *Die Theorie der Gesetzgebung – Die Idee der Evolution im Recht*, Haarlem: H.D. Tjeenk Willink.

Sirena, Pietro (2008), 'The DCFR: Restitution, Unjust Enrichment and Related Issues', *ERCL* 445.

Skouris, Vassilios (2007), 'Rechtskulturen im Dialog – Über Verständnisse und Unverständnisse, Risiken und Chancen einer internationalen Rechtsordnung und Rechtsprechung', in Junichi Murakami, Hans-Peter Marutschke and Karl Riesenhuber (eds), *Globalisierung und Recht*, Berlin: de Gruyter, 61.

Smits, Jan (2002), *The Making of European Private Law – Towards a Ius Commune Europaeum as a Mixed Legal System*, Antwerp/Oxford/New York: Intersentia.

Smits, Jan (2008), 'The Draft Common Frame of Reference, Methodological Nationalism and the Way Forward', *ERCL* 270.
Snow, David A., E. Burke Rochford Jr., Steven K. Worden and Robert D. Benford (1986), 'Frame Alignment Processes, Micromobilization, and Movement Participation', *American Sociological Review* 51, 464.
Staudenmayer, Dirk (2003), 'The Commission Action Plan on European Contract Law', *ERPL* 113.
Stein, Peter (1981), *Die Idee der Evolution im Recht*, Göttingen: Vanderhoeck & Ruprecht.
Steindorff, Ernst (1996), *EG-Vertrag und Privatrecht*, Baden-Baden: Nomos.
Study Group on Social Justice in European Private Law (2004), 'Social Justice in European Private Law: a Manifesto', *European Law Journal* 10, 653.
Stürner, Rolf (1996), Der hundertste Geburtstag des BGB – nationale Kodifikation im Greisenalter?, *Juristenzeitung (JZ)* 741.
Sunstein, Cass R. and Richard H. Thaler (2006), 'Preferences, Paternalism, and Liberty', in Serena Olsaretti (ed.), *Preferences and Well-Being*, New York/ Cambridge: Cambridge University Press, 233.
Taupitz, Jochen (1993), 'Privatrechtsvereinheitlichung durch die EG – Sachrechts- oder Kollisionsrechtsvereinheitlichung?', *Juristenzeitung (JZ)* 533.
Teubner, Gunther (1986), 'Autopoiese im Recht: Zum Verhältnis von Evolution und Steuerung im Rechtssystem', EUI Working Paper 1986/213.
Teubner, Gunther (2001), 'Legal Irritants: How Unifying Law Ends Up in New Divergences', in Peter Hall and David Soskice (eds), *Varieties of Capitalism: The Institutional Foundations of Comparative Advantage*, Oxford: Oxford University Press, 417.
Tidd, Joe, John Bessant and Keith Pavitt (2009), *Managing Innovation: Integrating Technological, Market and Organizational Change* (4th edn), Chichester: John Wiley & Sons.
Tversky, Amos and Daniel Kahnemann (1974), 'Judgment under Uncertainty: Heuristics and Biases', *Science* 185, 1124.
Ulen, Thomas S. and Nuno Garoupa (2008), 'The Market for Legal Innovation: Law and Economics in Europe and the United States', *Alabama L. R.* 59, 1555.
van Alstine, Michael P. (2002), 'The Costs of Legal Change', *UCLA L. Rev.* 49, 789.
van den Bergh, Roger (2007), 'Der Gemeinsame Referenzrahmen: Abschied von der Harmonisierung des Vertragsrechts', in Thomas Eger and Hans-Bernd Schäfer (eds), *Ökonomische Analyse der Europäischen Zivilrechtsentwicklung*, Tübingen: Mohr Siebeck, 111.
Van de Ven, Andrew H. (2007), *Engaged Scholarship – A Guide for Organizational and Social Research*, New York/Oxford: Oxford University Press.
Van de Ven, Andrew H., Harold L. Angle and Marshall Scott Poole (eds) (2000), *Research on the Management of Innovation – The Minnesota Studies*, New York/Oxford: Oxford University Press.
Van Erp, Sjef (2008), 'DCFR and Property Law: the Need for Consistency and Coherence', in Reiner Schulze (ed.), *Common Frame of Reference and Existing EC Contract Law*, Munich: Sellier European Law Publishers, 249.
v. Wangenheim, Georg (1995), *Die Evolution von Recht – Ursachen und Wirkungen häufigkeitsabhängigen Verhaltens in der Rechtsfortbildung*, Tübingen: Mohr Siebeck.
Watson, Alan (1974), *Legal Transplants: An Approach to Comparative Law*, Athens, Geo.: University of Georgia Press.

Watson, Alan (2006), 'Legal Transplants in European Private Law', Working Paper, www.alanwatson.org/legal_transplants.pdf, 20 July.

Wendehorst, Christiane (2006), 'Das Vertragsrecht der Dienstleistungen im deutschen und künftigen europäischen Recht', *Archiv für die civilistische Praxis* (*AcP*) 206, 205.

Wilhelmsson, Thomas (2004), 'Varieties of Welfarism in European Contract Law', *European Law Journal* 10, 712.

Ziller, Jacques (2006), 'The Legitimacy of the Codification of Contract Law in View of the Allocation of Competences between the European Union and its Member States', in Martijn Hesselink (ed.), *The Politics of a European Civil Code*, The Hague/London/New York: Kluwer, 89.

Zimmermann, Reinhard (2006), *Die Europäisierung des Privatrechts und die Rechtsvergleichung*, Berlin: de Gruyter.

Zweigert, Konrad and Hein Kötz (1996), *Einführung in die Rechtsvergleichung* (3rd edn), Tübingen: Mohr Siebeck.

10. Fitting the frame: an optional instrument, party choice and mandatory/default rules

Horatia Muir Watt and Ruth Sefton-Green

I. INTRODUCTION

1. Tool-box, Code or Mere Source of Inspiration?

The legal status of the proposed Common Frame of Reference is, to say the least, somewhat obscure.[1] A recent press release by the Council[2] now defines it as 'a set of non-binding guidelines to be used by the lawmakers at Community level on a voluntary basis as a common source of inspiration or reference in the lawmaking process'.[3] The academic Draft Common Frame of Reference[4] indicates, too, that it has been drawn up on the assumption that it could serve as a legislator's guide or tool-box, leaving open its destiny as a political text.[5] As a mere source of inspiration to which Community lawmakers may or not choose to refer, such a framework is clearly of seriously diminished interest. Indeed, in this perspective, it becomes entirely unimportant that whatever text emerges from the political process may not be a 'frame of reference' at all, in the sense

---

[1]   See von Bar, C., E. Clive and H. Schulte-Nölke (eds) (2008), *Principles, Definitions and Model Rules of European Private Law: Draft Common Frame of Reference Interim outline edition*, Sellier (henceforth 'DCFR') para. 6, admitting that it is mute whether and to what end and by what means there will be a Common Frame one day. See Reich, N. (2006), 'A Common Frame of Reference (CFR) – Ghost or Host for Integration?,' ZERP, Bremen, *Diskussionspapier* 7/2006.

[2]   Press Release of 18 April 2008, 8397/08 (presse 96) 18.

[3]   In this respect it could be considered to be a soft law instrument, which may be categorised into three (sometimes overlapping) types: interpretive (with a post-law function), steering (with a para-law function) and preparatory (with a pre-law function). See Senden, L. and S. Prechal (2001), 'Differentiation in and through Community Soft Law', in Bruno de Witte, D. Hanf and E. Vos (eds), *The Many Faces of Differentiation*, Intersentia, 181.

[4]   DCFR, n 1 above, para 4.

[5]   Ibid., para 60–70.

of 'principles, definitions or model rules'[6] but for the most part, like the academic version, a set of codified rules governing not only the validity, formation, interpretation and performance of contracts but also various other areas of private law.[7] Community lawmakers, for whom the reference to this text will take place 'on a voluntary basis', will be free in any event to prefer other sources of inspiration. In fact, much of the DCFR is borrowed from the Principles of European Contract Law ('PECL'), which it set out to improve on various points.[8] One would presume that Community lawmakers could, if need be, refer directly to the original sources – as well as many others, including the Vienna Convention on the International Sale of Goods or the Unidroit principles for international commercial contracts – and indeed, why not the American Uniform Commercial Code, doctrinal writings, the rules of Monopoly, etc. At this stage, it might reasonably be supposed – subject however to further clarification later on – that as a mere toolbox, the Common Frame of Reference would not be designed to affect the consumer *acquis* otherwise than through a process of '*mise en cohérence*' or consolidation, designed to ensure that the terms and concepts used in the various EC instruments in the field of substantive private law bear the same meaning throughout.

However, the Commission's own agenda, as set out in its 2003 'Action Plan' and its 2004 'Way Forward' paper,[9] seems to have been somewhat different. While the European Civil Code project, at one point much in vogue, had by then all but bitten the dust, the Commission nevertheless revealed its intention to explore the way of an 'optional instrument'. While it was not clearly stated that the instrument would in substance still resemble a set of model

---

[6]   Ibid., para 9.

[7]   On scope and policy for extension see DCFR, n 1 above, para 37, whose coverage is wider than the PECL.

[8]   DCFR, n 1 above nos 57–58 where it is indicated that the draft also draws its sources from the *Acquis* Principles. See *Principles of Existing EC Contract Law (Acquis Principles), volume Contract I – Pre-contractual Obligations, Conclusion of Contract, Unfair Terms* (2007) Sellier (henceforth 'ACQP'). Whether the DCFR actually constitutes an improvement on its sources is highly controversial. See, for example, Schulze, R. and T. Wilhelmsson (2008), 'From the Draft Common Frame of Reference towards European Contract Law Rules', 2 *European Review of Contract Law* 154.

[9]   One of the proposals contained in the Commission's Action Plan of 2003, COM(2003)68 final OJEC 2003 C 63/11, para 72, was to introduce an optional instrument called the Common Frame of Reference. This idea was reformulated in 'European Contract Law and the Revision of the Acquis: The Way Forward', COM(2004)651 final, 11 October 2004, para 3.1.3, p. 11 which referred to the CFR as containing 'fundamental principles, definitions and model rules', in order to serve as a 'legislator's guide' or 'tool-box'.

rules, it was apparently designed nevertheless to govern contracts, on either an opt-in or opt-out basis. The question of its normative status thus became somewhat enigmatic. Firstly, the form such an instrument might take remains uncertain. The Rome I Regulation refers, sphinx-like, to 'an appropriate legal instrument' by which the Community might adopt 'rules of substantive contract law, including standard terms and conditions' (recital 16), adding, curiously, that 'such instrument may provide that the parties may choose to apply those rules'. Since the authority of such a recital is decidedly unclear, and since it is also difficult to conceive that any non-binding instrument would have any auto-poietic authority to provide for parties to choose it, over and above the Rome I Regulation, it is highly likely that the appropriate instrument could only be another regulation, providing for its own applicability in cross-border contracts and prevailing over the choice of law provisions of Rome I Regulation under Article 22 (b) of the latter.[10] Whether or not it is realistic at this stage to expect sufficient political agreement to drape the Common Frame of Reference with this sort of formal normativity, one may wonder if these are entirely appropriate trappings for a purely optional regime. If parties are free to choose it or not, why bother to give it such a solemn form? The explanation for this curious situation may be linked to the resistance which became apparent during the drafting of the Rome I Regulation on the law applicable to contractual obligations, to allowing parties to a cross-border transaction to choose non-state law (including PECL, Unidroit Principles, *lex mercatoria*, etc.). However, since this – entirely anomalous – restriction clearly put an end to the career of any soft optional instrument, which would thereby be disqualified from governing cross-border contracts (even if they were specifically of an intra-Community variety), the only solution was to make such an instrument look as much as possible like state law.[11]

The shadow of the Rome I Regulation also casts further doubts on the scope of the envisaged rules. According to the Council's press release, the framework should cover 'general contract law and consumer contract law'. This implies that the content of the instrument is composed of both default rules and mandatory provisions, consumer law being presumably largely part of the

---

[10]   Under Art. 22 (b) of the Rome I Regulation, the provisions of that Regulation do not affect the application of other Community instruments which govern contractual obligations and which apply by virtue of the will of the parties in situations involving a conflict of laws. Tailor-made for the Common Frame of Reference, the latter would therefore apply with the permission of the Rome I Regulation, without any ostensible modification of the reach of the choice of law rule.

[11]   To the extent that any choice by the parties is, in any event, restricted by the internationally mandatory provisions (*lois de police*) of the forum (under Art. 9 of the Rome Regulation), it is very difficult to see any justification for not allowing them to choose non-state law.

latter. This of course creates another enigma as far as parties' freedom to opt out of mandatory provisions is concerned, which is in turn further complicated by the fact that it is still not clear whether the proposed instrument is designed to extend to domestic contracts, and thereby provide an alternative to the normally applicable provisions of national domestic law, or whether the freedom to set aside domestic law by opting in to the instrument is limited to cross-border contracts – where choice under Rome I is already, barring the state-law requirement, unlimited.[12] This answer is of considerable practical import, since Article 3 of the Rome I Regulation does not allow parties to a purely domestic transaction to contract out of rules which are mandatory under domestic law, thereby creating considerable discrepancy between the extent of party choice – and by the same token, the definition of mandatory rules – in internal and international contracts.

2. Method, Policy and Design

However, given the difficulty of distinguishing domestic and cross-border contracts and, among the latter, of drawing the line between intra-Community and world-wide transactions, it would no doubt be judicious not to attempt to restrict the scope of the Common Frame of Reference. Indeed, if its justification lies in its dual ability to eliminate existing diversity of contract laws (perceived as an obstacle to the single market) and promote consumer and business confidence (necessary for the smooth functioning of the internal market),[13] then it should logically have as wide a scope as possible, since this is the only way towards eliminating diversity – although, of course, if parties remain free not to choose the instrument, then such a justificatory discourse is hardly convincing anyway. But we then find ourselves once again confronted with the initial conundrum, since domestic mandatory rules are unwaivable in domestic contracts under Rome I. All these difficulties tend to suggest that the idea of the Common Frame of Reference as an optional instrument raises various important methodological issues, the common denominators of which are the controversial distinction between mandatory and default rules, and its relationship to both party choice and the optional nature of the proposed instrument. The first part of this chapter will attempt to clarify such issues, particularly in view of the fact that, as we have seen, the recitals of the Rome I Regulation allow the Common Frame of Reference to become an additional

---

[12]   Rome I does not distinguish international or cross-border intra-Community and extra-Community (worldwide) contracts.

[13]   See Wilhelmsson, T. (2004), 'The Abuse of the Confident Consumer as a Justification of EC Consumer Law', *Journal of Consumer Policy* 317, who refutes the idea that increased consumer confidence is a valid justification for EC consumer law.

object of party choice in cross-border contracts.[14] It may well be, however, that any attempt to fit mandatory rules of national or Community origin into a set of facilitative provisions set out in an optional but binding instrument proceeds in turn from a mistaken premise. Contemporary integrated approaches to European law-making, currently advocated under the aegis of 'new governance', show that the stark alternative between mandatory and purely facilitative rules can no longer appropriately account for the way in which law actually impacts on social conduct or indeed, ultimately and importantly from the Commission's instrumental or competition-biased perspective on contract law,[15] shapes the market.[16] It might be that the Common Frame of Reference could find its place as a hybrid constellation of hard and soft contract law within the Commission's 'open method of coordination'[17] and that the very concept of default rules requires serious overhauling. Thus, the second part of this chapter seeks to explore the internal relationship between the Common Frame of Reference and the dichotomy between mandatory/ default rules.

II. THE DESIGN AND FIT OF PARTY CHOICE AND THE COMMON FRAME OF REFERENCE

1. A Tool-box Which is Not a Tool-box

If one supposes that the legislative 'tool-box' will take the official form of what is euphemistically characterised by the recitals of the Rome I Regulation as an 'appropriate instrument', and if one supposes further, by elimination, that such an instrument would be, more likely than not, a Regulation,[18] the real issue is the mandatory or facilitative nature of the proposed Common Frame of Reference (whatever it may contain). This question makes sense, of course, and the debate is worth entering, only if the tool-box is not a tool-box, in the

---

[14]   The issue arises as to the authority of these recitals, which actually create an implicit conflict with the Regulation itself to the extent that it is generally considered that parties may choose only state law.

[15]   Micklitz, H. (2005), 'The Concept of Competitive Contract Law', 23 *Penn St. Int'l L. Rev.* 549.

[16]   See Trubek, D., P. Cottrell and M. Nance (2005), '"Soft Law", "Hard Law" and European Integration: Towards a Theory of Hybridity', *Univ. Wisconsin Madison, Law School, Legal Stud. Res. Paper Series, Paper no. 1002.*

[17]   This idea is voiced by N. Reich, n. 1 above.

[18]   Since a directive would clearly not allow the desired uniformity of any common framework and any other purely inter-institutional arrangement would not lend itself to private party choice, as we have seen above.

sense that it is recognised as being able to govern private contracts (and indeed perhaps other private law relationships, such as tort and property),[19] whether domestic or cross-border, business or consumer, etc. The crux of the matter is therefore the relationship between the envisaged Common Frame of Reference and existing provisions within the laws of Member States which cannot be waived by contract. Beyond constitutional or human rights provisions of whatever origin (EC Treaty or Social Charter, European Convention on Human Rights, national constitutional provisions) relevant to the regulation of contracts, such as the principle of non-discrimination, and indeed Community or national rules of market regulation, such as competition law, such mandatory law might be composed of the Community private law *acquis*, specifically in the field of consumer protection, and of national rules, particularly those which have extended the protection afforded by minimum-harmonisation consumer directives. How, then, is a comprehensively drafted Common Frame of Reference to accommodate these sources of law?

2. First Way of Framing the Frame: Fitting into the Space Left for Dispositive Rules

At first sight, the better question might be to reverse the terms of the question and ask how these various blocks of existing mandatory law can accommodate a Common Frame of Reference. The answer is apparently simple. Thus, in cross-border contracts, the Common Frame of Reference, chosen by the parties under Article 3 of the Rome Regulation, could fit into the space left to party autonomy by Articles 5, 6 and 9 of the Regulation or any other applicable choice of law instrument which prevails over the Rome Regulation for certain categories of 'special' contracts under Articles 22 and 23 (sale of goods, insurance contracts subject to insurance directives, posting of workers, etc.). In such a case, the Common Frame of Reference would enjoy a status identical to that of any system of national law chosen by the parties under Article 3, or indeed, on this point at least, to the Vienna Convention on the international sale of goods, the opt-out provisions of which prevail in Contracting States over the Rome I Regulation for that particular category of contracts.[20] The vocation of the Common Frame would therefore be fairly extensive in B to B contracts, where the scope of derogatory mandatory rules applicable by virtue of Article 9 of the Regulation is essentially limited to public market regulation. Indeed, the bulk of 'ordinary' private contract law

---

[19]   See Reich n. 1 above.

[20]   The Vienna Convention gives way to the mandatory rules applicable in the forum under the Rome Regulation. This is without prejudice to its opt-out status and the primacy of incompatible contractual clauses.

rules are considered to be dispositive for the purposes of party choice in international contracts.[21] In consumer or employment contracts, on the other hand, the body of mandatory provisions, applicable under Articles 5 and 6 of the Rome I Regulation, is of course considerably more substantial. Thus, in the case of consumer contracts, by virtue of Article 5, the mandatory provisions of the country of the consumer's habitual residence will prevail over the chosen law if that law is less protective. If the Common Frame of Reference incorporates the consumer *acquis*, then one can presume that the relevant regime mirrors the case where the chosen law is the law of a Member State (supposing that it has transposed the relevant directives).[22] In such an instance, the scope for conflict (that is, for setting aside the chosen law in the name of greater protection afforded by the country of residence) appears where the Member State in which the consumer resides has extended the protection afforded by a minimum-harmonisation directive. Here, if the Common Frame of Reference is less protective than the law of the country where the consumer resides, it should therefore give way to the more protective provisions of that law. According to the same approach, in purely domestic consumer contracts, if the parties were to choose to have their contract subject to the Common Frame of Reference, such a choice would be constrained by whatever the forum characterised as mandatory or unwaivable within domestic contract law – which may of course vary as between jurisdictions.[23] Here again, the situation would be similar to the one arising from the choice of a foreign law in a purely domestic contract under Article 3 of the Rome Regulation: such a choice cannot 'prejudice the application of the rules of the law of that country which cannot be derogated from by contract'. This means that the Common Frame of Reference would have to fit into the space defined by reference to domestic dispositive rules.

---

[21]   Difficulties may arise however as to the status of principles of good faith or fair dealing which in certain jurisdictions will be applied by the court whatever the position of the governing law. The Unidroit principles endorse this approach, when they provide (Art. 7) that (at least, if they are applicable), that:

(1) Each party must act in accordance with good faith and fair dealing in international trade.
(2) The parties may not exclude or limit this duty.

[22]   If the chosen law is the law of a third state, then the Community *acquis* must prevail whenever there is a close link to the Community (which is the case – though not exclusively under *Oceano* – when the consumer is resident in a Member State). However, this last instance concerns the problem of the mandatory nature of the common frame of reference when it prevails over the chosen law and not when it is itself the chosen law.

[23]   The question of how national legal rules are characterised as default or mandatory rules will be considered below.

2.   Second Framing of the Frame: Conflicts of Mandatory Rules

However, this approach is probably too simplistic, in view of the fact that the Common Frame of Reference is apparently intended to be more than just a set of dispositive rules which, as seen above, would apply to domestic contracts subject to contrary party choice, and to cross-border contracts in the absence of incompatible provisions of internationally mandatory law or *lois de police*; indeed, it seems to be designed to incorporate the Community *acquis*, and might indeed borrow certain provisions from the European or Unidroit principles which are self-characterised as overriding (such as the good faith provisions).[24] Therefore, unlike the Vienna Convention, which simply provides a set of self-effacing facilitative rules for international sales of goods, subordinate both to contrary party choice and to the stronger normative claim of *lois de police* applicable in the forum, the Common Frame of Reference could then actually generate a conflict with other mandatory sources of law. The issue will arise in cases where either (if the Common Frame of Reference adopts an opt-in mechanism) parties have specifically chosen to subject their contract to it, or (if the Common Frame becomes an opt-out instrument) they have not drafted clauses on specific points in domestic contracts, or have not made any specific choice of the applicable law within the terms of Article 3 of the Rome I Regulation, in the case of cross-border contracts. In the latter hypothesis, however, the status of the Common Frame as an opt-out mechanism would require extensive adjustment, for consumer contracts, of the default solution of Article 5 (application of the law of the consumer's habitual residence in the specified circumstances), and, in B to B contracts, of the default rule under Article 4.[25] Since such adjustments have not been made by the Rome I Regulation (which nevertheless envisages the possibility that parties may, at some future date, choose the substantive common rules contained in an appropriate instrument to govern their contract), it may therefore be simpler to assume that the Common Frame of Reference will be applicable on an opt-in basis, through party choice. This assumption does not modify the terms of the potential conflict between the chosen Common Frame of Reference in its own mandatory provisions and the otherwise applicable mandatory rules originating in the laws of Member States

---

[24]   See Unidroit principles, Art. 1–7 cited above and Lando, O. and H. Beale (eds) (2000), *Principles of European Contract Law,* Kluwer, Commentary H to Article 1: 201 PECL, which states that the Art. is mandatory.

[25]   Until now, under the Rome Convention, this was the law of the country of the establishment of the party providing the characteristic performance of the contract, but this rule has undergone a radical face-lift in the Rome I Regulation, which contains a series of specific connecting factors for specific categories of contracts.

(a) More protective national provisions: exeunt in domestic cases?

To a large extent, this conflict raises, in turn, once again, the issue of the status of national provisions relating to consumer protection, which go beyond the requirements of minimum harmonisation in a specific field. Let us suppose that parties to a domestic contract have chosen the Common Frame of Reference, which incorporates the consumer *acquis* along the lines traced by Community directives. Let us suppose, too, that the country in which this transaction takes place has increased consumer protection in its domestic law. Is it conceivable that the Common Frame of Reference could diminish the level of protection thus afforded? Hardly so, under Article 3 of the Rome I Regulation, which provides, as we have seen, that the mandatory provisions of the local law will prevail. Quite clearly, as certain writers have already pointed out, to the extent that the Common Frame of Reference aims to contain more than default rules, it necessarily goes hand in hand with a policy of maximum harmonisation and therefore a potential reduction of the level of protection provided in Member States' laws.[26] Otherwise, its provisions would be neutralised in situations which belong to the domestic sphere of Member States.

(b) Exeunt in cross-border cases

And what of cross-border contracts? Let us suppose that parties to an international contract (or, under Article 3 of the Rome Regulation, a contract of which all the elements are not located in a single country) choose the Common Frame, creating a conflict with the more protective, derogatory provisions of the law of the country of the consumer's habitual residence. To what extent should these prevail, as they undoubtedly would if the parties had chosen, say, the less protective provisions of the law of a third state? Does the mandatory content of the Common Frame of Reference signify that, on the contrary, more protective national measures will no longer benefit the cross-border consumer? Once again, it is difficult to see how the Common Frame of Reference could coexist with Article 5 of the Rome I Regulation if it does not unify – thus potentially diminishing – the level of protection in the laws of the various Member States.

It may be, however, that, thus framed, the terms of this alternative are once again misguided. Indeed, independently of the Common Frame of Reference, Stefan Grundmann has suggested that in areas which have been harmonised (albeit by directives which have not capped the authorised level of consumer

---

26   Reich, n. 1 above, Lurger, B. (2007), 'The Common Frame of Reference/ Optional Code and the Various Understandings of Social Justice in Europe', in Wilhelmsson, Thomas, Elina Paunio and Annika Pohjolainen (eds), *Private Law and the Many Culture of Europe,* Kluwer Law International, 177.

protection), specific principles pertaining to the functioning of the internal market come into play to prevent the application of the higher level of protection of the consumer's residence in respect of a supplier established in another Member State. In such a case, the supplier could oppose the country of origin principle to avoid being subjected to the more stringent rules of the consumer's residence. Although the relationship between the country of origin principle and the conflict of laws is extremely controversial, it is quite apparent that there is a potential clash between internal market principles and ordinary choice of law principles, so that in the current perspective of the Commission's 'competitive' contract law,[27] diversity of levels of protection is perceived as an impediment to the smooth running of the cross-border business and may well need to be regulated otherwise than through the ordinary operation of Rome I.

It is clear, however, that the articulation of Rome I and the Common Frame of Reference is designed as a matter of legal technique, yet the real issue raised by the legal status of the Common Frame of Reference is a political one, and concerns the orientation of the Commission's policy in the field of consumer protection. We have just seen that a static analysis of the fit between the Common Frame of Reference and the existing provisions on party choice suggests that the Common Frame is being designed in the perspective of Commission's competitive contract law. This conclusion is confirmed when the analysis of the Common Frame as an ostensibly neutral tool-box is conducted from the more ideological standpoint of the social function of default rules. As we have seen, recital 16 of Rome I Regulation indicates that 'such instrument may provide that the parties may choose to apply those rules'. One is tempted to ask whether this freedom (if it were to exist) could actually be exercised. Who chooses to opt in or out? Our view is that the 'stronger party', the party offering standard terms, exercises the choice. This will lead to social dumping[28] and also may have the effect of surreptitiously converting minimum harmonisation into maximum harmonisation, as has been pointed out above.[29]

---

27   Micklitz, n. 15 above.
28   Rutgers, J. (2006), 'An Optional Instrument and Social Dumping', 2 *ERCL* 199.
29   Lurger, n. 25 above.

III. THE DESIGN AND SOCIAL FUNCTION OF THE DEFAULT RULES OF THE COMMON FRAME OF REFERENCE

When considering appropriate or desirable levels of protection from a maximum/minimum harmonisation perspective, the crux of the matter is to identify which domestic rules are default rules, so that the Common Frame of Reference can be fitted into them. It may be useful at the start to consider what the category 'default rules' actually covers.

1. Distinguishing Default and Dispositive Rules

In order to clarify the debate it is necessary to make a distinction between the existence of default rules and their nature. Default rules, such as implied terms in English law, or, for instance, an implied duty to negotiate in good faith[30] in French law, are gap-filling rules. In this respect it should be recalled that comparatists often consider implied terms (in English law) as a functional equivalent of good faith, which exists as a general duty or principle in civilian systems.[31] Such rules are necessarily made (or, one is tempted to say, made up) by the judges or the legislator in the absence of express explication by the contracting parties. In other words, the parties do not choose these terms; they are supplied, in the absence of their choice. This is one of the reasons why the theory that the parties have implicitly consented to such terms (or would have, had they thought about it) is denounced as being artificial or fictive. However, although these rules exist by default, this does not make them exclusively non-mandatory in nature. This proposition can be illustrated in the following ways.

Let us imagine a B to B contract of sale under English and French law respectively. Under the English Sale of Goods Act 1979, combined with the Unfair Contract Terms Act 1977, for instance, a seller acting in the course of business can exclude or limit an implied term as to satisfactory quality of the goods,[32] only to the extent that it is reasonable to do so.[33] In other words, the parties cannot derogate unqualifiedly from these terms. Under French law,

---

[30]   Note that under the DCFR the duty to negotiate in accordance with good faith is not a default rule; and *a fortiori* cannot be waived: DCFR II-3:301 (2): 'A person who has engaged in negotiations has a duty to negotiate in accordance with good faith and fair dealing. This duty may not be excluded or limited by contract.'

[31]   Zimmermann, Reinhard and Simon Whittaker (eds) (2000), *Good Faith in European Contract Law*, Cambridge, CUP, 45–46.

[32]   S. 14 (2) Sale of Goods Act 1979.

[33]   S. 55 Sale of Goods Act 1979 and ss. 6 (3) and 11 of the Unfair Contract Terms Act 1977.

such a seller guarantees that the goods are free from hidden defects. The guarantee, stated in Article 1641 of the Civil Code, is dispositive since a seller can derogate from, or exclude, this guarantee under Article 1643 of the Civil Code. To circumvent such exclusion clauses, French case law assimilates a seller acting in the course of business with a seller in bad faith,[34] which has had the effect of rendering the guarantee almost mandatory. Assimilating the 'professional seller' with a seller in bad faith affects the seller's knowledge of the defects in the goods: it means that the seller is deemed to know about the defects in the goods, so the exclusion clause is treated as being invalid. The irrefutable presumption is laid down by the courts as a substantive rule,[35] and can be compared to an implied term. It is a default rule from which the seller cannot derogate. A seller can exclude the guarantee only when the buyer is acting in the course of business and is of the same speciality as the seller.[36]

The first implied term as to satisfactory quality under English law can be qualified as a default rule but can be derogated from only partially. It is neither mandatory nor non-mandatory but somewhere in between. The second, the seller's guarantee against hidden defects under French law, looks dispositive but is not always. In fact the seller can only derogate from this rule depending on the circumstances of the sale, the status and nature of the buyer, etc. The third implied default rule, that the seller is in bad faith, is not waivable. The corollary, that it is not possible to derogate from a default rule of good faith, is also true.

In order to illustrate the proposition that it is not possible to derogate out of good faith, which looks less like a default rule and more like a mandatory one, another illustration will be used. Under French law, a party cannot derogate out of his duty to negotiate in good faith, even when the duty has been judicially implied. As is well known, French judges have a tendency to supply good faith by default when interpreting the contract, just as they can imply terms by virtue of Article 1135 of the Civil Code.[37] However the parties cannot derogate out of the implied duty of good faith, as this would have the effect of negating its *raison d'être*. This example shows, once again, that qualifying a term as a default rule is not at all equivalent to qualifying the term as waivable or derogative.

---

[34]   Civ 1, 24 November 1954 (1955) *La semaine juridique II 8565*, note H.B. This is now *'jurisprudence constante'*.
[35]   Ghestin, J. (1983), *Conformités et garanties dans la vente*, Paris, LGDJ, no. 260f.
[36]   Com, 8 October 1973 (1975) *La semaine juridique* II 17927, note J. Ghestin. The principle has been reaffirmed on numerous occasions, and is also *jurisprudence constante*.
[37]   For a succinct overview of the judicial use of good faith in French law see M. Fabre-Magnan, *Les obligations*, vol 1, PUF, 2008, no. 36, p. 75.

Furthermore, in addition to classifying rules as default and mandatory and examining their normative basis, it may be useful to examine their source, i.e. to identify from where the mandatory and default rules are derived. Does it make a difference if it is the legislature, the courts or private organisations (trade organisations, i.e. private regulation) which fashion these rules and, if so, why?[38] In other words, we need to explore the margin for manoeuvre judges have when applying both of these kinds of rules. To adopt a schematic approach at the outset, common lawyers would tend to indicate that most of the gap-filling, illustrated by implied terms, to take an obvious example, is carried out by the judiciary. In civilian systems, judges also fill in the gaps and articulate party choice in lieu, but by working from a written *règle dispositive*, such as Article 1135 of the Civil Code. Another example would be the guidelines for interpretation of contracts, where judges have room to fill in the gaps, though their starting point (a subjective or objective approach) may be different. There may be an argument for saying that the legal system (common law/civilian) is not a relevant criterion of distinction. As explained above, this sort of default rule, the purpose of which is to fill in the gaps, may differ in nature from the dispositive rules that parties can consciously deviate from (e.g. exclusion clauses, etc.). The Common Frame of Reference's dispositive rules will derive from a legislative source. These rules will have to sit side by side with national dispositive rules which may derive from a variety of sources: legislative, judicial and private regulation.

In sum, default rules can be mandatory and derogative, as shown above. The apposite criterion is not then between default and mandatory rules but between rules which can be derogated from (dispositive or derogative), and those which cannot. The classification of default (or non-mandatory) and mandatory rules relates much more to how these rules come into being and is, ultimately, not only unhelpful but also misleading.

2.   When are Mandatory Rules Needed?

Hans Schulte-Nölke[39] has identified EC permanent regulatory density, both in B to B and B to C contracts, in the pre-contractual phase and in the phase concerning withdrawal and unfair terms. It is inferred that regulatory density indicates that there are EC mandatory rules in these areas. In contrast, conclusion of contract mechanisms and remedies for non-performance are areas where there is a low regulatory density pattern. This could be taken to mean

---

[38]   Riley, C.A. (2000), 'Designing Default Rules in Contract Law: Consent, Conventionalism, and Efficiency', 20 *Oxford J Legal Studies* 368.
[39]   Schulte-Nölke, H. (2007), 'EC Law and the Formation of Contract – from the Common Frame of Reference to the "Blue Button" ', *ERCL* 332.

that national legal rules are dispositive or non-mandatory in these domains. Under this hypothesis it follows that a minimum standard of remedies, as under the consumer sales directive, suffices. However the existence of diversity of legal rules on a national level and the absence of EU regulation is not tantamount to the proposition that all these national rules are dispositive rules. For a start, the existence or not of EU regulation is determined by questions of competence and cannot be equated with the classification of rules as mandatory or not. It is quite clear, for example, that the reason there is no EU regulation of national procedural rules about remedies is due to a lack of competence.[40] Lack of regulation is not necessarily because harmonisation is not required in certain areas; or, more specifically, because these rules are not mandatory. Indeed, it is not certain that this question is always properly addressed in empirical research.[41]

Remedies for non-performance or breach of contract are considered to be default or non-mandatory rules, but their non-mandatory nature needs to be verified. In French law, it is not possible to opt out of *l'exécution forcée* as a judicial remedy over damages. A party cannot contractually prefer one judicial remedy to another (e.g. damages instead of enforced performance, or enforced performance instead of judicial termination). A party can deviate from Article 1184 of the Civil Code only by replacing a judicial remedy with a conventional or self-help remedy. For instance, a party can include a *clause pénale* – to fix damages on breach in order to circumvent a judicial award of damages; the same reason lies behind the insertion of an exclusion or limitation of liability clause. The rule is non-mandatory in that derogation is possible but not all derogations are possible. How much freedom parties have depends on the content and nature of rules of national legal systems. In English law, the question of deviating from specific performance does not arise in the same circum-

---

[40]   See Rott, P. (2007), 'Effective Enforcement and Different Enforcement Cultures in Europe', in Wilhelmsson, Paunio and Pohjolainen, n. 25 above, 305, 314–315.

[41]   See Goode, R. (2003), 'Contract and Commercial Law: The Logic and Limits of Harmonisation', vol. 7.4 Electronic Journal of Comparative Law at: www.ejcl.org/ejcl/74/art74-1.html who suggests that, when asked whether diversity constitutes an obstacle, businesses tend to favour harmonisation on the basis that mandatory rules are the subject of discussion. See Voganauer, S. and S. Weatherill (2006), 'The EC's Competence to Pursue Harmonisation: an Empirical Contribution to the Debate', in Stefan Vogenauer and Stephen Weatherill (eds), *The Harmonisation of European Contract Law – Implications for European Private Law, Business and Legal Practice. Studies of the Oxford Institute of European and Comparative Law,* Oxford, Hart Publishing, 105, 138–139 where it is admitted that this question was not asked. '[W]e did not touch on business attitudes to the inclusion and the status of mandatory, rather than non-mandatory, rules in the optional instrument.'

stances. It does not make sense to formulate this in terms of deviating from the rule, since it is not a rule in the first place, but an exception. This point seems to have been overlooked. Conversely, under English law, a party cannot opt into specific performance, in preference to claiming damages. Such clauses are not recognised as being valid by the English courts.[42] In contrast, however, a recent French unpublished decision implicitly recognised, *obiter*, that a clause giving preference to enforced performance over damages was valid.[43] However, since this is an unpublished decision where the clause was not actually recognised, it seems unwise to give too much value to it. These heteroclite examples simply show that the classification of rules as mandatory/default rules, such as the suggestion that rules on non-performance do not need to be regulated at a European level, i.e. through harmonisation, since they are non-mandatory rules, is simplistic and does not take account of the reality of contract law rules. It is not the categorisation of these rules that matters but how they work in practice; a repetition of the distinction between 'law in books' and 'law in practice'.

Furthermore, it has also been suggested that the dual classification of mandatory/default rules is more complex than appears at first sight. Duncan Kennedy suggested that the dividing line is quite blurred in practice.[44] Following on from this analysis, Martijn Hesselink has suggested that parties cannot deviate from non-mandatory rules *de facto* because of unequal bargaining power, so that many rules are *de facto* mandatory.[45] Taking this interpretation to its limits, a threefold category of mandatory, non-mandatory and *de facto* mandatory rules could be created. However, although there is no doubt some truth in this assertion, it must be qualified. This proposition seems to assume that non-mandatory rules are inevitably favourable to strong parties, but the validity of the assumption needs to be verified. This partially depends on their normative basis. C.A. Riley,[46] for example, has shown that there three normative explanations for default rules exist: consent, conventionalism and efficiency. Although we may disagree about which of these normative foundations explain default rules: the consent analysis fails to be truly convincing.[47] Following Riley's conclusion that default rules are mostly, though not

---

[42]   This is considered to be an indirect ouster of jurisdiction clause.
[43]   Civ 3, 27 March 2008, no. 07-11721, unpublished.
[44]   Kennedy, D. (1982), 'Distribution and Paternalist Motives in Contract and Tort Law. With Special Reference to Compulsory Terms and Unequal Bargaining Power', 41 *Maryland Law Review* 563.
[45]   Hesselink, M.W. (2005), 'Non-Mandatory Rules in European Contract Law', 1 *ERCL* 44, 73.
[46]   Riley, n. 38 above.
[47]   Contra, Barnett, R.E. (1992), 'The Sound of Silence: Default Rules and Contractual Consent', 78 *Virginia Law Review* 821.

exclusively, based on a consensualist position, it follows that non-mandatory rules, reflecting social norms, would be somewhere in the middle between the wishes of strong and weak parties. It would follow therefore that even if weak parties are not able to deviate from non-mandatory rules in practice, strong parties are indeed able to do so. This means that the rules are not *de facto* mandatory in the absolute, they are *de facto* mandatory from the point of view of one of the contracting parties. It can be inferred that an optional instrument will be highly dangerous from the perspective of social protection. Categorising a rule as non-mandatory may enable the stronger party to derogate from what might otherwise be a protective rule for the weaker party. In short, the ambit and content of mandatory and default rules are highly complex, dependent on numerous casuistic factors and inextricably linked with maintaining a consensualist level of protection, acceptable to society.

3. The 'Blue Button': Lowering Social Protection

In view of this range of contract law where domestic non-mandatory rules exist Schulte-Nölke has suggested introducing an optional instrument in a specific field of application for e-commerce sales, B to B and B to C, otherwise known as the 'blue button'. 'More precisely, the optional instrument would be applicable only for the sale of goods and would have to contain certain rules on 'scope and definitions, pre-contractual obligations, conclusion of contract, content and interpretation of contract, validity ... withdrawal, unfair terms ... remedies for non-performance ... Many of these provisions would be applicable for all contracts, as non-mandatory rules, whereas they would be mandatory in B2C cases ... If the client chooses the 'Blue Button', the optional European Law would derogate the law which otherwise were applicable according to the conflict of law rules (and which would be in B2C cases – under the actual and probably also under the future Rome system very often the law of the consumer's home country).' According to Schulte-Nölke, the 'blue button' would be 'politically attractive' as well as providing an 'evident utility for market integration and consumer choice'.[48] The term 'politically attractive' is highly ambiguous. As demonstrated above, the blue button will be politically attractive only for those who are in favour of lowering standards of protection for the weaker party. Of course the blue button could be politically attractive in terms of its visibility; the Common Frame of Reference would thus be a transparent instrument for businesses and consumers alike. However, in view of the preceding discussion about the Rome I Regulation it should now be clear that the blue button proposal is a

---

[48]   Schulte-Nölke n. 39 above, 349.

mere figment of imagination. Consumers cannot choose the Common Frame of Reference, non-state law, or to prevail over the mandatory provisions of the law of their home country. So fortunately – for those who do not wish to lower standards of protection– this pipe-dream may be set aside, at least for the time being.

It may be helpful to illustrate the above propositions by examining a provision of the DCFR. The following hypothesis examines the implications of the premise that remedies for non-performance are dispositive rules, even if it has been shown above that this premise may not always be well founded. Imagine a B to B contract of sale where the seller is English and the buyer is French. The seller is selling on his standard terms and for the purpose of the example the seller is *de facto* the stronger party, though it is not assumed that this is necessarily the case. The seller's standard terms and conditions choose the DCFR as the law governing the contract. The remedies for non-performance of contract under the DCFR differ from English law. The relevant provisions are set out below:

> DCFR III-3:302 (1): the creditor is entitled to enforce specific performance of an obligation other than one to pay money.

> DCFR III-3:102: Remedies which are not incompatible may be cumulated. In particular, a creditor is not deprived of the right to damages by resorting to any other remedy.

A French buyer could interpret this provision as allowing him to claim specific performance for late delivery and any damages arising out of the fact that the delivery was late. Suppose that our seller has foreseen this possibility and realises that it will be less costly to pay damages for his own breach, rather than specific performance plus damages for late delivery. Suppose also that the seller has unspecified goods to sell.[49] Since remedies for non-performance are generally considered to be dispositive rules, the seller will derogate out of the rule on specific performance as it suits him. To return to the analysis made above, the seller is able, or free, to derogate, since he is *de facto* the stronger party. The effect of waiving this default rule for the seller will be to put him back in the position he would be in under English law. In practice, the effect of adopting such a Common Frame of Reference may be futile, or perhaps perverse. The buyer thinks that a neutral law governs the contract and that he is not getting the seller's law but, under the hypothesis outlined above, he may end up doing so. More to the point, a great deal of diversity of legal rules will

---

[49]   This fact-hypothetical is necessary to avoid the application of s. 52 of the Sale of Good Acts 1979 which exceptionally allows a buyer to claim specific performance of specified goods 'if the court thinks it is just and equitable'.

continue in the EU and new diversity will be introduced. It is difficult therefore to ascertain what gain will be made by introducing the Common Frame
of Reference, if one of its aims is to eliminate legal diversity. Moreover, if the
rules on remedies for non-performance in the Common Frame of Reference
are considered dispositive, certain mandatory rules protective of the buyer
(existing in both English and French law even though the content differs) will
be dismantled.

This example illustrates a flaw in Schulte-Nölke's argument, namely the
assertion that 'the degree of uncertainty about the applicable remedies may
disturb, but not really impede, cross-border transactions'.[50] Assigning remedies to procedural, and thus unimportant, law which does not require EU regulation may miss the point. The choice may or may not be deliberate. First,
there may be a lack of competence to regulate this issue; secondly, trying to
harmonise enforcement regimes may not always be effective.[51] Thirdly, and
most crucially for the purposes of the argument, it may suit certain actors on
the market that this diversity exists. The conclusion that regulation of remedies is not necessary has flowed partly from an erroneous assumption that
rules for remedies on breach of performance are dispositive rules. Even if this
were the case and even if the uncertainty concerning the diversity of remedies
merely disturbs cross-border transactions, not more, it does not necessarily
follow that the parties should be able to increase this uncertainty, by choosing
the Common Frame of Reference. It would follow that the Common Frame of
Reference will exacerbate the situation, not only increasing uncertainty, but
also counteracting harmonisation goals. Once again, the Common Frame of
Reference, as an optional instrument, would end up having unintended consequences which are counterproductive to the stated goal of making European
contract law more coherent and more uniform. Moreover, the social function
of this optional instrument needs to be clarified: it has been demonstrated that
if many rules of contract law are classified as non-mandatory this will enable
the stronger party to derogate from these rules to his advantage, thus giving
preference to the stronger party while lowering the standard of protection
available to the weaker party.

In conclusion, if too many areas of contract law rules are categorised as
default or, rather, dispositive rules, then freedom of contract will prevail,
which is perhaps what the Commission really wants.[52] If, however, default
rules are restricted to real gap-filling rules, as suggested above, the parties'
choice and margin for manoeuvre are severely curtailed. Reducing party

---

[50]   Schulte-Nölke, n. 39 above, 338.
[51]   Rott, n. 40 above.
[52]   DCFR, n. 1 above, para. 25, where freedom of contract is stated to be a fundamental principle.

choice may sometimes be necessary and can often be justified on the grounds of social justice. If a more accurate analysis is carried out to identify which rules are really dispositive, then the whole idea of an optional instrument may fall apart. In short, offering the parties an additional choice of an optional instrument runs the risk of dressing up a market-functional liberal ideal of contract law in sheep's clothes.[53] Caveat emptor!

---

[53] The metaphor is borrowed from Lurger, n. 25 above.

Index